Good Governance in China – A Way Towards Social Harmony

Good governance is necessary for effective public administration and delivery of public goods and services. This is an important issue for all countries, but in particular for rapidly developing countries such as China where reform of governance and public administration is a key element of the public policy agenda. This book explores the key issues in governance and public administration facing China's policy-makers today. Edited by Wang Mengkui, the former President of the Development Research Center of the State Council, and currently Chairman of the China Development Research Foundation – one of China's leading think-tanks – it contains thirty-six papers selected from nearly 300 case studies presented by participants in the China's Leaders in Development Executive Program. The authors are outstanding and experienced officials, and together represent the voice of China's new rising generation of leaders, policy-makers and officials. The cases are based on first-hand information and experiences from either the officials' personal involvement or their own in-depth investigations. The chapters cover a wide range of issue areas, such as institutional reform, urban construction, social governance, crisis management, resource and ecological environmental management, education and public health, and economic reform and development. Taken together, it provides an invaluable resource for anyone seeking to understand China's own thinking on its governance and public administration.

Wang Mengkui is former President of the Development Research Center of the State Council, and is currently Chairman of the China Development Research Foundation.

Routledge studies on the Chinese economy

Series Editor: Peter Nolan, University of Cambridge
Founding Series Editors: Peter Nolan, University of Cambridge, and
Dong Fureng, Beijing University

The aim of this series is to publish original, high-quality, research-level work by both new and established scholars in the West and the East, on all aspects of the Chinese economy, including studies of business and economic history.

Good Governance in China – A Way Towards Social Harmony

Case studies by China's rising leaders

Edited by
Wang Mengkui

Routledge
Taylor & Francis Group

LONDON AND NEW YORK

中国发展研究基金会
China Development Research
Foundation

First published 2009
by Routledge
2 Park Square, Milton Park, Abingdon, Oxon OX14 4RN

Simultaneously published in the USA and Canada
by Routledge
270 Madison Ave, New York, NY 10016

Routledge is an imprint of the Taylor & Francis Group, an informa business

© 2009 The China Development Research Foundation

Typeset in Times New Roman by
Taylor & Francis Books
Printed and bound in Great Britain by
T.J.I. Digital Ltd, Padstow, Cornwall

British Library Cataloguing in Publication Data
A catalogue record for this book is available from the British Library

Library of Congress Cataloging in Publication Data
A catalog record for this book has been requested

ISBN 978-0-415-46278-5 (hbk)
ISBN 978-0-203-88768-4 (ebk)

Contents

x *Contents*

Illustrations

Tables

Figures

Contributors

Sun Baohou, Auditor-in-Chief, National Audit Office

Gao Zhili, Deputy Director General, Finance Bureau, Hebei Province

Li Chun-yan, Director General, Department of Information Industry, Jiangxi Province

Zhai Tianshan, Deputy Director General, Organization Department of Municipal Committee of CPC, Hubei Province

Huang Xuming, Director General, Department of Finance, Zhejiang Province

Sun Guoxiang, Secretary, Liaoning Provincial Committee, Chinese Communist Youth League

Piao Yi, Secretary General, Harbin CPC Committee, Helongjiang Province

Wang Xueqin, Deputy Director, Department of Communication, Committee of Beijing CPC

Zhang Sujun, Vice Minister, Ministry of Justice

Liu Guoqiang, Deputy Secretary, Municipal Committee of CPC, Neijiang City, Sichuan Province

Wu Shixiong, Director General, Bureau of Finance, Beijing Municipality

Wang Huimin, Assistant President, Xinjiang Uygur Autonomous Region; Director, Office for Finance Affairs, Xinjiang Uygur Autonomous Region

Fang Li, Mayor, Baicheng City, Jilin Province

Zhong Mian, Secretary, CPC Ziyang Municipal Committee, Sichuan Province

Chen Qingliang, Deputy Director General, Tourism Bureau, Shaanxi Province

Yang Shuping, Deputy Secretary General, Jiaozuo Municipal CPC Committee, Henan Province

Chen Zhongbo, Deputy Director-General, Science and Technology Department of Hunan Province

Zhang Lei, Director General, Department of Foreign Trade and Economic Cooperation, Jiangsu Province

Zhang Miaogen, Director, Construction Department, Zhejiang Province

Zhao Jin, Director, Yunnan Daily Press Group

Xu Jun, Secretary General, Hainan Provincial Government

Lu Gang, Director General, Department of Education, Hubei Province

Wang Chunqiu, President, Shandong University of Science and Technology

Kang Ning, Director, China Education TV

Yu Xinrong, Vice Mayor, Shaoyang City, Hunan Province

Dong Yong'an, Mayor, Anyang, Henan Province

Xu Songnan, Director General, Communication Department, Ningxia Hui Autonomous Region

Zhang Jianjin, Director General, Food and Drug Administration, Tianjin Municipality

Chang Xiaochun, Vice Chairman, Development and Planning Commission, Jilin Province

Zeng Yu, Director General, Provincial Food and Drug Administration, Hainan Province

Chen You'an, Assistant Governor, Gansu Province; President, Provincial Union of Rural Credit Cooperatives, Gansu Province

Bu Xiaolin, Secretary, CPC Alashan Prefecture Committee, Inner Mongolia Autonomous Region

Zhang Xiaolian, Secretary General, Mudanjiang CPC Committee, Helongjiang Province

Chen Weimin, Deputy Secretary, Jiangxi Province Government; Director, Foreign Affairs Office, Jiangxi Province

Wu Zhenglong, District Head, Wanzhou District, Chongqing

Li Lecheng, Director General, Organization Department, Jinmen CPC Municipal Committee, Hubei Province

Foreword

Strengthening and improving public administration is an important point of penetration for deepening reform and also essential for building a socialist harmonious society.

In order to enhance public administration and with the approval of the Organization Department of the Chinese Communist Party Central Committee, the Development Research Center of the State Council has been holding an annual advanced training course on public administration since 2002 in cooperation with Tsinghua University in China and Harvard University in America. Most of the trainees are bureau leaders from central and regional government. The training courses combine theoretical study with practical experience summarization, and each trainee has to write a case study paper based on personal work experience upon graduation. This book contains thirty-six papers selected from the case studies presented by over 300 trainees. The contents cover the reform of the government administration system, urban construction and management, crisis management and group incidents, resources and ecological environment, education and public health, and economic reform and development. The papers are all about concrete events, but their messages are of universal significance.

Our thanks go to these leaders who have voiced their ideas about how to build a harmonious society. With great zeal and in light of the practical conditions in their regions and departments, these leaders have provided us with vivid case studies on how to strengthen and improve public administration, coordinate relations of interest, solve social contradictions and promote social harmony. A harmonious society is by no means a society without contradictions. Complex contradictions exist in the preliminary stage of China's socialism and in the course of reforming the economic system, changing the mode of economic growth and transforming society. The process of reform and development is also a process of constantly solving social contradictions. While old contradictions are solved, new contradictions will emerge under new conditions. The goals of reform and development can be smoothly realized only when contradictions are carefully analysed and properly solved, when problems of partial implications are prevented from becoming those of overall implications and non-antagonistic contradictions are prevented from becoming antagonistic ones, and when maximum efforts are made to reduce the factors causing social disharmony and to increase the factors promoting social harmony. This should be a thread that runs through the whole process of building a socialist harmonious society and achieving modernization.

I highly recommend this book. It is a book full of pragmatism. The case studies are all personal experiences. They are descriptive, frank and highly readable. The readers will greatly benefit from them.

Wang Mengkui
Formerly President of the Development Research Center of the State
Council and currently Chairman of the China Development
Research Foundation
10 September 2006

Part I

Reform of the government administration system

1 Why private coffers are rampant

Sun Baohou

The term 'private coffer' is so well known in China that everybody understands what it means. But while nearly everybody believes no unit should have a private coffer, nearly everybody hopes his or her own unit can have one. While nearly everybody supports crackdowns on private coffers, nearly everybody hopes the private coffer affecting him or her will survive. While nearly everybody is fully aware of the harms of private coffers, nearly everybody hopes his or her personal interests associated with the private coffer will not be affected. The state has repeatedly banned private coffers and cracked down on them annually. Yet instead of being banned, private coffers continue to thrive, both in number and in value. Why? Can private coffers be effectively contained?

History of private coffers

Commonly called 'private money', private coffers have a long history in China. In old society, married women had no status or rights in their families. They had to hide some money in order to support their parents. Following the founding of the People's Republic of China, while women saw their status rising sharply, men saw their status dipping, and had to hand over all their wages and bonuses to their wives. While doing so, they naturally hid some money to pay for smoking, drinking and social activities. If the private coffer could stop there, it was only a private matter, which at most would disturb family harmony but would have no social implications.

The 'private coffers' we are talking about here are those established by government organs, public institutions and enterprises. They are beyond the control of the normal financial revenue and expenditure and the mandatory account books. They are called 'off-balance-sheet accounts'. According to state financial laws and regulations, the revenue and expenditure departments of government organs, public institutions and enterprises are required to draw up budgets that must be examined and approved in advance through certain procedures. While pending approval, the budgetary items and contents must be executed and entered in the mandatory account books. Afterwards, financial statements must be compiled and submitted. If these rules are observed, there will be no room or reason for the private coffers to exist. They are called 'private coffers' because they remain outside normal financial revenue and expenditure. They do not require strict budget compilation, examination, approval and execution. They embezzle, withhold and hide various forms of revenue and falsify costs and expenditure. These funds are transferred out of the mandatory account books and financial statements of their own institutions and privately deposited.

For a long time after the founding of the People's Republic of China, financial management in various institutions in general was fairly strict. There was no question of 'private coffers' at the time. However, in the late 1970s and early 1980s, a series of reform measures were introduced, such as separating government function from enterprise management, decentralizing powers, liberalizing control and fiscal decentralization. As a result, government organs, public institutions and enterprises began to exercise greater economic autonomy, and 'private coffers' mushroomed.

Private coffers are huge in number and value

At first, private coffers were not huge because of limited financial sources. For the government organs and public institutions, the private coffer largely comprised the revenue from selling old books and newspapers. For the enterprises, the private coffer largely comprised the income from selling left-over materials and redundant equipment. Those who were bolder claimed more overtime pay and night-duty allowance, and used this money to buy cigarettes and tea to entertain visitors, to visit patients or to have a year-end dinner party. However, this practice was carried out only piecemeal.

But human desire knows no limits. Once there is a beginning, there will be no end. The private coffer is like strong-smelling fermented bean curd, some people noted: everybody knows it smells offensive but they all like it and enjoy eating it. After over 20 years of evolution, the private coffer is no longer what it used to be in terms of scale, even though it still carries the adjective 'small'. As the desire to accumulate wealth is getting stronger, money is needed in more and more areas, and the ways of enriching the private coffer become increasingly disguised. As more and more money is accumulated, people become bolder and bolder in spending that money.

For example, a hard-working plant of a large company has an annual output value of more than 300 million yuan, but its private coffer is as large as 30 million yuan. A security company in Sichuan Province has 103 private coffers that hide funds totalling 227.89 million yuan. The private coffers of some departments of the General Administration of Civil Aviation of China have 87.84 million yuan in funds. A team at the sports management centre of the General Administration of Sport has 24.13 million yuan factored into the unit's unified financial account, but the balance of 4.38 million yuan is deposited in cash or in banks in personal names. In Jiangsu Province, thirty-seven of the forty-six institutions of higher education have private coffers worth 50.96 million yuan. The Guomaocheng case in the city of Harbin reveals that the former general manager has a personal private coffer of over 7.2 million yuan. Worse still, Hu Zhizhong, former chief procurator of the Zhongyuan District Procuratorate in the city of Zhengzhou, was not a high-ranking official, but his personal private coffer enriched with public funds was over 47 million yuan.

Private coffers do not exist in just a few units. In fact, many units in all walks of life have private coffers, and each unit can have many private coffers of its own. A unit has subunits, and the subunits have sub-subunits. If a unit is divided into several levels, private coffers exist at the same number of levels. If the former leaders of a unit have private coffers, the successors of the unit and their successors will continue to have private coffers. Some private coffers are inherited and others are newly created. Like snowballing, government organs, public institutions and enterprises all have large numbers of private coffers that hide huge amounts of funds. This is an open secret and also an indisputable fact.

How many private coffers are there nationwide, and how large are they in scale? Nobody can tell and nobody can conduct a thorough investigation. Some regional newspapers made bold estimations about the scale of private coffers nationwide. They claimed that nationwide there are about 500 billion yuan, or 5 per cent of the country's gross domestic product (GDP), entering the private coffers annually. This is an astonishing figure.

How can the private coffers contain so much money? From what sources do they obtain their money? In what forms do they exist? And who controls them? These are also questions nobody can answer clearly. An article once asked: where does the money in the 'private coffers' come from? Some of it comes from arbitrary charges, some of it comes from withheld fines, some of it comes from lapping funds, and some of it comes from the support funds swindled from higher authorities. In short, the money in the 'private coffers' all comes from public funds, publicly or privately, legally or illegally.

There are many sources for private coffers to draw money from that may go beyond the imagination of ordinary people, but these sources are familiar to those involved. There are even alternative forms of the existence of private coffers. Some are in the form of false accounts, some are off-balance-sheet accounts, some do not have accounts at all, some are formally deposited in bank accounts in personal or fictitious names, some are in bundles or boxes of notes, some exist in piles of vouchers, some in bundles of IOUs; some do not even have IOUs, while others are personally handled by leaders, some by accountants, and some are managed by other people.

The cases unearthed indicate that private coffers have five sources from which to obtain money and they exist in five forms.

1   *The private coffers with withheld funds.* The funds are not entered into the mandatory account books of the relevant units. They include the incomes from enterprises' production and operations, labour and service

charges, surcharges, fines, normal or abnormal discounts, concessions, commissions and kickbacks, extra-budget revenue of the government organs and public institutions (sometimes illegal charges), foundation incomes, institutional incomes, incomes from leasing or selling fixed assets, incomes from selling waste, and funds from donations and sponsorships. They exist in cash or are deposited in banks in personal or fictitious names, or are deposited into special bank accounts. In general, they exist in separate account books or in similar carriers.

2 *The private coffers with false accounts.* False accounts are used to transfer funds from the mandatory account books of the relevant units; fake invoices with no real business background are used to falsify costs and claims so as to raise cash illicitly, which is either kept separate or immediately distributed. Most private coffers do not have account books or similar carriers.

3 *The private coffers with offset funds.* The rents, contracting fees and investment profits that should be received and entered into the mandatory account books are kept with other institutions or in foreign countries; the resulting income is directly offset by the costs of meals, accommodation, gas and electricity, and attendance at conferences; expenses are directly reimbursed from the leasing, contracting or investing units; or the income may be directly reinvested. These incomes are not recorded or reflected at all in their own institutions.

4 *The private coffers with current accounting items.* Income is temporarily entered as a current account item in the mandatory account book, and expenditure is entered as an opposite item in the same current account. The original income and expenditure invoices are kept separately or destroyed. Thus, what appears to be a normal current cash flow hides the real contents of the receivables and payables.

5 *The private coffers with outward and inward allocations.* The institutions that have the power to distribute budget outlays allocate the funds to their subordinates or other institutions in the name of fund distribution, under the precondition that part of the allocated funds is only managed by the receiving institutions but has to be used by the allocating institutions. The private coffers of this type carry no traces of the allocating institutions. Alternatively, the allocating institutions request the receiving institutions to transfer the allocated funds to designated places for the use of the allocating institutions. The private coffers of this type may be recorded in the separate accounts of the allocating institutions or be transferred to other institutions and managed on their behalf.

Private coffers are used for diverse purposes

The scale of the private coffers is large and the sources of their income diverse. But what are they used for? They are used for all sorts of purposes. The following are just a few examples.

1   Some departments or enterprises crack down on private coffers annually, yet private coffers continue to thrive. Why? It is mainly because they can be cunningly used for many purposes. First, a private coffer is tantamount to a coffer from which the leaders or management personnel can take and use the money in any way they want. Is there anybody who does not want to use money without restraint? Second, when an enterprise has a private coffer, it can hide income and pay less in taxes. Third, the private coffer has become a 'cistern' or 'adjuster' for an institution or enterprise to ensure a stable source of welfare bonuses. Currently, the government generally allocates basic funds to the institutions under its budgetary control according to the number of people employed by those institutions. To some institutions, the allocations based on the number of employees are inadequate, and they are obliged to raise funds themselves for the welfare, allowances and bonuses payable to their employees. To make up the fund gap, these institutions have to find new sources of income. As the sources of self-raised funds are unstable and the amount of the raised funds varies from year to year, these institutions have to save the surplus funds left over from the good years and use them to stabilize the welfare of their institutions on a long-term basis. The surplus funds left over from the good years are set aside and enter the private coffers. Fourth, private coffers are indispensable for eating, drinking, entertaining and other social activities. Private coffers can play important roles. Without the lubrication of the private coffers, it will be impossible for institutions to have their projects approved or their fund allocations increased. To win the favour of one's leaders in order to seek promotion, one has to develop good relations with them by going to restaurants, teahouses and dance halls. The private coffers can make all this convenient and easy. Fifth, private coffers make it convenient for some people with ulterior motives to embezzle state-owned assets.

2   The funds of the private coffers are spent in the following ways. First, to finance kickbacks, commissions, royalty and service charges secretly. Second, to entertain guests and buy gifts. Third, to pay reception and tourist expenses. Fourth, to pay bonuses and welfare costs above the set standards. Fifth, to purchase or construct office buildings, large halls and guest-houses above and beyond the set standards and plans. Sixth, to settle other expenses that cannot be paid for from the official accounts, including corruption, embezzlement, illicit distribution and other office-related crimes.

3   The private coffers have stayed outside the control of the financial systems and have spread to various social strata in China. Official media call them 'black holes' of corruption, and ordinary people call them the 'green passages' for corrupt officials at various levels. The fund circulation of private coffers takes place in four steps: abnormal expenditure of the institutions → small amount of corruption by leading officials → rampant embezzlement by leading officials → joint corruption by collective leadership.

4 Where do the funds in the private coffers go? Some of the money is used for extravagant eating and drinking, some for secret purposes, some for the personal enjoyment of leaders, some to curry favour with superiors, and some to buy official positions. In short, private coffers are 'secret accounts' (or no account at all in some cases) outside the official accounts and are in fact the 'personal purses' of the leaders of institutions. These leaders can spend them in any way they choose.

5 The private coffers are used for 'black spending' and 'grey spending'. The latter was mainly used to pay welfare costs, allowances and bonuses to employees of the institutions, for receptions and gifts of a general nature, for 'tributes' paid to the higher authorities or some powerful departments, for gifts or gift money sent to leading officials, or 'special' people for 'special' occasions such as wedding or funeral ceremonies, hospitalization, public holidays and children's schooling, and as various forms of job-related consumption by the leaders of institutions and departments.

6 The private coffers are used for entertaining guests and buying presents, for publicly funded tourism, for extravagant eating and drinking, for buying luxury consumer goods, for starting up private business and for directly replenishing personal purses. In some cases, the expenses of family consumption, saunas and massages are claimed from the private coffers. Worse still, some people use the money from private coffers to gamble or to keep mistresses. The private coffers are regarded as personal purses and may be used for any purpose.

On the basis of the above descriptions, the uses of private coffers may be summarized as follows: (1) they are used for the reasonable and unreasonable benefit of the majority of employees in the institutions, such as welfare costs, allowances and bonuses; (2) they are used for some necessary and unnecessary expenditure of institutions, such as supplementing office expenses, project investments and collective activities, and for reception, liaison, gift and other items designed to develop markets, seek support and improve relations with higher or related institutions; (3) they are used for the personal gain of some people or even certain employees of institutions, such as for extravagant expenditure, illegal distribution, buying official positions and even bribery and corruption.

Private coffers inflict great harm on society

The harm done by private coffers to the economy and society is well known. But what are the specific harms?

First, private coffers stay outside the normal management of the institutions and beyond the supervision of the financial department, the audit of the audit department and the vision of the tax department. They are controlled by a few leaders and the persons in charge, and are used for entertaining guests, buying gifts, corruption, embezzlement, unreasonable welfare payments and bonuses. The harm done is great.

Second, the existence of private coffers not only causes distortion and falsification of the accounting documents, but also leads to huge losses of state fiscal revenue. Meanwhile, it fosters luxurious consumption, waste and corruption, and undermines the Party conduct and social atmosphere. Therefore, it has become a social problem that cannot be ignored in our political and economic life. Private coffers are harmful for the following reasons: (1) most private coffers are used for issuing bonuses and allowances in kind, causing the consumption funds to run out of control; (2) private coffers are noted for chaotic management and incomplete formalities, so that use of the funds is decided by a few leaders and is prone to misappropriation, corruption, bribery and other illegal activities; (3) the accounts of private coffers are mostly running accounts whose items can be entered in every possible way. These accounts are not kept for certain years and can induce various economic crimes.

Third, there are a huge number of private coffers in existence, and nearly all of them hide something not fit to be seen. (1) They hide 'confusions', including both income confusion and expenditure confusion, both financial confusion and business confusion, and both management confusion and system confusion. (2) They hide 'waste'. A glance at the accounts of private coffers can reveal that, apart from replenishing office expenses in a few cases, most of the funds are used for eating, drinking, sightseeing, bonuses and welfare costs of the employees of these institutions or enterprises. In some cases, the funds are used to hold conferences, purchase cars, build houses and buy office facilities above the set standards. (3) They hide 'bombs'. These are legal and disciplinary bombs rather than chemical bombs. Everybody knows that power without supervision breeds corruption. The use of the funds of private coffers is a form of power that escapes the supervision of the financial and audit authorities. The leading officials of the institutions or enterprises have the final say over what to spend and how to spend it. Accordingly, the heads who have the final say regard the money of these private coffers as their pocket-money and spend it like water. But one day, when some institutions are investigated, these officials will explode like 'bombs'. The first sacrificial victims are those leaders who 'have the final say'.

Fourth, most of the money in the 'private coffers' is used for illegitimate consumption. For example, the expenses arising from guest entertainment, gifts and pleasure trips for the leaders of some institutions are paid for from the 'private coffers' because they cannot be claimed through the normal financial channels. As this technique is 'convenient' and is not subject to external supervision, it can easily breed corruption and economic crimes. Some leaders or handlers are found to have committed corruption, misappropriation and illegal distribution of public funds.

Fifth, the 'private coffers' not only poison the social atmosphere, but also cause inequitable distribution of social interests, and can directly induce or evolve into corruption cases. Meanwhile, they can also cause confusion in people's values and moral outlook, reduce the public trust of society and seriously affect the building of a harmonious society.

Sixth, today, corruption is what the Chinese people hate most. And corruption occurs largely among the officials who have real power, and causes public resentment at Party and government levels. This has attracted the attention of various circles. But why has corruption become a chronic disease that cannot be cured? One key reason is that the 'private coffers' existing in public institutions and enterprises, big or small, urban or rural, have provided an endless financial source for corrupt officials.

In summary, private coffers are harmful for the following reasons: (1) they result in a huge loss of state-owned assets, national tax revenue and other incomes; (2) they cause inequity in distribution which favours certain individuals who desire a luxurious lifestyle; (3) they cause confusion in financial management and distortion of accounting information, and seriously disturb the normal economic order; (4) they undermine the solemnity, public trust and restraint of the laws, regulations and Party and government disciplines; (5) they escape the supervision and inspection of the financial, tax, audit and other departments; (6) they foster extravagance, waste, economic crime and corruption, distort the working styles of the Party and government, and poison the social atmosphere (the statistics of a province indicate that private coffers are involved in 63 per cent of corruption cases and 42 per cent of bribery cases; the investigation of a provincial capital indicates that as many as 90 per cent of economic irregularities relate to private coffers).

When can private coffers be effectively contained?

Everybody knows that private coffers are illegal and extremely harmful, and the relevant state departments have also taken action to contain them. But they continue to be a chronic disease. Why? And when can the spread of private coffers be effectively contained? Some people emphasize the priority areas, some people hope both the outward symptoms and the root causes will be treated, while others demand a comprehensive solution. Some are optimistic, some are sober-minded, others are pessimistic. Let us see how the media, academic community and government officials react to this problem.

To begin with, we will go through six typical media comments.

First, it is not difficult to contain and eliminate private coffers. The key measure is to punish without leniency. Laws and regulations should be improved to treat the use of private coffers as an economic crime. Specific standards for punishment should then be set, ranging from imposing Party and government disciplinary sanctions to prosecuting for criminal liabilities. With this firm determination and iron hand, private coffers will not be so difficult to contain and eliminate.

Second, media reports on the audit and punishment of holders of private coffers are not surprising. The government organs and enterprises have long had their own private coffers. Despite repeated efforts to ban them, they have continued to mushroom. As time goes on, the general public is no longer surprised by the media reports on the audit of private coffers. They have become disillusioned.

Third, we must realize that many social problems and systems-related chronic diseases reflected by private coffers have profound historical reasons and a complex social background. These problems cannot be thoroughly resolved by several audits at the present stage.

Fourth, some units continue to act as they choose, even though the state has explicitly banned private coffers. The reasons are as follows: (1) Some comrades believe that, in a market economy, 'emotional investment' and 'economic leverage' are indispensable for accomplishing something. Private coffers stay outside fiscal control and can precisely play full roles in this respect. Without private coffers, it would be impossible to accomplish certain things. (2) Some comrades believe that private coffers are in the interests of the units and that banning them may bring losses to the small collectives. As long as the money does not go into personal pockets and as long as it is spent in the areas known to everybody, private coffers will have a reason to exist. (3) Some people keep their private coffers simply because other units maintain them. In this large backdrop, banning private coffers will become difficult.

Fifth, one of the important reasons for the existence of private coffers is that the departmental budgets have run out of control. For example, one man can eat a quarter of a kilogram of meat for a meal but then you give him half a kilogram. When he cannot eat it all, he will save the surplus. Equally, if a department has a budget that is more than enough, it will put the surplus money into a private coffer. This is because all the expenditure items of a budgetary unit are arranged by the government fiscal budget. How can you have a private coffer when you do not have money to put into it? Therefore, the success of private coffers is due to the fact that departments or units are given too large a margin when the departmental budgets are compiled or when the construction projects are examined and approved. If private coffers are to be completely uprooted, we must 'give the right prescription for the right illness'. At present, it is imperative to conscientiously implement the instructions of the central financial authorities on the reform of departmental budgets, and exercise strict control over them.

Sixth, I personally believe that there are two main reasons for the existence of private coffers in many places and in many institutions. One is the mentality that the law fails where violators are legion. Most private coffers are collectively approved by the leaders under the pretext of supplementing office expenses and improving employee welfare. Therefore, the leaders take it for granted when they approve private coffers. They believe that as long as the money does not go straight into their personal pockets it will not have serious consequences, even if these private coffers are discovered. The other reason is the attitude of leaders at the higher level, who turn a blind eye to or even support the efforts of those units to 'earn money' to ease local fiscal pressure.

Therefore, treating the outward symptoms alone cannot fundamentally solve the issue of private coffers.

The academic community places more blame on system defects for the issue of private coffers. They believe that, if government revenue and expenditure are used as the parameters for statistics, there are at least three types of revenue and expenditure: budget revenue and expenditure, extra-budgetary revenue and expenditure, and extra-system revenue and expenditure. The control over budget revenue and expenditure is quite standard. They are regulated by unified systems, included into budgets and reviewed by the people's congresses at various levels. The control over extra-budgetary revenue and expenditure is less strict. They are regulated by relatively unified systems, partially reflected in budgets, partially staying outside of budgets and not wholly reviewed by the people's congresses at the various levels. The control over extra-system revenue and expenditure is completely substandard. Various institutions and departments establish their own rules, and earn and spend the money as they choose. From the perspective of standardizing the behaviours of the market economy, the extra-budgetary and extra-system revenue and expenditure are not standard. Their use is closely related to personal and departmental interests, and a considerable portion goes to the private coffers and becomes the 'personal purse' of a few leaders. The money is used directly to cover the spending that cannot be covered by the normal expenditure budget. Worse still, the money can become the target of some corrupt leaders through diverse channels. Therefore, Professor Gao Peiyong of the Chinese Academy of Social Sciences suggested in an article that a complete and unified government budget system should be established to eliminate extra-system government revenue and expenditure, and to include extra-budgetary revenue and expenditure into budget control so that the government budget could cover all government revenue and expenditure. He also noted that one of the reasons for the current widespread illegal expenditure by government departments was that these departments drew their financial resources through a double-track system. In addition to fiscal appropriation, government departments still have to 'earn revenue' to cover part of their expenditure. The 'revenue-earning' methods naturally stay outside the existing systems. As long as the double-track system of fiscal appropriation and self-financing continues to exist, government departments will inevitably play the double role of both social administrator and profit earner, and will accommodate the double motives of serving public interests and partial interests. Accordingly, this will create excuses and provide fertile ground for illegal revenue-earning and money-spending behaviours designed to serve personal and departmental interests. Experts suggest that government departments should rely on a united fiscal 'supply system', under which all their financial resources come from fiscal budget appropriations. Even if the double-track system cannot be abolished all at once in view of national conditions, the 'supply system' should be taken as a goal and be achieved step by step by creating appropriate conditions. The audit institutions have made lots of fruitful efforts in investigating the private coffers. Li Jinhua, Auditor General of the National Audit Office of the People's Republic of China, has made significant contributions to the investigations. Famed as an 'impartial and incorruptible auditor general', he was voted person of the year for 2004 by China Central Television. When asked how to deal with the 'private coffers' that re-emerge following each crackdown, he said frankly, 'The only thing we can do is to crack down again whenever they re-emerge'.

When this case study was nearly completed, I consulted a senior government official who had been engaged in cracking down on private coffers over how to contain them. He believed that, while education and punishment are naturally important, system improvements should become a priority if private coffers are to be effectively contained. First, the ownership system should be clearly defined. One unique feature of China is that the country has a huge amount of state-owned assets. The drain of the state-owned assets and state-owned revenue constitutes both a precondition and a result of the existence of private coffers. Therefore, reforms should be stepped up in establishing a truly well-defined state ownership system. Second, we should have a fund-guarantee system. Some of the state policies have long become outdated. For example, the standards for travel expenses are too low, and some income gaps are ignored. There is a wide income gap between central and regional government organs in the same city, and the incomes of powerful departments are higher than those of ordinary departments. Sometimes, when new policies on wages and welfare are set forth, no fiscal resources are given. If these problems are not solved, there will be no basic condition for cracking down on private coffers. Of all the expenses coming from the private coffers, a reasonable proportion of institutional and personal expenditure should be covered by the government budget instead of being raised by the units themselves. Third, the systems should be open and transparent. The openness of government affairs refers not only to the openness of administrative affairs, but also to the openness of financial affairs. This openness should have system support. The most striking feature of the private coffers is that they are concealed. The normal fiscal relationship between private coffers and the government's coffers is that the former is the destination and the latter the source. The most fundamental problem is that the government's coffers that should be open are not. For this reason, we must first of all make the government's coffers open and transparent and place all the fiscal revenue and expenditure of the government organs and public institutions under public supervision. Bringing the main revenue and expenditure into the open and blocking the illegal drain on the government's coffers can, to a very large extent, cut off the financial sources of the private coffers and thus facilitate the solution to the issue of private coffers. These system improvements are of an elementary and fundamental nature and will take a while to accomplish. They cannot be achieved overnight.

Written in 2006

2 An experiment in radical and holistic change

Gao Zhili

Budgeting officers' dilemma

Why are the revenues and expenditures of public finance always in a tense situation, whereas the allocative efficiency of public resources and the performance of public expenditure are pervasively low? Why does the spending level differ widely from one department to another within the same tier of government, with some having more to spend and some having less? Why are those spending departments keen to build close relationships with finance departments in order to get more resources, and budget has virtually no meaningful control over spending? Why is the finance department always seen as the focus of every contradiction, making enormous efforts without receiving any recognition in return? What are the significant factors affecting and constraining the allocation of the budget? Where on earth is the way out? In the year 1998, the budgeting officers of Hebei Provincial Finance Bureau (HPFB) experienced these problems.

Difficult fiscal status

Although Hebei Province is one of the largest provinces in China in terms of land area, population and economic scale, the fiscal capacity has been placed in only the middle and low levels of the whole country historically. Between 1994 and 1998, the average annual growth rate of overall revenues of the province was 21.4 per cent, and the average annual growth rate of disposable resources was 16.8 per cent. Such surging growth rates, primarily accredited to policy factors – incentives brought by a tax-sharing system and something that had rarely happened in Hebei Province over the many years since the foundation of New China – cannot be sustained in the long run. Nevertheless, total revenue per capita calculated on the basis of the whole population in 1998 was ranked only seventeenth in the country, while expenditure per capita was ranked twenty-third. More seriously, revenues per capita of nearly half the county-level governments in Hebei can only meet the minimum operating demand, and the resources in some counties were not even able to cover the expenditure for public employees' standard salaries.

The tensions of this contradictory situation have grown and are aggravated by the increasingly deepening economic system of reform in China and the expanding coverage of services provided by public finance. Specifically, almost all state-owned enterprises were downsized in an attempt to reduce employees' efficiency in the process of transformation. At the same time, properly settling those redundant employees of state-owned enterprises and getting them re-employed has added new pressure on the government. In fact, the problem basically tackled by the social security system in Western industrial countries has to be addressed by public resources in the case of China where the social security system is still in its early stages and employees of state-owned enterprises are seen as another form of government support; all redundant employees have to depend on the government financially. Similar social protection such as poor urban populations, the elderly, sick or disabled people in rural areas as well as public services including utility infrastructure, public health and compulsory education are a drain on public resources together with social and economic development.

In addition, some of the accumulated liabilities including huge government borrowings, delayed payments for agricultural products and salary arrears of public employees have become a heavy financial burden for the government, adding further pressure on expenditure. From time to time, the public funds of provincial and some municipal or county-level governments were coming close to the warning line, and borrowing 'revolving funds' from upper-level government to cover the need to continue to operate became a common occurrence.

The decision-makers and budgeting officers of HPFB believe that there are no other ways to address this difficult financial position than by finding additional channels of resources or cutting expenditures. Under the circumstance that there is no potential for increasing revenues, cutting back on expenditure seems to be the only choice. As budget is the driving force of public resource allocation and the critical device in solving fiscal problems, the greater potential of improved expenditure is achievable through enhanced budgetary management. Consequently, solving fiscal problems through reforming traditional budgeting practice was the consensus reached by the management of HPFB at that time.

Pitfalls of traditional budgetary management

The managers of HPFB rested their hopes on reforming traditional budgetary management, but is this an effective approach? While giving a positive judgement, the management of HPFB prudently required the budgeting division to carry out a comprehensive study and analysis. The results were startling. The analytical report written by budgeting officers taking into account their day-to-day working experiences has summarized the principal deficiencies of budgetary management under the planned economy and concluded that reform was inevitable, irrespective of whether the original objective of solving financial difficulties was achievable or not. A budgeting official involved in the study commented: 'You would never expect that there are so many problems associated with traditional budgetary management, you cannot even imagine the worst effect that current practise can lead to if the same pattern will be followed continuously'.

Detailed research was carried out on each stage of the whole budgeting process – preparation, execution and supervision – and many issues were identified following the research.

The most obvious issue was the simplicity, lack of detail and low quality of the budget, which may be seen in the budget proposal submitted to the provincial National People's Congress (NPC). According to the law, provincial government has to submit an annual budget proposal to the provincial NPC, the superior local authority. The proposal comprises no more than a dozen pages containing several thousand words: a few tables presenting revenues by tax category and expenditures by functions, without any detailed information such as how much expenditure is budgeted for each specific department, project or line item. What was virtually reviewed by the NPC was some highly abstract information and aggregated figures; for example, one of the representatives from NPC noted that the budget proposal 'is hard to understand by a layman and hard to know clearly by a specialist'. Why? The reasons were quite straightforward, the budgeting officers and researchers believed. As Budget Law stipulates, budget preparation for the following year is prepared every November, which is 2 months before execution. In most foreign countries, in contrast, the budgeting process will take at least 1 year to accomplish, and is even longer in the USA, at 18 months. So it is not surprising how poor the quality of the budget could be when it is prepared within such a short time. With more careful study, it was also found that historically there had never been a departmental budget, nor has it been a requirement of the Chinese government. Although Budget Law states that the government budget is constituted of departmental budgets, no matter how approximate the budget figure, it is still within reasonable range of system design.

Of course, after the proposal is approved by provincial NPCs, some expenditure will be allocated to line items, but this will still be a very rough approximation. On the one hand, the spending units with the budgeting authority at each level will set aside some reserves, so the funds allocated to departments and items in reality are only a part of the budgeted amount. With respect to block funding, except for reserves allowed by law, an additional amount is put aside with the excuse of covering unforeseen expenditures, and the 'secondary public finance department', the spending units' holding allocation authority, will squeeze some funds from the budget for contingency. Similarly, spending units will hold some funds without allocating the budget fully to its subordinate units using the same argument. Under this 'reserves' mechanism, it was solely the decision of managers without any prior review and approval process. As a result, the percentage of 'reserves' is naturally high. Once reserves are set aside by each level, only less than half of the budgeted amount at the beginning of the year can be allocated to line items.

The reason behind the simplicity and low quality of the budget is that it is not prepared in a scientific manner. As there is no requirement for detailed budgeting, the budget is prepared in block funds and on a 'base plus incremental' approach. This oversimplified method aggravates the contradiction between demand and supply of public funds because the budget is not a response to actual need; rather, it is based on the benefits that have already been attained plus an equalized increase. Meanwhile, this approach solidified the allocative pattern of public funds among spending units and also put a barrier to the adjustment of economic structure and the pattern of social development. The expenditure base of some spending units was improperly determined at the beginning, and it was becoming more and more irrational under this 'base plus incremental' approach. Apart from this, the way in which the budget is allocated both by the nature of funds (NPC budget) and by department (internal budget of administrative branches) led to many disputes, which weakened the allocative function of public finance and made it harder to distribute the limited resources effectively. More importantly, the separation of on-budget and off-budget has resulted in the incomplete nature of the government budget.

Another significant issue was that the format of the budget cannot fully reflect the whole funding policy of the government. Internationally, the government budget consists primarily of departmental budgets and functional budgets, where the functional budget refers to the budget that is categorized by the function of revenues and expenditure. The departmental budget is the budget managed by the category of department. The functional budget details the distribution of public funds in terms of nature, reflecting the policy objectives that the government intends to achieve in political, economic and social areas. It shows directly the structure of fiscal capacity and the area of resource allocation of government spending, which depicts the whole picture of revenues and expenditure to the public and makes it easier to carry out analyses on certain aspects of government revenues and expenditures. The functional budget, however, has its disadvantages; for instance, it is too abstract that resources allocation cannot be explicitly presented by departments and units, which is difficult not only for budget preparation and execution but also for an accurate assessment by the government and general public of the status of revenues and expenditures of one particular department. In particular, when the functional budget is used as the only tool for budgetary management, the problems loom larger. First, because the focus of the functional budget is on the overall scale of public funds in different functions, it has no requirement for detailed budgeting. As a result, the budget prepared is vague with no incentives for improved quality. Second, under the functional budget, most of the funds cannot be allocated to specific expenditure items at the beginning of the financial year and have to be determined during the implementation stage, which will have an adverse impact on regular disbursements throughout the year. Third, frequent adjustments during execution resulting from the vague nature of the functional budget have caused major difficulties for supervisory departments in reviewing and monitoring the use of public funds. Fourth, the decreasing involvement of spending departments in the budgeting process under the functional budget approach provides no incentives for spending units to manage their resources actively. Fifth, the lack of detail of the budget under the functional budget approach triggers unfair competition for public funds through abusive lobbying activities.

The pitfalls in budgeting subsequently lead to problems in budget execution and supervision. Because the funds are not approved and assigned to the specific items at the beginning of the year, the allocation of funds has to be delayed, as has the execution of the budget; in fact, most of the earmarked funds are spent during the last quarter of the year. Owing to a lack of transparency in the budgeting process, in the early months of the year, the spending units have no idea how much total funds are available or how much their share of expenditure is; consequently, they ask for supplements throughout the year. In reality, the situation is 'one year budget, budgeting all over the year'. Moreover, the finance department performs neither effective follow-up in examining the subsequent performance of spending units, nor careful evaluation after the final accounting.

In addition, the dispersed accounts of the spending units create low efficient distribution of budget funds. As much of the daily efforts of the finance department were spent on reviewing and approving supplementary requests from spending departments, it is hard to study some profound public expenditure issues and in turn to achieve an improved level of budgetary management.

Choice of reform scheme

After carrying out detailed and extensive analysis, the decision-makers and budgeting officers of HPFB seemed to see bright prospects for the reform. The consensus was swiftly reached among the decision-makers that 'The pitfalls of the traditional budget won't automatically disappear, there is no other way than reform'. There were three options under consideration as to how the reform would be implemented.

The first option was simply to keep the same pace with the reform programme at national level, given that the Ministry of Finance knew exactly what was wrong with the current system and would not allow it to exist in the long run. If this option was selected, the reform would be pursued in accordance with the unified reform scheme of national government. This way, it would not only win strong support from the upper level of government, but it would also have better institutional conditions. The reform would be easier, and the obstacles would be fewer. On the other hand, however, this option was too passive, suitable neither for market economy-oriented reform nor the actual conditions of Hebei Province.

The second option was to implement partial reform, focusing on only one or two major but less complex aspects of budgetary management to start with – for instance, zero-based budgeting or comprehensive budgeting – as colleagues in other provinces had done. This option would not touch the basic framework of traditional budgeting; therefore, the degree of foreseen obstacles and difficulties would be much less in both reform design and implementation, and was within the firm control of the finance department. The disadvantages of this option, however, were that piecemeal reform within the framework of traditional budgeting would not bring anticipated outcomes and substantial change. It would also be hard to push the reform further, as already proved by other localities in China.

The third option was to introduce holistic and radical reform. Consistent with scientific, standard and highly efficient objectives, the reform would break radically with the traditional budgeting framework by changing the format, operating scheme, preparation approach, execution procedures and supervision. From the perspective of significance, this option was the most desirable and, if successful, the implications and significance were enormous. It was believed that the significant effects of such reform would be as follows.

First, it would facilitate the construction and development of a socialist market economy. Through the introduction of budget reform, the budgetary management system would be put on a legal, standard and scientific track, which would firmly push the reform in the areas of planning, investment, the national economic accounting system as well as the decision-making process, and foster the completeness and development of a new economic management system.

Second, it would enhance the transparent public expenditure management in accordance with the law. A new model of budgetary management would greatly enhance the legal structure and harden the constraints of budget, effectively regulate the behaviour of finance departments in fiscal management and ensure efficient use of pubic funds by spending units. Meanwhile, preparing the budget in an open and transparent way would strengthen the democratic process for decision-making in resources allocation, and facilitate the review and supervision of NPC representatives by exerting real power in participating and consulting during the policy-making process.

Third, it would help to enhance the macro-management capacity of government. Through introducing a comprehensive budget, the range of the government budget would be expanded and the size of funds allocated would be larger. A zero-based budget would help to break the base of long-term attained interests of spending units so that resource allocation would be more rationalized. The adoption of a treasury single account would improve the control capacity of government in providing a useful tool to strengthen macro-adjustment and regulation.

Fourth, it would help to improve the overall level of financial management. After the new model of budget preparation and execution has been approved and adopted, finance departments can shift their focus from the daily review of supplements to being more deeply involved in the process of sector planning, selection and determination of programmes as well as supervision of the use of funds. At the same time, implementing departmental budgets will hold the spending units accountable for some basic responsibility of budgetary management and require them to pay more attention to financial management, to be more responsive to the requirements of reform, to enhance management in various aspects, particularly when establishing development objectives and prioritizing programmes, and they should be more able to take into account the budgeting arrangements, and plan and perform tasks in line with the budget.

Fifth, it would help to set up an anti-corruption scheme, which would pave the way for preventing corruption at source. Through the establishment of a distributing and allocating scheme of public funds, one-off allocation in an open, transparent and fair manner would ensure the scientific, fair and logical allocation of resources and avoid 'black box' activities. In addition, expenditure methods including government procurement and treasury single accounts would ensure that fiscal funds would be managed in a more scientific, standard and transparent way, which would greatly reduce the possibility of a breach of law or disciplinary violation, preventing corruption at source and establishing clean government.

The decision-makers and budgeting officers of HPFB, however, were also clearly aware of the extent of the difficulties and risk that this option entailed. Holistic change called for the overthrow of traditional budgeting, but the long existence of convention implied that the role of factors supporting the system was still in play, and the deep-rooted inertia of an entrenched tradition would strongly fight off the change. Naturally, due to the unpredictable outcome of reform, higher level decision-makers were not in a position to offer definite support to radical change, given their major concerns over the possible side-effects that the reform might bring, a pattern of thought that can be traced back to the 'middle way' of traditional Chinese philosophy. Although numerous beneficiaries of the traditional system would agree theoretically with the necessity and importance of change, on the other hand, they would not like to see reform coming too soon because change always means a reshuffle of interests among various stakeholders, and they would prefer to enjoy the various good things embedded in the traditional system. Consequently, they would not wholeheartedly welcome the change, and it would be fortunate if there was not much resistance. Therefore, reform not only requires great determination and courage, but also a thorough consideration of the readiness for reform including whether adequate manpower, knowledge and techniques are in place, whether the contradictions or conflicts of interests from various stakeholders can be handled properly and, more importantly, whether the prerequisites for reform exist.

Reform in context

As Stephen P. Robbins, the famous management specialist in the USA, once observed, there are two types of change: one is to imagine the organization as a large boat sailing on a peaceful sea. The captain and crew know exactly where they are heading because they have made many voyages like this before, and changes only occur in stormy weather. The rest of the trip is predictably smooth. Another kind of change is to view the organization as a raft on a stormy river. There are half a dozen crew on the raft, but they have never embarked on this journey together, nor do they know the geography of the river. They don't know where to go and, what is even worse, they have to travel at night.

Which kind of change did the budgeting reform in Hebei Province belong to? Let us look at the situation at that time.

Institutional environment

Since the foundation of New China, several reforms have been implemented in adjusting the fiscal system, such as the unified collection and allocation of funds by the state, fixed lump sums for each administrative level, separate financing and tax-sharing system reforms in 1994, which all centred on adjusting the distribution of resources vertically. Even though, in 1998, the establishment of a public financial framework was proposed at the annual public finance working conference, the focus of reform was still on the vertical fiscal relationship. Horizontal budgetary reform related to the effectiveness of public expenditure was not an item on the agenda. Similar to other provinces, before 1998, the reform effort in Hebei was concentrated on a deepening and refining of the tax-sharing system, while budgetary reform was not a priority.

Although it was decided in China to transform from a planned economy to a market economy, there was no substantial progress in aspects of planning and management until 1998. National economic planning still starts quite late during the year with no close coordination with government budgeting, as most senior officials and departments believe that the budget should be prepared on the basis of planning; therefore, planning was the most significant factor affecting budget preparation. If the planning system remains as it is, early and detailed budget preparation would be difficult. On the other hand, the Ministry of Finance at the central level still follows the conventional approach of budgetary management. If Hebei moves ahead beyond the scope of the traditional framework, the immediate question would be how compatibility can be attained.

Management practice symbolizing a command economy has been deeply rooted in many aspects. Public funding, in most cases, was arranged through the command economy. Phenomena such as personal, imprudent or on-the-spot decisions were common and far from the requirements of a scientific, standard and early preparation of budgets.

Theory and competence

Theory is needed to guide the reform. When HPFB decided to implement the reform, theories that could be used to direct the reform were few. Because it was in a special transition period from a planned economy to a market economy, the budgeting theory originated under the planned economy was obviously not suitable for guiding the reform, whereas Western budgeting theories are not effective enough to guide reform in China because of big differences in terms of the political and economic systems between China and Western countries. Moreover, the formation of Western theories has developed over a very long period of time. At that moment, few relevant studies or research projects had been conducted in China, and the introduction of practices and theories regarding budgetary management in foreign countries had only just begun; even now, the budgeting theory combining Chinese characteristics with Western concepts is not mature enough. Consequently, the theoretical base for reform was inadequate.

Without the guidance of available theories, following the successful experiences of others is a practical way to proceed. However, at that time, domestically, the focal point of fiscal reform was on how to rationalize the fiscal relationship vertically between central and local government. Budgetary management reform was not started on the whole; some approaches such as zero-based budgeting and comprehensive budgeting were tried only in certain fields by some provinces, with no locality implementing holistic reform. Further, internationally, because of different conditions among Western countries, specific budgeting management practices differ from one to another. Therefore, it is not proper to just simply 'copy' the experiences of others. Budgetary management reform in Hebei province needs a breakthrough over the traditional framework; the big challenge was that, while the practice of Western countries cannot be fully 'borrowed', a new way of budgetary management consistent with the progress of economic reform must be found.

When the decision-makers in HPFB finally determined to make reforms with conscience and a sense of responsibility, they found that the prerequisites for reform in terms of manpower, financial resources, knowledge, techniques, authority and space were not freely available. Those staff in the Budgeting Division holding key responsibility for the design and performance of the task of reform did not have sufficient budgeting experience. In terms of authority, as a department under the provincial government, HPFB has limited room to promote the reform, and its role in the decision-making process of major economic policy was no less strong than that of some other departments. The only controllable authority is to reform internally and to take over 'revolutionary' measures. It was obvious, however, that there was also resistance from insiders.

Culture and tradition

Stakeholders are always very sensitive to reform where a reshuffle of interests takes place. Previous piecemeal reforms have already aroused disputes, and some have claimed that 'budgetary reform is a process of making the power more centralized towards the finance department', 'the finance department cannot serve as the sole representative of government in deciding resource allocation', and that 'since reform reduces the fiscal power of spending for departments, care should be taken that small corruption does not become very significant corruption'. It is easy to imagine the upheaval caused by a holistic and radical change.

The initial objective was to remove the pitfalls of the traditional practice and at the same time introduce advanced budgeting methods. But how, and by what means, to achieve the objective, which route to take and what operation to select appeared to be truly critical. Different routes with the same objective may lead to different outcomes. There is no doubt that radical reform would bring significant changes, given the environmental constraints; however, it was no surprise that many people adopted the attitude of 'looker-on' as they were not so sure whether the model chosen and the design for reform would lead to success.

On the one hand, too many unpredictable factors made it harder to control the variables that determine the success; on the other hand, as reform touched upon the interests of stakeholders, they would naturally resist. The more intense the change, the more risky the reform became. Historical experiences had shown that a few reformers became well known as a result of the success of their reform, while others became utterly discredited because they were unsuccessful. There were many more examples where reformers were 'dead' before success or reform itself was a success, while the reformer was a loser for whatever reasons. Budgetary reform in Hebei Province was an unprecedented event entailing double risks: the fate of reform and reformer.

Organizing and implementing reform

Notwithstanding the risks, after thorough consideration, the decision-maker and budgeting officers of HPFB decided without hesitation to move ahead with the third option – performing radical and holistic change of traditional budgetary management. They had planned and organized the reform in a cautious manner to ensure its smooth progress and implementation.

Designing the reform

It took more than a year to prepare the reform, from the start of design in March 1998 to the official completion of the reform proposal in June 1999. During the initial design period, a careful study was made regarding the latest theories of reform in China and the reform measures taken by other provinces. Meanwhile, the advanced concepts and budgeting practices of

Western countries were borrowed; moreover, extensive consultation was sought from various departments and units. Instead of making minor adjustments or revisions to conventional practices, they intended to go beyond the old system and make a breakthrough in building a new model of management framework consistent with a market economy system. The principal objectives of the reform included: first, to strengthen budgetary management by adopting departmental budgets; second, to establish a budgetary management operating system with the separation of preparation, execution and supervision; to legalize and standardize each stage of budgeting, from preparation and execution to supervision; third, to adopt a scientific budgeting approach, to open the budget up to the public gradually and to endeavour to prepare the budget scientifically and democratically; fourth, to tighten budget constraints and manage expenditure in accordance with the law; and fifth and finally, to strengthen the supervision of budgets by building a multi-tier budget supervision system.

Strategically implementing the reform

Given the complexity and difficulty of reform, reformers have developed strategic implementation plans using great determination and courage. They have actively absorbed international budgeting theories and successful experiences. At the onset, they contacted the World Bank, International Monetary Fund (IMF) and other international institutions for advice. In 1999, they met those experts and specialists and listened to their comments and suggestions. The confirmation from international experts regarding reform measures played an important role in lessening the concerns of the senior officials and gained their support for the reform. Subsequently, reformers put a lot of effort into preparation. Early in 1999, a complete investigation and evaluation of assets was conducted for each department directly under the administration of the provincial government to gather basic information regarding staffing and assets, following which a budgeting database was established. Considering the time scale and complexity of reform, a 'starting first, refining later' approach was adopted, the specific reform measures being continuously fine tuned during implementation in line with primary objectives. In parallel with borrowing international practice, the unique circumstances of the province were also given full consideration. On the condition of adhering to basic principles of reform, enough time and room was left to allow stakeholders to understand the reform. For instance, with respect to budget preparation, the new requirement is a one-off allocation of the budget at the beginning of the year but, given that the Ministry of Finance was still maintaining the old approach, departments were allowed to keep some reserves as counterpart funding for transfer payment of central government, and additional flexibility was also offered in the form of contingency to cover unforeseen expenditure during the year.

Getting support

In September 1999, the key leader of HPFB reported to the Ministry of Finance (MOF) about the ideas for reform that had attracted the attention of the senior officials of the MOF who also intended to adopt similar reforms, and since that time the strategy of HPFB has been supported and given particular attention as a reform pilot by the MOF. HPFB subsequently forwarded the comments of the MOF to the high-level officials of the Provincial Party Committee, NPC, provincial government and provincial Chinese People's Political Consultative Conference (CPPCC) to help them understand more about the reforms, and almost all key officials commented positively on the budgetary management reforms, which was crucially important in removing the obstacles and facilitating the reforms. Meanwhile, reformers were also aware of the significance of cooperation and coordination with various spending departments – without their support, it would be hard to implement departmental budget reform. Therefore, in both design and implementation stages, the comments and opinions of various departments were given full attention. Key leaders of HPFB made visits to some departments to exchange opinions and information frankly and, finally, the understanding of spending departments was attained. Moreover, managers of HPFB tried their best to help spending departments in implementing budgeting reform and organized a great deal of training in all aspects of technical and software application. In addition, they invited officials from the Budget Working Commission of National NPC, Central Committee for Discipline and Inspection and the MOF to Hebei to guide the reform, and an IMF mission was also invited to Hebei to conduct research.

Creating a favourable public opinion environment

To address different opinions and voices about the reform which originated from misunderstandings, importance was given to the dissemination and promotion of the reform by taking many effective measures. For instance, key high-level officials of the province were invited to be present at the finance and financial management conference in order to achieve consensus among spending departments. Information regarding reform was made available to the public through the major media or at national-level conferences. Working closely with the media, budgetary reforms were extensively covered on CCTV, the *People's Daily*, *China Economic and Financial Daily*, *Public Finance*, HTV, *Hebei Daily* and so on.

Progress and results of the reform

Starting from 1998, the reform has primarily experienced two stages in 6 years, namely creating a new system framework and pursuing improved performance for expenditure. At present, with the completion of the first stage, the reform has reached the second stage.

The first stage of reform

From 1998 to 2002, the task of the first stage of reform was to dismantle the old model of budgetary management and, in the meantime, to build a new management framework consistent with the socialist market economic system with a specific focus on reforming the format, operating mechanism and framework of budgetary management. It included the following four steps:

1   *Preparation and mobilization.* In March 1998, the new management of HPFB decided to implement radical and holistic budgetary reforms. Within HPFB, and in cooperation with the relevant line divisions, the Budgeting Division took the lead in preparing a reform proposal. In August, the document *Implementing Opinions of Managing Public Expenditure in Accordance with Law by Reforming Budgetary Management* was completed. In November, this document, a guideline for reform, was circulated to various departments with the approval of the provincial government.

2   *Implementation.* The reform officially kicked off in early 1999. In February, the document *Opinions on Reforming Operating Mechanism of Budget Preparation, Execution, Supervision and Development Management* was issued and disseminated. In mid-February, the Budgeting Review Centre was established; in mid-March, it was announced that the departmental budget for 2000 was to be prepared. In early June, the document *Hebei Province Provincial Level Budgetary Management Reform Proposal* was issued. After a year, a new framework in which budget preparation, execution and supervision were separated from each other was established, and Hebei was the first province in the country to prepare a new departmental budget.

3   *Refining and rolling out.* When preparing the 2001 budget in March 2000, HPFB made further improvements to the reform proposal and measures by incorporating problems and issues encountered during the budget execution of the previous year. First of all, the departmental budget system was refined by consolidating the presentations of the budget; second, a detailed budget was implemented and a project budget composed; third, improvements were made to the technical supporting system by developing software used in delivering basic information and data, budget reviews, quota management and direct salary payments through commercial banks. In August 2000, the document *Guiding Opinion on Pushing Budgetary Reform in Hebei Province* was disseminated to guide the municipalities and counties to accelerate reform by following the model of HPFB.

4   *Institutionalization.* Early in 2002, once the new budgeting model had been preliminarily established, HPFB decided to make a thorough examination and review of the documents issued over the past years

regarding management measures and methods. After 1 year's review and revision, a whole new set of budgetary management regulations consisting of forty-seven 'measures' was published and came into effect upon the approval of the provincial government. Meanwhile, technical standards regarding five aspects such as information systems, departmental budget texts, functional budget texts, operating expenditure quotas, project budgets and so on were also developed.

The second stage of reform

From 2003 until the present, the priority of reform has been to complete and perfect the decision-making process of budgets, to mobilize public resources on key projects and to improve public expenditure performance.

1 In 2003, in line with the objective proposed at the 16th National CPC to 'Complete and refine the budget decision-making process and management system' and the requirements of the provincial Party Committee and the provincial government, HPFB made ten recommendations to deepen budgetary reform and standardize budgetary management. The provincial government consecutively issued a series of documents including *Some Opinions on Deepening Public Finance Reform and Standardizing Budgetary Management at Provincial Level, The Block Funding Mechanism of Hebei Province to Manage Earmarked Funds by Category and Sector, Hebei Province Management Measures on Integrated Application of Earmarked Funds* and *Hebei Province Review and Approval Measures for Reserves.*

2 In 2004, in order to improve the effective use of public funds by addressing the tendency to give greater weight to allocating over managing for performance, HPFB decided from the 2005 budgeting year to experiment with performance budgeting at the provincial level by borrowing international practices as well as the experiences of other provinces. From this, the *Hebei Province Provincial Level Performance Budget Reform Proposal,* the *2005 Provincial Level Performance Budget Pilot Reform Proposal* and the *Notification of HPFB on Preparation of a Three Year Budget 2005–2007* were developed.

3 In 2005, the provincial government issued the *Hebei Province Regulations on Provincial Level Budgetary Management.*

Recognition and positive comments on the reform

Senior officials from the Budget Working Committee of the National NPC, the Central Committee for Discipline and Inspection and the MOF have visited Hebei successively to conduct the study and investigation on its reform experience, and asked HPFB to present its reform experience at national-level conferences.

Within several years, HPFB had received about 300 study tour delegations from other provinces. The IMF mission visited Hebei in August 2000 and gave full recognition to it.

HPFB reform was covered extensively by major media including CCTV, the *People's Daily*, *China Economic and Financial Daily* as well as local media in Hebei Province, either as a major news item in the first edition or as a follow-up report.

Representatives from provincial NPCs commented positively on the thick budget book covering more than 100 departments, and noted that it was the first time they had seen a real budget. Some people from the National NPC even observed that budgetary reform in Hebei Province was of epoch-making significance.

Food for thought

China is facing enormous challenges when transforming its planned economy to a market economy, not only in terms of institutional obstacles during operation but also pitfalls within the general framework. Practically and realistically analysing and solving the problems are the original motivations for development and reform. No matter the minor issues or major problems, if one really means to solve the inevitable problems with courage and suitable strategy, one will find a way and make a breakthrough.

Originated in 2004, revised in 2006

3 A case of construction of the governmental information network in Jiangxi

Li Chun-yan

The successful practice of a governmental information network in Jiangxi has aroused the concerns of relevant authorities in the state and other provinces or cities. The leaders of the National Development and Reform Commission, Information Office of the State Council, Confidential Affairs Bureau of the General Office of the Communist Party of China (CPC) Central Committee, Secretary Bureau of the State Council, National Administration for the Protection of State Secrets and other departments, as well as the leaders of more than twenty provinces, municipalities and autonomous regions have at some point organized investigation tours in Jiangxi Province. They have fully affirmed the success of the practice in Jiangxi, and the experts also speak highly of e-government in the province. The experts point out that, as a result of many years' efforts, Jiangxi has established the first e-government network in China fully in accordance with the *Guiding Opinions of State Informatization Leading Group Regarding E-government Construction in China* and carved out a successful path of e-government construction in economically less developed areas, which features the advantages of excellent programmes, complete functions, satisfying effects, but less investment, really the first model of its kind in China.

Spring awakens on the apricot branches

In the 1980s, informatization was still in its initial stages in China, and the paperless office eventually settled down, following initial frenetic activity. Then, at the very beginning of the 1990s, a new global information technology (IT) revolution gradually began to thrive. The USA worked out a full set of national information plans one after another, such as *Information Superhighway, National Information Infrastructure (NII)* and *Global Information Infrastructure (GII)*. The European Union (EU) subsequently published the *Action Plan for Information Society Development* and *Electronic Europe*. Canada put forward the *Connecting Canadians Strategy*. Japan, India and governments of other countries formulated action plans for informatization. China also formulated a rapid response and, since 1993, it has proposed to construct the *Golden Bridge* and a series of other informatization projects; as a consequence, four major internet network structures have been put into place, *China Science and Technology Network, Golden Bridge Network, Chinanet* and *China Education and Research Network*; informatization operated from then on. For the sake of interconnection and interworking of the four major internet networks and phasic success in the *Golden Custom, Golden Card* and *Golden Bridge*, informatization in China has entered a vigorous phase never seen before, and its applications and management march ahead together. Currently, director J from Jiangxi Provincial Planning Commission has received an order of transfer to act as the director of Jiangxi Provincial Information Office and concurrently as director of Jiangxi Provincial Economic Information Center, where he is assigned to be responsible for the acceleration of informatization across the province. As an expert who has been engaged in economic information for some time, director J is clearly aware that informatization is now ready to go ahead in Jiangxi.

Thanks to the popular use of the internet and Golden Projects by the ministries and commissions of the state, informatization has spread rapidly in China. The departments directly under the provincial government were all enthusiastic about it and prepared the working plans to construct the necessary information infrastructures and to build up local area networks (LANs) and wide area networks (WANs) of their own, in which they held on to their own views, and their plans for the same purpose were radically different. Thus, it seems to be the time of 'the spring awakening on the apricot branches'.

In April 1997, the First National Working Conference of Informatization was held in Shenzhen, where representatives summarized their experience of national informatization since 1994 and studied in great depth the principles, policies and informatization plans as proposed by the different trades, departments (or commissions) and provinces (municipalities or autonomous regions). The vice premier of the State Council and concurrently head of the National Informatization Leading Group subsequently put forward a guiding principle consisting of twenty-four Chinese characters; that is to say, to plan as a whole and under the leadership of the state, unify the standard, construct on a joint basis and interconnect and interact to share the resources. The vice governor of Jiangxi Province also attended the conference. Afterwards, the provincial government immediately changed the original Jiangxi Provincial Joint Meeting of Informatization to the Jiangxi Provincial Informatization Leading Group in which the executive vice governor H acted as the group leader, vice governor Z as deputy to the group leader and, as a subgroup, established the Office of Leading Group with Mr J as director. Soon after the group was set up, it began to prepare for the group's first meeting to discuss mainly how to initiate the information network of the CPC Jiangxi Provincial Committee and provincial government. Director J was keenly aware of the importance of the meeting and convened several meetings to discuss network construction and certain major policies and measures, organized experts to investigate the relevant departments of the state and other provinces or municipalities, and drafted and then submitted to the leaders of the province the *Scheme for Construction of a Uniform Platform of E-government Network in Jiangxi Province.* The scheme clearly specified for the first time the guidelines for the construction of a uniform platform of e-government network, and it elaborated the perspective, objectives, contents, appropriate measures and financial preparations for the construction of such a network. Afterwards, the Jiangxi Provincial Economic and Trade Commission, Jiangxi Provincial Post and Telecommunications Administrative Bureau, Jiangxi Provincial Electronic Industry Bureau and Jiangxi Provincial Radio and Television Bureau and other departments of the province also put forward and reported to the leaders of the province their respective tentative plans for network construction, like 'the Eight Immortals going across the sea, each in his or her own way'.

By the end of 1997, the Jiangxi Provincial Informatization Leading Group convened its first meeting, and a heated argument was to focus on two issues: first, whether or not to set up a uniform platform of networks. According to some departments, it was not feasible to achieve the interconnection and information exchange of governmental offices only through a uniform network. On the contrary, it is important that the departments set up private networks of their own linked with their higher authorities. Another issue rested on who should and how to construct such a network and its financial support. The Provincial Post and Telecommunications Administrative Bureau, Provincial Radio and Television Bureau and other departments of the province wished to set up a network based on the current public network platforms of post and telecommunications and radio and television. Some departments even proposed not to set up the said network, but instead to tackle the interconnection of government offices via the internet and networks of telecommunications operators.

Following a full consideration of opinions from each side, the executive vice-governor H, leader of Jiangxi Provincial Informatization Leading Group, clearly stated his position:

> Generally speaking, the Party and government offices of the province must be equipped with a network platform of their own, and a specific department must be responsible for the construction, operation and maintenance of the network. In my opinion, the construction must not be decentralized among the Party and government offices of the province. On the contrary, we must make concentrated efforts to the construction of a network platform to solve the interconnection of the Party and government offices and of the whole province. Proceeding from the objective facts, many departments may have the capacity to undertake this project. But I think it is better to assign this job to the provincial economic information center for the following three reasons: Firstly, no need to further enlarge its body size. One hundred and twenty-eight staff there have long engaged in the technical work for that purpose, and no

more training of technical personnel [is necessary] in this regard. Secondly, there is no need to construct more computer rooms. A new building was constructed one year before, and the office rooms and computer facilities are available now. Thirdly, a loan from the Japanese government can be used for the construction of information network of the province.

Afterwards, the platform of the Party and governmental information network at the provincial level was formally constructed.

By the end of 2000, a horizontal interconnection of over 200 departments of the CPC Jiangxi Party Committee, Provincial People's Congress and provincial government was accomplished via the special optical cable of the provincial governmental information network in the major city N, which constructed a uniform platform of governmental networks at the provincial level. In addition, each municipality with districts across the province initially built the platform of governmental information network at the municipal level, and many departments directly under the provincial government also built up LANs for their own use. Some departments even extended their networks downward to their corresponding individual units of cities and counties. From then on, the e-government network of the province began to take shape and to win universal approval.

Coming events cast their shadows before them

Jiangxi launched the reform of governmental institutions in 2000. Another governmental institution, namely the Jiangxi Provincial Department of Information Industry, emerged at the right moment to take charge of the manufacture of electronic information products, the software industry and telecommunications across the province and to carry forward the information-based national economy and social services of the province. Director general L of the Jiangxi Provincial Department of Information Industry was also the deputy group leader of the Jiangxi Provincial Informatization Leading Group. The establishment of the Jiangxi Provincial Department of Information Industry and director general L's assuming office were actually of significance to the promotion of provincial governmental network construction and, since that time, the informatization management system has been set up preliminarily in the province.

However, bottlenecks appeared gradually in the network construction of the province, although the network was enthusiastically accepted by all. Despite the fact that the network platform at the provincial level was about to be completed in the province, the network in the departments directly under the provincial government had to be extended downward to the cities and counties, and they applied one after another to the provincial government for approval and financial support. In order to meet the urgent need for network construction in these departments directly under the provincial government and to have a thorough understanding about the investment in network construction, director general L, the newly elected deputy group leader of the Jiangxi Provincial Informatization Leading Group, conducted an investigation into the above together with director J. However, the results of this investigation astonished not only director general L, but also director J and even the provincial leaders. As shown in the investigation, every department in SH, a place with the best practice of informatization throughout the country, has built up the network independently, and its derived services extend to the grassroots units, but investment in hardware alone exceeds RMB 1 billion yuan. Although SH has a great financial capacity, it is becoming increasingly aware of its huge lack of funds with each passing day. In addition, the independent networks can only meet the need for linking up with departments or systems of their own, and cannot or will not solve the problem of trans-departmental or trans-network interconnection. The erection of an independent network would cost about RMB 30–60 million yuan on average, in addition to more than RMB 2 million yuan of communicating costs and operating maintenance costs per year. According to these figures, the erection of independent networks in fifty departments of the province needs approximately RMB 2 billion yuan, and the communicating costs plus operating maintenance costs are as high as over RMB 100 million yuan annually. Undoubtedly, it is still a heavy burden for Jiangxi, a province that is not financially strong.

Armed with this depressing investigation report and a series of other problems, executive vice governor H, director general L and director J attended the first meeting of the National Informatization Leading Group in April 2001. A dialogue between the executive vice governor H and one of the deputy directors from the State Information Center played an important role in the construction and development of the e-government network in Jiangxi. In the dialogue, the executive vice governor H asked: 'What's your favourable advice to us for a local support necessary on the present occasion of extending the networks of ministries or commissions of the state?' The deputy director of the State Information Center replied: 'of course, every province must render necessary support to the promotion of informatization and e-government in the ministries or commissions. But it's exactly unnecessary for each department of the province to prepare an independent network. You may concentrate your efforts on a uniform platform of networks to cover the whole province and link up with each department of the province. You may give priority to the preparation of supportable internal office automation and LAN systems. In fact, it is just to build up a uniform platform of networks to cover the province'.

The executive vice governor H, director general L and director J were greatly inspired by the reply of the deputy director of the State Information Center. According to the deputy director, in order to construct a uniform network platform, the province must be creative and economical. However, it was still necessary to demonstrate its feasibility, applicability and security in a further step. At the request of director general L, therefore, director J convened a meeting to demonstrate its feasibility and listen to opinions and advice from authoritative experts. At the meeting, the experts said that to construct a uniform network platform was not only feasible technically, but would also avoid the presence of information islets or information independence and benefit information sharing and coordination in work. Moreover, the internal network can be isolated physically from the external network, and the external network can be isolated logically from the internet, which in turn would enable the adoption of security techniques and measures on a uniform basis and assurance of network and information security. However, the experts also pointed out that e-government was not solely a technical problem, but a problem associated with systems and management. Great importance needed to be attached to the balance of interests and control of repeated construction in every department. Besides, it was of practical significance to rearrange appropriately the networks and systems already constructed.

Soon after the first meeting of the National Informatization Leading Group, the General Office of the CPC Central Committee issued the *Directive Opinions on the Construction of E-government in China*. This helped to speed up the construction of a national e-government network, and the programme for a uniform network platform in Jiangxi entered a stage of further study and intense but orderly demonstration. Unfortunately, at that precise time, the Jiangxi Provincial Development and Reform Commission intended to construct its independent network to cover its own system. The proposed development and reform commission is an administrative authority of investment in the province and also a deputy group leader unit of the Jiangxi Provincial Informatization Leading Group. The construction of its independent network will inevitably have rather negative effects on the programme for a uniform network platform in the province. Immediately after listening to an important report on the above issue from director J, director general L went with him to visit director S of the Development and Reform Commission, where they repeatedly expounded their views supporting a uniform network platform rather than an independent network and stressed that only through the concentration of great effort on a uniform e-government network in the province will the interconnection of the Commission itself be accomplished in a proper way. Thanks to the patient explanations of director general L and director J, director S finally changed his mind, and the two major departments under the Provincial Informatization Leading Group reached unanimity over the construction of a uniform network platform in the province. To win more support from the provincial leaders, director S, director general L and director J reported specifically to Mr H, who was subsequently promoted to the post of governor, and then to executive vice governor A, who served as group leader of the Provincial Informatization Leading Group at the time.

Afterwards, executive vice governor A called director S of the provincial development and reform commission, director general L of the provincial department of information industry, director X of the provincial radio and television bureau, director J of the provincial economic information center and other leaders from the relevant major departments to discuss the programme for a uniform e-government network for the province and, in the end, they reached agreement, and the discussion enabled executive vice governor A to make a firm decision to promote the implementation of the project. The executive vice governor A told director general L and director J: 'the construction of a uniform network platform is exactly what the provincial leaders are certain about, and it must be done as soon as possible. You may call on me at any time for further help, if necessary'.

Just like a stone tossed into the water raises a thousand ripples, the decision to build up the uniform information network of the Party and government offices seemed to stir up a thousand ripples among the departments directly under the provincial government. Some were in favour, but the opposing voices also continued. The general office of the CPC Jiangxi Party Committee, the general office of the provincial government and many other departments directly under the provincial government proposed to build up their own special networks and extend them to their local systems in order to solve the problems of internal information delivery to each city and county (or district) and to realize horizontal and vertical interconnections through their own networks in order to share information and coordinate their work. One department directly under the jurisdiction of the central government even claimed that, through improved interconnections with higher authorities at ministerial or commission levels and a better assurance of information security, it is necessary to build up a network of its own, and that the ministry or commission of central government will provide sufficient funds for that purpose. It has nothing to do with local government and, based on the official document issued by the competent authorities in the ministry or commission of central government, it claimed to build up the network separately. A department in charge of confidential affairs stressed the particular importance of maintaining secrecy through an independent network. Even if a uniform network platform has been built up, no one will dare to use it because they will be liable if something goes wrong. Some departments announced that they would build up special networks of their own and had already established links with the ministry or commission of central government and city or county. If they decided to employ the uniform network platform instead of the existing special networks, a huge waste of resources would result. Some departments even produced various excuses to highlight the necessity of special networks, saying that, as there had been no previous case of a uniform e-government network platform anywhere in the country, Jiangxi need not create a precedent in this regard. A few departments asserted that it was impossible to accomplish a uniform e-government network platform in the province. Even among the departments who agreed to use the uniform network platform, some suggested that they would build up independent networks of their own, if the uniform network could not be completed as soon as possible.

The general office of the provincial government even went a step further towards the construction of its independent network. For example, a construction plan was proposed, and division director D from the general office, who was quite familiar with the network, drummed up support for his idea to seek financial support from provincial leaders. As soon as director general L and director J got to know of this plan, they entered discussions with the division director and deputy division director of the general office of the provincial government, where they expounded the significance of a uniform network platform and the plan for that purpose, saying that they could build the network fully in accordance with the general layout. However, the network construction plan proposed by the general office of the provincial government had already been submitted for a two-way review on account of the extraordinary efforts of division director D. Although there existed a divergence of views over an independent or uniform network among those on the judging panel, the construction plan for an independent network was seemingly a foregone conclusion due to division director D's prior consultation among some of the judges. As an expert invited to participate in the review, director J stood up to clarify his position, saying: 'the construction of a network is favored by us, but it must rely on the provincial governmental information network to cope with the practical requirements of the departments themselves, other than the repeated construction of independent networks. In fact, I hold the greatest esteem for every individual from yours and I would render my support to you in work. But unfortunately there exists a divergence of views between us. If you insist to build an independent network again, I won't sign to approve it'. It was due to the firm position of director J that the review failed to reach a conclusion over the network construction.

Following the review, director J prepared a report entitled *Relationship of Governmental Information Network with Three-Networks-and-One-Databank* and submitted it to director general L. Subsequently, director J and director general L reported to the leaders of the provincial government, expounding the importance, necessity and feasibility of construction on a unified basis. On the contrary, some leaders from the general office of the provincial government still went on record in support of the construction of an independent network, and every department directly under the provincial government hesitated and made no move to wait for a final decision from the provincial government. The turbulent wind precedes the mountain storm, and subterranean flow rises in a surging tide. The leaders of the provincial government, director general L and director J, were the focus of public attention, and the e-government network of Jiangxi had reached a crossroads before the onset of numerous queries.

Regarding the construction of a uniform network platform, both director general L and director J were puzzled about its necessity, construction methods, feasibility and financial support, and were also perplexed by the control of independent networks arising after the platform network of uniform government was erected and the many other problems concerning the special networks and systems that had already been built up.

Epilogue

Following plenty of investigations and feasibility studies, director general L and director J reported again to executive vice governor A and governor H and, immediately after this discussion, the provincial leaders considered that the construction of a uniform network platform was based on the realities of the province and fully in accordance with the fundamental principle put forward by us in 1997. At the second meeting of the Jiangxi Provincial Informatization Leading Group in April 2002, it was decided to concentrate efforts on the construction of a vertical governmental information network as the uniform platform of the governmental information network of the province, for which a summary of the meeting was issued in the name of the general office of the provincial government, and so the uniform governmental information network was formally initiated in construction.

As shown in the summary of the second meeting of the Jiangxi Provincial Informatization Leading Group, the uniform e-government network platform in Jiangxi must adhere to the principle of Five Unifications, i.e. unified organization and leadership, unified planning and implementation, unified standards and criteria, unified platform of network and unified security management. It must centre on the construction of a uniform e-government information network platform to solve the networking problems of the CPC Jiangxi Party Committee, Provincial People's Congress, provincial government, Provincial People's Political Consultative Conference and other Party and government offices across the province, rather than accepting repeated construction in a haphazard fashion, but in a planned way in order to push forward the construction of a platform and application systems for an e-government network step by step. The following major measures will be adopted to construct the uniform platform for an e-government network in Jiangxi:

- The constructing and operating costs of the governmental information network in Jiangxi must follow the principle of 'whoever uses it must construct it'. The constructing and operating costs of a governmental information network at the provincial level must be listed as the financial expenses of the province, and the constructing and operating costs of a governmental information network of the municipality including districts must be listed as the financial expenses of the same municipality itself.
- Joint efforts must be made to control the independent network of every department while in the process of examination and approval for project and financial arrangements. All the e-government projects must be subjected to technical demonstrations. Any repeated WAN projects will not be approved by the Jiangxi Provincial Development and Reform

Commission or funded by the Jiangxi Provincial Financial Department without exception.

• The departments directly under the provincial government must not arbitrarily extend their networks downward without prior consent. The newly built service systems must be based on the uniform network platform. The service systems and networks completed by those departments must be transferred gradually to the uniform network platform.

Nowadays, all the departments of the province rely on the uniform e-government network platform to construct their application systems, without the presence of any repeated physical WANs in a haphazard way. Depending on the uniform e-government network platform of the province, each department has achieved marked effects in the development and utilization of information resources and the construction of application systems. For instance, horizontal and vertical applications have been launched among 200 or more departments and another twenty or more departments directly under the provincial government. Over 100 meetings have been held through the completed e-governmental video conference system. The functional e-mail system has 100,000 registered users in the province, and the video on demand (VOD) system and other public application systems have been highly praised by departments across the province. Favoured by the uniform e-government network platform of the province, every department is undergoing the construction of its internal application systems and professional databases. Moreover, some trans-departmental application systems are steadily progressing, such as the decision support system (DSS) for the provincial government, Advanced Talents Databank of the province, Credit Jiangxi system, Digital Certificate System, Emergency Commanding System for Public Emergent Cases, E-port System, Expertbank for Bid Evaluation, and some other trans-departmental application systems have been completed or are under construction. The achievements in the construction and practice of a uniform e-government network platform are mainly: (1) less investment, cheaper operating maintenance costs and good economic benefits achieved; (2) 'information islets' were avoided at the very beginning, which facilitates information sharing and coordination in service; (3) the adoption of security tactics and security technical measures on a uniform basis, which ensures the network security of the uniform platform.

The energetic development of e-government will play an inestimable role in institutional reforms, such as the transformation of governmental functions, integration of services, institutional reorganization, procedure re-engineering and managing innovations, in Jiangxi, which will largely promote the efficiency and quality of administration, enhance the government's abilities in supervision and service and drive the rapid development of the national economy and social informatization in Jiangxi.

Indeed, the construction of a uniform e-government network platform in Jiangxi is a remarkable achievement, but it is still faced with numerous problems, such as the fact that the present uniform e-government network platform is actually hard pushed to meet the needs of all departments along with the continuous extension of its applications, and some departments are demanding an independent network. Without immediate upgrading and improvement, it will be hard to drive forward the construction of e-government in Jiangxi, and resistance to the control of an independent network will be continuously on the increase; second, the gradual shifting of networks is not yet fully in operation; third and finally, the outlay is still a major bottleneck to restricting the development of a uniform e-government network platform in Jiangxi.

Written in 2006

4 A study of how to improve the system of civil servant performance evaluation

Zhai Tianshan

No gain without pain. This is an attitude towards work, and also a basis for harmonizing social interests and building mental balance. But in the area of public administration, the wish of public servants for a balance between gain and pain and between input and return is often merely an expectation.

As the socialist market economy improves and the competition in the government's administration ability becomes increasingly fierce, establishing and improving the value-oriented mechanisms and the incentive and restraint mechanisms for the management of civil servants has become increasingly important in strengthening the ability of civil servants and enhancing the innovation ability and work efficiency of the government. From the introduction of the *Provisional Regulations on State Civil Servants* to the promulgation of the *Civil Servant Law of the People's Republic of China*, China has enforced the civil service system for over 10 years. During this period, the constant improvement of the civil servant management system has greatly promoted the development of the cause of public administration and the improvement of the civil service. But how to measure the performance of civil servants in the course of managing them, and how to establish a scientific performance evaluation and incentive system for civil servants that conforms to the features of administrative work remain two puzzling issues.

Three civil servants' comments on 'performance'

Civil servant A (formerly a university official and professor and now a leading official of a functional department of a provincial government):

> Somebody once asked me how I felt after I came to work in the government. I told him I had lots of feelings. One deep feeling was that working in government requires greater dedication and care for the people. When I worked at the university, I felt I was having a full life and a strong sense of fulfillment. Each class, each paper and each research was fruitful, both in fame and in gain. On the other hand, working in government involves greater responsibility but less pay. And I

can hardly have a sense of fulfillment. At the end of a day, I don't even know whether my effort is fruitful. This is a puzzling feeling. I know the work performance of a civil servant cannot be measured directly with pay and welfare. But I should have the satisfaction over my dedication and sense of achievement. Otherwise, how can a civil servant be enthusiastic about his work?

Civil servant B (a secretary general of a prefecture government):

All my work performance does not belong to me. I have worked for more than half of my life and I have written lots of documents and articles. But not a single piece belongs to me. I made lots of remarks, but none of them belongs to me. I did a great deal of coordination, but the result does not belong to me. As far as work performance is concerned, my feeling is that making as less mistakes as possible in my work is my performance. And giving no thought to personal gains or losses is also my performance.

Civil servant C (formerly a provincial government officer and now working as a deputy town chief):

A grass-roots civil servant has too many things to care and to do. Whatever difficulty or trouble the townspeople have, they will come to us. Every day, you have to reconcile various contradictions and solve many specific problems. But all these cannot be cited as 'performance'. The higher authorities set two main indicators to measure our performance. One is the investments attracted and the economic projects launched. The other is that no major problems occur to disturb local law and order and political stability, no people die, the number of people involved in collective disturbances and complaints is on the decline. These are our performance. As the two are rigid indicators, we have to pay high attention to them. The other issues will become less important. For example, we launched a chemical plant and our fiscal revenue increased visibly. Everybody says this is good. But when talking about contributing money to controlling air and water pollution, everybody was hesitant. Everybody hopes to have a fine performance and to be promoted sooner. But what else can you do if you don't act like this?

Analysis of existing methods and their effectiveness

Most people believe that civil servants are a leading force in social administration and social development, that their work performance is easy to evaluate and that their work has far-reaching social influence. A good civil servant is naturally publicly respected and loved. In particular, some outstanding political leaders can be loved and extolled by the public from generation to generation. In reality, however, the ordinary civil servants find it impossible to enact direct and all-encompassing social effects because most of their work is to do with service, business and coordination. With regard to how to evaluate their work performance and stimulate their work enthusiasm and creativeness, the competent authorities of the Chinese government and the civil servants themselves have made many useful explorations over the years.

From the perspectives of the relevant state laws and regulations (see Appendix: *Civil Servant Law of the People's Republic of China* at the end of this chapter) and the practice of civil servant management in various parts of the country, we could see that the existing methods of evaluating the work performance of civil servants may be summarized in the following categories. First is annual evaluation. The evaluation is comprehensive, covering the morality, ability, diligence, performance and integrity of civil servants, with the emphasis being on the evaluation of work performance. The process is that the individuals first present their personal evaluation, their immediate leaders make comments and propose evaluation grading on the basis of hearing mass opinions, and the leaders of the unit or the authorized evaluation committee set the evaluation grades. The evaluation grading is divided into four categories: excellent, competent, basically competent and incompetent. The outstanding grade is generally controlled at a ratio of about 15 per cent. The result of the annual evaluation is used as the basis for adjusting the positions, ranks, wages, rewards, penalizations, training and dismissal of civil servants. The second category is to evaluate the management (responsibility) targets or special indicators. For those civil servants who are in leading positions or project leaders, quantitative evaluation of the preset responsibility targets and task indicators is conducted on a regular basis, the rankings are set and corresponding rewards or penalizations given. The third category is to evaluate by selection. In light of work requirements, selections and citations of advanced workers, outstanding civil servants and other honorary titles are carried out on an irregular basis, and rewards are given to the civil servants for their outstanding performance.

The existing evaluation methods have played positive roles in stimulating the civil servants to improve their qualifications and fulfil their work responsibilities. But there are many problems. First, the standards for annual evaluations are too general and are difficult to verify. Such evaluations in general can only be based on an overall impression, and the grades are set by mass voting. Those with better relations with the masses in general can achieve higher grades. Besides, the 'outstanding' ranking is sometimes rotated in order to strike a balance. This is unfair. A senior civil servant who has not received the 'outstanding' ranking for many years complained: 'When evaluation was not introduced, I was rather mentally balanced because I did my job out of my conscience and Party character. Now the annual evaluation makes me not know what to do. I don't know where I am wrong and where other people are right. However, I don't plan to change my personal character just to win more votes. And I have to be content with the "competent" ranking for ever'. Second, although the evaluation of management (responsibility) targets and special indicators has clear-cut standards, these standards are not enough to comprehensively evaluate the work performance and effects of a civil servant. More often than not, economic indicators (such as GDP growth) or stability indicators (non-occurrence of disastrous incidents and other safety problems) are used to replace other management targets. This tends to encourage short-term behaviours and induces people to maintain the status quo and neglect reform and development. For example, the mayor of a county-level city launched several major projects and built a large square during his tenure of office. For that, he won accolades and was promoted. But he left a heavy load of debts to his successor. Besides, the efficiency of these projects was not good and all were losing money. The ordinary people had many complaints against him, but to no avail. Third, although evaluation by selection (citing advanced persons) can stimulate the advanced civil servants to continue to make contributions, this stimulation plays only limited roles in the majority of civil servants.

Problems in work

When discussing the difficulties of evaluating the performance of civil servants, a section chief who has been engaged in the management of civil servants summarized three major problems in this respect:

- The contradiction between the necessity of evaluations and the difficulty of evaluations is hard to solve. The reform, opening up and development of the market economy have set higher requirements for the qualifications and ability of civil servants and for the efficiency of government administration. But as the status quo that civil servants are underpaid is difficult to change (cultivating integrity with high pay is impossible to realize quickly because there are high ratios of jobless and low-income people and the number of civil servants is too high), these major requirements are incompatible with the low pay received by civil servants. As a result, some civil servants are in a mental disequilibrium. In addition, the absence of the reform of the examination and approval system and the market system has led to some power–money 'collusions'. At present, it is imperative to introduce an effective performance evaluation and incentive system to help civil servants select the right values and to overcome their value deviation with the lure of dedication, sense of honour and promotion (in fact, purely using money returns to stimulate civil servants does not conform to the occupational characteristics of the public administration personnel and is difficult to realize). On the other hand, as civil servants have diverse work targets (having both the efficiency target and the equity requirement, and both the pursuit of reform and development and the necessity of stability), this makes it very difficult to accurately evaluate the performance of civil servants. In particular, it is difficult to quantify the effects of some public interest and long-term work. Besides, as many civil servants are engaged in coordinating and indirect work (helping other people to produce results), the results of the evaluation items that can be quantified are difficult to attribute directly to individual civil servants.

- The contradiction between the rationality and feasibility of evaluations is difficult to harmonize. The government work done by civil servants is of a guiding, overall and basic nature. For this reason, the evaluation of their work performance should be comprehensive (in standards) and omnidirectional (in ways and methods). Being comprehensive means the evaluation should include work attitude, work input and work efficiency. In addition, the evaluation of work efficiency should also take into account efficiency in economic development, political civilization, cultural construction and social progress. Being omnidirectional means that the evaluation should cover multiple perspectives. Combining the evaluation by leaders with the evaluation by co-workers and service recipients and running an omnidirectional examination can ensure its truthfulness and accuracy. However, this comprehensive and omnidirectional evaluation is hard to implement. This is because the explicit indicators for economic development are easy to evaluate whereas the implicit political and cultural efficiencies are difficult to measure. While short-term effects are easy to spot, the long-term efficiencies are difficult to predict. In the meantime, an omnidirectional evaluation is both time- and energy-consuming and cost-inefficient. Besides, the evaluation opinions from different parties are difficult to measure and balance. Therefore, a rational, comprehensive and omnidirectional evaluation is unrealistic when information technology is not widely used.
- The internal validity and external efficiency of evaluation results are difficult to unify. Theoretically, there should be a unity between the internal validity (which means that the evaluation targets are measurable, the tools reliable and the results credible) and the external efficiency (the evaluation results can bring about an improvement in government work and personal promotion and development) of the performance evaluation. But in reality, this unity is difficult to achieve because of the influence of various subjective and objective factors. There are two main reasons. First, government work is of an exclusive and monopoly nature, which makes it difficult to conduct horizontal comparison within a region. Therefore, it is difficult to decide whether a specific evaluated person should be rewarded or promoted according to a specific effective evaluation result. Next, the tenure system and the change in government work requirements make it difficult to achieve the external efficiency of evaluation results in a timely manner.

Suggestions on how to improve the evaluation system

Comrade Z works in the department responsible for managing civil servants. He believes that the evaluation of civil servant performance deserves further exploration. He thinks that if he can make some contributions to the solution to this difficult issue, it will be a considerable achievement. To this end, he has reviewed lots of research papers and conducted field investigations. In particular, he participated in the Advanced Training Course on Public Administration jointly held by the Development Research Center of the State Council, Tsinghua University and Harvard University. Subsequently, he used the integration of the three circles of 'value, ability and support', the 'adaptability' challenge and other theories on strategic decision-making he had learned to make innovations in systems for improving civil servant performance evaluation. Accordingly, he organized a small research group. On the basis of full deliberations, they put forward their suggestions that the value orientation of civil servant performance evaluation should be redefined and the evaluation contents, methods and support mechanisms improved. The improvement measures they suggested are as follows:

- To give play to the value stimulation roles of dedication, break away from the stimulation of pure monetary feedback and promote the 'evaluation mode highlighting dedication stimulation'. Simply put, a civil servant's performance = environment for pioneering work + dedication + ability. The evaluation of a civil servant's work performance should emphasize the stimulation of his dedication and should break away from the restraint of commercial mentality that relies purely on monetary returns for stimulation. Of the three factors that have an impact on performance, the main one that impedes the stimulation of personal dedication and the display of personal ability is that the environment is not so liberal for pioneering work. The management grades are too rigid, which adversely affects the display of the creativeness and personal character of civil servants. With the deepening of the reform of the administrative examination and approval system, the change in government functions and the building of a learning-oriented government, a liberal work environment that can encourage civil servants to innovate and render active services is being formulated. In this environment, those who wish to make contributions are given opportunities, those who can make contributions are given promotion and those who make significant contributions are given status. This will provide a practical basis for introducing the 'evaluation mode highlighting dedication stimulation'.
- The selection-based evaluation activities should be minimized and standardized, and permanent mechanisms should be established for evaluation stimulation, appointment and promotion. The work performance of civil servants is realized in the course of collective coordination, and evaluating the performance of civil servants should emphasize the long-term efficiency of overall optimization. In the past, evaluation by selecting outstanding and advanced candidates was overused in evaluating civil servants, which could easily cause mental disequilibrium among most civil servants. They tended to feel that their ability was lower than other

people's instead of learning from the more advanced civil servants, because they also worked very hard but could not become advanced themselves. In fact, at a time when post competition is not full, the result of selecting outstanding candidates cannot truly reflect the degree of personal effort and ability. Therefore, the internal selection of outstanding and advanced candidates presided over by the government departments should be reduced as much as possible. If the selection of outstanding candidates is really needed, it should also be standardized so that they can radiate a positive effect on others. We should concentrate more of our energy on the regular evaluation of regular management (responsibility) targets and management responsibilities so as to stimulate every civil servant to advance through regular evaluations. Specifically, the institutionalized annual evaluations should be improved and should take the meeting of work responsibilities and the achievements of innovative work as the basis for evaluations. The results of annual evaluation should be recorded in the personal files of performance and credit, which will serve as the information basis for future appointment, promotion or reward. The citation and rewarding activities that emphasize immediate honouring should be reduced.

- Post-related contributions should be used to evaluate work performance, with the emphasis being placed on the behavioural performance of duty fulfilment and the results of work innovation. The evaluation of civil servant performance is different from the test of employment qualification and the test of academic achievements. It cannot become an evaluation of their general qualifications. Instead, it should emphasize the adaptability, creativeness and contribution of civil servants to their work. There should be different qualification and ability requirements for people at different levels and of different categories. The generalized evaluation of morality, ability, diligence, performance and integrity cannot reflect actual conditions. In fact, as long as civil servants have the basic educational and professional qualifications, their work and results should not only reflect their performance but also their ideological qualifications and abilities. Besides, emphasizing the evaluation of post-related performance and contributions can discourage the development of the weak tendency that some people can talk and write but do not or cannot actually carry out certain practical tasks.

- To promote the openness of government affairs and political achievements, widen channels for public participation in civil service evaluation and establish mechanisms for public opinion survey, social accountability, non-governmental evaluation and timely rewarding (for example, establishing a public fund to reward people for their brave actions for just causes and policemen for loyal service). The government's public administration undertaken by civil servants is in fact a cause of rendering services to the general public. Therefore, when evaluating the work performance of civil servants, the evaluation should not be limited to self-evaluation within the government. Instead, it should be open to the general public and allow them to participate in evaluating and rewarding the service and work performance of civil servants. This can fundamentally meet the mental requirements of civil servants for their sense of honour and fulfilment, and can stimulate and encourage civil servants to dedicate their lives to the cause of public service and establish a value system of sharing joy and sorrow with the general public.

- The wage and welfare system for civil servants should be improved. While the wage levels should be properly raised, the emphasis should be placed on improving their working conditions and on establishing a sound preferential pension system for them.

The above points constitute the important external conditions for introducing the 'evaluation mode highlighting dedication stimulation'. As civil servants render social and public services, they should be provided with sufficient working conditions to ensure that they can perform their duties effectively. Improving their learning (such as increasing training opportunities) and working conditions (such as increasing office automation) can help them to work in a creative way and to be stimulated by their career achievements. Meanwhile, establishing a preferential pension system can help to prevent them from carrying out undesirable short-term measures in order to win immediate money returns, which is detrimental both to social and public interests and to the prospects for their career development. Besides, it can stimulate them to devote their lives to the cause of public administration and services and to realize their career expectations and life values.

Unfinished tasks and new progress

Comrade Z and his research group believe that the above suggestions and countermeasures should serve as a feasible work plan instead of a proposal. Naturally, this plan requires further appraisal and improvement. Comrade Z said to the group members, 'As long as you know what you want to do, you should do it sooner than later. I believe in the old saying: "where there's a will, there's a way".' But when Comrade Z reported to a competent leader on this issue, the leader cautioned him with all sincerity: 'Your ideas are well founded and very good, and can be experimented on a limited scale. But don't change the nature of annual evaluation, for it has been institutionalized by state laws and regulations. Besides it is closely related to the personal interests (wage and promotion) of the civil servants. The selection-based evaluation should also continue as usual. The activity of selecting the "civil servants to the people's satisfaction" is a national event and cannot be abolished. In addition, the evaluation of the management (responsibility) targets and special indicators are personally controlled by the government leaders at various levels. We cannot change it'.

On hearing that, Comrade Z clearly realized how difficult it would be to improve performance evaluation. He even doubted whether he had the ability to carry on his investigation. However, after thinking things through for some time at his desk, he picked up his pen and began to write the Plan for the Experiment on Reforming the Evaluation of Civil Servant Performance.

Fortunately, the Organization Department of the Party Central Committee formulated the *Provisional Regulations on the Comprehensive Evaluation of the Performance of the Regional Party and Government Leading Groups and Leading Officials in Light of the Requirements of the Scientific Approach to Development*. The document, formulated in 2006 at the request of the Party Central Committee, was to be implemented in the re-elections to be held on the expiration of the term of office of the regional Party and government leading groups. Reorienting the past evaluation tendency that overemphasized economic development, this document emphasizes that the performance of the leading groups and officials should be comprehensively evaluated from the diverse perspectives of economic construction, political construction, cultural construction, social construction and Party building. To improve evaluation, new tools such as democratic evaluation, public opinion survey, field inspection, performance analysis and integrated evaluation have been added to the traditional method of democratic recommendation and individual interview. Currently, Comrade Z is leading an evaluation inspection group in implementing the methods of comprehensive evaluation in a prefecture city. The experience arising from this field experiment will provide new inspiration for evaluating the performance of ordinary civil servants working in non-leadership capacities.

Personal feelings

As I have been doing personnel work and civil service management for many years, I personally feel that the responsibility is great and the tasks are difficult. At a time when the human factor and the scientific approach to development are emphasized in modern social development, how to understand, stimulate and safeguard people's legitimate rights and interests and promote the comprehensive development of human beings will be a new topic for organization and personnel workers. Evaluating the performance of civil servants is only a subtopic of this major subject, but it has extremely important impacts on the mental balance and work enthusiasm of civil servants. Although I have carried out certain investigations, ideas and experiments, I have not been very successful. Fortunately, I have maintained my interest in scientific exploration that was developed when I was working at university. I will continue to study and think through my busy daily chores and to examine the resulting issues in an academic way so that my work can be more exploratory, more predictable and more independent. My conviction is that pursuit is more important than possession!

Originated in 2003 and revised in 2006

Appendix: *Civil Servant Law of the People's Republic of China* (excerpts)

Chapter V Evaluation

Article 33   The evaluation of the civil servants should comprehensively cover the morality, ability, diligence, performance and integrity of the civil servants according to the management jurisdiction, with the emphasis being placed on the evaluation of actual work performance.

Article 34   The evaluation of the civil servants comprises routine evaluation and periodic evaluation, with the latter being based on the former.

Article 35   The periodic evaluation of the civil servants without leading capacities is done on an annual basis. First, the individuals should summarize their work according to their positions, responsibilities and the related requirements. After soliciting mass opinions, the immediate leaders set the proposed evaluation rankings. Finally, the unit leader or the authorized evaluation committee sets the evaluation rankings.

The periodic evaluation of the leading members is handled according to the relevant rules of the competent authorities.

Article 36   The results of the periodic evaluation are divided into four rankings: excellent, competent, basically competent and incompetent. The civil servants should be notified in written form of their periodic evaluation results.

Article 37   The results of the periodic evaluation are used as the basis for adjusting the positions, ranks, wages, rewards, training and dismissal of the civil servants.

5 Controversy arising from the experiment on expanding the powers of the town and township governments in Shaoxing County

Huang Xuming

The organizations of the town and township political power are at the lowest level of political power in Chinese rural areas. Passing the instructions of the central government directly to the rural areas and the peasants, these organizations are a link between the Party and the government with the people. They are the footholds of the Party and government work in the rural areas and play important roles in promoting the implementation of the lines, principles and policies of the central and provincial authorities, in increasing the Party's ability to rule and in building a socialist harmonious society in rural areas. But after China deepened its reforms and, in particular, after it reformed rural taxes and fees, the organizations of political power in the towns and township have revealed some problems that cannot be ignored. They include the heavy debt burdens of the town and township governments, the inability of the town and township governments to provide sufficient public products and services and the contradictions between the town and township governments and rural society.

In order to consolidate the results of the rural taxes and fees reform and to attempt to solve the difficulties and problems confronting the town and township grassroots organizations, we began experiments in 2005 on integrated rural reforms. These experiments highlighted the reforms of five major systems: the systems of the town and township institutions, the management systems of rural compulsory education, the financial systems of the county and township governments, the settlement of the debt burdens of the town and township governments and the improvement of the operational mechanisms of village-level organizations. In Zhejiang Province, Shaoxing and three other counties (districts) were selected for experiments. In the course of these experiments, Shaoxing County conducted experiments on 'expanding the powers of the town and township governments', in which part of the enforcement powers of the functional departments of the county government were decentralized to the town and township level in the form of entrusted enforcement. This experiment was conducted against the backdrop that the town and township institutions nationwide are universally streamlined and the town and township level has no enforcement institutions or power. This move has attracted widespread attention.

'Too much responsibility with too few powers'

In Zhejiang Province, county economy is relatively well developed, with Shaoxing County being one of China's top ten economic counties. It has nineteen towns (neighbourhoods) and over 10,000 enterprises. In particular, ten of its towns have fiscal revenues of over 100 million yuan each. While the development of the town and township economy has been relatively rapid, the county's administrative and public services are still controlled by the county-level institutions. 'Many of the administrative powers have been centralized, the enforcement power is mainly controlled by the county-level institutions, and the town and township administration has a vacuum in some areas'.

In June 2005, a mountain dweller captured a pangolin and took it to a nearby holiday village to sell. After receiving a tip-off, the town's government sent some people to dissuade the man. But he refused to listen. Subsequently, no sooner was the pangolin released than it was captured again. If this case had been reported to the higher authorities, it would have been a long time before the forestry department of the county government could have sent people to release the creature.

Fish-pond contractors complained, 'Most of my fish ready for sale are dead due to the pollution of a nearby printing and dyeing mill. I reported this to the town government, but the officials there said they did not have the power to investigate and punish the enterprises that illegally discharged pollutants'. 'As the town and township governments have no environmental enforcement institutions or enforcement power, the only thing they could do was to report to the county environmental department and request them to come and handle the case. But as the county environmental bureau had too many towns and townships to take care of and was understaffed, they were unable to handle these problems in a timely manner. But if a serious pollution occurred, the town officials would be to blame'. The deputy secretary of CPC Pingshui Town Committee in Shaoxing County said, 'We can see the problems but we cannot handle them'.

As to the 'Sunday Project' involving illegal house construction in rural areas, the deputy secretary also remarked with deep feeling, 'When we went and talked to them during the working hours, they would stop. But at weekends when all the officials were resting, the peasants would work like hell and build a house in just two days. You couldn't do anything about it'.

On the other hand, most of the production safety accidents, food safety accidents, birth control, civil affairs and many other difficult problems happened at the town and township level. According to instructions from the higher authorities, the town and township officials would be punished if production safety accidents occurred there. 'We have too great responsibilities, but too little powers', said the deputy secretary. The main problem is a mismatch between the powers and the responsibilities.

Decentralizing powers to towns and townships

To solve the 'mismatch between powers and responsibilities', Shaoxing County decided to focus its priorities on a change in government functions and reform of the town and township institutions. Beginning in late August 2005, the county entrusted the inspection and supervision powers and partial approval and punishment powers of the county departments in charge of environmental protection, safety supervision, labour and social security, and forestry to the specially established town integrated enforcement station. The experiment was done in three towns, in keeping with the decentralization principle and the principle of 'unified management, town and township operation and departmental guidance'. The decentralized enforcement powers covered the areas where incidents occurred frequently and had direct impacts on rural stability, and which were beyond the reach of the county institutions. With regard to matters such as approval and punishment, the competent county authorities only have the power to affix official seals.

The integrated enforcement station is a nominal body, with the administrative and institutional personnel of the 'four offices and two centres' working concurrently as its enforcement staff. The four offices and two centres were the Party and government office, the economic development office, the social undertaking and support office, the rural construction office, the mediation and service centre and the village guidance centre, all directly under the town Party committee and government. In general, each station was staffed by between six and seven people, thereby incurring no additional fiscal spending. The functional departments of the county government signed written entrustment agreements with the town integrated enforcement stations, specifying the entrusted powers and responsibilities in administrative enforcement. The experiment was led by the office of the county leading group for integrated rural reform, and the duration of entrusted administrative enforcement was temporarily set for 2 years, beginning on 27 September 2005. Once the experiment was completed in the three towns and townships, entrusted enforcement would be popularized county-wide.

By the end of 2005, the authorization was largely completed in Shaoxing County. The relevant county functional departments decentralized powers according to the practical conditions of each town, and signed different entrustment agreements with fifteen towns. They mainly covered four functions: environmental protection, safe production, employment and urban construction supervision. Specifically, the departments of labour and safety supervision signed entrustment agreements with fifteen towns, the departments of environmental protection and construction signed entrustment agreements with twelve towns, and the department of forestry entrusted three powers including quarantine and transport to four mountain towns.

To ensure the quality of enforcement, the county selected ninety-five professional and responsible officials to work as enforcers and organized professional training courses, including six courses on specific topics, for the town enforcement personnel. In particular, the County Construction Bureau organized the town enforcement personnel for training at the Provincial Construction Department, and the county departments in charge of safety supervision and labour compiled operational manuals and distributed some of them to enterprises. These included *Manual for Inspecting Safety in Production, Collection of the Contingency Plans for Unexpected Public Incidents in Shaoxing County, Manual for Administrative Enforcement over Safety in Production, Reader of Laws and Regulations on Safety in Production* and *Procedures for Labor Supervision and Enforcement.*

Results

Authorization through entrustment helped solve the problems that were beyond the reach of the county government. It also effectively solved the mismatch between the powers and responsibilities of the town and township governments, promoted a change in the functions of the towns and neighbourhoods and strengthened public administration and social services. For example, in dealing with the environmental regulatory vacuum at the town and township level, Article 3 of the agreement specified that the enforcers might 'conduct investigation into and obtain evidence about the illegal pollutant discharges by the enterprises and public institutions within the jurisdiction and put forward punishment proposals'. The environmental enforcers in Pingshui Town discovered that they were receiving strong backing. They could handle illegal sewage discharges in a timely manner as long as they presented the relevant enforcement certificates. They could also directly report to the town and township governments if they found any instances of illegal housing construction. In addition, the town and township government could immediately issue 'stop construction' notices to prevent illegal construction from expanding further. Statistics indicate that, by the end of 2005, the towns across the county had handled a total of 649 cases (seventeen in environmental protection, 495 in labour, five in safety supervision, eight in urban construction and 124 in other areas), thus contributing to social stability in the rural areas. In the past, the county labour supervision brigade comprising ten staff had been constantly on the run but still could not manage. Now they could concentrate on certain major matters. The public administration and service centre of Yangxunqiao Town waged a month-long joint rectification campaign, which swiftly improved public order in the Jiangqiao region and won the approval and support of the local people. Administration over the implementation of urban construction planning was also proceeding in an orderly manner. In the first 5 months of 2006, a total of ten proposals on site selection for construction projects were issued; eleven permits on land use for construction totalling 7.35 million square metres were approved and issued; and sixteen permits on construction engineering totalling 10.93 million square metres of gross floor space were approved and issued. This has been very convenient for the grassroots units. In the meantime, punishments for illegal acts were intensified. In all, eight illegal construction projects were investigated, six of which were demolished, involving 750 square metres of gross floor space.

This move has also been convenient for ordinary people. Marriage registration is a new item entrusted to the towns and townships by Shaoxing County. According to the new Marriage Law, marriage registration can only be done in the Civil Affairs Bureau of the county government. On 4 January 2006, the bureau established a marriage registration station in Pingshui Town to handle marriage registrations for Pingshui, Jidong, Wangtan and Fusheng, the four towns and townships in the southern mountainous regions where transportation is inconvenient. Another marriage registration station was set up at the county seat of Shaoxing at the same time to handle marriage registrations for the remaining towns and townships. Accompanying his fiancée, a girl from Guizhou Province, to the marriage registration station in Pingshui in late January 2006, a villager from the town said, 'It's very convenient. It's on my doorstep. In the past, we in the southern mountainous regions had to climb mountains to the county seat for marriage registration. It was both troublesome and strenuous'.

Wang Fang, registrar of the Pingshui marriage registration station, said the service was very convenient for local people. 'As the Spring Festival is approaching, there are many people coming here for registration. Since the station was opened on January 4, more than 60 couples have come and registered in less than 20 days. Sometimes, as many as ten pairs were registered in 1 day. This is unprecedented here in this town'.

Controversies arising

Nationwide, the government institutions at the town and township level have been universally streamlined. Some experts have even called for the abolition of the town and township governments. At a time when the town and township governments have no enforcement bodies or enforcement powers, Shaoxing County has massively decentralized its enforcement powers through entrustment. This move has attracted extensive attention.

The proponents believe that this move helps intensify enforcement. However, opponents believe that the move runs counter to the current trend, that its disadvantages could outweigh its advantages, and that it can work for the time being but cannot have any lasting effects.

'This is not necessarily a move to strengthen the powers of the town and township governments', said Professor Mao Shoulong of Renmin University of China. 'We have to see the result of this experiment. If there is a strong restraint, it will be a useful exploration'.

Other people said, 'If we look at the positive side, the move is useful to elaborate the enforcement work at the grass-roots level of towns and townships'.

The relevant provincial departments have conducted repeated investigations and discussions into decentralization and have divergent views on the issue.

On 17 August 2005, a provincial symposium on the reform of town and township institutions was held in Hangzhou, with the jurisdiction over town and township administration and the county and township law enforcement system being the main topics. During the discussions, some people suggested that the law enforcement departments should have representative offices in towns and townships. But this proposal was not so realistic in terms of human and financial resources, and was also rejected because it ran counter to the general trend of the reforms. As a result, the towns and townships gradually reached consensus on authorization through entrustment. Some people from the Provincial Legal Office outlined the difficulties of entrustment. Various laws and regulations already have provisions on enforcement power and therefore there is no need for increased authorization. Besides, the responsibility following authorization still rests with the county-level departments. The issues of jurisdiction definition, organization and supervision should also be carefully considered. Although the relevant laws specified that powers can be entrusted (for example, Article 19 of the *Law of the People's Republic of China on Administrative Penalty* provides that powers can be entrusted to the institutions in charge of public affairs), the towns and townships as the grassroots level of government are not included.

He Bing, Professor of the China University of Political Science and Law and a scholar in administrative law, believes that how much legal force a 'guiding opinion' of a county-level department and the related entrustment agreement carries remains a question.

'Although the move taken by Shaoxing County has legal grounds, it is only based on the reference to the major provisions of the relevant regulations, and neglects the minor provisions. In jest, it's a borderline practice in law, which can induce inequitable enforcement and invite new problems'. An expert in government governance said, 'If the detailed provisions on entrusted enforcement are carefully examined, the move taken by Shaoxing may fail to meet the conditions of entrustment'.

The legality of authorization is facing challenges. On the one hand, the reformists hope to solve the mismatch between the powers and responsibilities of the town and township governments and to optimize law enforcement mechanisms. On the other, the legality of the law enforcers at the town and township level is questionable, and this could lead to new problems such as the abuse of powers and illegal examination and approval.

What course to follow?

Reform at the town and township level is an important component of ongoing rural integrated reform. It is important to the social stability and long-term development of the rural areas, and also to whether the building of a new socialist countryside can effectively promote the achievement of the goal of comprehensively building a well-off society. What course should the experiment on decentralizing powers to the towns and townships take under current conditions? Let us try to find answers from the following analyses.

Should the functions of the towns and townships be weakened or strengthened?

Decentralizing powers to the towns and townships by Shaoxing County is in essence designed to strengthen the functions of the towns and townships and promote rural governance through entrustment. Currently, it has become a consensus that the town and township institutions should be reformed. But how should they be reformed? And what is their future? Both academic and administrative personnel have different views. In general, one view favours weakening their functions, because the political powers at the town and township level should be of a transitional nature. The town and township political powers could be abolished or have their institutions and staff reduced so that they would become the representative bodies of the county (municipal and district) governments. This would help to reduce government functionaries and cut administrative expenditure.

The alternative view favours strengthening their functions, believing that, through reforms, the political powers at the town and township level should be further strengthened and their functions changed so that they can play even more comprehensive and important roles in maintaining social and political stability, and fostering the development of the economy and other undertakings in the rural areas.

In practice, there have been no explicit provisions as to the reform of the town and township institutions which is going on in various parts of the country. As the core content of integrated rural reform, the reform of the town and township institutions was initially put forward as a supporting measure for the reform of rural taxes and fees. The main purpose was to suppress the huge administrative operational costs of the towns and townships and to consolidate the results of the tax and fee reform by reducing both personnel and spending. Therefore, many places interpret the reform of the town and township institutions as merging the towns and townships and reducing institutions and personnel. The theoretical basis for this reform is that towns and townships are the chief culprits responsible for the heavy tax burden on the peasants. If the peasants' burdens are to be eased, the first target should be the towns and townships, which are noted for inflated institutions and overstaffing. At this level, the ratio between officials and citizens is grossly unbalanced, with too few productive people supporting too many unproductive people. Under the tax-sharing system, the towns and townships should raise their financial revenue from their respective jurisdictions. When there are too many people to be paid, the town and township governments have no alternative but to demand more revenues from the peasants. This is a direct reason why the peasants' burdens are so heavy. Accordingly, if the peasants' burdens are to be eased, the town and township institutions and personnel must be reduced and some of the functions of the towns and townships weakened.

In reality, easing the peasants' burdens and the financial difficulties of the towns and townships should not become the reason for abolishing or reducing the town and township governments. If there really are many functions that must be performed by the town and township governments and at the same time the town and township governments have not sufficient financial resources to perform these, what should be reformed is the financial system. The town and township governments should not be abolished. In some places today, some towns and townships have been merged in order to meet the rigid reform targets of 'abolishing and merging towns and townships and reducing institutions and personnel'. As a result, the properties of some towns and townships have been sold or divided, which has not only caused loss of state-owned assets but also produced harmful impacts on rural administration and construction. In the meantime, a pure pursuit of personnel and assets reduction can render the town and township governments unable to perform their function of public administration and to exercise their public powers, and further adversely affects the normal operation of the town and township governments and lasting social stability in rural areas. If the functions of the town and township governments are weakened under the pretext of exercising 'administration according to law', no villages will intervene and no towns or townships can intervene if unexpected group incidents occur in rural areas. The contradictions will escalate, become increasingly serious and eventually undermine the harmony and stability of rural society. In China, nearly 60 per cent of the population live in rural areas. The coordinated development between urban and rural areas and the building of a new socialist countryside require the grassroots government to implement and realize its powers. It is possible that one day the rural nongovernmental organizations (NGOs) will play a part in the government of the populations. In the long run, it is also a possible trend. However, currently, the town and township institutions are all required to actually maintain the rural market economic order, handle interest contradictions and disputes, manage public resources, control various epidemics, organize rural education and training, construct rural culture and release public information. The goal and starting points of rural integrated reform are both to consolidate the results of burden reduction and to increase the ability of the grassroots governments to provide social management and public services.

Scholar Liu Shangxi believes that, in the new historical period, the reform of the town and township institutions should be designed to reconstruct the functions of the towns and townships so as to provide services to rural residents. Based on this view, it is quite in order to abolish and merge some towns and townships with a view to providing better public services to rural residents. Means serve objectives. But if the towns and townships are massively abolished and merged and are even turned into the representative bodies of the county governments in order to reduce the burden of town and township finance, it is tantamount to placing the cart before the horse. Mass abolition and merger of towns and townships and mass reduction of personnel do not solve the 'real issue' (i.e. reconstructing the functions of the towns and townships), and run counter to the general orientation of building a new socialist countryside.

Accordingly, the most pressing goal of reforming the town and township institutions should be to solve the mismatch between the real functions and the mandatory functions of the towns and townships. In other words, it is an issue of how to enable the towns and townships to truly perform the function of serving both ordinary people and society by taking active reform measures. While reducing the institutions and personnel of the town and township governments, Shaoxing County has decentralized some administrative enforcement powers to the towns and townships. Without increasing personnel, institutions and spending, the move strengthens the functions of the towns and townships to provide public services and public administration in rural areas. This general orientation conforms to the practical conditions of rural areas.

Problems arising from decentralization

The experiment conducted by Shaoxing County is an unprecedented reform move across the country. However, the reform process has also encountered the following main problems.

Different professional qualifications of the town and township law enforcement personnel have different impacts on enforcement efficiency and quality. Despite repeated specialized training, the enforcement personnel still lack professional knowledge. In addition, most of them are too old, have too many concurrent duties and are quantitatively insufficient. Let us take the enforcement personnel for town and township safety supervision as an example. Shaoxing County has thirty-one people on the regular payroll. While twelve of them are full-time, nineteen are part-time. They are on average 42 years old and only 52 per cent of them have received college or higher education (including academic credentials obtained through correspondence courses). As to the environmental enforcement personnel at the town and township level, only the towns of Anchang and Qianqing have two or three personnel. Each of the remaining towns has only one environmental enforcement officer.

Proximity law enforcement tends to affect impartiality. The town and township governments have diverse responsibilities, such as expanding insurance coverage, soliciting educational donations and asking people to subscribe to newspapers and magazines. These tasks cannot be accomplished merely by administrative orders. The enforcement personnel have to take into consideration themselves, their future work and their other tasks. Therefore, case handling could become 'personalized', and law enforcement could fail to strike home or could be treated with partiality.

The powers the departments intend to bestow do not match the powers the towns and townships demand. Investigations indicate that currently some of the enforcement powers the towns and townships would very much like to achieve carry strict legal provisions and can only be exercised by the law enforcement departments at the county level. They include some enforcement powers of the departments in charge of environmental protection, labour and safety supervision. On the other hand, some powers that have been decentralized by departments are the powers that the towns and townships do not want, because they are troublesome or too weak. They include the power decentralized by the forestry bureau that 'felling of less than five cubic metres of timber should be approved by the town and township government'.

A more important and prominent problem is that the legal provisions and policy restrictions on enforcement entrustment still exist, and the status of the towns and townships as the law enforcer has not been confirmed, even though enforcement experiments have been conducted for nearly a year. The legality of decentralizing power to the towns and townships by Shaoxing County has not yet been confirmed by the provincial or higher governments. Meanwhile, after decentralization, the departments at the county level entrusted their inspection, supervision and partial administrative enforcement powers to the towns and townships through the signing of formal contracts. However, in keeping with the principle that power should match responsibility, the responsibilities will be borne by one side, the towns and townships, instead of the two sides in the past. As a result, the towns and townships will face the double test of power and enforcement.

Solutions

The experts believe that provincial legislation can provide legal grounds for decentralization and thus remove the legal barrier to this exploration.

'No matter how great the pressure is, it is surely a good thing for the towns and townships in Shaoxing County', said Sheng Guofeng of the Policy and Law Section of the Agriculture Bureau of Shaoxing City. 'Under the existing administrative enforcement system, some town and township officials feel they are helpless. Even though they have performed their responsibility of supervising and reporting to the county-level departments, they are bound to be blamed if something goes wrong. But now with the enforcement powers in their hands, the towns and townships find themselves in a fully advantageous position and can solve the problems whenever they emerge. They are willing to do so even if there is pressure'.

In order to improve the quality of law enforcement, the relevant departments of Shaoxing County have not only signed entrustment contracts with the towns and townships, but also requested that the integrated enforcement stations of various towns and townships must exercise strict management that emphasizes 'access qualification for personnel and dual management for work posts'. The entrusted enforcement stations are located in the 'four offices and two centres' of the towns and townships, the personnel come from the town governments, the operations of these stations are controlled by the relevant enforcement departments, and the enforcement personnel must be selected from the administrative and institutional personnel who have obtained the corresponding enforcement qualifications. The relevant data indicate that, by January 2006, staffing had been preliminarily completed for the integrated enforcement stations of the towns and townships in Shaoxing County, and 70 per cent of enforcement personnel had received the corresponding enforcement qualifications. 'Currently, those who have not received qualifications are not allowed to take up their posts. The enforcement that should be done by these people can only be done on their behalf by other qualified personnel. This is a precondition set by the county for decentralizing enforcement powers', said the town's deputy Party secretary.

Conclusion

Practice over the past year indicates that, despite the tangible effects, it remains to be seen whether the experiment on decentralizing powers to the towns and townships, the first ever in the country, will succeed and be confirmed.

At present, the relevant departments of the Zhejiang provincial government are largely positive about the experiment conducted by Shaoxing County. They believe that, as a unit for reform experiment, Shaoxing County can go ahead of the others, even though the *Provisional Regulations on the Entrustment of the Administrative Enforcement Powers to the Town Governments by Some Administrative Enforcement Organs in Shaoxing County* do not fully conform to the existing relevant administrative laws and regulations. The adjustment of the administrative enforcement system will be studied further by the relevant provincial departments and handed to the provincial government for consideration before being submitted to the provincial people's congress for legislation.

Sheng Guofeng remarked: 'We still have to wait and see whether the bold reform conducted by Shaoxing County can break through the existing legal limits and achieve good results, or whether the reform can promote legal changes, or whether the reform experiment will fail in the end because the towns and townships are unable to control the qualification of the enforcement personnel and cause enforcement inequity'. Currently, this experiment has not been conducted in other places in Shaoxing County, but Sheng Guofeng will closely follow the trend of reform in Shaoxing County.

As the reform executors, the town Party committees remain upbeat about the integrated enforcement stations: 'We are still in a run-in phase and it is quite normal that some problems will emerge. But I believe the result will point to the right direction'.

Written in 2006

Part II

Urban construction and social administration

6 New stories of old shantytowns

Sun Guoxiang

In Liaoning, 'Shantytown' is the name for the city areas where dilapidated buildings are clustered together. The dwellings in these areas are mainly earth–rock or brick–wood buildings built in the early period after the People's Republic of China (PRC) was founded. Some of them were even built during the Japanese occupation and Manchukuo period as servants' quarters or simple houses. Most of these buildings are more than 50 years old, and almost all of them are dilapidated. The reconstruction of the shantytowns was once a historical problem for Party committees and government at all levels in Liaoning. The Party committee and government of Liaoning Province started to reconstruct the shantytowns early in 2005, although they encountered difficulties at every stage of reconstruction – from financing to building demolition, from construction to distribution, from moving in to habitable living conditions. Because effective management and proper measures were adopted, we have accomplished the phased objectives of the 'Shantytown Reconstruction'. In 2005 alone, the eleven cities in the provincial plan of shantytown reconstruction demolished 7,650,000 square metres of shanty buildings, started to construct 7,580,000 square metres of buildings for returnees, completed 3,340,000 square metres and allocated 104,002 shantytown residents in total. The residential conditions and environment of the shantytown residents were greatly improved.

Background

While row upon row of tall buildings, roads extending in all directions and flourishing streets comprise the modern style of city development in Liaoning, there is still some discord at the edges of cities. These are the shantytowns that greatly contrast with modern city lives. It is hard to imagine that these areas, which have barely changed for decades, still exist in cities in the twenty-first century.

Not long ago, the developers of Liaoning established the foundations of Chinese industry. As an important raw material industry province, the coal enterprises of the major coal production areas, such as Fuxin, Fushun and Benxi, made a major historical contribution to the construction of China.

During that period, holding the belief of 'production first, personal life second', these labourers worked with their lofty sentiments and sweat under considerable hardship, including poor living conditions. At the end of the twentieth century, facing constitutional and structural problems, Liaoning started reform of the state-run enterprises comprising the old industrial base, including the enterprises once directly owned by the Chinese central government. Most of the coal enterprises in Liaoning were owned by the central government, so the areas were isolated and the living and working areas comparatively independent. After these enterprises were given to the local governments, many difficulties and problems began to surface. As the resources were being increasingly depleted, many coal-mines in cities such as Fuxin, Benxi and Fushun were facing closure or bankruptcy. Many employees of these enterprises had been laid off and their living conditions were getting worse. It made the task of paying back the historical debt much more complicated and difficult.

The shantytowns in Liaoning are mainly in Fushun, Benxi, Fuxin, Chaoyang and Yinkou; coal-mine shantytowns are the most typical, and have problems rooted in history. The oldest buildings were built around 1920. The common characteristics of these shanty buildings are their small plots, high density, poor construction standards and high inhabitant density. Almost all these buildings are dilapidated. There is usually no public sewage system, heating or gas services, and the sanitation is poor. The residents have problems with drinking water, using lavatories and transportation.

Most shantytowns serving the coal-mines were built along with the excavation of the mines and are located at the edges of cities. The commercial development value of these places is low due to the poor location, high density of buildings, sloping sites and high development costs. These shantytowns are mainly located in the cities where resources are depleted, and these cities have limited local financial budgets (Fushun, Benxi and Fuxin, for example, have budgets of more than one billion RMB or even only hundreds of million RMB). These cities cannot afford the investment needed for the reconstruction task, and the financial capacity of the local enterprises and their employees is also very low. Many coal-mines were on the edge of bankruptcy and could not afford to invest in residential construction, while their employees were not able to purchase apartments because of their low income. Seventy per cent of families in shantytowns are low-income families. Even the everyday lives of these residents depended on the succour of the government, so they were unable to afford to rebuild their houses or purchase new ones. According to a survey in Fushun, only 1.34 people in ten families in shantytowns have jobs, and a large number of city residents live below the poverty line. During the reconstruction process, only 12 per cent of all coal-mine employees could afford RMB 10,000, and more than 65 per cent had no money at all.

Since reform and opening up, the Chinese Party Central Committee and State Council have given great consideration and support to the shantytown reconstruction project in Liaoning Province. Liaoning Province has continuously reconstructed shantytowns under the instruction of relevant departments. By the end of 2004, 26,620,000 square metres of shantytowns had been reconstructed and the housing problems of 783,000 families – 2,636,000 people – had been resolved. The total area of remaining shantytowns over 50,000 square metres is 9,800,000 square metres, including 4,415,000 square metres of shantytowns involving 143,000 families and 459,000 people that originally belonged to the coal enterprises which were owned by the central government.

In 2005, the completed residential area in Liaoning Province was 2,200,000 square metres, and this increased by 1.4 per cent in 2006. The real estate investment reached RMB 70.1 billion and the average living space per person 19.9 square metres. Liaoning Province continued to promote the healthy development of real estate and to improve the housing conditions of residents in 2006. The real estate investment will be RMB 70.8 billion and will increase by 1 per cent. The completed residential area is forecast to cover 2,220,000 square metres and will increase by another 1 per cent. The average living space per person will be 21.6 square metres – an increase of 0.7 square metres. However, the average living space per person in shantytowns is only 2.14 square metres, and the housing environment and conditions are terrible.

Emergence of the problem

With the background of rejuvenating the old industrial base and building a harmonious society in Liaoning, the biggest shantytown reconstruction project in the history of the province started in 2005 and became one of the most important events for the rejuvenation of the old industrial base.

It is not strictly correct to say that reconstruction began in 2005, because the historical date was 26 December 2004, when the new secretary of Liaoning Provincial Committee of the Communist Party of China, who had only been in the position for 12 days, went to Fushun. Fushun was once called the 'coal capital' of China but is now facing the problem of resource depletion. That day when he visited Modigou shantytown in Xintun Community, Dongzhou District, the temperature was -29°C. Most of the houses there were more than 50 years old and were extremely shabby, dark and small. Their foundations had seriously settled, about 35 centimetres, and rainwater seeped into the houses. Because of leaning house supports, cracking walls and rotten roofs, cold winds blew into most of these houses in winter and rain leaked in during summer, making them dilapidated and uncomfortable. The residents had problems obtaining drinking water as well. Many people drank untreated reservoir water and some depended on well water. There was one public toilet for 790 families on average. The roads were narrow and were all dirt roads. They were dusty on sunny days and muddy in rainy weather. There were no street lamps and so it was totally dark in the evenings. The distance between many houses was less than 1 metre and fire engines had access problems.

Wenzhang Wang, 79 years old, worked as a coal-miner for 40 years and was a Grade 8 technician. He was a famous 'top technician' in the national coal industry and was invited to the National Day Ceremony at Tiananmen as an honour. He gave up his chance for relocation to other people several times because of his generous personality and thus had lived in Modigou for 50 years. He said with great feeling: 'My house was originally a work shed, made of yellow mud bricks. It is only a little more than 20 square metres and the walls are only 25 centimetres thick. The wind comes in from all directions in winter and there is water everywhere when it rains in summer. The walls crumble when you touch them'.

The secretary, realizing that the old workers who contributed their youth for the benefit of their country were still living under such conditions, told Wenzhang Wang: 'Our Party and government will provide for you to live in new houses as soon as possible'.

The promise to the shantytown residents touches a problem that is very difficult to solve. As an old industrial base, Liaoning has a great number of shantytowns covering a large area. This problem was not resolved during the planned economy period. After our country entered the market economy period, state-owned enterprises were busy extricating themselves from difficulties and were not able to resolve this problem. Although delayed, this problem has to be solved, but how? The shantytown problem has had a negative influence on the harmony of society and the development of the economy in Liaoning. It affected reform and opening up and the rejuvenation of the old industrial base. It has to be solved.

The reconstruction of shantytowns is easy to talk about but extremely costly to carry out. The government wanted to solve this problem but was unable to do so due to lack of funds. The investment needed for this shantytown reconstruction project was estimated to be RMB 18.7 billion. It was very difficult for government at all levels to raise such a large sum of money. If only from the economic point of view, there would be virtually no return and it could be a non-effective investment, so is it worthwhile to pay the history debt now with such a large amount of money? However, the Provincial Committee of the Communist Party of China and the Provincial People's Government have a clear understanding of this issue: the most urgent problem for the people is the most urgent problem for the Committee of the Party and the government.

The reconstruction of shantytowns is not only a historical problem left over by the old industrial base and urgently needing a solution, but also an unavoidable challenge for realizing overall development. The only right choice for the Committee of the Party and the government of Liaoning is to face the challenge and shoulder the responsibility.

On 30 December 2004, the Provincial Committee of the Party and the government studied and weighed up the situation, and made the decision that the reconstruction of the connected shantytowns in the cities of Liaoning would be basically completed in 2 to 3 years starting in 2005 during the Eighth Session of the Ninth Provincial Committee of the Party and the Provincial Economic Working Conference.

On 16 May 2005, the provincial government issued *The Implementation Plan of Reconstruction of Connected Shantytowns in Cities of Liaoning Province*. A coordinating group for the shantytown reconstruction was established. This group comprises seventeen provincial departments including the Department of Construction; the group leader is the governor. Executive groups for shantytown reconstruction were formed in every city or district and the group leaders are the mayors. The following working groups were established by officers from relevant departments: comprehensive, demolition, letters and visits, programming and investment attraction.

Source of funds

The total investment required for this shantytown reconstruction was calculated to be RMB 18.7 billion. The financial gap was very wide for Liaoning Province. The Committee of the Party and the government of Liaoning introduced the idea of 'marketization operation, government backup'. The funds were raised by a number of methods: provincial and city government subsidies, loans from banks, individual investment of residents, land transfer fund reduction, tax and expense reduction policies, transference of cleared land and commercial building development. The provincial government gave RMB 1.335 billion to the cities as start-up capital. Governments of the cities borrowed RMB 5.44 billion from banks, solving the problem of circulating capital for the shantytown reconstruction project. For the shantytowns with commercial development value, reconstruction was based on a real estate comprehensive development model and the real estate enterprises were selected by bidding. For those shantytowns that were more difficult to reconstruct and without commercial development value, the construction expenses of infrastructure and public installations were paid for by government and those coal-mining enterprises that could afford it.

Yingkou City adopted the marketization operation comparatively early. It started the marketization operation of shantytown reconstruction in 1999 and has accumulated several years of integrated experience. It got rid of the old idea of 'using money in the pocket' and publicly transferred all the projects and land of the shantytown reconstruction by bidding, auctions and quoted sales. In order to reduce the development costs of shantytown reconstruction, relevant policies of land bidding and auctions were developed, and thus land price manipulation and 'real estate bubbles' were avoided. The buildings for relocated residents of shantytown reconstruction were built according to the standards specified in the contracts, and the government bought them back according to the construction costs, equipment charges and land price according to land area. A new pattern – namely that the main contractors for shantytown reconstruction were real estate developers while the government carried out a combination of macro-economic control, policy support and management by supervision – was formed through marketization operation. Therefore, the city shantytown reconstruction process was improved. Adopting the pattern of main contractors being real estate developers with government support by marketization operation, Yingkou City mobilized social power and raised funds, especially starting funds, from various channels. It transferred land for shantytown reconstruction with commercial value by bidding, auctions and quoted sales, and eleven land contracts were completed. The land area was 1,570,000 square metres, the demolished building area was 500,000 square metres, and 16,000 families were relocated.

The experience of Yingkou City was popularized quickly throughout the province, and most cities did well on the shantytown project by using the marketization operation. However, the marketized operation could not completely solve the problem for the coal-mine shantytowns in Fushun and Benxi, and the government had to foot the bill.

Fushun reconstructed seventeen shantytowns in 2005. Because six of these shantytowns were located far from the city and house prices were low, the marketization pattern was useless and investment of government subsidies was adopted. The total investment for the shantytown reconstruction in Fushun in 2005 was RMB 1.3 billion. Despite facing a financial shortfall, the city government provided RMB 0.8 billion through loans, financial subsidies, taxes and expense reduction and exemption, and free use of land. Other funds were raised by loans, interest concessions from construction enterprises in the project, charges on areas extending beyond the original ones and investment from enterprises. Through the marketization operation, Dandong attracted eight enterprises with investments worth RMB 0.2 billion and land assignment of RMB 74.46 million. Jinzhou tripled the available amount of reconstruction area through the marketization operation. Panjin used the marketization operation for all six of its shantytowns, and the government invested RMB 123 million for the basic infrastructure and environmental construction in order to help the development enterprises.

Shantytown reconstruction

Demolition is always seen as 'the most difficult issue'. Some residents did not understand the policies; some asked for increased compensation; some did not have house ownership; and some shanties were self-built and could not be compensated according to the regulations. About 40 per cent of the residents were in low-income families or families close to the low-income line. They had no money to buy an apartment. If these problems could not be solved properly, a lot of trouble would occur.

The Committee of the Party and the government of Liaoning not only made the demolition policies to protect the public wealth, but also to provide a practical solution to the problem. The operation not only reflected the authority of the government, but also emphasized the transparency of a just, fair and open process.

The demolition policies were based on the opinions of relevant departments and the representatives of shantytown residents. The provincial government made policies more favourable than the policies of economically affordable housing after much investigation and many calculations. The local government exempted fifteen items of administrative charges related to shantytown reconstruction and reduced the operational charges relating to the reconstruction. Different cities established specific execution schemes and regulations about relocation of residents and prepared detailed explanations of the provincial policies. Every city regulated that 1 square metre new housing would be returned for each square metre of old housing demolished and no price difference would be charged. If the metric area increased within the standards, only a favourable price of RM 600 to 800 per square metre would be charged. Liaoyang rented the apartments at a low price to families who could not afford the expense of buying the increased space. Yingkou invested in the construction of small family-type buildings for families with special difficulties. The local people gave great support and cooperation to the shantytown reconstruction. There were occasions when local people spontaneously lined up to return their houses in every shantytown. As for houses without ownership paperwork, all self-built houses, buildings constructed before liberation and buildings with a land licence but no building licence were verified and compensated. During the demolition, new apartment buildings were constructed first and then old houses were demolished. This not only solved the problem of temporary settlement, but also reduced the expenses of temporary settlement. Fushun regulated that there would be no charge for the area equivalent to the original area of the old buildings, a charge of RMB 600 per square metre for increased land area and the property rights would belong to the residents. Favourable policies were the premise, and the local people accepted them because they would lose nothing.

However, it was still not easy to relocate so many people and to make payments in such a short time. In fact, some residents had little idea of the intention of the policies and had unrealistic expectations of the demolition compensation. It made the difficulties encountered that much greater. Thus, there was still a lot of detailed work for government at all levels.

The idea of 'working out the details and demolishing in harmony' was emphasized. The issues of humanization, the spearhead function of leaders, integrated dispatching, area divisions, responsibility divisions and consistency of responsibilities within the system were quickly realized in the cities.

These cities repeatedly used all kinds of media to publicize the significance of shantytown reconstruction. The shantytown residents gradually realized that the Party's actions were well intentioned and that the project was moral and for their benefit. Fushun made full use of newspapers, radio, TV and billboards to broadcast special programmes and publish articles. The purposes, meaning, policies and stages of work on the shantytown reconstruction were well publicized, and a good atmosphere of advancing shantytown reconstruction was formed throughout the city. Fushun organized officers from the departments of construction, house property, planning and finance to go to demolition sites in the shantytowns in order to remove doubts by answering questions and mobilizing residents. While on site, they answered 1,720 questions. They also organized the community leaders and some shantytown residents to carry out ideological work with local people. Some 10,683 families moved out and 400,000 square metres of housing was demolished in only 40 days. It was a miracle in the history of Fushun.

Members of the standing committee were in charge of different cities, city leaders were in charge of the various shantytowns, and senior party members were in charge of families. The Committee of the Party and the government of Tieling took the shantytown reconstruction as a political task of poverty alleviation. More than 3,000 officers from seventy-three city departments and fifty-four district offices were chosen to be responsible for those families affected by the demolition. Some of these officers used their own money to help the relocated residents pay the housing system reform expenses and some helped them rent apartments. Through real consideration and help for the local people, a harmonious programme of demolition was realized.

Yunfeng Zhang and Ruocai Chen from the Bureau of Civil Affairs of Tieling were in charge of the family of Min Li, who refused to move out because of a misunderstanding of the policies. The bureau offered her counselling and, after listening to their explanation of these policies, Min Li not only agreed to move out, but she also helped other families come to terms with the situation. Min Li wrote to the Bureau of Civil Affairs of Tieling on behalf of ten relocated families. She told the Bureau that she had explained the policies in detail, and the local people had finally understood that the shantytowns were to be reconstructed for the benefit of the country and its people. In this way, society could develop comfortable and affordable living conditions for the local people.

There was one clay brick apartment building in the shantytown whose property rights belonged to the Shenyang Railway Administration. The City Committee Office of Tieling was in charge of twenty-two families who had to go to the Railway Administration office to complete the legal formalities. In order to minimize these people's troubles, the City Committee of the Party rented a minibus for the residents to travel to Shenyang and provided them with free lunches and bottled water. This was praised by the local people. All the residents in this building who had not yet gone through the formality signed the agreement within 9 days.

Jianying Zhang was disabled due to disease and was laid off. She had little income and lived in a shanty building with her son. She lived by gleaning and collecting scraps. After the coordination of the education office of Yinzhou District which was in charge of this area, a 35 square metre apartment was allocated to her family. In order to support the work of the government, she gave up her key in advance and moved to a deserted public toilet without water, electricity and windows as a temporary living place before relocation. Upon hearing of this situation, the education office initiated a donation for poverty alleviation and sent her RMB 500. The office also helped her pay the rent on a house and move there instead of staying in the deserted building.

The whole process was public and transparent. Fushun posted notices and established a computer database containing all the relevant information, including shantytown reconstruction compensation entitlement, house residual value assessment, order of relocation, compensation confirmation of houses without licences and building extensions, as well as design drawings of apartments for relocation. Tieling examined and verified the houses of low-income residents or houses without ownership through a four-stage system from community, street and demolition departments to the working group. Huludao conducted policies of 'eight publics': namely to make public the list of low-income residents in the reconstruction area, to make public relocation addresses of relocated residents, to make public the unauthorized construction list, to make public demolition orders, to make public payment numbers, to make public selected floor plans, to make public the evaluation of house prices and to make public interior decoration compensation. These policies were praised by shantytown residents. The supervision and inspection group made up of the City Committee of Discipline Investigation and Inspection Office followed and examined the whole process from the initial investigation of the situation, double-checking, signing demolition agreements and relocation of residents. There was a hotline for public reporting and supervision in order to investigate and discipline any person violating the law.

Let shantytown reconstruction be 'trustworthy' and 'excellent'

In order to ensure the safe use of funds, the provincial audit, supervision and financial departments supervised and inspected the provincial subsidies used as construction funds by different cities. These cities established monitoring and inspection systems, which included all important aspects such as an accountability system, prevention of crimes by taking advantage of duty, use of subsidies, compensation for demolition, bidding on projects and quality management. In this way, comprehensive judicial and administrative supervision was realized. The city leading group offices of shantytown reconstruction and city financial departments in particular kept strict accounts of the use of subsidies. The closed fund operation procedure was strictly followed, and special accounts for depositing the reconstruction funds were set up, so that the funds were transferred from cities to the construction enterprises directly and the leaking of funds was prevented. The reconstruction project was a project of honest and clean politics. Fushun invited bidding from all over the country to introduce enterprises from outside to stimulate its own construction market. It also put raw material purchasing by the government under transparent operation and saved funds equal to the cost of about 1,000 apartments in the process of purchasing water, electricity and gas meters.

In order to ensure the quality of the project, the provincial coordination group and the cities strictly executed the regulations and compulsory standards. Management of all staff, the entire process and all-round management were conducted to stop any possible leaks. Clearance on design examination, material and equipment, sealing work and completion tests was strictly required. Quality safety inspections were strengthened to ensure absolute safety. The provincial construction department organized experts to give free training to more than 150 quality safety management personnel for shantytown reconstruction in the different cities. The cities delegated responsibilities to the construction project quality supervision station and hired representatives of the residents as project quality supervisors. The cities involved emphasized the project's quality, safety and progress. The construction enterprises were required to self-inspect and examine, supervising departments had to conduct regular inspection, and the construction inspectors were detailed to adhere strictly to the regulations. Inspection evaluation, situation notification and quality safety cross-checking systems were simultaneously adopted. Inspection groups, based on a daily supervision management plan, were established to go on tours of inspection of the shantytown reconstruction project of each city. In some projects, the supervision was 'one person for one building', and resident representatives acted as full-time quality inspectors in every complex.

The government of Tieling took charge of all the purchases for the shantytown reconstruction project. Tieling is located in northern Liaoning and is a less economically developed area. It is rare for the government to be given responsibility for purchases for government projects in less developed areas. It was not an easy task for the government to be in charge of all the purchases for the shantytown reconstruction project. The purchase office director of the city financial bureau, Han Sheng, said: 'The government is in charge of the purchases for the relocation buildings, and auxiliary projects like roads, piping network and plantings. The purchase of main construction materials is also the government's responsibility. It means that we have divided the purchasing into two parts, project purchasing and material purchasing, according to the general requirements for cutting expenditure and the characteristics of the project'. The government purchasing budget for shantytown reconstruction was RMB 280 million in Tieling last year, 49 per cent of total purchasing funds for the city.

Ensuring that the inspection experts would operate impartially was not only important for the quality of the project, but also related to the image of the government. The purchase office director, Han Sheng, believed that Tieling adhered strictly to this line. He said: 'The inspection experts were drawn on the day of bidding every time from expert banks of different cities under the monitoring of the supervision committee made up from the disciplinary inspection, audit and financial departments. The bidding must be set on the day of bidding to ensure the justice, fairness and openness of shantytown reconstruction'. Up until June of this year, there were nine incidents of public bidding for the relocation buildings of the project and the purchase amount was RMB 283,360,000. There was not even one complaint from the suppliers. The contract purchase amount was close to RMB 100 million, a saving of RMB 17,960,000. The saving rate was 18 per cent. During the purchase of power boxes, for example, the first-stage budget was RMB 3.4 million, but the actual purchase was made using only RMB 1.7 million.

Because of the efficient management of the project, the relocation buildings for reconstructed shantytowns are of very high quality. The relocation buildings in many cities are of an even higher quality than commercial residential buildings.

Making apartments affordable for local people

Another key problem of shantytown reconstruction was whether shantytown residents living below the poverty line could afford new apartments. Most of the shantytowns in Liaoning are residential areas for miners. More than 40 per cent of the residents were low-income or close to low-income families. Nearly half the shantytown residents could not afford the expense of the relocation apartments. The provincial government issued policy documents such as *Instruction Opinion of Solving the Housing Problem of the Families under the Poverty Line in the Shantytown Reconstruction* and *Instruction Opinion of Management of Relocation Complex Residents of the Shanty Reconstruction*. The economic policies guided those shantytown residents who had only one residential place to choose property right exchange and solve the housing problem of shantytown residents once and for all. The unnecessary reconstruction after currency compensation was also prevented. Small family-type relocation apartments were built for families who could not afford to increase their living area. They were small but comfortable. Most cities built low-rent houses to solve the problem of families in extreme difficulties. Dandong not only constructed 10,000 square metres of low-rent houses, but also published a document setting out *Temporal Methods of Renting Management of City Low-rent Houses*, which regulated the support system of low-rent housing from different aspects, such as supply objects, construction control standards, purchase standards and strengthening of management.

In order to enable low-income families in shantytowns to move into new apartments, the provincial committee of the Party and government set up a fund which raised RMB tens of millions and asked the general labour union of the province to distribute the subsidies to these families. The families who could not afford the expense of the new apartments were given the first rights of occupancy with ownership after the arrears had been paid within the time limit. Self-help estate management was used to reduce the estate management charges and increase employment. Some houses were kept, and the income from these was used for housing subsidies, heating subsidies, estate management subsidies and other utility subsidies for the poorest families, or designated as a special fund and the fund and its interest used to cover these expenses. Municipal, environmental sanitation, health and legal services were organized to enter shantytown communities in order to solve management problems and reduce the costs to their residents.

Although they were happy to move into the new apartments, many of the shantytown residents still worried that they could not afford the new apartments without stable sources of income. City governments combined this complex management with employment of poor families, and employment bases were established to provide employment. The able-bodied people from poor families were trained for employment. Labour-intensive industries such as construction, construction materials and service industries were developed to ensure their livelihoods. In Liaoyang, shantytown residents could work in the positions of estate management, gardening, security and cleaning in the reconstructed communities. Some 850 laid-off residents of shantytowns are now employed in these jobs. Yingkou connected shantytown reconstruction with re-employment projects. The department of employment trained all the shantytown residents for nothing and established an employment service centre for them as well as special service windows. More than 20,000 were re-employed with this help. Anshan organized a series of activities to assist shantytown residents in finding employment. Free training courses such as bakery, welding and computer classes helped them gain certain skills. Many people joined these classes to learn more skills.

Postscript

After nearly a year's work by the Party committee and government at all levels, in 2005, the eleven cities in the shantytown reconstruction project demolished 7,650,000 square metres of shanty houses which covered 90.2 per cent of the total demolition area of 8,480,000 square metres. All eleven cities surpassed the annual demolition plan: 7,580,000 square metres of relocation construction was started and 3,340,000 square metres was completed. Some 104,002 families were relocated in various ways. The living conditions and environment of shantytown residents were greatly improved. The old shantytowns became pleasant places to live, and the 'project of people's lives' became 'the project of people's hearts'. By the end of 2006, the reconstruction of connected shantytowns will be finished, and the reconstruction of isolated shantytowns will be started next year and is planned to be completed in 5 years.

Written in 2006

7   The heating charges of 'Ice City'

Piao Yi

Located at latitude 44° 04′ to 46° 40′ N, Harbin is the coldest capital city with the highest latitude in China. Thus, it is famously known as 'Ice City'. To some extent, its harsh climate is the source of the city's wealth. The magical ice and snow are attracting more and more visitors from both home and abroad, and Harbin has become the most popular winter tourist city in China. After all, the harsh climate is also a severe test for the survival and developmental abilities of human beings. The inhabitants of Harbin have to spend extra money on dealing with the freezing conditions, such as purchasing heavy clothes, cleaning the ice and snow from the roads and putting on hold outdoor construction projects in winter. Among these expenditures, the biggest and most immediate one is heating costs.

In Harbin, the average temperatures in 66 days are usually lower than -22°C in wintertime, with a minimum temperature of -38.1°C. For about 6 months every year, the stipulated heating period is 183 days in total from 25 October to 25 April. Therefore, heating is a necessity for residents in Harbin, and is also an important task and responsibility for government at all levels. To maintain 'warm and cosy rooms in the season of ice and snow', a giant heating system is required. At present, there are 365 registered heat supply enterprises and 2,775 boilers for residential heating, which consume 3.9 million tons of coal every year. The total heating cost in Harbin is 2.12 billion yuan every year, with a unit price of 34.55 yuan per square metre of residence (usable floor area). Currently, heating charges are collected through two channels: 90 per cent of the charge is borne by the unit of each worker or cadre, and the other 10 per cent is borne by the worker or cadre him/herself. State-owned enterprises or institutions provide each worker or cadre with a heating subsidy of 10 yuan per month.

The difficulty in collecting heating charges is a noticeable problem in the urban heat supply of Harbin. Up to now, the uncollected heating charges have reached as high as 1.5 billion yuan. The low rate of heating charge collection has resulted in heavy debts and burdens and low credits of heat supply enterprises, which makes it difficult for companies to operate normally and has led to lack of maintenance of equipment, huge energy consumption, low thermal efficiency and potential safety hazards. In Harbin

Boiler Heating Company, there is even a boiler that has been in operation ever since the anti-Japanese War period. The conflict between the high demand for heat supply and the large sum of uncollected heating charges is currently confronting CPC Harbin Committee and Harbin Municipality.

Heat – welfare or a commercial article

The problem of heating charges did not emerge during the planned economy period. Since the implementation of public housing leases for workers and cadres, heat supply has been seen as a kind of welfare item under the overall rationing system over the decades. Before the reforms and opening up of China, most households in Harbin made use of hot wall, individual heating systems or hot floor heating if on their own. The unit would grant each worker or cadre a coal/heating subsidy of 30 yuan every year. A small number of residents living in centrally heated buildings did not receive the coal subsidy because their unit or house property departments were responsible for the entire heating supplies. In 1979, the centrally heated housing area totalled 300,000 square metres in the city, with a heating cost of 5.8 yuan per square metre and a total heating cost of 1.14 million yuan per year.

Since the reforms and opening up of China, the living conditions of people in Harbin have improved fundamentally. Most residents have moved into centrally heated buildings, and the centrally heated housing area has reached 80 million square metres with an increased heating cost of 34.55 yuan per square metre. Meanwhile, the annual heating charges borne by the unit have been increased to an average of 1,500 yuan from 30 yuan. However, the system used to collect heating charges has not been reformed accordingly. Under the housing reform system, most public housing leased to workers and cadres has been transferred to individually owned housing, but units still have to pay 90 per cent heating costs for each worker or cadre. Although the other 10 per cent of heating costs is borne by each worker or cadre individually, as the units grant a heating subsidy of 10 yuan per month to each worker or cadre, basically the units are responsible for all heating charges.

With a great increase in heating area and cost, the collection of heating charges is becoming increasingly difficult.

First, units are experiencing more financial difficulties in paying heating charges. 'Unit' is a form of address relating to the planned economy and is usually affiliated with state and public ownership. Under the traditional system, a worker or cadre living in a unit depended on that 'unit' for both work and living conditions. Heating was naturally no exception. Harbin has been experiencing problems in terms of reform because, as an old industrial base, it has a large proportion of state-owned enterprises. At present, large and medium-sized state-owned enterprises have remained the key targets in the collection of heating charges. With the development of a market economy, the mechanism problems of traditional state-owned enterprises have increasingly emerged. Some of the state-owned enterprises directly under the central government or provincial government have trouble operating, and 219 enterprises out of the 517 key industrial enterprises under the municipal government have stopped production or are on 50 per cent of production. These enterprises have great difficulty paying their workers and cadres without having to pay their heating costs as well. In many cases, when staff from heating companies attempt to collect money owed for heating charges, some workers or cadres will refuse to pay the whole amount in advance for fear that they will not get the 90 per cent reimbursement later from their units. The uncollected heating charges that large and medium-sized state-owned enterprises owe total 500 million yuan, and tend to be continuously rising. Compared with private enterprises, which do not have to pay the heating charges for their employees, some leaders of state-owned enterprises complain that it is a heavy social burden for them to pay the costs.

Second, the notion that heat is a welfare product is deeply rooted in some people's minds. They believe that a socialist country will definitely not see people die from cold without doing anything about it. Some heads of units refuse to pay their employees' heating bills even when they are financially capable, deliberately acting against the relevant policy in the hope that the bills will be settled by the government. As for the residents, it is a fact that some poverty-stricken families cannot afford their heating bills. However, many are unwilling to pay their share of the bills simply because they regard heat as a welfare product supplied for free by the public or the units. These people hide themselves from the heat suppliers' bill collectors when they visit their homes, saying, 'I will pay after all the others have paid' or 'I just don't have the money, what can you do to me?' Some of them intimidate, abuse or even attack the bill collectors. Every winter will see frequent newspaper reports that the bill collectors suffer injuries from such attacks.

Third, there still exists relatively serious unfair distribution. The groups that do not enjoy heat subsidies are the first to feel hard done by. The heat subsidies are only enjoyed by the registered employees of the units. Other groups, including the self-employed, non-governmental enterprise employees and the unemployed, have to pay the entire heating bills themselves. At present, the number of people without heat subsidies is increasing because more and more people are employed in a non-traditional way. These groups have to pay 100 per cent of their heating bills while employees in the state-owned enterprises only need to pay 10 per cent, resulting in a ratio of 10:1. This imbalance, not only practically but also psychologically, has seriously eroded the enthusiasm of the without-heat-subsidy groups for paying their heating bills. They question the bill collectors who visit their homes, often asking them, 'why do we have to pay when those enjoying the heat subsidies refuse to pay their share?' Another imbalance occurs between different units and between different employees in the same unit. The current heating bill collection system has caused the scenario whereby the units that have supplied their employees with houses or are financially capable pay more in heating bills than those that have not supplied houses or are financially incapable. As for the individual employees, those who have been supplied with larger houses benefit more from heating subsidies. The unfair distribution has led to a lack of enthusiasm for paying heating bills, not only for units but also for individuals.

Fourth, the traditional way of supplying heat has an added advantage for those who refuse to pay their heating bills. The early heat supply system was single tubes connected in a series without separate equipment for supplying and measuring heating to individual homes. This way of supplying heat is the result of the planned economy, compatible with the notion that heat is a welfare product. A boiler house supplies heat to one or several, sometimes dozens of, buildings. The heat users of one boiler house are bonded as a group, all of whom can receive heat whether they have paid their heating bills or not.

Owing to the above problems, Harbin municipal government has been giving top priority to heat supply and heating bill collection. Every year, when the heating period is approaching, the government will routinely convene on heat supply where the mayor and the vice mayor concerned make speeches specifying explicit and detailed requirements for heat supply tasks. The municipal government and relevant subordinate departments every year issue several documents on heat supply. During the New Year's Day and Spring festivals, it has become a routine task for the leadership of Harbin to inspect the heat suppliers' workshops, visit families to monitor their indoor temperatures and talk to heating bill collectors. In order to bridge the enormous gap in heating bills, the municipal government, while trying every means to collect bills, has appropriated 130 million yuan in heat subsidies since 1995. The municipal government has also obtained 110 million yuan in special heating subsidies from central and provincial government to support heating suppliers' operations. The heating suppliers, in order to complete the task of supplying heat, have to borrow money to purchase coal. Most are running at a loss, with 68.3 per cent having net liabilities. Taking Harbin Boiler Heat Supplying Company as an example, it owes 120 million yuan in bank loans. New customers are generating heating bills, while the original bills remain unpaid, making heat supply a thorn in the side for suppliers. It is not acceptable to stop supplying heat, nor is it acceptable to continue supplying heat in this way.

The government of Harbin is realizing that heat is a commodity and that treating heat as a welfare product has led to heavy social burdens. Neither the government nor the heating suppliers can afford these burdens. Even if they could afford them this year, they cannot in the future. The market economy principle has to be followed; that is, heat has to be purchased, otherwise it will not be supplied. The notion that heat is a welfare product must be abandoned. Heat must be commercialized and costed. Only then can the future of urban heat supply be fostered in a healthy way.

A campaign in the heating period of 1998

'Heating is a kind of commodity'. This phrase grew increasingly loud and resonant in October 1998. After achieving the success of the biggest anti-flood war in 100 years, Harbin was soon to enter a new heating period. The relevant departments, already exhausted from collecting heating bills, had suggested to the municipal leaders that Harbin should launch a massive heating cost collection campaign, to raise the collection rates and to resolve the stalemate situation of the heating programme once and for all. This was no doubt a very valuable suggestion. Soon, it had been adopted and the campaign had begun.

'Heating is a kind of commodity. Heating service must be paid for'. This was a striking proposition stressed repeatedly at various heating meetings at different levels of city government in 1998. It had also become the focus of the local media for some time. The heating departments and all the governments of the different districts had sent out a large force of collectors to visit residents and repeatedly confront them with the new policy. Some people were very optimistic about the campaign. They believed that the residents, with their memories of the anti-flood war, would surely understand and support the government's stance to overcome the difficulty together.

'If you don't pay the heating bills of your working staff, you'll have to step down'. This was the warning given to leaders of all enterprises and public institutions in the city. The municipal government had clearly demanded that all the relevant departments of the city and district governments should assume responsibility for guaranteeing heating payment. The task of heating payment should be divided into different portions, and each should be assigned to an individual leader similar to the approach taken during the anti-flood war. And no 'dead angle' charge should be allowed. All the enterprises were to guarantee their staff reimbursement of their heating bills. Regarding those enterprises in difficulties, they should refund their working staffs' heating bills in various forms, such as selling cars, houses or asking for a bank loan. In addition, some relevant departments would adopt certain strict measures to help supervise and control the heating payments of the enterprises. For example, the Municipal Finance Bureau and Labor Bureau would not permit any bonuses or purchases of new cars for those enterprises that failed to reimburse the heating bills for their staff. Furthermore, the Harbin Foreign Affairs Office would refuse to accept applications from the leaders of those enterprises to travel abroad on business. And the Municipal Auditing Bureau would follow up auditing the accounts of those enterprises whose leaders were capable of but failed to reimburse the heating bills for their employees, and would mete out serious punishments accordingly. Harbin Intermediate Procurator, Harbin Intermediate Court and other related judiciaries would be resolute in penalizing those enterprises and individuals who obstructed or hindered the heating payments. The Organization Department of CPC Harbin Committee would take the settlement of heating payments as an important reference in the assessments of unit leaders. The municipal leaders emphasized repeatedly that the leaders should be held responsible for not taking positive measures to reimburse the heating bills of their employees. Those leaders were subject to punishment or even dismissal.

These measures were more comprehensive and forceful than ever before in previous heating campaigns.

'Payment first. No payment, no heating'. 'No heating in cases of less than 70 per cent of heating payments'. This was the policy clearly indicated by the municipal government. It was an unprecedented measure. In the previous year, by 25 October, which was the starting date of heating services stipulated by the municipal government, the average heating payment was only between 10 per cent and 20 per cent, and the remaining heating payments were collected over the whole winter. By the end of the heating period, the heating payments could have reached 60 per cent at most, and very occasionally 70 per cent. This time, however, the municipal government clearly indicated that 70 per cent of the heating payment was the premise of providing heating services. The heating companies could offer heating services only after obtaining 70 per cent of the heating payments. The remaining 30 per cent of payments should be collected during the heating period.

Could the heating companies really refuse to offer heating services in cases of less than 70 per cent of payments? Some residents responded to the government's call to pay the heating bills of their own accord, but many others had taken a wait-and-see attitude. By 20 October 1998, only 5 days before the stipulated starting date of heating services, the heating payments had reached only 14.3 per cent, and many residential zones with poor records of heating payments had been exposed by the media. Once again, the relevant departments warned that residents in those zones would not qualify for heating provision in cases of payments below 70 per cent before 25 October. On 21 October, a municipal leader visited a heating fee collector who had been attacked and injured by residents refusing to pay their heating bills. He clearly reiterated the government's firm stand on the issue of heating payments; namely, payment 'first', and 'no heating services in cases of less than 70 per cent of heating payments'.

By 25 October, which was the starting date of heating services stipulated by the municipal government, the total heating payments of the city amounted to only 26 per cent. There still existed a wide gap between it and the bottom line of providing heating services set by the municipal government. Apart from the 778 buildings that had made 70 per cent of heating payments, the majority of the residential zones in the city had not been supplied with heating.

By taking such unusual and definitive measures, the municipal government had conveyed a very clear message to the public. That was: 'Heating comes after payment. There's no room for discussion on this point'. A cartoon in a local tabloid depicted the situation as two hands engaged in wrist wrestling. The larger, more forceful hand, on which was written 'No payment, no heating', represented the government. The other, smaller and weaker hand represented those people who owed heating payments.

On 29 October, the municipal Party committee and the municipal government held an emergency meeting with a view to launching an urgent campaign to promote heating payments and to ensure heating services for the whole city. It also requested that all the departments of the municipal government take the lead to reiterate three points: first, to try to secure 70 per cent of the heating payments; second, to provide heating services for the whole city by 1 November; and, finally, to provide heating at a temperature of 16°C. Although the tone remained firm, some attentive people could observe two different sets of information: namely, the request for 70 per cent of the heating payments remained unchanged, while people were asked to try their utmost to fulfil this goal. Second, for the first time, the municipal government announced that, by 1 November, heating services would be provided for the whole city with no exceptions. And the heating services were guaranteed.

Why? Because, behind the 'wrist wrestling of the two hands', the situation was very complicated, and the public mood was unpredictable.

'It's OK to step down. I'm already tired of this job', said some leaders of those enterprises experiencing difficulties. These enterprises were in such trouble that they dared not promise to reimburse the heating bills for their employees, while other leaders had paid no attention to the municipal government's warning of stepping down, because they were affiliated enterprises of Ministries of the State or of the provincial government. The appointment and removal rights of these leaders rested with the ministries or the provincial government.

'We would surely pay the heating bills. But we are in such difficulties that we cannot pay them at the moment. Please provide the heating first. We will pay later'. Quite a large number of enterprises and residents said this. Among them, some were no doubt lying, but many told the truth. When the relevant departments clearly expressed that later payment would not be allowed, those in difficulties were dismayed.

'We have paid our heating bills. Why should we stay in a cold house without heating?', said those people who had already paid their bills. Because the heating payment of certain residential zones was under 70 per cent, the whole zone could not be offered heating. Those residents who had paid their heating bills would be in the same position as those who had not paid their bills and have to endure 'cold houses'. Thus, those people felt that they had been treated unfairly and became angry.

'The government had stipulated that the room temperature should be above 16°C during the heating period. But every year we had always been below 16°C. So we could only pay after the temperature reached the standard. Otherwise, we wouldn't pay', said those who had not paid. Of course, some of them probably used this as an excuse to refuse to pay the heating bills, but the rest were telling the truth. Because some heating facilities had fallen into disrepair over many years, and the service and management of the heating systems was very poor, the quality of some of the heating services could not be guaranteed. As heating is a kind of commodity, according to the principle of exchange at equal value, it seemed reasonable to refuse to pay for the substandard heating services.

For quite some time, 80 per cent of the complaints had focused on heating issues. Many flocked to the provincial government offices to complain about the 'cold houses' issue. At that time, some of the former important leaders had begun to voice concerns, and some People's Congress representatives and members of the CPPCC had expressed their opinions about it. They had believed it absolutely necessary to intensify the heating payments. But, with people's interests at stake, the heating issue had to be settled appropriately.

Meanwhile, we should also note that, being the subject of the collection of heating fees, the heating providers had taken the administrative orders of 'no payment, no heating' to collect heating bills. To some extent, they were inflexible, rigid and mechanical. Especially for those groups experiencing difficulties, they lacked patience and the necessary favourable policies. Besides, some of the residential zones of the related Ministries of the State or of the provincial government, who were by no means refusing to pay the heating bills, had become unhappy about the mechanical nature of the heating fee collectors' methods.

It is natural that different people have different opinions and voices. Given time, they would gradually reach consensus. However, the cold weather would wait for no one. All the people in the city were watching the result of the campaign.

On 1 November, the municipal government issued an order for companies to provide heating services unconditionally for the whole city. This was 6 days later than the stipulated starting date of heating. By then, the heating payments had reached a level of 35 per cent, much higher than that of the previous year. However, it was still only half of the standard stipulated by the municipal government. By the end of the heating period of 1998, the heating payment had reached 71.4 per cent.

People were very clear that the large and forceful hand of the cartoon had not won an overwhelming victory. From then on, no one mentioned the saying, 'No heating in case of less than 70 per cent of heating payments'.

Solutions – deepening the reforms under the guidance of scientific development outlook

The experience of the winter of 1998 had made the policy-makers of the city more rational and mature. Especially after the 16th Party Congress, the central committee of the Party set the goals of a scientific development outlook and establishing a harmonious socialist society, which served as a scientific guideline for Harbin heating system reforms. In 2003, the central government released an important document, *The Guiding Opinions on the Urban Heating System Reforms Pilot Projects*, which included Harbin in the list of pilot cities. Under the guidance of the scientific development outlook, as well as under the leadership of the central government and provincial government, Harbin has made further efforts in seeking the best solutions for the heating system reforms.

- To positively carry out the reform of the heating payment system. The perception that 'the heating service is a kind of commodity' is absolutely right. Insisting on the practice of 'heating comes after payment' is also correct. The key point is that the heating payment problems should not be settled by continuing to rely on the traditional welfare heating systems as well as administrative orders. After years of deliberation, the municipal government has worked out the *Implementation Plans on Heating Payment Subsidy Monetization*, expected to be published in 2007. The general idea is as follows. To annul the traditional system of 'employees consuming heating, while enterprises pay the bills', which was left over from the planned economy, and to establish a new system of heating payment subsidy monetization, the heating consumers would pay the heating bills directly to the heating providers. The heating expenditures would be brought into heating consumers' personal consumption categories.

- Establish an urban heating guarantee fund system. According to the request of a people-oriented scientific development outlook, settlement of heating payments guaranteeing security for those social groups experiencing difficulties is the foundation of heating system reforms. It is also of vital importance to social stability. Since 1999, Harbin has begun to implement the heating fee subsidy policy for those social groups in financial difficulties. Among those who can enjoy the benefits from the policy are: those who enjoy the privileges of a minimum living standard guarantee while other family members are unemployed; those subsidized or compensated who are identified by the municipal civil administration; unemployed and exempted people; the blind or the severely handicapped who work in municipal state-owned welfare enterprises; veterans who joined the army before 1949 and had no working units after demobilization or the working units were incapable of paying their heating bills. The heating bills of these people would be fully covered by the corresponding state revenues according to their relations of administrative subordinations. Meanwhile, some enterprises and individuals could also enjoy benefits from the policy, such as retirees from the closed, suspended or bankrupted state-owned enterprises of the city, as well as retirees from the bankrupted state-owned enterprises who receive pensions from social insurance funds. A proportion of their heating bills, which would be borne by the retirees' working units, would be covered by the corresponding state revenues according to their relations of administrative subordinations. In addition, the state revenues could also cover the partial heating costs of the retirees who enjoy the privileges of the minimum living standard guarantee, which should be borne by the individuals, as well as 50 per cent of the partial heating costs of disabled employees from the state-owned welfare enterprises of the city, which should be borne by the enterprises. According to this policy, during the heating period between 2005 and 2006, there were 31,434 families enjoying subsidies worth RMB 32.364 million. In addition, according to incomplete statistics, in Harbin there are still 130,000 families who are incapable of paying their full heating costs, but who fall below the standard of the subsidy policy. If 50 per cent of the heating costs of the 130,000 families were to be subsidized by the state revenues, they would still need an expenditure of RMB 60 million. At present, the municipal government is working on making relevant guarantee policies.

- Gradually push for the transformation of separate heating on an individual family basis. In recent years, Harbin has stipulated that all new buildings should be designed and equipped with new heating systems with functions for separate measurement for individual families and temperature control. In addition, to gradually implement payment according to the actual heating requirements of each family. In the case of old buildings, in order to create favourable conditions for payment on the basis of the actual heating consumption of each family, to gradually push for the renovation project of separate heating for each individual family. Since 2002, old buildings with an area of 16 million square metres have been refurbished. This practice showed that heating bills have been greatly reduced for families who have carried out these refurbishments. In order to carry out the renovation of the remaining old buildings of more than 80 million square metres, they will need an estimated expenditure of RMB 2 billion.

- Tighten the reforms on heating providers and improve the quality of heating services. Since 1998, the municipal government has no longer insisted on the practice of 'heating service comes after payment'. Instead, the government has invented the slogan, 'Win the hearts of the residents by providing quality heating services, and promote the heating payment by providing quality heating'. The heating authorities and providers have introduced an emergency service and handle consumers' complaints around the clock. In cases of accidents and breakdown, the heating authorities and providers undertake to settle the problems on the spot. The municipal government has further strengthened the supervision of heating providers. The government authority has adopted a 'watchdog' system on heating, and worked out the quality standard for heating services and technical standards as well as assessment and supervision methods. The government has gradually established a supervision mechanism with citizen involvement and government monitoring. The government has also planned to gradually introduce a franchise system for heating. The government hopes to break the monopolization of the heating market by state-owned heating providers and to push forward the structural reforms of state-owned heating providers in order to improve their services.

- Collect heating fees according to the law and deal with cases of dodging heating payments. The municipal government has set up a heating supervision and law enforcement team to help heating providers to collect heating payments according to the law. For those enterprises and individuals who deliberately avoid paying their heating bills, the law enforcement team will, if necessary, collect the payments owing by force. In this way, the serious nature of the heating regulations has been defended.

Through concerted efforts from many sides over recent years, the heating services and heating payment collections have worked better than previously. People have become more satisfied with the heating services. For five consecutive years since 2001, the total heating payments of the city have reached 80 per cent. The bosses of the heating companies are quite satisfied with this result, which was rare in the past. Meanwhile, people's attitudes towards this issue are gradually changing for the better. According to a recent poll of 5,000 families, 85.3 per cent were in favour of the commercialization of heating services and the reform of heating payments.

However, the total debt from heating payments has been increasing continuously. Being a city with the most difficult problems of heating reforms in China, these reforms are still in the initial stage. There is still a long way to go, with more difficulties and anomalies to come.

Written in 2004

8 Internet cafés

What else can be done in addition to rectification?

Wang Xueqin

Internet cafés have been developing rapidly in China since the end of the twentieth century as a result of the global breakthroughs in information technology. This is an area where the technological gap is quite small between China as a developing country and the developed countries in the West. However, the gap in the number of Internet surfers is extremely wide. After the first Internet café in the world came into being in Britain in 1994, the business sites of Internet access services began to mushroom in China. Incomplete statistics indicate that, by early 2002, there were a total of 200,000 Internet cafés across China, with less than half being legally registered. Beijing had 2,992 Internet cafés. While only seventy of them had the required certificates and licences, 889 had only certificates or licences and 2,033 had neither certificates nor licences. Internet café administration (especially the administration of illegal Internet cafés) has rapidly become a major social problem that the competent government departments have to solve as soon as possible.

Unexpected accident

The date of 16 June 2002 was generally believed to be an auspicious day in China. But a tragic accident occurred when the whole of Beijing was asleep. It was the most serious accident in the city since the founding of the People's Republic of China.

At about 2:40 a.m., a fire broke out in the Lanjisu Internet café in Haidian District, Beijing. Many witnesses discovered after daybreak that all the bar's windows were covered with burglar-proof bars, each having ten one-metre-long steel rods and fixed with eight large screws. The only door was locked when the fire broke out.

As many as twenty people died instantly in the fire, and five of the seventeen injured died later in hospital. According to China News Service, nine of the dead and three of the injured were students at the preparatory school of the Beijing University of Science and Technology.

An official from the Beijing Municipal Public Security Bureau told a press briefing on the same day that the café had been in operation for less than 1 month, with no business licence or fire control equipment. The public security organ was investigating the cause of the fire.

At 9:00 a.m., Liu Qi chaired a meeting attended by the leading officials of the relevant departments of the Beijing Municipal Party Committee and the municipal government, and those from the districts and counties. It was decided at the meeting that a clean-up and rectification campaign be launched immediately against all the Internet cafés and cultural grounds across the city. Step one was to effectively restrict the development of Internet cafés. The relevant departments were to revise the regulations on Internet café administration and rectification and should work out strict administrative measures. Step two was to screen the Internet cafés one by one. Step three was to immediately mobilize forces to crack down on illegal Internet cafés and confiscate their illegal proceeds and operational tools. Those that had committed serious violations would have their business licences revoked and would be included in the industrial and commercial credit monitoring system. In the meantime, the general public would be mobilized to report illegal Internet cafés to the authorities, and illegal operations would be firmly banned. Step four was that all the Internet cafés and other public entertainment grounds must meet the fire control requirements. Step five was that all the district and county governments, all the subdistrict offices and all the town and township governments must participate in the Internet café rectification campaign. They should comb all the Internet cafés, and no illegal Internet café should be left unpunished.

In its report on this accident, a Xinhuanet reporter paid special attention to Liu Qi's announcement: 'From now on, all the Internet cafés in Beijing will suspend their businesses for rectification, and Beijing will not encourage the development of Internet cafés in the future'.

After the fire, the Beijing Municipal Public Security Bureau established in its investigation that the remnants of the fire contained gasoline. Combining spot investigation with technological appraisal, a special investigation group established that the fire was arson. On 18 June, two boys suspected of setting the fire were arrested. According to the public security organ, the two suspected arsonists were 13 and 14 years old. They were students of a junior middle school and often played truant due to the lack of family control after their parents divorced. They often went to the Internet cafés. After a quarrel with the café attendants, they decided to take vengeance and bought gasoline to burn down the café.

The fire turned the Internet café problem into a social concern. Media reports began focusing on Internet cafés and the children addicted to Internet cafés. Some called for 'saving the children', and others argued over whether Internet cafés should be banned altogether.

Although the accident on 16 June was found to be a case of arson, was this incident inevitable?

History of administration

Internet café administration began when Internet cafés appeared.

Some media described the Internet cafés in Beijing as a 'hottest holiday landscape'. They said, 'Most Internet cafés are filthy, full of smoke and with no fire control equipment. Although the posters banning the entry of minors are pasted on walls or doors, most of them were just for appearance's sake. According to the regulatory rules, the business permit and business licence should be hanged in a conspicuous place, but none of the Internet cafés has complied'. 'Most of the Internet café visitors are students and especially university students. This is why there are so many Internet cafés around universities. Of course, middle school students and even primary school children are also frequenters'.

Shang Xiuyun was the deputy chief of the No. 2 Criminal Tribunal of Beijing's Haidian District People's Court and one of China's top ten female judges. At the Fifth Session of the 9th National People's Congress in March 2002, she said the crackdown on illegal Internet cafés should be intensified in order to establish green Internet cafés for primary and middle school students. She said parents often visited her in tears, saying their children had left home for several days and were spending their time in one of the illegal Internet cafés. 'In an illegal Internet café beside a middle school, I saw that those sitting at the computers were all students. They had their eyes glued to the screens, many holding cigarettes. The Internet café operators had boarded up the windows of their small rooms to escape official inspections. The light was dim and the air unpleasant. The computer programs provided were all about sex, violence, superstitions and other harmful contents, and all the children looked infatuated'. In fact, the relevant government departments began exercising administration over Internet cafés as soon as they appeared.

In April 2001, the General Office of the State Council issued the *Notice on Further Strengthening the Administration of the Business Sites of Internet Access Services*. Later on, the Ministry of Information Industry, the Ministry of Public Security, the Ministry of Culture and the State Administration for Industry and Commerce jointly promulgated the *Regulations on the Administration of the Business Sites of Internet Access Services*. This document specifies that the Ministry of Information Industry under the State Council is in charge of exercising administration over the business sites of Internet access services, the Ministry of Public Security is in charge of inspecting their safety and investigating and punishing Internet security violations, the Ministry of Culture is in charge of investigating and punishing the business sites of Internet access services whose computer games contain harmful contents about sex, gambling, violence and superstitions, and the State Administration for Industry and Commerce is in charge of issuing business licences to the business sites of Internet access services, and investigating and punishing those that operate without licences or beyond the limits of their business licences.

Also in April, Beijing issued the *Notice of the General Office of the Beijing Municipal People's Government on the Rectification and Administration of the Business Sites of Internet Access Services* in the city. The document requests the communications department to lead a 3-month intensive rectification campaign against the business sites of Internet access services across the city. In addition, a joint conference system was established for the leaders of the municipal communications administration bureau, the information office, the public security bureau, the cultural bureau and the industrial and commercial administrative bureau. The office of the joint conference was housed in the communications administration bureau.

Did the rectification campaign meet with initial success after 1 year?

On 30 April 2002, a special national video conference on the rectification of harmful information was held. At this conference, the Ministry of Public Security, the Ministry of Education, the Ministry of State Security, the Ministry of Information Industry, the Ministry of Culture, the State Administration for Industry and Commerce, the State Council Information Office and the National Administration for the Protection of State Secrets jointly promulgated a document entitled the *Plan for a Special Crackdown on Harmful Internet Information*. As a result, a nationwide intensive crackdown on harmful Internet information was launched, with the emphasis being placed on the Internet cafés and other business sites of Internet access services. For the first time in history, the central authorities decided that the departments of culture would be in charge of exercising administration over the Internet cafés and other business sites of Internet access services and would be vested with the responsibility of strengthening the day-to-day supervision and administration of the business sites of Internet access services, including cyber games, cyber audiovisual products, art products, performance activities and Internet cafés.

On the same day, the Beijing Cultural Bureau conducted a joint inspection of three Internet cafés in Beijing's Dongcheng District in collaboration with the departments in charge of public security and industrial and commercial administration. On 4 May, they launched another inspection on four Internet cafés in Haidian District. The officials from the city's cultural bureau were upset by what they saw during the inspection. They immediately reported to the deputy mayor who had recently been transferred to take charge of cultural work. The deputy mayor requested the cultural bureau to prepare a document for the longstanding administration of Internet cafés and to refrain from campaign-style administration.

On 10 May, it was announced at the video conference on a special city-wide crackdown on harmful Internet information that a special crackdown would be launched on the Internet cafés and other business sites of Internet access services under the leadership of the Beijing Cultural Bureau in cooperation with the departments in charge of public security and industrial and commercial administration. On 14 May, the deputy mayor who had been in post for only 3 days led the personnel from the departments of culture, public security and industrial and commercial administration in investigating and inspecting the Internet cafés in Haidian District (again!).

Ten days later, the cultural bureau and other departments held a symposium on the longstanding administration of the business sites of Internet access services. The members of the non-Communist parties, the municipal committee of the Chinese People's Political Consultative Conference and the cultural market supervisors were invited to voice their opinions and suggestions. Many of the suggestions became the measures of this crackdown and future administration.

On 11 June, Beijing set up a steering group for the special rectification of Internet cafés and other business sites of Internet access services, headed by the deputy mayor. The group was given the task of exercising unified leadership over the special rectification.

At a meeting held on the same day to launch the special rectification campaign, two documents were issued and the mailbox and hotline for reporting illegal Internet cafés were announced. The two documents were the *Plan for the Special Rectification of the Internet Cafés and Other Business Sites of Internet Access Services* and the *Publicity Programme for the Special Rectification of the Business Sites of Internet Access Services*. A total of 450 people attended the meeting. They included the leaders of Beijing's administrative departments, the leaders of district and county governments, the leaders of the district and county departments in charge of culture, public security and industrial and commercial administration, and the legal personnel and managers of the Internet cafés and other business sites of Internet access services. *Beijing Evening News*, with a circulation of nearly one million, carried detailed reports on this event under the headline 'Crackdown on Illegal Operations, Beijing Focuses on Special Rectification of Internet Cafés'.

On 14 June, the deputy mayor again led an inspection of four Internet cafés in Dingfuzhuang Area in Chaoyang District, at the head of the officials of the departments in charge of culture, public security and industrial and commercial administration. Beijing's initial steps to rectify Internet cafés won full affirmation from the Ministry of Culture, which believed Beijing to be the first city in China to take this action.

However, as noted by Liu Qi at the meeting on 16 June, the accident occurred precisely in the month dedicated for Internet café rectification and for safety in production. While efforts were made to carry out the rectification, the accident killed many people. The lessons were profound. The documents issued and the steps taken by the relevant departments of the Beijing municipal government all indicated that Beijing was truly among the forerunners in terms of setting guidelines and taking practical steps in this respect. But what were the lessons learned?

Devastating strikes

The accident on 16 June speeded up Beijing's work and intensified its rectification.

Step 1: An emergency notification was issued, ordering all Internet cafés in the city to suspend their operations for rectification. First, the total number of Internet cafés was established, and lists of Internet cafés and especially the illegal ones were compiled. With regard to the Internet cafés and other business sites that had all the required certificates and licences, the inspection focused on safety. With regard to those that did not have all the required certificates and licences, they were ordered to suspend their operations and sever their physical connections with the Internet. With regard to those that were set up without permission, they were banned and their equipment confiscated.

Files do not indicate how many illegal Internet cafés had been investigated and penalized. Does this mean that there were no illegal Internet cafés?

One month later, the first group of thirty Internet cafés that had passed safety inspections and had all the required certificates and licences began operating after signing the *Letter of Commitment on the Standard Operation of the Internet Cafés and Other Business Sites of Internet Access Services.* The contents of the *Letter of Commitment* included the establishment and improvement of the site safety inspection system, with minors being prohibited from entering the business sites, the business sites registering all individuals who accessed the Internet, and the installation and use of the computer security management software.

Who could be sure that there were only thirty Internet cafés operating in Beijing at the time?

Step 2: Vertical and horizontal efforts were combined to intensify integrated administration and increase regulatory tools in order to deal with the weak links of Internet café administration. In other words, the combination of local administration with day-to-day administration was emphasized. Industrial administration was combined with administration by districts, counties, subdistricts, communities and units. The segments of this industry strengthened their coordination. Supervision by the industrial authorities was combined with that of public opinion. With regard to the re-registered qualified Internet cafés and the banned ones, the districts, counties, subdistricts, communities and other administrative bodies were to cooperate with each other in functional administration and should leave no 'blank spot' in administration. In strengthening social supervision, the names, addresses, legal personnel and owners of the Internet cafés were published in the media, and the community security activists and the public were mobilized to participate in Internet café supervision, administration and comment. The hotlines for reporting illegal Internet cafés were published and the prominent problems exposed. In using high-tech tools to strengthen the monitoring of Internet cafés, monitoring systems were established, monitoring software developed, and a computer hook-up monitoring system was also established for the cultural market.

Following this, the media did expose the illegal operations of a few Internet cafés. But was it enough?

Step 3: This was a really devastating blow. After the accident on 16 June, the relevant departments of the State Council were busy drafting the administrative regulations. In only 3 months, Premier Zhu Rongji of the State Council signed the State Council Decree No. 363 on 29 September 2002 to promulgate the *Regulations on the Administration of Business Sites of Internet Access Services*. The document came into force on 15 November 2002.

According to media interpretations, the document explicitly provides that minors will henceforth be barred from entering Internet cafés, computer pubs and other business sites of Internet access services and that Internet cafés will also be banned from operating within a 200-metre radius of primary and middle schools and from the residential buildings (compounds). The most important regulations were that minors under 16 were prohibited from entering Internet cafés, that Internet cafés should not be established within the 200-metre safety zones and should not be set up next to schools, that Internet access records should be kept for 60 days, and that each computer should have a 2-square-metre safety space and doors and windows should not be locked.

The *Regulations*, containing such specific quantitative requirements, were designed to be a longstanding mechanism.

In keeping with the *Regulations*, Beijing soon formulated its own implementing rules. In particular, it established an enforcement accountability system to prevent 'passing the buck' to others. In addition, it worked out a plan for establishing a special integrated enforcement body for the cultural market to reduce enforcement costs and increase enforcement efficiency. Other measures included preparations for the establishment of industrial associations and the opening of free and healthy Internet access sites for young people.

Striking at the root of a problem as well as its harmful effects has always been an ideal solution, but issuing documents is also imperative. Does moving from special rectification to integrated administration represent a dredging or a blocking? Which of the effective steps are designed to dredge or block and which are more important?

Rising here and subsiding there

Following the Lanjisu accident, some media commented on the allegation that half the Internet cafés were illegal. 'Illegal Internet cafés accounted for an astonishing ratio of 50 percent. How could half of the Internet cafés escape the administration by the three major departments in charge of industrial and commercial administration, culture and public security? It is hard to understand'. 'The efforts to rectify the Internet cafés always rose here and subsided there. Once there was a tragedy, a rainstorm of inspections would be launched. Then everything would become calm and tranquil, and administration and operation would return to their usual tracks, where enforcement and illegal operations were at peace with each other. How effective are these administrative blitzes?'

An official at the marketing section of Beijing Cultural Bureau also admitted that weak links existed in administration. The first weak link was that examination and approval were out of control. Why were they out of control? (1) The administrative rules and regulations were unsound. The *Regulations on the Administration of Business Sites of Internet Access Services* issued in April 2001 provide that a legal Internet café should have three certificates and one licence, namely the approval documents issued by the public security department and the cultural department, the business operation permit issued by the telecommunications department and the business licence issued by the department of industrial and commercial administration. But these departments failed to dovetail their approval procedures to form a complete system. (2) The research and planning of the Internet cafés and other business sites of Internet access services were insufficient, the development of the Internet cafés was underestimated, and the administrative guidelines were inconsistent. (3) Examination and approval failed to strictly comply with the relevant provisions of the *Regulations on the Administration of Business Sites of Internet Access Services*, over-emphasized economic interests and provided access services to some business sites that had not obtained any certificate or licence.

By the end of June 2002, according to some officials, the city's department of industrial and commercial administration had issued business licences to seventy business sites, which explicitly described their business scopes as 'providing Internet access services'. The city's telecommunications department issued permits for the business sites of Internet access services to 127 sites. The city's cultural department issued permits for Internet cultural operations to 303 sites. And the city's public security department issued the opinions on the safety inspection of the business sites of Internet access services to 920 sites. In addition, there were 2,033 illegal Internet cafés providing Internet access services but with no certificate or permit.

The *Regulations* of the State Council constituted the discretionary powers for Internet café administration. Are there any weak links, confusing procedures or blind spots?

On 19 February 2004, the State Council convened a working conference on Internet café rectification. State Councillor Chen Zhili urged participants to fully understand the necessity and urgency of the special rectification campaign and to treat the rectification as one of the most important items on their agenda from the perspective of being responsible for the Party, the people and posterity, building the Party for public interests and ruling the country for the people. In addition, participants should be determined and dedicated to tightening up this special rectification so as to effect fundamental improvements in the operational order of the Internet cafés and create a healthy social environment for young people.

The conference decided that the rectification would be conducted from February to August. The emphasis of the rectification was identical to that launched 1 or 2 years before. Allowing minors in, operating longer than permitted and other illegal operations would be severely penalized. Illegal Internet cafés would be resolutely banned, and the acts of operating business sites of Internet access services under the guise of computer schools, occupational and technical training courses, electronic reading rooms and computer classrooms would be severely penalized. Illegal Internet cafés seemed to have spread into school campuses.

Xinhuanet once again carried a special report on the implementation of the decisions made at this conference. 'Beijing introduces effective measures to rectify Internet cafés; those accepting minors twice will be suspended'. This was another devastating blow for the industry.

However, the ensuing comments once again focused on the Internet café issue and even the whole social administration.

The *Beijing Star Daily* first disclosed in a signed article: 'We learned from Beijing Juvenile Reformatory that 70 percent of the inmates there had been to Internet cafés and 30 percent of them had committed crimes due to playing Internet games or surfing porn websites in Internet cafés. And most of their crimes were of a violent nature. In particular, about 25 percent of the inmates were from single-parent families'. Meanwhile, Xinhuanet quoted the Hongkou District Procurator in Shanghai as saying, 'Internet cafés have become an important place for juvenile delinquents and in particular for crimes committed by primary and middle school students'.

The *China Cultural Daily*, the official newspaper of the Ministry of Culture, carried an article arguing that 'regarding Internet cafés as the common enemy and even regarding the legal Internet cafés as a dreadful monster are tantamount to giving up eating for fear of choking'.

Under the headline 'Why 10 departments cannot control one Internet café?', Xinhuanet again criticized the phenomenon of 'too many people being involved in administration but nobody being responsible'. This report sparked lots of Internet comment.

In the meantime, some law-abiding Internet café operators had much to complain about. According to the regulations, the existing business hours for Internet cafés are from 8:00 p.m. to 12:00 p.m., so they had to close just when business was thriving. The 20 per cent tax rate for Internet cafés was designed for the entertainment industry, but Internet cafés were in fact a service industry, for which the tax rate should be 5 per cent. As the tax rate was too high, some Internet cafés had to make a profit by opening beyond normal business hours and accepting minors. This was because operating according to the regulations is not profitable.

After only 3 months, Chen Zhili again convened a meeting of the coordinating group for the special rectification of Internet cafés on 18 May. She told the meeting:

> The Party Central Committee and the State Council have attached great importance to the administration of Internet cafés and have given a

series of important instructions on this matter. Within the 3 months, a total of 15,900 illegal Internet cafés have been banned and the illegal operations such as accepting minors have also been contained to some extent. The rectification has made initial progress and won public support. But the whole rectification task remains formidable. All regions and all departments must focus their attention on two major issues: illegal Internet cafés and acceptance of minors. In addition, law enforcement must be strict. Effective measures should be worked out to resolutely contain the spread of illegal Internet cafés into rural areas. At the same time, longstanding mechanisms should be established, legislative research should be intensified, censorship over the contents of the Internet cultural products should be strengthened, and necessary human and funding support should be provided for the special rectification campaign.

Here, I do not attempt to discuss the specific aspects of Beijing's rectification work and the practical problems arising from implementing the state council resolutions. One year later, the National Coordinating Group for the Administration of Internet Cafés convened a conference on 8 July 2005, the main topic being the experiment of establishing a longstanding mechanism for Internet café administration. Chen Zhili told the conference,

Since the special campaign to rectify Internet cafés was launched in 2004, the order of the Internet café market has improved, which has won public welcome and support. But the task of Internet café administration remains arduous and requires constant efforts. All departments and the governments at all levels must fully understand the importance of strengthening Internet café administration from the perspectives of ensuring the healthy growth of minors, building a harmonious society, fulfilling government functions and enhancing administrative ability. It is imperative to further consolidate the results of the special campaign of rectifying Internet cafés, and to take the establishment of a longstanding mechanism and the strengthening of Internet café administration as an important matter in safeguarding the people's interests and ensuring the healthy growth of minors. The efforts should be effective and result-oriented.

She emphasized:

Strengthening Internet café administration is a long and arduous task. Currently, it is imperative to focus the work emphasis on establishing a longstanding mechanism for Internet café administration. One, law enforcement should be strict and supervision should be effective. Two, social supervision should be improved and industrial self-discipline should be promoted. Three, the educational responsibility of families and schools and in particular the responsibility consciousness of parents being the 'primary responsible persons' for minors should be empha-sized. All the experimental cities should intensify their organizing and leading function to strengthen the responsibility of dependency administra-tion. All relevant departments should strengthen coordination and coopera-tion to create a working pattern featuring division of labor and overall interaction. The National Coordinating Group for the Administration of Internet Cafés should strengthen guidance over the experiment and sum-marize experience and popularize it in a timely manner so as to ensure that the experiment will be successful.

In discussing how to establish a longstanding mechanism, Beijing's deputy mayor who attended the conference put forward a four-point proposal. He said that, under the precondition that minors are prohibited from entering Internet cafés, the restrictions on the business hours of the law-abiding Internet cafés should be removed. In addition, the *Regulations on the Administration of Business Sites of Internet Access Services* should be revised so that the document would become more feasible and operable.

In fact, media reports said earlier that the Ministry of Culture had been soliciting opinions from various circles including Internet café owners on how to revise the *Regulations*. Some reports said that, although the *Regulations* had rectified the environment for Internet access, the excessively strict provisions could lead to a slowdown in the development of China's Internet café industry. The *China Cultural Daily* even noted that revision was imminent.

However, what was particularly noticeable to the industry was that official media reports said, 'Chen Zhili stressed in conclusion that all places in the country should continue to implement the *Regulations on the Administration of Business Sites of Internet Access Services* and strengthen the administration of Internet cafés'.

Does the bottleneck to Internet café administration constitute a turning point for the Internet café industry?

What should the competent government departments do and not do in the face of government administration and market development and in parti-cular in the face of the dual character of Internet cafés as both a cultural industry and a cultural undertaking?

Latest efforts

In April 2005, the Beijing Enforcement Contingent for Cultural Administration was officially established. In August, the contingent formally began operating. Internet café administration, formerly part of the functions of the municipal cultural bureau, became part of the integrated enforcement.

In October 2005, the *Plan of Beijing for the Experiment on the Establishment of a Long-Standing Mechanism for Internet Café Administration* was formally launched.

In May 2006, Beijing removed the restrictions on the business hours of Internet cafés according to the new *Regulations of the People's Republic of China on Administrative Penalties for Public Security*; Internet cafés could operate 24 hours a day. In the same month, Beijing launched a 90-day special campaign for Internet café rectification. The Beijing Association for Business Sites of Internet Access Services urged all Internet café operators in the city to resolutely refuse to accept minors under the age of 18. By June, the legal representatives of more than 1,000 Internet cafés had received training in relevant laws and regulations, 800 Internet cafés had been ordered to conduct rectification and reform, twelve Internet cafés had been ordered to suspend operations for rectification, and six Internet cafés have seen their business licences revoked.

In July 2006, the National Coordinating Group for the Administration of Internet Cafés believed when inspecting Beijing's Internet café market that the longstanding mechanism innovation was working and that its achievements were real.

In August 2006, Beijing mayor Wang Qishan filed his comments in a report that called for banning all illegal Internet cafés: 'Our city will continue to work hard to rectify and standardize Internet cafés'. Newspaper reports also said that the cultural market development centre of the Ministry of Culture had formally established an office for planning the promotion of the Internet café industry, and the office had formally put forward the *Plan for the Promotion of the Internet Café Industry*. But shortly afterwards, it was claimed that the reports were untrue, and that the policy of the Ministry of Culture had been constant and that the ministry had not introduced any new policy or requirement recently.

The Ministry of Culture disclosed that the state would formally begin revising the *Regulations on the Administration of Internet Cafés* this year [2007] and that the basic principles specified in the *Regulations* would not be changed. The revision would focus on some provisions that were ineffective in administration. At the same time, some good practical experience would be added to the *Regulations* and explorations would be made on the issue of minors visiting Internet cafés. But when the *Regulations* would be revised and how to solve the sensitive issues such as whether the ban on minors should be lifted were still undecided.

Originated in 2005 and revised in 2006

9 The road to community correction

Zhang Sujun

Community correction refers to the general concept of alternative penalties to imprisonment, which deprives sentenced criminals of their personal freedom. It has been widely applied in Western countries since the 1960s and 1970s. Now it is a major means of criminal punishment, which covers over half the penalties of sentenced criminals in many countries. Since the second half of 2003, China has begun experiments on community correction. In this case, in light of the actual situations of the experiments in different provinces and cities, I will discuss the achievements, problems and anomalies of community correction through narration of the designated roles.

Introduction of main roles

Wang Fang: aged 32, male, sentenced to 8 years' imprisonment for a violent crime, having served for 3 years of his sentence, 18 months' commutation of his sentence was made during the term with 3 years and 6 months' imprisonment remaining. He was selected as one of the first targets of community correction in S city on trial and granted parole.

Ms Li: aged 47, female, director of the subdistrict office where Wang Fang lives, which is one of thirty-five experimental communities in S city.

Professor Su: unknown age, male, Doctor of public administration from the Kennedy School of Government Administration, Harvard University in his early career, and Dean of the Department of Social Science at a famous university in S city, the major designer of community correction in S city.

Community worker Xiaogao: aged 22, male, a graduate from the regular college course run by Professor Su, employed by the social group of community correction 'Xinhang Service Group' as a social worker under a 3-year contractual term, in charge of the education of such people as Wang Fang and other targets of community correction.

Wang Fang awoke from another nightmare to spring sunlight shining through the gap in a curtain in a small crowded room of a two-storey old building located in S city. His wife was still sleeping like a log and, on a camp bed by the wall, his 8-year-old daughter murmured something in her sleep. The division curtain hung in the middle of the room was already open, which apparently revealed that Wang Fang's parents had left for their morning exercise.

Crowded as it was for five family members in a room measuring only 7 to 8 square metres, Wang Fang still felt safe, warm and comfortable. In comparison with the time when he was in prison 2 years ago with twelve people in a cell that was filled with six bunks and sundry personal articles, the area of his home might not be much larger; however, it was free from the gloomy atmosphere in prison.

The scene of 2 years ago was still engraved in Wang Fang's memory. That afternoon, he, who had been charged with negligent injury and sentenced to 8 years' imprisonment and had served his term for 3 years, never expected that he would be given a lucky break. The moment when the section chief of Prison Politics announced the first targets of community correction and that he was one of them, he really could not believe it.

Wang Fang remembered one day 5 years ago when he was 28. He had returned to his factory to claim his living allowance and had quarrelled and fought with a workmate. At that time, his family was having a run of bad luck. The factory where his wife worked went bankrupt, his 60-year-old parents were sick and the factory where he worked had also ceased production for many months. As a result, he was so furious that he beat his workmate with an iron bar and caused him serious injuries ...

During the term of imprisonment, encouraged by his relatives and cared for and educated by government officials, Wang observed the rules of the prison, studying hard, working positively and complying with the prison authorities. Such good behaviour earned him the title of 'he who is active in reform' each year, and 1.5 years' punishment was commuted once.

Wang Fang had planned to strive for a further commutation of 1 year's imprisonment through industrious reform, so that he would have been released 2 years in advance. It never occurred to him that he would be listed as one of the first targets of experimental community correction. Thinking of the twists and turns in the 2-year community correction, Wang Fang remembered vaguely that his nightmares these days were concerned with failure of correction, and the re-detention and reform of himself.

The previous Sunday, Ms Li, director of the subdistrict office, had spoken of one matter in the weekly ideology course for the three prisoners who were the targets of community correction. The communication correction programme in S city had yielded major social repercussions in society as well as protests from many people. Therefore, she told them, they must not cross the line, as failure to comply with the terms of community correction would result in their imprisonment and reform again.

Director Li, aged 47, who had served as director of the subdistrict office for 10 years, was delighted when her superior designated the neighbourhood where she worked as one of the first experimental areas for community correction. Leaders in the city government lectured in training courses on community correction that a vital condition for the trial plan of community correction set forth by the Ministry of Justice included the complete organization of the community and the high quality of officials at the basic level with advanced ideas and sound administration ... Being selected proved that the leaders recognized the advancement of the residential district under her administration.

In relation to the selection of the three targets of community correction including Wang Fang, Li also played an essential part. These three boys had grown up in the community under her administration and she knew them well. She was aware that they were good in nature and committed crimes negligently as first-time offenders. Once sentenced, they all left old parents and small children at home, and the residential district invested a lot of energy and money in order to solve their family problems. When community correction was carried out, the district issued them individual business permits and allocated them stands in the agricultural and trade market with priority. Although they earned only a small wage, their basic living standards were secure, which also relieved the residential district of economic pressure. On a weekly basis, they would also work for the community for free for 2–3 hours, taking care of the repairs to water and electricity appliances in the Home for the Aged for 2 years, which was greatly appreciated by the elderly.

However, Li's husband, who worked in a branch of the Public Security Bureau, brought her the news that he had received many letters and calls, which complained that 'kids in the courtyard dared not go out to play due to criminals' service of penalty at home', 'This was equal to setting the criminals free and would disturb the stability of society again'. Some regarded the correction as worship and blind faith in foreign things and the appropriation of Western standards which propagated false human rights to China: 'Now that the criminals' human rights are to be protected, what about those of the mass and stability of society?', asked some policemen. They deemed that on one side we had carried out a 'strict strike' and on the other we had 'released criminals', creating a 'safe community' while enforcing community correction.

Director Li thought that criminals such as Wang Fang were unruly and had been making trouble since childhood. Wang Fang, in particular, had a hot temper and frequently got involved in fights with others. If he lost his temper and injured others again, a failure of experimental community correction would thus be made and even the sound reputation of the residential district for more than 10 years could be damaged. In thinking these matters through, Director Li felt a little bit regretful of having actively requested to participate in the experiment. 'If the experimental plan develops successfully, we are sure to promote it, otherwise we will give up', said Professor Su in the training course. 'Professor Su, as a researcher, might work out the dissertation anyway, but if we fail, we lose face!' thought Ms Li. 'I had to warn and remind them constantly and should not rely on such measures as "psychological guide", "psychological treatment or correction" as adopted by the "SW"[1] Xiaogao. In whatever sense, we should stand up to this and not make any mistakes'.

Professor Su, Dean of the Department of Social Science at a famous university in S city, actively engaged in public policy and had achieved a great deal of respect in policies of criminal justice in the transitional stage. He was the pioneer of domestic community correction theory and a promoter and supporter of community correction in experimental areas. He is also the major drafter of the community correction plan for S city and a member of the Community Correction Expert Group of the Ministry of Justice. In the mid-1980s, Professor Su was awarded the Doctor's degree of public administration from the Kennedy School of Government Administration, Harvard University, and he went to the University of Maryland (USA) as a visiting scholar at the end of the 1990s. There he explored criminal justice policy for 1 year where his special topic was on 'community correction and its prospects in China'. Professor Su deemed that community correction, which was begun in the 1960s and 1970s in Western developed countries, reflected a general rule and development trend of criminal justice policies in human society. Similar to the market economy system, which is not unique to capitalist or socialist societies, community correction may be used in both societies as it is an effective tool for curbing crime in communities. It has four strong points compared with imprisonment: (1) it may prevent the passing on of crime skills among criminals, and prisoners' mental and physical injuries arising from imprisonment; (2) it may be good for criminals to be adapted to society and pave the way for their return to the community, enhancing the effect of correction; (3) it is beneficial to secure the stability of a criminal's family and reduce the social burden; (4) the related expenses will be only one-third to one-fifth of those for imprisonment, which would save on public resources.

In the 3-year experimental period, China has altogether received over 60,000 criminals in community correction. We have saved costs equivalent to building twenty large-scale prisons with a capacity of 3,000 inmates. The saved expenditure amounted to billions of RMB. More importantly, less than 1 per cent of the criminals receiving community correction would commit crimes again, and the ratio is much smaller than that for imprisonment. In the process of industrialization, urbanization and marketization, there are more and more floating population and social controversies and, for a long period of time, the crime rate has been increasing. In particular, when we enter a social transitional period in which per capita annual average income goes above US\$ 1,000, such trends will be accelerated. A correct criminal justice policy should be one that will achieve the most effective results of curbing crime with limited and scarce public resources. We should apply community correction to those who are negligent first-time offenders with penalty terms below 5 years who make up 50 per cent of all prisoners, most young criminals and the old, the weak, the sick or disabled prisoners who are not appropriate for imprisonment. Meanwhile, we should apply imprisonment, which is relatively more costly, to offenders committing severe or violent crimes, and this should be the inevitable choice of an efficient criminal justice policy. These also embody the social values of community correction.

In terms of competence, Professor Su reckoned that organizations at the basic level had been well developed after reinforcement of community construction in recent years. S city and many other areas have developed some social organizations under the auspices of government for community correction. Professionals majoring in social science, psychology and education such as Xiaogao were employed by those organizations. Several years ago, Professor Su had offered a course of community correction in the department, and Xiaogao was among the first graduates to take it up. Moreover, a group of volunteers with professional knowledge, social experience and enthusiasm for public welfare undertakings have joined the organizations. The human resource capacity has been installed for expanding the experimental areas. Over the past 3 years, the pilot project has gradually explored a management mode that is in line with our national conditions and a set of rules, institutions, procedures and standards have been established step by step. The standardization of the guaranteed capacity of community correction has been gradually completed.

People's support is the main problem. There are still some people who have doubts; some policemen and law enforcement officers cannot accept community correction from the angle of their work and fail to cooperate; some leaders also have different ideas. However, community correction has been included in the reforms of the judicial system and working mechanism, and the sampling survey has reflected that social recognition is steadily improving. All these factors show that community correction has gained more and more support.

Overall, when Professor Su analysed community correction with his 'value – capability – support' three-circle theory model (Figure 9.1), he believed that, although current community correction stayed in the left-hand side with insufficient support, it would move to the 'NIKE' area[2] where the three circles overlapped, with the expansion of experimental areas and the strengthening of public awareness. By then, community correction can be brought into full play.

Social worker Xiaogao is an excellent student of Professor Su; he became a social worker in the 'Xinhang Service Group' 2 years ago under a 3-year labour contract and was responsible for the education and reform of a group of correction targets including Wang Fang. During his vocational training, the 22-year-old man brought into play his strong points as a graduate of social science. In particular, Professor Su added a community correction course to the students' curricula and familiarized Xiaogao with his functions and duties more quickly than other social workers from the same major. Xiao met the correction targets regularly, reviewed their files and visited their former working unit, neighbourhood officers, some of their relatives and neighbours, and devised different correction plans for each target using his professional knowledge. Two and a half years ago, he was quite confident

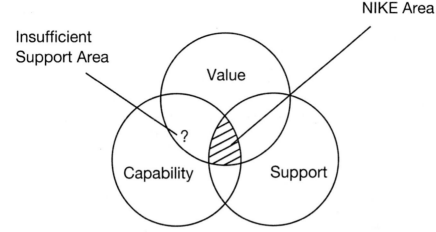

Figure 9.1 The three-circle theory model refers to the 'value – capability – support'
policy analysis tool.

of Professor Su's optimistic estimation, and felt that he had entered into a
brand new NGO in the early stage of his career and was imbued with hopes
of a bright future.

After two and half years, Xiao encountered challenges in his work and the
cruelty of reality. First of all, the correction plan devised for each target was
not as applicable as it had been when they were in prison. Sometimes, the
targets were absent for various reasons; some had no available time, and
some were absent-minded during discussions. They were not the same as
prisoners in terms of obedience and cooperation. Second, the subdistrict
officers, thinking that the government paid him for his services as if paying
for the purchase of commodities, criticized his work and expected instant
results. They objected to his scientific measures such as 'analysis of personality categorization' and 'psychological measurement'. In addition, according to current laws and regulations, administration power over the correction
targets was in the hands of the Department of Public Security. If the target
does not appear to violate the law, it is hard for the Public Security
Department to approve requests for applying the correction programme.
What made him doubt the feasibility of the 'government – society – volunteer' correction plan as set forth by Professor Su was an e-mail from his
classmate Xiaozhang from B city. B is also one of the six experimental cities[3]
of community correction selected by the Ministry of Justice. Yet B city's
correction plan is featured as a 'judicial bureau – policeman – volunteer'
model. Xiaozhang had been recruited as a uniformed civil servant of the
judicial bureau. The 'Sunshine salary' plan adopted in 2006 increased his
income dramatically, which was already much greater than Xiaogao's. S city
also aimed to carry out this salary plan, but the public service units were
excluded, not to mention such NGOs as the Xinhang Service Group.

In Xiaozhang's e-mail, he said that the community correction plan was going well in B city. The previous year, all communities had participated in the plan. The number of targets for community correction also increased from 100 at the beginning to more than 5,000 currently. The key to B's success is the 'judicial bureau – policeman – volunteer' correction plan. Orders were promulgated to define the jurisdiction of the judicatory bureau over community correction targets. In addition, over 100 prison guards were deployed temporarily to each experimental community. Those targets could not tell policemen from public security stations from prison guards, and thus behaved themselves whenever they saw policemen nearby. Xiaozhang worried about what would happen after the prison guards withdrew at the end of the correction plan.

Xiaogao strongly sensed that the key to community correction was a prompt and special mandate of legislation, making clear that the power and jurisdiction of correction organizations and the power of administration, education, reward and penalty would all belong to one single organization.[4] Xiaogao also agreed with Professor Su that more support was essential. But Xiao also believed that the practical effect of and solution to problems served as a precondition of obtaining support. The urgent matters to address were not to expand experimental areas, as stressed by Professor Su, but to solve problems exposed from current work through legislation. Legal guarantee is the ultimate support. Moreover, Xiaogao had the feeling that the creative measure that Professor Su was very proud of – bringing in NGOs and the government paying for their services – was actually the same as the 'outsourcing practices' often adopted by Western counties. Is it suitable for government to outsource such a core business as reforming criminals? Especially in China where most public services and utilities were still under the charge of the government, is it appropriate to contract out such work as in disputes even in Western countries? Can B city's practice, namely using NGOs to organize volunteers and giving civil servants administrative power, better comply with our national conditions?

It occurred to Xiaogao that several days ago when Professor Su visited his area for research purposes and told him that he was invited as one of the representatives of S city to the 'conference of community correction in experimental spots' held by the Ministry of Justice, Professor Su had already prepared a detailed 'work plan of fully pushing forward community correction' and had done his best to call for the expansion of experimental areas for community correction.

Xiaogao indeed admired Professor Su for his solid foundation of theory, international vision, enthusiasm for work and creative thinking; however, he deemed it an obligation to report to his tutor various difficulties and problems he had encountered during his work at the front line. Thinking of this, he immediately started writing …

Night fell and the lights in S city gradually went out. A misty spring rain fell in the city while Xiaogao was still absorbed in his report …

Written in 2004

Notes

1 SW is an abbreviation for social workers in S city. They engage in social surveys, community correction, drug addiction treatment, etc., and they belong to different social groups, which are privately run and non-profit organizations for the public good, similar to the NGOs in Western countries. These groups recruit social workers on a contractual basis.

2 The three-circle theory model refers to the 'value – capability – support' policy analysis tool. In general, the 'NIKE' area of 'Community correction' in this chapter lies in the "?" area in Figure 9.1 (overlapped by two circles), meaning it has value and capacity yet insufficient support.

3 The Ministry of Justice of the People's Republic of China chose Shanghai, Beijing, Jiangsu, Shandong, Tianjin and Zhejiang as the first pilot areas in the second half of 2003. And in the first half of 2005, the Ministry of Justice chose another twelve provinces (districts and municipalities) including Hebei as the second set of pilot areas.

4 According to the pilot plan, community correction is conducted for the following five types of targets in line with the current laws and regulations: probation, parole, control, temporary execution of the sentence outside prison and deprivation of political rights. At the same time, the plan prescribed how education and correction work should be conducted by judicial administrative organs. Thus, different departments are in charge of different work: management, education, awards and punishment and so on. To solve this problem, we need to amend some basic laws such as criminal law and criminal procedure law. Community correction law and its supporting laws and regulations should also be enacted.

Part III

Crisis management and group incidents

10 Twenty-six days and nights for the pollution of Tuojiang river

Liu GuoQiang

Tuojiang river, the mother river of the Neijiang people.
Tuojiang river, the life river for the 800,000 population by its side.
But, an unexpected pollution incident had occurred at the upper reaches of it.

The pollutants were from the Qingbai river. On 1 March, 2004 at 10:00 p.m., the Environmental Protection Bureau received a complaint from a native of the Jiangyang area of the Tuojiang river who had discovered a large amount of dead fish, meaning that the Neijiang area of the same river was probably polluted. The Environmental Protection Bureau reported the news to the People's government in the shortest possible time. Almost simultaneously, vice mayor Z received similar news from another channel. Mayor Y immediately issued an order to send specialists to collect water samples for analysis. By 11:30 p.m., specialists had collected water samples from the garden shore at the central business district (CBD), Zizhong Yinshan town and Shunhechang town.

On 2 March at 2:00 a.m., examination results showed that there was no excess mercury, arsenic, lead or cyanogens, but the amount of ammonia nitride was in excess by seven to fifteen times, which meant that the water was unfit to drink by both humans and animals.

At 8:30 a.m., the government called for an emergency meeting. Mayor Y was named director, related leaders of the city as deputies, and those in charge of the relevant departments as members. By this time, a water pollution emergency headquarters had been set up.

Secretary Q, who was attending the national people's representative meeting, contacted the relevant leaders immediately after hearing the news. He ordered that effective measures be taken and to use every conceivable means to ensure the safety of the people's drinking water.

It was decided that: everyone must stop getting water from the polluted river; the course of water supply should be altered, which meant that there would be a limited amount of time for people to obtain drinking water at designated points; the use of water for industrial purposes would be stopped at those points to ensure a sufficient amount of drinking water; and the water company, environment protection and health departments were to set up an emergency programme as soon as possible, and to define and open up a second water resource.

After the meeting, the city government immediately reported to the provincial government, applying the immediate cut-off point of the polluted area and suggesting that water be obtained from Dujiangyan and reservoirs by the side of the river; the amount and velocity of water in the middle and lower reaches of the Tuojiang river should be controlled; and hydroelectric power plants and water conservancy projects should release water in order to strengthen the self-purifying ability of the Tuojiang river. It also called for more specialists to direct operations in the affected areas.

On the afternoon of 3 March, the provincial government reported that the main reason for the pollution was that the second fertilizer factory located in the Qingbaijiang district of Chengdu was implementing transformations in techniques, and that a fault in the equipment had caused the discharge of ammonia nitride into the river. As the Tuojiang river was experiencing a drought, the self-purifying ability of the river was low, which resulted in the pollution. The provincial government decided to close down operations to cut off the pollutant.

Seeking water on a rainy night

The 800,000 population in the affected area of the Tuojiang river had entered a state of emergency. The second water company stopped supplying water on 2 March. Some 40,000 tons of water were available at noon and during the night, but there were only 7,000 tons in storage. The city district population of Neijiang needed 8,000 tons of water daily, and 7,000 tons in storage meant that, after 3 March, a city of 30 square kilometres had no water for its people.

Because it was an emergency, there was no water storage equipment in people's houses, and even cooking had become a problem. Some schools, homes for the aged and child welfare institutions lacked water; farmers from Zizhong town sold water for RMB 20 per pole; on the night of 2 March, it started to rain and people began to collect water in pots placed under their roofs.

The pollution continued ...

The environmental protection and health departments were monitoring the situation day and night. The level of ammonia nitride was still seven to ten times over the acceptable amount, and there was no sign that it would fall.

The report from the Ministry of Water Resources (MWR) showed that the velocity of the Tuojiang river was 0.17 m/sec. The distance was 300 kilometres from the source of the pollutant to Neijiang city; according to this velocity rate, if there were no outside forces, the polluted water would reach

Neijiang in 500 hours' time, in about 20 days. Zhang Xuezhong, the provincial secretary attending the national people's representative conference, enquired about the situation several times after hearing of it. The governor had commented on the Neijiang's government report. The secretary of Neijiang made numerous calls for members of the government to get in touch about the situation and issued repeated warnings: we must at any cost ensure the people's use of water, fire safety and social stability.

The emergency meeting of the government believes the use of the second water resource is extremely urgent …

After consultation and discussion, it was decided that Wuxing reservoir, which is 7 kilometres from the district and has a storage capacity of 600,000 cubic metres, was the best choice. However, before the alternative resource could be accessed, the only way to send water from it to the district was by tankers.

We can send out at most five firefighting vehicles to transport water, each holding 8 tons, after retaining the necessary water for firefighting equipment.

OK! Ordered firefighting vehicles are on stand-by.

Spot reconnaissance discovered that the second water supply area was too low to access water, so the proposal to pump water from Daqingliu river was abandoned.

At 12:30 a.m., the Zigong government was contacted.

The Neijiang and Zigong firefighting teams reported to the SiChuan Provincial Fire Department, which immediately put the plan into action. Eleven firefighting vehicles from these two cities set off for Dashanpu.

It was raining heavily. Nearly a hundred soldiers braved the wet and the cold winds as they made repeated journeys between Neijiang and Dashanpu. Vice mayor D of Zigong government directed operations on the spot from the shelter of his umbrella,

At 1:50 a.m., the first vehicle with its full load of water had reached Neijiang, a sign of the compassion and friendship between Neijiang and Zigong.

At the same time, the environmental protection and health departments had reported the test results at Wuxing reservoir – the water was drinkable.

Provincial leaders go to Neijiang

On the morning of 3 March, at the Wuxing reservoir in Dongxing district, vice mayor Z joined designers and engineers who were investigating the pollution spot. Even calculating the fastest time, the channel installation programme was estimated to take at least 48 hours. But what happened during those 48 hours? Eleven firefighting tanks transporting water for 10 hours was way off the target at just 370 tons of water, far short of the population's needs.

For the sake of protecting the people's rights and to avert disaster, the government issued emergency notices ordering public entertainment bodies and water-supported units to cease operations and strictly prohibited the selling of water. In addition, every unit was ordered to check out fire hazards.

The government suggested that people should buy more vegetables and fruit, prepare more solid food and for the preparation of cooked food to be simpler; no bathing was to be allowed during the emergency, but only minimal washing to maintain cleanliness.

However, the problem was that there were only 2,000 tons of water stored in the second water factory, which was much lower than the deadline; therefore, the water supply had to be totally cut off. The Neijiang population was undergoing a serious test.

At 8:00 p.m. on 3 March, vice-governor ZH visited Neijiang and, after checking the actual situation, he decided to send more vehicles to transfer water to flush out the Tuojiang river to help Neijiang overcome its difficulties. He then returned to Chengdu that evening to carry out the plan.

Neijiang was facing a difficult situation, but it was not alone. On the afternoon of 4 March, the fire control headquarters sent out six firefighting vehicles, Luzhou station sent out two, and Chengdu environmental protection department sent out seventeen street watering tanks. In all, there were thirty-eight water-transporting vehicles mobilized to help Neijiang. More vehicles joined them later.

By 5:00 p.m., Tuojiang Theatre, Guihu Street, Minzu Road and immediate areas had twenty-three water supply points altogether. People carrying all sorts of containers lined up in an orderly fashion to wait their turn. There were no grumbles, no quarrels. Leaders from the government took it in turns to oversee operations, and the police and community cadres made every effort to publicize and explain the situation, to maintain order and look after elderly and young people. At 7:40 a.m. on 5 March, Chengdu military region sent out twenty water-transporting vehicles to Neijiang by order, and soldiers immediately set to work. Third-grade petty officer Zhangbangdong and first-grade petty officer Hanxintao drove a vehicle carrying 12 tons of water to Baima district and cement factory to supply 800 residents with drinking water, and continued to the appointed areas to supply water to other people in need ...

On the afternoon of 5 March, the deputy commander of Sichuan military region contacted Neijiang to find out more about the situation and to reassure the public that operations would not cease until the disaster befalling Neijiang was over.

At 8:00 p.m. on 5 March, the water conservancy department reported that, until 6:00 p.m. on 5 March, Tuojiang river's velocity had speeded up to

0.31 m/sec. The provincial government clearly pointed out that all water conservancy projects had to discharge without any condition. The process of purifying the Tuojiang river had speeded up.

At 11:00 p.m. on 5 March, after over 40 hours of operations, the Wuxing reservoir temporary channel had settled down, and new water resources had flowed into the second water factory.

At 12:30 a.m. on 6 March, accompanied by cheers from the residents, the supply of water was restored. On the morning of 6 March, in Wulong town, Zizhong's second water resource exploration project was completed.

We have the confidence to fight the water shortage

Getting water from the Wuxing reservoir has eased the emergency need for water. Although the district government had only limited powers to help people fight the disaster, it still did its best. But who knows how much hardship was caused by the water shortage?

In her own fight to combat the disaster, Zhang Yuanling, a female engineer with the Neijiang Water industry, walked back and forwards a few hundred times over a distance of 3 kilometres, walking over 100 kilometres altogether. Despite falling down several times in the mud because of hunger and tiredness, she kept on working. At the same time, her elderly mother was dying and was anxious to see her daughter for one last time. Facing the wrath of her relatives, she could only grieve silently, because she knew there was something more important for her to do. When everyone was cheering for the reinstallation of the water, Zhang knelt down in front of her mother's portrait and cried silently: 'Mum, please forgive your daughter … '.

For the sake of the people of Neijiang, there were many who contributed just as much as Zhang.

Cheng Jianzhang, a farmer from Zizhong town, abandoned a 100-dollar income to contribute his own boat so that the specialists could extract water samples for analysis. Because the specialists had to examine the water hourly, Cheng Jianzhang did not sleep or eat properly for 9 days.

From city to town, cadres to people, residents to soldiers, adults to children … every street, every community, every water supply point told impressive stories.

Donxing district secretary, Zeng Shengwen, accompanied by his few cadres, starting on 5 March, kept on sending water to about twenty elderly residents who had lost their children. They also had made a special contact list for the elders in case the elders had any emergencies.

Firefighting

There was a further serious problem facing the Neijiang people at the time of the water shortage – firefighting.

There being no water in the city's storage system, the consequences of fire were so serious that no similar scenario had ever occurred anywhere in the world.

On the night of 6 March, a decision had been taken in the daily meeting headed by the deputy mayor and vice head of the emergency headquarters L as the firefighting director, emphasizing that preventing fire was as important as fighting the water shortage, that no slackening would be tolerated and that all must use every means to ensure fire safety.

To ensure fire safety, two proposals were put forward. First, to use contaminated water from the Tuojiang river to fight fires and put up notices to remind residents that this water was undrinkable. However, following discussions, it was decided that this proposal would not ensure that residents would not drink the contaminated water, and it was possible that people could be poisoned as a result. It was therefore decided to use the second proposal, namely that the 40,000,000 tons of reserved water would be used for firefighting, fire stations would have staff on 24-hour standby and to activate the emergency act in the event of fire. On the basis of suspending the business of 820 public entertainment places, everyone in the city had to be vigilant in their efforts to help prevent the possibility of fire breaking out. Nine investigation groups were set up, and police patrolled schools, hospitals, hotels, shopping malls and so on. During this period, 230 strict punishments were issued to those infringing the temporary act. Community centres used all kinds of ways to remind their residents of the dangers. Astonishingly, there was not even one incidence of fire during the water shortage!

However, as time passed, the situation was worsening. According to specialists, there was only enough water in the Wuxing reservoir to supply residents for 20 days.

Leaders of the province and city visit the spot again

At 10:00 a.m. on 9 March, another emergency meeting was called by the provincial government. Deputy governor ZH pointed out that all water conservancy projects next to the Tuojiang river must be opened. The government sent out specialists and related cadres to monitor the situation.

At 6:30 p.m. on the same day, fire stations from all over the province sent out twenty more water transport vehicles to Neijiang.

On the afternoon of 11 March, Liu Peng, deputy secretary of the province, vice governor ZH and other relevant people visited Neijiang. After investigating all aspects of the situation, Liu Peng pointed out that maintenance of the water supply to all residents was the most important priority; all water power plants in the upper reaches of the river had to open their dams to let out water to dilute the contaminated water; and to use artificial rainfall if at all possible.

By 16 March, there were altogether 101 water transport vehicles in Neijiang to ease the situation.

On 17 March, some good news was received from the provincial environmental protection department. Following further water sample analysis, the content of ammonia nitride had dropped from 36.6 mg/L on 11 March to 1.65mg/L and was continuing to fall.

Success is just around the corner

On 18 March, the situation had eased to such an extent that the relevant department decided, starting from 8:00 p.m. on 19 March, to increase the amount of water supply to the city area, and that this water would also be used in production, firefighting and other related aspects. Water supply points were also increased to forty-one.

Some 101 water transport vehicles were continuing to be driven between Neijiang and Zigong non-stop. Vice governor L commented emotionally,

> In the fight with the disaster, the Municipal Committee, people's government, People's committee of Neijiang have led its people to fight the disaster bravely, and you have ensured the safety of your own properties. I represent the Provincial Municipal Committee and government to convey my heartfelt thanks to the Neijiang government and related departments, also to the soldiers, who have fought at the first line of the disaster. I hope the people of Neijiang will continue to fight the disaster till it is over! I wish you all the best!

At 6:00 p.m. on 27 March, a moment that the entire Neijiang population had been waiting for, the government formally announced: 'THE DISASTER IS OVER, ALL USAGE OF WATER IS BACK TO NORMAL!'

As the last water transport vehicle drove away from the water supply point, the people cheered and clapped. At last, the terrible disaster was over. By this time, more than 400 people and 101 water transport vehicles had been deployed making 7,809 journeys to carry over 62,781 cubic metres of water since 3 March.

At this time, when Neijiang people turned on their water taps, they could finally see clear and purified water flow again.

Adults cheered, children laughed, and elders murmured through their tears, 'Water! Finally there is water again!'

What an eventful period of 26 days and nights: they will never be forgotten by the people of Neijiang.

Postscript

Two and a half years on, I recall happiness when overcoming a difficulty, but also there are fears for the risks we have taken after the event.

The municipal committee and the government made immediate, fast and accurate decisions so that there was not even one poisoning case. There was unprecedented unity and order.

However, because there was no water in the 30 square kilometre city storage system, the hidden threat of fire was ever present. If there had been a fire, the consequences would have been too dreadful to contemplate. Looking back on it now, the first proposal when setting up the firefighting plan would probably have been the safest and most scientific.

Written in 2004

11 Emergency response in the city management

Wu Shixiong

Having suffered the epidemic disease of 'severe acute respiratory syndrome' (SARS) in 2003, all levels of government departments in Beijing have now made emergency plans to respond to such emergency incidents. The emergency preparations mechanism has proved effective in dealing with certain emergencies.

On 3 January 2006, a large part of the street road surfaces subsided near the Jingguang Bridge in Dongsanhuan (the Third Loop Route East). The city government immediately initiated the emergency control scheme for serious accidents. The government quickly contained the situation and won wide praise from all walks of life in the city.

However, 6 months later, on 31 July, a rainstorm hit Beijing city and, although the relevant departments immediately implemented emergency measures, floods occurred under some cloverleaf junctions. Both directions of the expressway to the airport were blocked, which resulted in 200 aeroplanes being delayed. A lot of the public criticism about this matter pointed to the government. The effectiveness of the emergency control plan was widely doubted.

Beijing government successfully implemented the city emergency scheme to treat the road surface subsidence accident at Dongsanhuan

Event: A large area of road surface subsidence at Dongsanhuan

At around 12:40 a.m. on 2 January 2006, eight workers of the tenth subway route construction site were preparing to spray concrete slurries under Dongsanhuan Road between Hujialou Road and Guanghua Road when they suddenly saw that some water was welling up from the construction site. The workers immediately warned the other forty workers to evacuate the site as quickly as possible.

At about 2:00 a.m. on 3 January, the surface of the side road of Sanhuan Road situated over the construction site subsided, causing a large depression 10 metres in length.

At 6:00 a.m., the depression enlarged to more than 50 square metres. Sewerage started to back up, causing the depression to widen even more.

By around 9:00 a.m., the depression covered an area of over 100 square metres. At about 10:00 a.m., while two excavators were digging out the collapsed surface of the side road of Sanhuan Road, a major city water supply pipeline was uncovered. Subsequently, all the underground pipelines and cables were exposed.

By that time, the depression had enlarged to 18 metres long, 14 metres wide and 12 metres deep. The accident resulted in traffic jams on the main and side roads of Sanhuan Jingguang Bridge and Chaoyang Road. All the tenth subway route constructing operations between Hujialou Road and Guanghua Road were halted. Five backbone optical cables belonging to Beijing Telecom Company and four optical cables of Beijing Mobile Communication Company were struck, affecting over fifty major telecommunications clients, and more than 10,000 household telephones and broadband users living in twelve communities were cut off. The forty-eight-cable backbone telecommunications pipeline of Beijing Network Communication Company had subsided. The heating supply for 205 households adjacent to the accident area was switched off.

Treatment: Rapid response to the emergency

At around 2:00 a.m. on 3 January, a telephone in the City Emergency Control Centre rang. Chaoyang District reported that the road surface on the southeast side of Jingguan Bridge on Dongsanhuan Road was subsiding and the sunken area was enlarging. The relevant top official of the city government was informed of the report immediately from the centre, and the responsible officials of all the relevant government departments were asked to go immediately to the accident spot. Those departments included the Beijing Commission of Communication, Beijing Municipal Bureau of Public Security, Beijing Municipal Bureau of Construction, Beijing Municipal Administration Commission, Beijing Administration of Work Safety, the publicity department of the Beijing Municipal Committee of CPC and Chaoyang district government.

The Communist Party secretary of Beijing and the mayor of the city paid close attention to the handling of the accident. They asked the departments concerned to adopt effective measures to contain the damage. The emergency scheme was implemented immediately, the mayor remaining in the emergency centre to command and coordinate action. Meanwhile, two assistant mayors were sent to the spot to take direct command of emergency operations.

At 4:00 a.m., in an office building to the east of the accident spot, emergency headquarters were set up, consisting of responsible officials from the above-mentioned government departments and two associate mayors directing operations. The headquarters was divided into the emergency control team, the expert group, the public security and traffic management team, the social workers' team, the publicity team and the information team.

Every unit went immediately to their respective positions to deal with the emergency.

The depression was steadily growing larger, and the situation was becoming urgent; following discussion with the experts on the spot, headquarters decided to take the following measures immediately.

Control of traffic to ensure citizens' safety

The accident black spot at Jingguang Bridge on Sanhuan Road and the affected areas at the centre of all the main and side roads from Guomao Bridge to Hetaoyuan Bridge on Dongsanhuan Road were closed. All vehicles except for buses and authorized vehicles were prohibited from Xiaozhuang Crossing and Guandongdian Crossing on Chaoyang Road. Around the controlled roads, eighty-seven traffic signs were set up to signpost the diversion. All the intersections were controlled by the police to direct the traffic flow.

Bus companies implemented an emergency transportation service. Nine bus routes were affected, with buses not allowed to make stops while passing through Chaoyang Road. Another thirty-two bus routes made a detour to avoid the accident area. Over 300 workers were sent to adjacent bus stops to keep order and to help those passengers getting on and off the buses. Those passengers affected by the accident deciding to take the subway increased by over 10 per cent. The subway company shortened the departure intervals on the second subway route from 3.5 to 3 minutes and put another 50 trains into temporary operation. The departure intervals on the thirteen subway routes and the Batong route were shortened from 5 minutes to 4.5 minutes. Meanwhile, at the major subway stations such as Guomao and Jianguomen, over 300 workers were seconded to guide passengers and direct the traffic. In general, the traffic flow was maintained.

Urgent repair operations

The main sewage pipelines leaked and the outflow increased steadily. It was very difficult to block the pipelines and pump out the water. Worse still, the accident spot is geologically complicated as it is located on sandy soil. Under the sunken road surface, there were heating, electric power, communication, telecommunication optical cables and pipelines. Except for the subsiding road surface at the southeast corner of Jingguan Bridge, the cavities appeared in the southwest, northeast and northwest directions. If the accident was not dealt with correctly, there would be severe consequences. A wide area of communications would be interrupted; the water supply, electrical power and heating supplies would be terminated. It would probably jeopardize the safety of the whole area around the bridges.

After discussions with the experts in subway, bridge, water conservancy and construction emergency, headquarters took urgent measures. First, to cut off and fill in the bidirectional sewage pipelines and lead the outflows. Second, to fill in the depression with concrete and pour in cement to reinforce the soil body, recover all pipelines and the protection wall. Third, to drill holes into the sunken surface of the tunnel, fill them with concrete and mix the cement mortar to reinforce the surface. Fourth, to pump the water from the subway tunnel. Fifth, to monitor round the clock the road, bridge, water supply, heating supply, gas supply, electric power, communication cables and pipelines to prevent the possibility of further disasters.

To keep citizens informed of the accident

The publicity team comprised the officials from the relevant government departments and the chief editors from the press units to urgently inform citizens of the accident by means of mobile telephones, radio and television broadcasts, outdoor electronic bulletin boards and newspapers.

Mobile text message: This is the fastest and most convenient way to submit information. On the morning of 3 January, most Beijing citizens received a mobile text message from *1860 Station*. The message read: 'According to the traffic department, a sewage leak accident occurred this morning at the southeast corner of the side road of Jingguan Bridge on Dongsanhuan Road. The traffic control measure was taken around Chaoyang Road, Jingguang Bridge on Dongsanhuan. Please avoid this area. Thanks for your cooperation and help'. It was the first time in Beijing that traffic administration informed citizens of an accident through mobile text messages.

Beijing Radio Broadcasting Station: The traffic information was broadcast frequently. From 5:00 a.m., Beijing Traffic Broadcasting Station and the City Administration Broadcasting Station repeatedly broadcast news updates regarding the sunken road surface at Jingguan Bridge to remind drivers to avoid the area.

Beijing Television Station: Continuous reporting of the notice of traffic control. At intervals of 30 minutes, Beijing Television Station broadcast the notice of traffic control, showed a map of the affected area, a map of the bus route changes, the cross-section picture of the accident spot and updated reports of the accident treatment operation, and interrupted programmes with scrolling news of the changing traffic situation.

Mobile television and outdoor traffic guide bulletin: The traffic information was scrolled to broadcast. It reported the latest news from the traffic control area, relevant information for citizens' reference, and notified viewers of developments.

Newspapers: In the afternoon, *Beijing Evening News* and *Legal Evening News* issued updated news of the accident and the traffic control with a map of the traffic control area and the list of bus route changes. On the morning of 4 January, all the capital's media reported the road surface depression on Dongsanhua Road.

In addition, headquarters held a press conference every day and notified the media of the latest situation in order to maintain calm.

Evacuating the neighbouring residents

Near the accident spot, there was a building scheduled to be demolished. Four families still lived in the building. At 5:00 a.m. on 4 January, headquarters ordered them to leave the building as soon as possible, and the street-managing office was asked to arrange for the affected families to stay at Chaoyang Hotel. At 6:30 a.m., all four families had been evacuated.

Emergency control: Everything was carried out and order maintained

In the early morning of 3 January, a meeting was held in the emergency headquarters and tasks assigned. Every relevant department began operations and worked together closely; the treatment operation was running to schedule. At 3:30 p.m., the leaking sewerage pipelines were filled in, and outflows were basically controlled. At 9:00 p.m., the area around Jingguang Bridge received a TV signal again.

At 5:00 a.m. on 4 January, the sewage at the accident spot was pumped out, and concrete construction work started. At noon, telecommunication and heating pipelines were recovered. Meanwhile, square sewer channels were built, and the tunnels beneath the depression were reinforced. By 5 January, the square sewer channels were finished, sewer tubes repaired, and the depression was filled and paved with pitch.

At 6:00 a.m. the following day, the traffic on Chaoyang Road returned to normal, including the side roads.

At 6:00 a.m. on 7 January, two main westbound roads on the external sides of Dongsanhuan were reopened. The following day, the depression on the main side road of Dongsanhuan was filled in, and the main road protection wall building and road surface cleaning work was completed.

On 10 January, when the water level fell to 1.8 metres below the transom, over seventy firefighters entered the tunnel by boat, carrying video cameras and signal transmitting devices to check the status of the internal surface of the tunnel structure.

At 7:00 p.m. on 11 January, about 20,000 cubic metres of water in the subway were pumped out, and on 12 January, the tunnel ventilation and internal surface disposal work began. At 4:30 p.m., the team of experts conducted an inspection to confirm that the internal surface was in good condition and met the requirements to reopen the side road to traffic.

At 5:00 a.m. on 16 January, the side roads of Jingguang Bridge were opened in both directions. Thus, halted traffic, telecommunications, heating, water and sewerage pipelines were all reinstated.

Effect: Positive feedback from all sides

Most citizens expressed understanding

Mr Zhen, who lived near the area of the accident spot, told reporters: 'It is the longest closure of main roads of Dongsanhuan I've ever seen, vehicles on the side roads are moving very slowly, but the traffic looks in good order'. Mr Wang, who was waiting at a bus stop, said that, because of the receipt of the timely mobile text message from the municipal traffic department, despite the inconvenience, he understood that the measures taken were necessary. As of 11:00 a.m. on 4 January, the municipal traffic management department had not received any telephone complaints about bus route changes. Some citizens sent text messages saying that they would travel to work on foot instead of driving.

Positive comments from the experts

The director of the Capital Research Institute for Social and Economic Development, Xin Xiangyang, said, 'I noticed that the government immediately organized and coordinated all relevant departments to work together to respond to the emergency and postponed the accident investigation until later. They deserve praise'. Xin told the reporter, 'I believe that operating the emergency control mechanism would become the routine work of the departments concerned'.

Praise from net friends

Net friend A: To be honest, the emergency control action taken by the government is good; especially as citizens were quickly informed about the accident through MSM. Not everyone would have been watching TV and only the car drivers would listen to the traffic broadcasts. MSM was the best way to relay the information because almost everybody has a mobile phone, it costs little but it is effective.

Net friend B: In an emergency such as this, the most important thing is the trust and cooperation between the government and the public. Beijing is a developed city, and by means of the modern media such as broadcast, TV, internet, mobile phone and outdoor electronic bulletin boards, the government was able to distribute the information to the public in a transparent way. With the understanding and the cooperation from the public, the difficulties could be easily overcome.

Net friend C: When the accident occurred, the government implemented the emergency scheme immediately, and different government departments responded to the emergency quickly and worked together closely. While dealing with the emergency, the government departments concerned did their best to provide road diversions for citizens which prevented their daily lives from being disrupted due to traffic jams. The government served the people conscientiously during the emergency period.

Positive and objective reports from the media

Xinhua News Agency: After the Jinguang Bridge accident, the government actively informed the citizens of the situation through both media news reports and MSM. It not only ensured the citizens' right to know the whole story of public events, but also reduced the possibility of traffic jams. The government won a lot of respect from Beijing citizens.

Renmin Network: Considering it was such a major accident, it was astonishing that nobody was killed or injured, no serious traffic jams occurred in the affected area, and the residents around the accident spot received good care. Obviously, the emergency response measures taken by the city government were powerful and effective.

Guangming Network: Because the top government officials paid close attention to the road surface subsiding accident and the city government departments concerned worked together closely to do the repair work, the problem of the accident around East Third Ring Road was solved. The sewage pipe leakage was effectively controlled, normal traffic flow resumed, and the direct influence on citizens' life by reason of the accident has been minimal. The Beijing government has shown a strong capability to respond to an unforeseen public emergency and has won acknowledgement and praise from the media and citizens.

The central government is focusing on treatment measures

The Capital Academy of Science Decision and Beijing Leader Decision Information Centre issued a 'Reference for Decision' on 1 January 2006, which said that the public information transmission through MSM during the emergency measures was subject to close attention from the central government including the Department of Civil Administration. On 4 January, an official from the Department of Civil Administration said that the MSM application solved the difficulty of letting all citizens know when a public emergency had occurred in the city. To transmit the message in time before the possibility of disaster, the Department of Civil Administration decided to extend and improve the MSM applications in the early warning and forecasting of such disasters throughout the whole country.

Accumulated rainwater cut off the airport expressway to challenge Beijing's emergency control mechanism

Beijing's major accident control scheme proved successful in dealing with the road surface subsidence around Jingguang Bridge in Dongsanhuan.

However, 6 months later, another accident was to further test the emergency treatment mechanism of the city government.

On the morning of 31 July 2006, a rainstorm filled up many low-lying places on the airport expressway. There was a 1.5-metre-deep accumulation of rainwater under the Yingbin Bridge, which cut off the expressway for about three and a half hours. The vehicles backed up along the motorway for 15 kilometres. The vehicles leaving Beijing transformed the road into a huge car park. This was the first time in 10 years that the airport expressway had been cut off in both directions. In order to catch their scheduled flights, many passengers had to leave their cars on the road, collect their luggage and walk several kilometres to the airport along the expressway.

The Capital Airport set in train the flood emergency measures. They commandeered one of the main runways to divert vehicles through the southern airport area and into the airport building to avoid the accumulation of rainwater on the expressway. A hundred armed policemen lined both sides of the diversion to maintain order. The airport staff went to the south Yingbin Bridge to help passengers. One person was posted every 50 metres to guide people through the diversion. The airport also ran transit buses to ferry those passengers arriving at the airport on foot to the airport building. The airport also updated the public through the media as to the latest situation, guided latecomers to the respective reception desks of the airline companies for their flight transfers and kept reminding passengers to arrive earlier than usual and to detour the blocked section.

At the same time, the Capital Airport sent out urgent calls for more equipment to pump out the water. The two emergency control teams from Beijing Tap Water Group Company and Beijing Environment Protection and Sanitation Group Company were urgently sent to assist the airport and speed up the operation. At around 1:50 p.m., the airport expressway had reopened to traffic.

Because the accumulated rainwater flooded the airport expressway, more than 360 flights were delayed, sixty cancelled, forty-two landed in airports outside Beijing, and three flights had to return to the departure airport. According to the Capital Airport, about 70 per cent of flights were delayed due to the rainstorm.

Comparing this incident with the emergency treatment of the road surface subsidence around Jingguang Bridge in Dongsanhuan, the public offered very different views.

Net friend A: At 10 o'clock this morning, I drove my friends to the airport for London from Haidian. We set out three hours ahead of schedule and thought the time should be quite enough. But I was really disappointed. The distance from the Siyuan Bridge to the toll station of the airport expressway took us three and a half hours. At that time the airport real-time electronic bulletin board showed that the flight was delayed about one and half hours, and finally my friends decided to go to the airport on foot. Carrying their baggage, they walked 3 kilometres in the drizzle to the airport. Today there must be many passengers who experienced this kind of hardship. The ten-mile expressway from Dashangzi to the airport really became a big parking lot. It was 3:00 p.m. when I left the airport, but the traffic situation got no better. What a disappointing experience!

Net friend B: Today I was stuck on the airport expressway for five whole hours! I have never met this kind of situation since I drove years ago. It was raining a little, the so-called 'First Road in Beijing' was blocked that long! Where was the emergency planning? Beijing government should make a reassessment of the situation. Otherwise, how to realize its promises for the 2008 Olympic Games? I saw some foreigners walking from the airport building to the toll station where they were lucky to get a taxi. The cab was just turning around (today's situation was unique, and cars were permitted to turn around in front of the toll station to return to the city). I couldn't imagine what impression they would get. Altogether it wasted a lot of people's valuable time. If the Beijing government cannot learn a lesson from this and take effective measures to improve, that would be our greatest disappointment.

Net friend C: On 31 July, a rainstorm cut off the bidirectional airport expressway for the first time in the past ten years. The flight passengers had to walk all the way with their luggage to the airport. I watched a large crowd of passengers and their vehicles crawling along in the rain and could not help feeling depressed. The roads in Beijing are wide enough, and there are sufficient cloverleaf junctions, so why should a rainstorm cause such chaos? When will Beijing be able to cope with flooding? How could a cloudburst cause a modernized city such as Beijing such problems?

Newspaper New Beijing: The rainstorm tested the capital's ability to handle an emergency. Although the departments concerned issued an early warning of flooding, and some necessary prevention measures were taken, if we ask citizens to give the Beijing government marks out of ten for the way it handled the situation, it would not score highly. It is worth mentioning that the economic loss the city suffered during the rainstorm caused by the traffic jams on the airport expressway should be calculated. The loss must be striking. We do hope this accident will encourage the government departments concerned to learn from these past lessons and mistakes.

The Xinhua Network: The phenomenon of a 'traffic jam in a rainstorm' in Beijing tested the municipal emergency mechanism to its limits. On 31 July, our reporter saw on the big screen in the control centre of Beijing Traffic Administration Bureau that heavy rain on the airport expressway had led to long queues of traffic. The worst affected area was closed to traffic, causing a succession of traffic jams in other areas. Policemen sent to direct the traffic told the reporter that it would not be enough to rely on the traffic police to solve the problems, and that the solution would be to build a long-term effective mechanism.

That same evening, the Beijing government took urgent measures to improve the emergency planning. Considering the possibility of heavy rainfall in wider areas in recent days, the departments concerned were tasked with setting up more water pumps under bridges to strengthen the drainage capability. Meanwhile, they passed a regulation that all heavy repair construction would be performed during the night to avoid traffic being blocked again by the accumulated water.

Counter-thinking: How to deal with the relationship between the emergency scheme and emergency prevention in city management

Two emergency schemes were implemented for two emergency situations, but each yielded different results. What was the problem?

As early as 2003, the Beijing government had established a general scheme for public emergencies. According to this general scheme, every county, every district, every department and every unit has its own emergency scheme. Jin Lei, the associate secretary general of the Disaster Preventability Commission of China, told the reporter from *Liaowang Weekly* that the Beijing government had made great achievements and breakthroughs in the construction of an emergency planning system, and 'the emergency examples' of Beijing city were providing management experiences to the metropolitan cities in China.

However, with the advent of the rainstorm, although the government set in train the emergency scheme and took the necessary measures – laying on more policemen to direct the traffic, pumping water – the traffic jams on the airport expressway still occurred. What was the problem? The public began to doubt the reliability and safety of the rainwater drainage system of the city.

The severe flooding of the airport expressway occurred because the rainfall exceeded the rainwater drainage capability. Feng Lei, the associate general manager, said that the original drainage capability of the rainwater under Yingbin North Bridge was designed to cope with rainfall of 50 millimetres per hour. However, the actual rainfall on the morning of 31 July was over 80 millimetres per hour, which far exceeded the capability of the rainwater drainage, so that severe flooding occurred under the bridge. Since the previous flooding of 10 years ago, there had not been such a large amount of accumulated rainwater under the bridge. In 1996, there was also flooding under the bridge which blocked the airport expressway.

'The existing rainwater drainage of Beijing city is not a sufficiently integrated system', claimed Qi Jingjun, the section chief of the water drainage department of Beijing water authority. In recent years, Beijing city has been developing rapidly. To meet the development needs of the city, a series of related municipal projects and construction programmes should be put in place and improved in a synchronized way. However, many parts of the city have not carried out the programme in time. Many problems have occurred because the development plans and original programme of the city have not been realized. The key reason for the flooding and traffic jams on the roads around Huaxiang Bridge and Majialou Bridge is because there is no rainwater drainage near the bridges.

Wang Yi, the chief engineer of the Command Office of the Flood and Drought Prevention of Beijing, told reporters:

> The standards of the flood prevention and drainage system are set very low. They are much lower than the standards in advanced foreign large cities. In addition, along with the development of the city, the drainage construction work is increasingly dropping behind, which cannot catch up with the speed of road development; therefore the circumstance shows that drainage construction cannot meet the development of the roads and the city riverway treatment. The downtown area which has insufficient drainage accounts for more than 80 per cent of the total area. So the heavy rainfall must result in a lot of traffic jams.

He continued:

> Part of the reason why flooding occurred on the airport expressway is that the ongoing road repairs in that area destroyed the drainage pipelines. Therefore, the lower section of the road accumulated a lot of water.

It seems that the flooding problem on the airport expressway cannot be completely solved by relying only on the emergency scheme. In any case, the emergency scheme is passive. No matter how powerful the measures taken, the final result would just be to reduce the chaos. Prevention schemes are active. The government should take all the necessary measures as early as possible in advance to reconstruct and improve those infrastructures of the city that have proved to be deficient. In this way, we could reduce substantially the incidence of flooding. However, we were reliably informed that such an emergency could not be avoided completely, no matter how thorough the preparations. Therefore, in the management of the city, the government should 'take measures in advance, nip problems in the bud, look to the future, and eliminate the potential troubles and not only deal with the problem, but also prevent the emergency in the first place'. The government should take measures to both prevent and control the emergency.

Following the flooding of the bidirectional airport expressway, citizens are expecting the government to issue as early as possible a scientific, logical and integrated emergency prevention scheme.

Written in 2006

12 Analysis of the efficiency of government participation in restructuring high-risk listed companies

Wang Huimin

Because of the public nature of listed companies and their prevalent 'guarantee chains', their risks and ensuing crises have wide-ranging and far-reaching impacts on the regional economic and financial environment and on social and political stability. Correctly handling the crises of the problem listed companies and ensuring economic and social stability have become important responsibilities of regional governments.

Pijiuhua Co. Ltd (subsequently referred to as Pijiuhua) is a leading enterprise in Xinjiang's agricultural industrialization. Founded in 1993, it was listed on the Shanghai Stock Exchange in 1997. The company specializes in the production of hops, beer, barley and carrot juice, and enjoys resource, industrial and technological advantages. In particular, it produces and sells 6,000 tons of hops annually, or over 60 per cent of the national total. It is the largest raw materials supplier for beer breweries in China. In 2001, the company acquired the Xinjiang Beer (Group) Company and had a market share of over 50 per cent in Xinjiang. But on 30 October 2003, Ai Ke La Mu· Ai Sha You Fu, chairman of the company, left the company suddenly and without notice. As a result, many problems that had long been hidden began to surface. Investigations indicate that, by December 2003, Pijiuhua had 1.08 billion yuan in assets and 1.94 billion yuan in liabilities. In particular, its external guarantees totalled 1.44 billion yuan, of which 800 million yuan was not disclosed. The company was seriously insolvent. The creditors who were eager to claim their dues descended on the company, and immediately had Pijiuhua's accounts, stock rights, land, plant buildings, equipment and other assets frozen, sealed off and preserved. The company's employees became highly agitated and its production was paralysed.

Pijiuhua's mutual guarantee could trigger a regional financial crisis

Pijiuhua's insolvency and even bankruptcy would first of all cause a worsening of the huge amounts of bank loans and a rise in the non-performing loans of the financial institutions in the region. Xinjiang had four listed companies at the time (Tianshan Stock, Youhao Group, Xinjiang Joinworld and Huitong Group). Together, they offered a guarantee of 445 million yuan for Pijiuhua. In addition, another group of enterprises (including Tianshan Textiles and China Colored-Cotton) provided a guarantee of 1.56 billion yuan for the four listed companies. The four listed companies owed 4.28 billion yuan in bank loans. The joint and several guarantee liability would entail a repayment of bank loans totalling 6–7 billion yuan. This would trigger a collective debt crisis involving both the above four listed companies and their affiliated enterprises, a domino effect in risk spread, a blowout rise in the non-performing loans of the banking system and systematic risk and turmoil in Xinjiang's financial market. Therefore, restructuring Pijiuhua and cutting off the guarantee chain became an important issue for overall financial stability (see Figure 12.1).

1   Social and political stability would be affected. Once Pijiuhua went bankrupt and was liquidated, over 3,000 employees would be laid off, and the investments of numerous public stockholders would disappear.
2   The banks would lose their relatively high rates of loan repayments. A comparison of different disposal plans indicated that, if the company went bankrupt and was liquidated, the rate of loan repayments of the creditor banks would fall to about 10 per cent. As far as Pijiuhua was concerned, the company's resource, industrial and technological advantages and its market, brand and other intangible assets were sufficiently favourable for the credit banks to safeguard their claims and to achieve a relatively higher rate of loan repayments through restructuring than through bankruptcy liquidation.

Analysis of the necessity of government participation in restructuring

1   Market efficiency would be higher. If the market mechanism was to play its role effectively, it would require a relatively complete market system. However, currently, China's market system is unsound. In particular, the market mechanism still cannot fulfil its role independently and effectively in the course of corporate restructuring. Therefore, government intervention is required to make up the deficiency in the market mechanism.
2   Market blindness could be avoided. Game theory stipulates that selection by a person or an enterprise is subject to the influence of other people or enterprises and, conversely, influences the selection of other people or enterprises. The individual utility function depends not only on one's personal selection, but also on selection by other people. The optimum selection by a person is the function of the selection by other people. In essence, game theory can be divided into cooperative game and non-cooperative game theory. The difference between the two is whether the parties can reach a binding agreement when human behaviours interact. If they can reach such an agreement, it is a cooperative game. Conversely, it is a non-cooperative game. A cooperative game emphasizes group rationality, efficiency, equity and fairness, while a non-

cooperative game emphasizes individual rationality and individual optimum decision-making. The result can be either efficient or inefficient.

It is quite common for individual rationality to lead to group irrationality. In the fundamental sense, the best way to solve the conflict between individual rationality and group rationality is not to deny individual rationality. If a system arrangement cannot satisfy individual rationality, it will inevitably lead to market confusion and cannot be truly practised. But individual rationality must accommodate group rationality so as to form a basis for cooperative game theory. An example of this is when people are trapped in a house in the event of a fire. Everybody wants to escape as soon as possible, but they all rush for the door at once, thereby blocking their escape route. The eventual result is apparent. At this time, an authoritative person should assume charge and maintain order so that greater losses or casualties can be avoided. In the case of Pijiuhua's restructuring, because of the conflict of interest between the creditor banks, the restructuring parties and the target company, the behaviour of individual rationality is highly likely to lead to a result of group irrationality and cause the restructuring to fail. At this time, the regional government should become the 'authoritative person'. This is because the current unsound market economy still does not have a legal and systematic arrangement to ensure a cooperative and win–win game theory. When the creditors know the risks, they naturally adopt various measures to protect their respective rights and interests, and try to make their own loans a priority. The liquidity problem makes it difficult for an enterprise to survive. But bankruptcy liquidation can cause greater losses to the creditors and

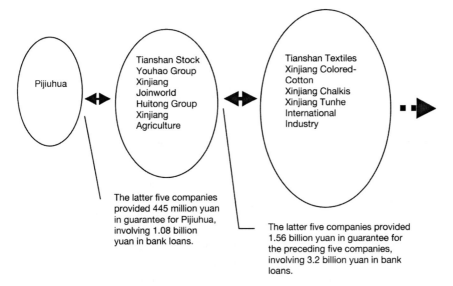

Figure 12.1 Spread of Pijiuhau's mutual guarantee risk.

entail higher social costs. To solve this problem, the government's administrative forces should step in to take charge of the situation.

In Pijiuhua's case, the regional government must take charge in the following areas

The regional government should mobilize social resources to ensure the normal operation of the enterprise. If the creditor's rights are to be fundamentally protected and the restructuring is to proceed in an orderly manner, an authoritative department must be on hand to control the situation and ensure the normal production and operation of the enterprise. This role belongs exclusively to the regional government, as only the regional government can mobilize various social resources to contain the looting of creditors, ensure the normal production and operation of the enterprise, ensure the maximization of the common interests of the creditors and create conditions for an orderly restructuring.

The regional government should communicate and cooperate with the relevant departments. The restructuring of a risk listed company is a complex system engineering endeavour, involving strict compliance with the relevant policies, many links and complicated procedures. The facts indicate that no other department or intermediary institution can replace the government in providing policy services and guidance, and in conducting effective communication and coordination with relevant state departments, commercial banks, creditors' committees and relevant enterprises.

Restructuring itself requires the support of the regional government. In the course of restructuring, the regional government should properly resettle the laid-off and retired employees and at the same time strengthen macroguidance in light of the requirements of industrial policies and corporate development strategies so as to prevent short-term corporate behaviours and effectively safeguard the credit environment and social stability.

Functional definition: effective methods of government participation in restructuring

The relationship between the government and the market

Government participation in restructuring a risk listed company inevitably involves the relationship between the government and the market. One practical issue is in what way the government should fulfil its role. If the government 'forces a marriage' (a common and unsuccessful practice in reforming state-owned enterprises in previous years), this practice will not have positive effects because it runs counter to the market rules and is inconsistent with the principles of Chinese laws and regulations, the regulatory authorities and the market-oriented economic reforms. Government participation in restructuring does not mean that the government should lead or replace the market. Instead, when the market malfunctions or is absent, the government should create conditions and stimulations for corporate restructuring by providing policy services, interest harmonization and information exchange. The Xinjiang government observed the following principles in the process of Pijiuhua's restructuring: market rules, administrative push, debt reduction and restructuring, risk control, industrial preservation and stability maintenance. Specifically, with the support of the Ministry of Finance, the People's Bank, the China Banking Regulatory Commission and other government departments, corporate restructuring should proceed according to the law and within the framework of the market rules. Stock rights transfer, debt relief and the settlement of other contingent debts involved in restructuring should be agreed upon by the relevant parties through negotiations and according to the market rules. The government's goal in negotiations between the stakeholders was to realize an effective balance, and the government's maximum interest was to preserve the industry, contain the risks from spreading and safeguard financial and social stability. On the other hand, the restructuring parties would have strategic opportunities for industrial integration, scale expansion and market occupation, and the creditor banks would boost their rates of debt repayment as much as possible.

The role of government when participating in restructuring

The government usually adopts the following measures when participating in corporate restructuring: (1) to promote cooperation between the restructuring parties and increase their risk-resisting capacities; (2) to establish a communication, coordination and administration mechanism for corporate merger and acquisition (M&A) and to offer administration and guidance over M&A and restructuring of the listed companies; (3) to set the plan and standards for the restructuring of the listed companies. For example, this would include the qualifications of the restructuring parties such as the industrial relevance, industrial status and competitive advantage of these parties, and the stock structure and minimum capital requirements of the new companies; (4) to provide the necessary assistance for debt restructuring, such as the debt relief offered by the creditor banks; (5) to adopt a series of measures to facilitate corporate restructuring, including legal assistance, tax relief and encouragement of outside capital's participation in corporate restructuring.

The government role in system rigidity and market restraint

Debt reduction was a key issue in Pijiuhua's restructuring

Debt reduction and the entry of the restructuring parties were a prerequisite to each other. The creditor banks, the enterprise and the restructuring parties should always maintain a cooperative relationship in their dealings.

The banks' difficulty in reducing debts lies in the fact that it has complex options when information exposure is not full. In fact, most banks have to face such options. They either agree to reduce debts, believing they can keep some loans through restructuring, or refuse to reduce debts because no one can guarantee that there will be no new risks after debt reduction. Perhaps some of the loans can be recovered by other means. In the actual process, all parties will do their best to safeguard their own interests. This not only depends on their value judgements but also on their interest comparisons. At this time, both the market and the banks require such a mechanism, under which information asymmetry will be reduced as much as possible and both parties to the game can cooperate. The regional government can precisely play this role: to persuade the creditor banks to face and accept the reality and, when necessary, to make the necessary sacrifices and choose to over-come difficulties along with the enterprise. This can minimize both sides' losses.

But the problem is always with the banks that emphasize fairness. 'As far as the creditor banks were concerned, Pijiuhua's crisis arose from its own excess speculations. There was no reason to ask the banks to bear the risks arising from the company's playing with fire'. Furthermore, the most difficult issue was how to define the roles of the regional government in structuring. Should the regional government act as an objective neutral force or as a game player representing regional interests? Or, more frankly, should the regional government make its selection out of consideration for regional protectionism? There had been no precedent for the banks to reduce debts through the market. This would require a breakthrough in China's existing legal system on credit management. The difficulty for the banks was that there was neither a legal basis for debt reduction nor experience to effect a practical solution. Many issues were involved in the decision-making responsibility. Article 37 of Chapter 7 of the *General Rules of Loans* provides that no creditor is allowed to waive loans without the approval of the State Council and that no unit or individual is allowed to force creditors to waive loans without the approval of the state. Article 46 of Chapter 9 provides that creditors have the right to participate in restructuring the debts of borrowers that are in the process of acquisition, bankruptcy or stockholding transfor-mation, and borrowers should be requested to arrange the repayment of both principal and interest. Therefore, in deciding whether the loans should be waived and what proportion should be waived, some banks are more concerned about who should assume the responsibility and how great the responsibility should be.

The issue becomes more complicated. Now we have to consider what the standard for debt reduction is. In other words, debt reduction should be oriented towards the restructuring need or towards the real risk value of the loans. Why should the debts be reduced to 30 per cent instead of 50 per cent or even higher? And can the debt reduction eventually pass the reg-ulatory and audit requirements? The fact that the banks have no mature operational guides for debt reduction can also cause doubt over the moral hazards in the course of debt reduction, including whether the motive of debt reduction is rational, whether the basis and procedures for decision-making are legal, and whether credit management has performed its duties. In a relative sense, the write-off of the non-performing loans operated by the creditor banks could be simplified. According to the existing state administrative regulations, the 'leave, death and escape of the loan borrowers constitute a condition for the banks to write off bad loans'. But Pijiuhua's problems were caused by market risks, and at least did not involve the responsibility of the credit management personnel. This makes the problem doubly difficult. If the loans were to be written off, the company had no alternative but to declare bankruptcy. And if corporate restructuring was chosen, the loan write-off procedure would not be feasible.

Even so, the creditor banks still reached agreement on Pijiuhua's plan for debt reduction and restructuring. On this issue, the government acted as a system innovator. Without government backing, the creditor banks would be reluctant to reduce debts and the existing rules would remain unchanged. In this sense, government participation in Pijiuhua's restructuring was an innovative move.

The rules and restraints of the creditors' committee

Establishing a creditors' committee for Pijiuhua represented a positive attempt to dispose of the non-performing assets of the banks according to the market rules. The committee was designed to serve as a mechanism for full consultation and communication, and to make it possible for the creditor banks to take joint and unified actions to maximize loan repayment. Pijiuhua's case indicated that, if the creditor banks could reach agreement on debt reduction and restructuring within the framework of the creditors' committee, 30 per cent or as much as 50 per cent of the loans could be repaid. And if the creditor banks emphasized their own interests and claimed loan repayment on their own, this would have a negative result. In other words, if the company were to declare bankruptcy and be liquidated, the eventual rate of loan repayment would be no more than 10 per cent. While some banks could have a slightly higher rate of loan repayment, others might get nothing at all. But a deal acceptable to all had to be done before the creditor banks could act in a truly concerted manner.

The practice of the creditors' committee for Pijiuhua indicated that it was absolutely essential for the rules to be explicit and acceptable to all the creditors. These included the nature of the committee, the rules of procedure, the rights and obligations of the creditors and the liabilities for breach of contract. Otherwise, the creditors would have no unified platform for exchange. Once the creditors' committee had established unified rules, all the member units had to unconditionally comply with the rules. Otherwise, the committee would be unable to form internal restraints and solve problems when they emerged. Accordingly, the committee would have no reason to exist. Article 5 of the agreement of the creditors' committee for Pijiuhua specified the rights and obligations of the creditor units. It provided that the member units of the creditors' committee had the right to request the revision or recompilation of the debt restructuring plan but were not allowed to violate the resolutions or the rules of procedure of the creditors' committee or to discuss the terms of reconciliation with the borrowers individually or collectively, or to take other debt recovery measures on their own (including but not limited to the exercise of the right to mortgage, hypothecation and lien over the properties or rights of the debtors, the attachment, garnishment and freezing of the properties of the debtors, and the initiation of litigation against ST Pijiuhua). Article 8 specified the liabilities for breach of contract: if the creditors committed breach of contract, they should correct it within the time limit set by the creditors' committee; if they failed to correct it within the time limit, they should assume the corresponding liability for damage compensation.

There were indeed some creditor banks that stretched out their hands to Pijiuhua, hoping to recover more of their money while waiting to share the fruits of the negotiations of the creditors' committee. This would cause fundamental damage to the interest basis for the creditor banks to take concerted action. But in practice, the rules were easily violated, thus making it truly difficult to ascertain the liability for damage compensation. This was because the approval of the whole debt reduction and restructuring plan must be signed by all the creditor banks. Once the liability for damage compensation was to be ascertained, the defaulting creditor banks would refuse to sign and the restructuring would have to stop there.

A typical case was a bank's unilateral disposal of the assets of the ZhongShiShennei (Langfang) Company, a Pijiuhua-held subsidiary company with assets totalling 30.5 million yuan. The subsidiary company had been included in the effective asset package for corporate restructuring and still owed 6 million yuan in loans to the Langfang Branch of the Industrial and Commercial Bank of China. But the Langfang Branch of X Bank requested the Langfang Intermediate People's Court to seek loan repayment through judicial action, and eventually a deal of 12 million yuan was struck. This move nearly called a halt to Pijiuhua's restructuring.

Another case was the creditors' refusal to join the creditors' committee. Pijiuhua provided guarantees to its affiliated companies for a 30-million-yuan loan from a bank in Fujian and for a 50-million-yuan loan from another commercial bank. These guarantees formed contingent debts. But the two banks refused to join the creditors' committee and were determined to claim debt repayment unilaterally through legal procedures. This would inevitably divide up Pijiuhua's effective assets and undermine the debt reconciliation agreement already reached by the creditors' committee.

Frankly, the rules of Pijiuhua's creditors' committee were sound but not very efficient. The government was needed to act as an interest mediator. In solving certain problems, the regional government could be more efficient than the enterprise in communicating repeatedly with the creditor banks. Practice proves that there must be such a mechanism, under which, if the creditors do not join, the rights and interests of the creditors' committee will not be guaranteed. Once they join the creditors' committee, they must comply with the rules of the committee. The agreements reached by the committee must be binding and, when necessary, such a binding force should receive administrative or judicial support from the power departments of the state. Any breach of contract must be corrected and assume the necessary consequences. Only by doing so can the relevant parties achieve cooperation.

'Popsicle effect'

On a hot summer's day, several people are hectically discussing how to divide a Popsicle: who has the first bite and how much he should eat. All of a sudden, they find that the Popsicle has melted. The so-called 'Popsicle effect' refers to the process whereby the non-performing assets reduce naturally. Practice indicates that the non-performing assets have a time value, and the disposal of the non-performing assets has a time limit. In general, the longer the time, the less valuable the non-performing assets will be.

In the course of negotiations over Pijiuhua's debt reduction, the regional government applied to the State Council in 2004 for a 50 per cent cut. This was based on the asset–liability indicator at the end of 2003. However, regrettably, the creditor banks failed to reach agreement by November 2004. According to the relevant regulations, the company's assets and liabilities should be reappraised and the rate of debt reduction reset. This was because, within that year, major changes had been made to the actual conditions of Pijiuhua's assets and liabilities. Regrettably again, the debts should now be cut by 70 per cent instead of the original 50 per cent.

Currently, the systems and regulations on asset management and in particular on the disposal of risk assets are unsound. For this reason, the policy-makers in some departments prefer to become the custodian of the non-performing assets instead of the value maximizer of the non-performing assets. They will try their best not to touch on the sensitive issues concerning the disposal of the non-performing assets. This 'ostrich policy' is based on the fact that, if the non-performing assets stay in the account books, they will not be expressed in real losses and, if they are disposed of, the responsibility issue will emerge. When solving problems of this nature, the only solution is to allow the regional government to intervene.

Information asymmetry and intermediary institutions

The key step in restructuring a company's debts is to effectively overcome the 'information asymmetry' between the stakeholders to the restructuring. In the leading developed countries in the West, mature intermediary institutions are used to solve the information asymmetry between the stakeholders to the corporate restructuring. In the course of Pijiuhua's debt negotiations, the restructuring parties attempted to scale down the effective assets and exaggerate the risk losses so that the debts could be reduced as much as possible. On the other hand, the creditor banks took the opposite view and used all sorts of excuses to explain why the assets were not at risk or why their risks were not as high as described by the restructuring parties. Their goal was to ensure that the range of debt reduction would not be too large. The creditors' committee, the risk company and the restructuring parties all had their own intermediary institutions to represent their interests and form their judgements over the company's risks. For example, the real conditions of all assets and the risk judgement over the receivables could involve some highly specific and elaborate issues. It would be extremely difficult to reach conclusions that were objective, fair and acceptable to all parties. This was, to a large extent, due to the tendencies of the intermediary institutions. The intermediary institutions that worked for their clients often made things worse instead of better.

As there are no intermediary institutions that have a high level of public trust and as the relevant laws and regulations are unsound, the government has to organize and coordinate the various parties involved. When necessary, the government must act as an information intermediary in order to reduce the information asymmetry between various parties to the restructuring and to ensure that the relevant parties can reach agreement and discuss the restructuring plan on the basis of commonly acceptable information.

In summary, the government can play diverse roles when participating in restructuring, and it has to do so under the dual constraints of the systems and the market. The government has the authority, public trust and executive power in economic society and can effectively organize social resources, correct market malfunction, effectively coordinate all stakeholders, promote understanding and cooperation, and optimize social goals.

Thoughts and suggestions

Government participation in the restructuring of high-risk listed companies must always comply with the market rules. Government participation in restructuring does not mean that the government should lead the restructuring and act as a patriarch to replace the market to participate in all decision-making, or that it should decide the restructuring matter by administrative means. Government participation in restructuring is designed to facilitate organization, guidance, communication, coordination, policy service provision and order maintenance so that the restructuring can proceed in an efficient and orderly manner. Nevertheless, this should be done under the precondition that the market should fully play its basic roles in resource allocation, the market rules are upheld and the enterprises make their decisions independently. Government participation in restructuring should proceed from the correct angles and should be performed to a proper degree and intensity. It cannot be underdone or overdone.

The government must set up a special institution for risk prevention and disposal. The restructuring of a listed company is a complex system engineering endeavour, and the restructuring of a risk listed company in particular involves timeliness and urgency. It has no mature model to draw on. Currently, the restructuring of risk listed companies in China is a major topic that requires constant theoretical and practical exploration and innovation. From contemplating the restructuring plan to choosing the working method and specific practical operations, the restructuring process involves many departments and requires repeated communication and coordination. This is particularly the case when the restructuring involves debt reduction and reconciliation among the creditors, the adjustment of interests among the restructuring parties, the maintenance and reconstruction of the regional economic, financial and credit environment, social stability, and the harmonious development of the regional economic, financial and ecological environment. Coordinating and solving these profound contradictions and problems requires an authoritative institution and a special team for the task. Such an institution must investigate the conditions of the listed company, control the relevant information, evaluate the risks, formulate a plan for risk disposal and make proposals as to risk prevention and solution. In addition, the institution must urge or order the relevant enterprises to prepare for potential problems and avoid risk accumulation and eruption. Once a risk breaks, the institution can provide relevant reference data for the competent departments and leaders to make decisions, put forward proposals on risk disposal and ensure that risk disposal can proceed in a standard and orderly manner.

It is imperative to correctly understand the impact of debt reduction and restructuring and establish a longstanding mechanism for risk listed companies: (1) it is necessary to reduce or avoid the risk eruption of the listed companies; (2) it is necessary to consciously safeguard the credit environment and the legitimate rights and interests of the creditor banks in the course of disposing of the risk listed companies. Maximum effort should be made to redeem bank losses and to build an honest and rule-by-law image for the government.

Regulatory resources should be integrated and an integrated regulatory system established for the listed companies. The risks of the listed companies have diverse causes. Unsound internal control mechanisms, an unsound corporate governance structure, insider control, senior managers' dishonesty, long, inefficient external supervision and many other factors led to Pijiuhua's difficulties. However, improving the internal control mechanism, improving the corporate governance structure, overcoming insider control and building market trust will be a long and historic task for the securities market in China which cannot be fundamentally solved overnight. With regard to external supervision, Pijiuhua's risks would be unlikely to have arisen if all the commercial banks could truthfully record and reflect Pijiuhua's loans and external guarantees, if the banking regulatory authorities could collect and gather together the overall loans and external guarantees, and if the banks, the banking regulatory authorities and the securities regulatory authorities could emphasize information sharing and cooperation, and realize 'information sharing, coordination and cooperation'. Therefore, in order to truly improve supervision over the listed companies and avoid the one-sidedness of the regulatory work, the relevant government departments, the regulatory institutions, the intermediary institutions and the banks must strengthen their contacts and communications, realize effective information sharing, establish an integrated supervisory system and comprehensively build up a joint regulatory force so as to exercise effective supervision over the listed companies. In addition, the government, the stock exchanges, the industrial and commercial administration departments, the customs, the banks and the social intermediary institutions should cooperate with each other and play their supervisory roles.

Written in 2006

13 Settlement of the taxi drivers' strike

Fang Li

In modern society, taxis are an indispensable means of public transportation in urban areas, and taxi drivers have become a special population group whose work has connections with people in all strata of society. Can you imagine what a city of one million people would look like if all its taxis stopped running? In fact, this did happen in the city of Jilin. This case may serve as useful experience for other municipal governments that have to deal with unexpected incidents of this nature in their cities.

The early morning of 15 September 2004 ushered in another new day and everything was running normally in Jilin, a northern Chinese city with unique appeal. As an important means of urban transportation, taxis carried people in all directions to every corner of the city. For pedestrians and those doing their morning exercises, it seemed no different from any other day. However, those seeking to take taxis instinctively discerned that there were fewer cabs on the streets than usual. Quite unexpectedly, all the taxi drivers refused to take fares from about 8:00 a.m., and dispersed in all directions or congregated in various meeting places. News immediately reached the executive deputy mayor F of the municipal government that all taxi drivers were on a strike.

Taxis famed as 'city's mobile business cards'

The city of Jilin has forty-three taxi companies and 5,800 taxis, which transport about 60 million passengers a year. In general, a taxi is driven by two people, one during the day and one at night. So the city has over 10,000 taxi drivers. As they are generally excellent, the office in charge of the city's taxi management had won a mention from the Ministry of Construction. More than 10 years previously, some taxi drivers had put a 'Leifeng Taxi' sign on their cars. Those taxis exhibiting this sign were noted for their positive attitude and service and for offering free rides to the disabled and those over the age of 65. Inspired by these pioneers, over fifty taxis voluntarily formed a 'Leifeng Taxi Fleet', and they further inspired other people. When a bus carrying passengers ran into the Songhua river, it was the taxi drivers who voluntarily and collectively conducted a rescue operation. In the fire disaster at the Zhongbai Plaza that shocked the whole country, dozens of taxi drivers, with no thought for their own safety, braved thick smoke to rescue people and then ferried them to nearby hospitals. During the annual season of university entrance examinations, all the taxi drivers did two things in unison: no horns for three days and free rides for examinees and their parents. This was the rule for every taxi driver in every year. As to other good deeds, such as not stealing items left in taxis by passengers and sending home those who lost their way at night, these were already taken for granted. The drivers continuously won honours for the city and were praised as the 'city's mobile business cards'. Accordingly, they also continuously won honours for themselves. Some became provincial or municipal model workers; some became deputies to the provincial and municipal people's congresses; some were encouraged by the municipal government to visit and holiday in other parts of the country; some were invited by the government to cut ribbons for the city's major newly completed roads and bridges. Yet, all of a sudden, over 5,000 'mobile business cards' stopped running.

Difficulties in confronting taxi drivers

- The real income of the taxi owners had dropped as a result of the constant rise in oil prices. From August 2003 to September 2004, fuel prices were increased four times, up 17 per cent from 2.88 yuan per litre to 3.37 yuan per litre. If one car consumed 30 litres a day on average, the fuel cost after 2004 was 101.1 yuan a day, which was 14.7 yuan higher daily, 441 yuan higher monthly and 5,292 yuan higher annually.
- Illegal motorcycles and tricycles lured passengers away with the promise of low fares. Operating without paying an administrative fee, these motorcycles and tricycles constituted opposition for the taxi market and put the taxi drivers in an unfair position.
- Diverse administrative fees consumed a considerable chunk of the taxi drivers' income. As a result, strikes by taxi drivers occurred from time to time in some Chinese cities.

Handling a letter of complaint

In late August, a taxi driver sent a letter of complaint to the municipal government, in which he put forward four demands with regard to fee payment. (1) The toll gates around the city should either be demolished or offer exemption to taxis. (2) The fee for industrial and commercial administration should be reduced. (3) The road toll should be reduced. (4) The membership fee of the self-employed taxi drivers' association should be reduced.

Immediately after receiving this letter, the deputy mayor instructed the Municipal Utility Bureau to investigate and put forward specific comments on these issues. In the meantime, the municipal government arranged for relevant personnel to act as taxi fares to acquire information from taxi drivers. Deputy mayor F and the deputy mayor in charge of municipal administration also did the same personally, and the information they gathered was largely identical to that reflected in the letter of complaint.

On 5 September, the Municipal Utility Bureau presented a report to the municipal government on the basis of its investigations and a comparison with other cities in the province. The report mainly reflected the requests of the taxi drivers to lower fee rates and to remove the toll gates around the city or to offer free passage for taxi drivers out of the urban areas. The report also conducted the following analysis. The city's road toll was the highest in the province, being 350 yuan per Jetta car per month and 330 yuan per Auto car per month. The city's industrial and commercial administration fee was slightly higher than in other parts of the province and was 10 yuan higher than in the provincial capital. The membership fee of the self-employed taxi drivers' association was flexible, but the city's rate was the highest. However, only the provincial authorities had the power to set the three fee rates and collect them.

On 12 September, deputy mayor F presided over a special meeting to discuss the four requests from taxi drivers and the related issues and made the following decisions. (1) With regard to the industrial and commercial administrative fee, the road toll and the membership fee of the self-employed taxi drivers' association, the relevant functional departments should immediately report to the higher authorities for inspection and support, and should act upon the reply from the higher authorities. (2) A crackdown on illegal motorcycles and tricycles should be launched, and the relevant departments should prepare a plan and submit it to the executive meeting of the municipal government for consideration. (3) The toll gates around the city should not be demolished because the three toll gates the taxi drivers requested to be demolished had borrowed a 400-million-yuan mortgage loan from the Bank of China, which would expire at the end of September 2012.

However, by 31 December 2003, the toll gates in the urban areas had collected a total of 182 million yuan, of which 120 million yuan was paid for loan interest and 62 million yuan was paid for loan principal. As an outstanding loan of 338 million yuan still had to be paid, the toll gates could not be removed. Free passage for taxi cabs was also difficult to implement. If buses and trucks entering and exiting the city sought the same treatment, it would threaten the social stability of the city. However, as the taxis were going in and out of the city frequently, it was proposed that the toll rate be reduced for them. The margin of toll rate reduction had to be worked out by the relevant department and reported to the executive meeting of the municipal government for consideration.

On 13 September, deputy mayor F chaired an executive meeting of the municipal government on behalf of the mayor to discuss the crackdown on illegal operations and fee reduction. The following decisions were made at the meeting.

- A city-wide crackdown would be launched on illegal operations. The vehicles reserved exclusively for disabled people would not be allowed to be used by non-disabled people. In addition, only one type of vehicle would be allowed for a disabled person as a means of transportation, and such a vehicle must carry a visible uniform sign. The cars, minibuses, motorcycles and motor tricycles engaged in illegal operations, the vehicles with fake business permits and the taxis operating locally from other areas would all be banned and severely penalized. To ensure that this crackdown would produce the expected results, a leading group for crackdown and rectification was established, and the principle of 'rectifying according to law and banning with care' was set. The steering group contained not only personnel from the bureaus of public security, publicity and municipal utility, but also representatives from the departments of labour and civil affairs, and the Federation of the Handicapped. The labour department had to register the owners of all the banned vehicles so as to recommend alternative jobs to them. The civil affairs department should handle the formalities for minimum living allowance for the qualified drivers whose vehicles were banned. And the Federation of the Handicapped would mainly do mentality work among disabled people.

- The urban toll rate would be reduced. In order to ease the burden on taxi drivers, the monthly toll rate of the three toll gates in the urban areas would be reduced from 160 yuan per month to 80 yuan per month. Those who did not buy the monthly ticket would pay 5 yuan each time (compared with 8 yuan each time for other vehicles).

On the afternoon of 13 September, the municipal government held a conference of the representatives of taxi drivers, at which deputy secretary general M briefed them on the decisions made at the special meeting and the executive meeting of the municipal government. The decisions were welcomed by the representatives of the taxi drivers. Meanwhile, the official also explained why the toll gates could not be demolished and why taxi drivers could not be offered free passage. This explanation also won the understanding of the representatives of the taxi drivers. Thus, the issues raised in the letter of complaint from the taxi drivers were satisfactorily solved.

An unexpected turn of events

On 14 September, the deputy mayor received an anonymous telephone call claiming that a few people were distributing leaflets to incite the taxi drivers to strike on 15 September. Investigations revealed that some people had distributed leaflets to the taxi drivers, in which they expressed dissatisfaction over the municipal government's refusal to abolish the toll gates around the city and to offer free passage to the taxi drivers, and they urged the taxi drivers to strike on 15 September in protest. In light of this situation, the municipal government adopted appropriate measures, and the radio and television stations broadcast the *Open Letter to the City's Taxi Drivers* issued by the city's association of the taxi industry and the *Proposal* issued by six prominent taxi drivers. The 'city 110' radio programme opened a direct dialogue between the host and the taxi drivers to offer them positive guidance. As a result of these efforts, most taxi drivers became emotionally calm and indicated that they would not participate in the strike.

At about 6:00 a.m. on the morning of 15 September, deputy mayor F and three other municipal leaders went to different parts of the city to monitor the situation and then returned to the municipal office to organize taxi management. The situation prior to 7:30 a.m. was normal, although the number of taxis on the streets was slightly lower than usual. However, the situation had changed dramatically by 8:00 a.m. Some taxi drivers became angry with those who were working normally and organized pickets to prevent the taxis from running on more than ten streets in the city. They even registered the licence numbers of those taxis that were running in order to settle accounts with them later. During this period, three taxis were destroyed and seven people were beaten, forcing many taxi drivers to park up their cars. Then, taking advantage of most taxi drivers' hopes of reducing or abolishing the relevant fees, these same people urged the taxi drivers to continue to press for removal of the toll gates around the city or offering free passage to taxis. As more and more taxi drivers were taken in by this, there were fewer and fewer taxis on the roads. By dusk, the city of two million people had only about 100 taxis running.

Dealing with the crisis

To prevent unexpected events from occurring on 15 September, the deputy mayor had already organized the relevant departments on 14 September to work out the Plan for Preventing and Dealing with the Strike by Taxi Drivers. In addition, police were deployed to maintain public order on 15 September. In all, the city ran an extra forty-seven buses and twenty mobile minibuses and shortened the running intervals from the normal 5–8 minutes to 3–6 minutes. The time of the last bus run along twelve main routes was extended from 8:00 p.m. to 10:00 p.m., and the running intervals were shortened from 15 minutes to 8 minutes. In addition, repairs, security, money box collection and money counting were also extended to ensure that public transportation would not be affected. The transit corporation arranged mobile vehicles at the railway station, hotels, hospitals and at schools where students were attending evening classes to meet the demand of people using public transport. The public security department not only focused efforts on patrolling vital communication lines, squares and bridges, but also conducted intensive patrols all over the city. The goal was to ensure there would be no mass taxi meetings and no taxi blocks to roads, bridges and gates; to ensure there would be no serious beatings, break-ins, looting or burning; to ensure the taxis would not go to the provincial and national capitals and stir up disturbances there; and to ensure there would be no improper law enforcement that could be used to incite new instability. The police force was deployed to guard against some dangerous vehicles and insecure areas, and they were detailed to reach the scene within 5 minutes whenever any beatings, break-ins or road blocks occurred.

Between 1:30 p.m. and 2:00 p.m. on 15 September, the municipal government received replies from the relevant provincial departments on reducing the industrial and commercial administration fee, the road toll and the membership fee of the self-employed taxi drivers' association in the city of Jilin. The industrial and commercial administration fee was reduced from 90 yuan per car per month to 80 yuan per car per month, the membership fee of the self-employed taxi drivers' association was reduced from 5 yuan per person per month to 3 yuan per person per month, and the road toll was reduced from 350 yuan per car per month to 280 yuan per car per month for Jetta taxis and from 330 yuan per car per month to 264 yuan per car per month for Auto taxis. After the replies were made public, some taxi drivers expressed their thanks to the government, while others argued that this represented a 'victory of the strike' and believed a 'greater victory' would be possible if the strike continued. Deputy mayor F chaired an emergency meeting at 4:00 p.m. and re-emphasized at the meeting that the toll gates would not be removed and no free passage would be offered to any vehicles. At the same time, arrangements were made for resuming normal transportation. (1) A municipal working group was set up, with Bai Jingjun as its leader. Bai was the deputy head of the bureau of urban management and integrated enforcement, and the former director of the office for taxi management. Bureau-level leaders were selected from the municipal federation of trade unions, the municipal Party committee and the municipal government's supervisory board to form a working group that would be assigned to the office for taxi management and oversee the office's work in an all-round way. (2) Eighty officials would be selected from the Municipal Utility Bureau and the office for taxi management to form eighteen groups that would be assigned to eighteen main taxi companies (together they accounted for 80 per cent of the city's taxis). (3) A meeting of backbone personnel from the taxi industry would be held, which would be attended by 110 taxi drivers who were either model workers or Party members. They were requested to play leading roles in publicity, guidance and street running.

After a whole day of negotiations, the taxis on the streets on 16 September increased to over 500 from a little over 100 the previous day. In the early morning, more than 500 policemen were deployed at all main intersections and along all main streets. They hailed taxis and entered them to escort the drivers. This was a special measure taken by the municipal government to ensure the safety of the taxis and their drivers. On the afternoon of 16 September, deputy mayor F accompanied the officials from the relevant departments to inspect the operation of the taxis along the main routes and in the main areas. At 4:30 p.m., he again convened a special meeting, at which five decisions were made. (1) The public security department would arrange the household register policemen of all police stations to visit the families of the taxi drivers and explain policies and publicize laws and regulations. (2) The managers of forty-three taxi companies would be called to attend a meeting, at which they would be requested to further improve the relevant work. (3) The staff of the office for taxi management would be called to attend a meeting, at which they would be requested to record the taxi dispatches by various taxi companies, identify the destabilizing factors and report them to the authorities in a timely fashion. (4) The working group would convene a meeting of taxi drivers. As the group leader had worked as the director of the office for taxi management, he enjoyed high prestige among taxi drivers. A total of 1,197 taxi drivers attended the meeting, at which relevant policies were further explained and the participants were urged to resume operations as early as possible so as to serve the overall interests and reduce personal economic losses. (5) The public security department would intensify investigations into those who incited and organized the strike. Those who violated the laws would be resolutely dealt with, and in particular those who were engaged in distributing illegal leaflets and in smashing up vehicles would be punished according to law. In the meantime, the municipal government announced that the taxis in the urban areas would be downscaled from 5,800 to 4,600, and those who failed to run their taxis for three consecutive days without permission would be among the first group whose business licences would be revoked.

On the evening of 16 September, deputy mayor F stayed in his office, which was located on the banks of the beautiful Songhua river. Seeing the light from his office, some inhabitants who were walking along the river telephoned him, saying:

> Don't be afraid of them. We the laid-off people do not stir up any disturbance. They [taxi drivers] who earn so much a month are making trouble. ... It doesn't matter if they do not work. We can ride bicycles, which is good for health and for sightseeing. ... Let them strike. When they begin to work, we will not take a taxi.

Throughout the day, the mayor's hotline also received repeated similar calls.

Ending of the incident

On the morning of September 17, as many as 1,300 taxis were on the streets and the figure rose to over 2,600 in the afternoon. Normal operations resumed on the morning of 18 September. The inhabitants were calm and public transport returned to normal. The reporters from Xinhua News Agency who rushed to cover the incident praised the effective government measures and the excellent results after witnessing the perfect order reigning in the city streets. A deputy provincial governor who arrived in the city at the head of the officials from the relevant provincial departments gave full affirmation over the handling of the incident. He believed the city's work had been active and its measures had been effective. Every link, every step and every incident had been handled in a proper and planned way.

On the morning of 18 September, deputy mayor F and relevant officials rode in four taxis consecutively as ordinary passengers. Sitting in the rear seat with his secretary in the front seat, the deputy mayor chatted with the drivers. The first driver said to him, 'I did not participate in those things and I have been operating every day. As there were fewer taxis, I had more passengers. I earned quite a lot in the past two days'. The second driver said, 'I suffered a lot this time. I did not work for two days, and the fee reductions offered by the government were not enough to cover the losses'. The third driver said, 'These people [taxi drivers] had no strong will. If they could hold out for a few more days, the government would have given more concessions'. The fourth driver realized that the person he was talking with was the deputy mayor. He talked a lot in favour of the government. But was it really a reflection of what he had in his mind?

Following this incident, deputy mayor F wrote the following remarks in his diary:

> as a public administrator, the government should constantly adjust or introduce relevant policies according to the changes in the environment. But there are three points that should be remembered. (1) The policies must be timely. Policies should be adjusted at the right moment. Early or late adjustment can produce unfavourable results. We should not do what is inopportune and unrewarding or shirk historical responsibilities and fail to do what must be done. (2) The policies must be rational. Any new policy when introduced must benefit as many people as possible and harm as few people as possible. Never do anything that benefits some people and harms other people. (3) The policies must be authoritative. When a correct decision is made, it should not be changed. A new policy is introduced out of necessity instead of disturbance. Legitimate demands must have legal means to back them up.

Written in 2006

14 Pension insurance demands of the former town and township temporary personnel

Zhong Mian

The demand of around 10,000 former town and township temporary personnel to be included in the pension insurance programme was both legally justified under the Labour Law and in conflict with the existing specific regulations on social insurance. These people had been laid off by the town and township government over the years. While the municipal and county governments had no financial resources for this purpose, meeting their demands could trigger a chain reaction from other related groups. But the demand had become stronger and stronger and the contradiction had become increasingly acute. As a result, increasingly disharmonious and destabilizing factors were brewing at the rural grassroots level. How to solve this issue, how to exercise administration according to law and how to fulfil the political responsibility of ruling the country for the people and building a socialist harmonious society had become a practical issue for the Ziyang municipal Party committee and government.

History and reality

Ziyang is a city located in the central hilly region of Sichuan Province. About 85 kilometres from Chengdu on the Chengyu expressway, the city has four counties and 171 towns and townships under its jurisdiction. It has an area of 8,000 square kilometres and 5 million people.

Like other cities in the province, the town and township governments and public institutions in Ziyang had employed large numbers of temporary personnel since the 1990s. Subsequently, many of them were laid off when institutional reform was carried out, but more temporary personnel were hired after the institutional reform. Again, when a new institutional reform took place, many of them were laid off.

The laid-off personnel totalled more than 10,000 people. They were mostly laid off by the so-called 'seven centres and eight stations', namely the sectors of farm machinery, livestock industry, broadcasting, family planning, health and public security. The majority were aged about 50.

In the second half of 2005, the former town and township temporary personnel began lodging complaints to the county and municipal governments and demanding inclusion in social pension insurance schemes. Since then, more people have joined in, and the scale of the complaints has expanded month after month. In addition, the complainants have become increasingly irritated and their demands have become greater and greater. They have even tended to bypass the immediate leadership and presented their complaints to higher levels and in groups. The complaints reached a climax during the period from New Year's Day to the Spring Festival in 2006. Some complainants even went to the provincial and national capitals to complain. In the meantime, they began pressing for compensation and other benefits.

The complainants cited the Labour Law that entered into force in 1995 as the main legal basis to back up their demands. Article 72 of the Law stipulated that the government organs and public institutions should establish a social insurance programme as from 1996 for those people in employment after 1995. It also explicitly stipulated that the government organs and public institutions should implement this law for those employees who had established labour relations with them. The document issued in 1996 by the Sichuan provincial people's government on implementing the Labour Law also contained relevant explicit and specific requirements.

However, since the Labour Law has come into force, Ziyang has so far only established a pension insurance programme for regular personnel. These employees had been included in the authorized staff by the government organs and public institutions while the temporary personnel were excluded. Accordingly, they did not establish a pension insurance programme for the town and township temporary personnel who had signed labour contracts with them. In addition, other cities in the province had similar problems.

These complaints attracted the attention of the municipal and county authorities. The complainants constituted a large social group, which had a fairly strong influence on society and especially at the grassroots level. In the face of their legitimate demand, their practical difficulties and the growing social contradictions, the Ziyang municipal Party committee and government realized that reform was both necessary and pressing.

Expectations and difficulties

After the 2006 Spring Festival, the Party committee and government began a systematic study on how to solve the issue.

Analyse the nature of the contradictions and problems

Being people-oriented and caring about the vulnerable groups constitutes a political requirement for the concept of ruling for the people. After being laid off and returning to the countryside, most of the town and township temporary personnel had difficulties supporting their families because they had no other skills. As they were getting older, their difficulties became more serious. In the past, they had made significant contributions to rural development and stability. Therefore, in implementing the important thought of the 'Three Represents' and the requirement of ruling for the people, the municipal Party committee and government were obliged to include their difficulties and reasonable demands in their agenda as an important item and to solve them as far as possible, as these people represented nearly 10,000 rural families.

Establishing a social security system to cover more social strata should become a priority system design in the course of deepening reforms. To solve this historical issue, it was undesirable to use the methods under a planned economy or take measures of a contingent nature. Instead, the methods must conform to the orientation of the reforms, help promote long-term stability and be institutionalized. Apparently, the demand of the former town and township temporary personnel to be included in the social insurance programme was consistent with the goals of the system designs and reforms that were designed to gradually establish a social security system that would cover the whole of society.

Solving the people's legitimate demand in an active and timely manner was an inherent demand for exercising administration and ruling the city according to the law. If the legitimate demands of the general public and especially a large social group could not draw public attention and were not effectively solved through normal channels and in a peaceful way, they tended to trigger group incidents and undermine social stability. Therefore, properly solving the demand of the former town and township temporary personnel according to law was also a political responsibility for the municipal Party committee and government in easing social contradictions and building a harmonious society. Based on the above public value judgement, the municipal Party committee and government believed that the demands of these people and the growing social contradictions and destabilizing factors should not be rejected under the pretext that they were historical issues, that financial resources were insufficient and that there was no province-wide solution to this common issue. Instead, they must face the demands squarely and solve them in a timely and proper manner.

Did the municipal authorities have the ability and power to solve this issue properly?

Evaluate the ability to solve the contradictions and problems

In general, the municipal authorities apparently had insufficient ability to solve this 'sensitive' issue through reforms and innovations until the provincial authorities had worked out unified policies. This was because this issue was highly political, wide-ranging and required certain financial resources. Ziyang and other cities in the province had long wished to solve this growing contradiction but had failed to take the first step in this direction.

Officials' understanding and ability. There were neither clearly defined policies and successful models or experience, nor suitable existing methods and policies for solving this complex and sensitive historical issue. Therefore, it was necessary to learn, explore and confront challenges. A new value preference should be adopted for reforms and innovations, for formulating flexible transitional policies, for seeking proper methods and for promoting common understanding so that a joint force could be formed for solving this problem.

Financial resources. The financial resources of the municipal and county governments were insufficient. By 2003, the towns and townships throughout the city had laid off about 11,000 people, of whom 3,000 were laid off before the end of 1994 and 8,000 were laid off from January 1995 into the first half of 2003 when the final institutional reform was carried out. In the event of these 8,000 people being included in the pension insurance programme, the government would have to contribute 50 million yuan if these people were treated as self-employed, or nearly 100 million yuan if they were treated as enterprise workers. Ziyang was a newly established municipal division, noted for a high proportion of agriculture and rural areas. It was a typical city living on 'subsistence finance'. The fiscal transfer payments from the higher authorities accounted for 70 per cent of the city's total fiscal spending. The standby financial resources of both municipal and county governments totalled less than 100 million yuan a year. Therefore, they were apparently in no position to spend 50–100 million yuan in a lump sum to buy pension insurance for a vulnerable group. Besides, if policy designs were unscientific and irrational, they could trigger chain reactions from other groups such as the former 'educated youth' and the former workers of the collective enterprises. This would not only further overburden financial resources but could also cause other social contradictions and induce new problems.

Reform and policy innovation. Solving this problem would undoubtedly entail a breakthrough from the existing policies on social security. In other words, to solve this historical problem, the authorities had to seek solutions in accordance with the principle of 'respecting history, facing reality, being legal and reasonable, and easing contradictions', and in reference to the existing relevant policies. However, strictly speaking, the municipal government had no power to formulate and introduce a new policy on pension insurance. For this reason, the 'soft ability' to solve this problem through reforms was also insufficient.

Therefore, it would be tantamount to a beautiful dream for the municipal authorities to take the initiative to solve this problem. To make the dream come true, they must try to seek support from the relevant sectors and pursue their common goal.

Analyse and contact the relevant sectors and involve them in solving the contradictions and problems

Initial feedback from analysis and contacts at this stage of the practical operation indicated that a solution to this issue had to deal with real and specific contradictions and difficulties. The situation allowed for no optimism.

The existing departmental regulations and policies were unable to give their full support. Despite the relevant provisions of the Labour Law, these former temporary personnel had failed to be included in pension insurance at the time as required by the Law. Under the existing departmental regulations and policies on social security, only the urban population could participate. The rural population could only participate in rural pension insurance. Most of the former temporary personnel went to live in rural areas after being laid off. If they were to be allowed to be included in the social security programme, this would represent a breakthrough from the existing policies.

The relevant provincial departments expressed limited support. After reading the reports, the relevant provincial departments believed that this was really a common issue for the whole province that had to be faced and resolved. They appreciated Ziyang's positive attitude and courage, and they agreed that Ziyang would establish the base figure and consider the solutions. But they refused to give clear-cut opinions exclusively for Ziyang and cautioned Ziyang against hasty actions because the issue had implications for the whole province. This meant that Ziyang had to take the first step but could not expect corresponding financial support. If anything went wrong, the whole province would be affected, and Ziyang had to assume the relevant policy risk and leadership responsibility.

The former town and township temporary personnel had high expectations. These people even demanded that they be included in the pension insurance programme as the current personnel of the government organs and public institutions or at least as employees of the urban enterprises. This would involve a greater policy breakthrough and a heavier financial burden. Social implications and chain reactions would be more wide-ranging, and the contradictions and problems more difficult to solve. Some of them even demanded that the government also pay their personal contributions to the insurance premiums because they were in economic difficulties after being laid off. The 3,000 people who had been laid off before January 1995 also demanded the same treatment.

The relevant municipal departments were both supportive and worrisome. All the departments indicated they would comply with the decisions made by the municipal Party committee and government, and would carry out the relevant work. But the financial department feared the fiscal burden would increase, the social security department feared the pressure on the financial pool would rise, the complaints and stability maintenance departments feared that failing to fully meet their demands would not solve the issue and fully meeting their demands could trigger other chain reactions.

The county governments were in a dilemma. These governments wanted to see the issue solved as early as possible, as the growing complaints had brought great pressure to bear on stability maintenance and grassroots work. But they also feared that the proposal to be introduced by the municipal authorities would shift all fiscal burdens on to the county governments, which were in no position to bear such burdens.

Proposal comparison and selection

In light of practical conditions, the municipal Party committee and government set up a working group, which would work under the direct leadership of the leading members of the municipal Party committee and government, and would ensure that the relevant leaders were responsible for concrete implementation. The group began investigating the overall situation, studying the regulations and policies, measuring and calculating financial resources, communicating with the relevant parties, selecting the proposals and formulating the working and implementation methods so as to lay the groundwork for the municipal Party committee and government to make decisions. After 3 months of hard work, including hearing the views of the temporary personnel and communicating with them, the group presented a full report to the municipal Party committee and government after the May Day holiday. The report contained the following.

There were three proposals for policy selection.

1   The government would introduce a new policy and the individuals would pay full premiums for pension insurance. In other words, the laid-off town and township temporary personnel would have to pay the annual social insurance premiums in arrears in the capacity of individual labourers from the date when they were employed after 1996, and would continue to pay insurance premiums until the age of retirement (or having paid insurance premiums for 15 full years) before they could receive the basic pension on a monthly basis (the government would contribute no funds but offer a preferential policy for them to pay the premiums later).

2   The government would offer a preferential policy and pay part of the premiums, with the bulk of the insurance premiums being paid by the laid-off town and township temporary personnel. The individuals would pay 8 per cent and the units would pay 12 per cent for the period from their employment to their lay-off, and the individuals would pay the full 20 per cent for the period after their lay-off. According to this proposal, the government would have to spend 50 million yuan, of which the municipal government would pay 10 million yuan and all the counties

would pay 10 million yuan each. Both municipal and county finances would transfer the funds into their social insurance accounts over a 5-year period.

3   These personnel would participate in pension insurance as if they were enterprise employees. The hiring units would pay 20 per cent and the individuals would pay 8 per cent. As the wage base would be higher, the government would have to pay about 100 million yuan.

The above three proposals all represented a breakthrough from the specific provisions of the existing policies on social insurance. In other words, these people would be insured as individual labourers. But if the issue was looked at from a historical angle, these proposals were consistent with the Labour Law and other laws and regulations. They only represented an improvement over the legal provisions that had not been implemented in the past. The three proposals had their respective merits and weaknesses. Under proposal 1, the government would have no financial pressures, the educated youth and other related social groups were psychologically balanced, but the demands of the former town and township temporary personnel could barely be met. Under proposal 2, the demand of the complainants could be met reasonably, instead of fully. But this proposal could induce chain reactions from related sectors and the government would also have certain financial pressures. Under proposal 3, the demands of the complainants could be fully met, but the government would have enormous financial pressures and the proposal could trigger even more chain reactions.

There were also three proposals for implementing method selection.

1   The municipal Party committee and government would set the proposal aside for a specified period after making a decision, and would implement the proposal once it was approved by the provincial authorities or if the situation spiralled out of control. There was no need to be the first in the province to take the risk.

2   After making a decision, the municipal Party committee and government would hold a conference, issue a document, set a time limit and exercise unified leadership to solve the issue as quickly as possible.

3   After making a decision, the municipal Party committee and government would neither issue a document nor consult the higher authorities. Instead, they would quietly convene a conference to arrange the implementation. One county would be selected for experiment, and other counties would follow suit if the experiment was successful.

After careful consideration, the municipal Party committee and government chose Proposal 2 (pending further improvement) and optimized Proposal 3 for implementing method selection. (1) No document would be issued and no public announcement would be made. (2) A report would be submitted to the relevant provincial departments without requesting their response and instructions. (3) A meeting would be convened to unify the policy, approach and method, and the proposal would be implemented simultaneously in all four counties once the relevant personnel had been trained. (4) No time limit would be imposed, no unified organization would be required, and no mandatory requirement would be set. The temporary personnel would handle the insurance formalities voluntarily, respectively and at any time.

Proposal implementation and preliminary results

The municipal Party committee and government completed the above decision-making process, worked out a package proposal in mid-June and decided to implement the proposal in late July. Prior to that date, appropriate methods would be adopted: (1) to brief the temporary personnel on this proposal, and organize them to discuss and release their expectations; (2) to monitor the reactions of other related social groups and begin considering their problems; (3) to consult the relevant provincial departments over this proposal and dovetail it with the relevant policies and work so as to further improve this proposal. Thanks to the efforts lasting for nearly a month, progress was made.

- As a result of further reports and communications, the municipal authorities received guidance and support from the provincial leadership and the relevant departments.
- By further discussing and analysing all the proposals with more representatives of the temporary personnel and by publicizing the proposal selected by the government, the temporary personnel were allowed to participate in solving the contradictions and problems. In fact, they were given the responsibility of solving the issue and thus knew their rights and responsibilities in the formulation of public policies both as equal participants and as direct stakeholders. Therefore, they were more cooperative.
- By paying more attention to the roles of the complaint leaders (it was important to regard them as the de facto leaders of the special interest group instead of the NGO leaders and to win their cooperation), and by strengthening communication with them, they knew their rights were respected and their legitimate demands heard. As a result, they had a stronger sense of responsibility and gradually became partners in implementing public policies.
- By paying more attention to the reaction of other stakeholders and in particular the reaction of the remaining 3,000 laid-off personnel and the former 'educated youth' and by actively studying the relevant policy issues, the authorities won their understanding and cooperation.

In late July, the policy and working proposals were formally introduced for the former town and township temporary personnel to be included in the social pension insurance programme and were implemented in various counties. By the end of August, about one-third of these personnel went to the county social security department to register and handle the formalities. An acute contradiction was finally solved. The overall reaction was good and social stability was not affected. Currently, this reform is progressing steadily and smoothly.

Written in 2006

15 How was a collective complaint arising from land acquisition solved?

Chen Qingliang

Historical background of the incident

The incident under discussion originated in 1986, when tourism was in the take-off stage. As China's reform and opening up advanced, the number of foreign tourists increased rapidly. The reception facilities, and in particular hotels, were not only quantitatively insufficient but also qualitatively poor and were unable to meet the requirements of the growing tourist industry. In order to accelerate development and improve tourist reception facilities, intensive efforts were made to attract foreign capital for hotel construction. At that time, an American investment company signed an agreement with a tourist company to build a top-rate hotel, named Sino–US Hotel. For this purpose, the foreign company and the Chinese tourist company (the company and the Tourism Bureau were in fact the same team despite having two names) established the Sino–US Tourist Co. Ltd, which was exclusively responsible for acquiring land for hotel construction. The company acquired 54.54 mu (1 mu = 1/15 hectare) of land from the third production team of the suburban Ruyi village, which meant that 187 people (the team had over 400 people at the time) would be shifted from agriculture to industry. According to the document of the municipal government at the time, these landless people could not work at the hotel because it had been funded by foreign investment. Instead, it was arranged that they would work at different enterprises in the city's second light industrial system. At the time, it was regarded as a huge advantage for these peasants to have the opportunity to become urban residents. It was a rare chance for them, and those who could be shifted from agriculture to industry would be major players in the production team. For this purpose, the company paid more than 1.4 million yuan to the third production team and Ruyi village, including land compensation, agriculture-supporting fees and crop compensation. According to the document of the municipal government at the time, land compensation and agriculture support fees were not allowed to be divided among the members of the production team. They could only be used for living allowances and job searches. In fact, members of the production team divided the relevant fees equally among themselves, and the company had to allocate additional funds for those who were to be transferred to the enterprises of the second light industrial system. The housing units of those peasants who would be transferred would become state-owned. However, as some housing compounds were shared by certain family members who would not be transferred, this made for difficulties. The municipal government also had a special policy at the time, called the economic yard system. Under this policy, a peasant household could have an additional lot for diverse operations such as raising pigs and growing vegetables, but these lots could not be used to build houses. By the time the land was acquired, some of the peasants who were due for transfer had already built houses on the additional lots after getting married and separating from their parents. As these lots had been turned into housing sites without policy permission, they could not become state-owned. In view of the above two reasons, an agreement was reached with the village whereby these lots would become state-owned later when conditions were ripe, and the charge for handling the relevant formalities would be paid by the company.

As time passed, most enterprises in the second light industrial system were mismanaged and had been closed down by the early 1990s. Accordingly, most of the peasants who had been shifted from agriculture to industry were gradually laid off. Then, as urbanization increased and the urban areas expanded, the price of suburban land skyrocketed and the suburban rural collectives and individuals became rich because of land acquisition. Therefore, the well-being of the peasants who were first shifted from agriculture to industry is worse than that of those who were not shifted. They became restless and suffered from mental problems. As they attributed their relative poverty to the land acquisition by the Sino–US Hotel, they began complaining to the Tourism Bureau in 1993, and their complaints became wider in scale and stronger in demand after 2000. They staged sit-ins, beat gongs and drums, and blocked the doors of the Tourism Bureau. They even broke into the bureau, smashed up doors and furniture, and attacked senior officials, preventing them from carrying out their normal duties.

Initially, the peasants put forward five demands. First, compensation should be paid to solve the employment difficulties of children under 16 at the time and to alleviate the poor living conditions of those people who had been shifted from agriculture to industry. Second, the acreage of the land acquired did not tally with the official figure. Third, the public reserve fund and properties of the production team when they were shifted from agriculture to industry should be divided equally. Fourth, the issues of the courtyard economy and property service charges when they were shifted from agriculture to industry should be resolved. Fifth, each person should receive 38,000 yuan for economic and mental compensation because of the failure to fulfil the promise that they would not be laid off within 3 years after being shifted from agriculture to industry. In all, 187 people should receive more than 7 million yuan.

The Tourist Bureau reported all these issues to the relevant government departments. As the complaints escalated, the Complaints Bureau considered the complainants' views in collaboration with the departments in charge of public security and other affairs, and prepared a five-point reply. First, the acquisition of the 54.54 mu of land from the third production team of Ruyi village made in 1985 by the unit under the Tourism Bureau conformed to legal provisions and procedures. With regard to compensation for land acquisition, the Tourism Bureau had made the corresponding compensation. Second, with regard to the allegation that the acreage of the land acquired did not tally with the official figure, investigations revealed that the acreage of the land acquired was surveyed and accurate. Third, with regard to the issue of the employment and compensation issues of the minors at the time when the land was acquired, Document [81] 67 of the municipal government provided that those under the age of 16 did not belong to those groups of individuals for whom jobs should be provided. Thus there was no question of failing to find jobs for the minors at the time or awarding them compensation. Fourth, with regard to the issue of the housing sites, it was suggested that the laid-off people who had shifted from agriculture and were experiencing poor living conditions should refer them to the relevant departments of the municipal and district governments, and these departments would handle them strictly in accordance with legal provisions. The issues that should be solved must be solved by all means, and the issues that should not be solved should be explained to the people. Fifth, the acts of staging sit-ins, beating gongs and drums and blocking its doors had seriously interfered with the normal work of the Tourism Bureau and violated the *Law on Assemblies, Processions and Demonstrations*, the *Regulations on Administrative Penalties for Public Security* and the *Regulations on Complaint Letters and Visits*. The complainants should take the overall interests of society into account and return to their homes immediately. If certain people were determined to continue their illegal sit-ins, they would be held responsible for the consequences.

Dissatisfied with the above reply from the Complaints Department, the peasants continued to lodge their complaints to the provincial government and the Tourism Bureau, and became increasingly radical. Later on, the personnel who interviewed them told them that, if they believed the government had violated the relevant regulations and laws, they should appeal to the court and solve their problems through legal channels. But the complainants said they would not go to court and the government could sue them if it believed they had violated the law. They would continue to lodge their complaints. One day when they visited the Tourism Bureau and blocked the bureau's doors, one official was trapped on a staircase by the complainants. As he had important official duties to perform, the official broke away from the crowd, causing a person to fall down the staircase. The person was only slightly hurt, but he exaggerated his injury and resorted to threats in order to coerce the official into eventually paying more than 10,000 yuan for his medical fees.

As the Tourism Bureau had no effective way of dealing with the radical behaviour of these complainants, they sought police help. But they were unable to resolve the issue and complained repeatedly to the government. The leaders of the provincial government held a meeting to discuss the issue and instructed the municipal government to set up a working group in cooperation with the Tourism Bureau. The working group reinvestigated the issue and summarized the related problems into three points. First, with regard to the compensation for land acquisition, the complainants held that the compensation for land acquisition should be divided solely among those who had been shifted from agriculture to industry, instead of dividing it among all the members of the production team including those who were not shifted from agriculture to industry. Therefore, they requested the government to redistribute, among those who had been shifted from agriculture to industry, the compensation fund that had been distributed among those who were not shifted. Second, they held that it was not right for the crop compensation not to include the crops grown on their private lots and thus additional compensation should be paid. Third, it was imperative to expedite the formalities to nationalize the housing sites. The additional lots should also be treated as housing sites and be nationalized.

Two more years passed and the officials changed. Because of the different views of either side, no solution was worked out. Over the two years, the complainants continued to stage demonstrations. They were not only emotionally radical, but also repeatedly issued death threats to officials of the Tourism Bureau.

With the accelerated construction of urban roads and commercial estates, new problems emerged. Some other land in Ruyi village was acquired for municipal projects. As a result, those people who had built houses on their additional plots and who had been shifted from agriculture to industry became more restive. This was because the new developers offered compensation of about 400,000 yuan for each property built on a housing site and compensation of about 100,000 yuan for each property built on the plots where houses had been constructed illegally. As a result, those complainants affected began to demand more compensation. When the developers refused to give in, the complainants turned to the government. They occupied the corridors of the Tourism Bureau building, eating there in the day and sleeping there at night. They came in their droves and locked the doors of the Tourism Bureau building several times, paralysing the normal office routine. In the face of this problem, the Tourism Bureau repeatedly requested that the Public Security Bureau intervene, but as the peasant issue was rather thorny, the police would only try to use their powers of persuasion. This placed the Tourism Bureau in a dilemma. If they upheld the principle, they would have no peace; yet they had no powers to give in and make concessions.

As the land acquisition was done according to the policies and regulations of the municipal government and with the approval of the municipal government, the complainants sometimes also went to the municipal and provincial governments. However, as the gates were guarded by armed police, the complainants had no way of getting in to seek out the relevant officials. In comparison, going to the Tourism Bureau was much easier (the bureau had no armed police to guard its gates), and the Tourism Bureau had no powers to deal with them effectively. The municipal government also felt that this was a difficult issue. Even though the provincial government had instructed it to deal with the issue, it tried to delay its resolution as far as possible. In short, the municipal government failed to take the issue seriously.

What could the Tourism Bureau do in this case? It could only resort to continuously reporting the matter to the relevant provincial departments and municipal governments. But no reply was ever given.

The large-scale complaints lasted for more than 4 years since they began in 2000. Over those 4 years, the Tourism Bureau suffered continual disruption. The first thing on officials' minds when the staff came into work in the morning was how to deal with the complainants if they had decided to demonstrate that day. How could this state of affairs continue? The chaotic environment had seriously affected the work mentality and efficiency of all the staff. What could the Tourism Bureau do? What decisions should the government make? The Tourism Bureau was totally helpless.

Result

In the face of this situation, the Provincial Tourism Bureau did not know what to do. Although the provincial government had instructed the municipal government to handle this issue, the municipal government failed to come up with a solution. Although the Provincial Tourism Bureau repeatedly contacted the municipal government, it was just as repeatedly given the brush-off by the latter. But the problem remained unresolved. In May 2004, the leaders of both provincial and municipal tourism bureaus went to talk to the leaders of the municipal government. At first, the leaders of the municipal government said they were too busy, and the leaders of the Provincial Tourism Bureau replied that, if no appointment was fixed, they would stage a sit-in in the building until something was done. This declaration frightened the leaders of the municipal government, who had no alternative but to assure them that a meeting would be held the following day to discuss the issue.

The next day, the municipal government held a meeting, which was attended by the leaders of the departments of land, complaints, public security, district government and the Tourism Bureau. After views had been fully exchanged, the municipal government realized that the complaints would continue endlessly if no fundamental solution was found. After repeated arguments, consultations and compromises, a consensus was reached that this issue could no longer be handled according to past principles.

As a result, the following decisions were made. First, the housing sites should be divided and nationalized according to the promise made at the time when the land was acquired. As the issue of the additional lots involved only a few people who had built houses on them because they were homeless at the time, their economic interests should not suffer in the course of land acquisition. Even though the district government introduced no new policies, the deficiencies in compensation should be made up by the government. Second, as the compensation for the crops on the private lots did not amount to very much and did not affect the execution of other policies, it was decided that additional compensation should be given. Third, the compensation for land acquisition should not be increased according to relevant policies. However, in light of the real difficulties of the complainants, some money would be paid, as relief rather than compensation, in order to end the dispute and ensure social stability. In all, the relevant government departments would contribute 750,000 yuan, and the shortfall would be made up by the municipal government. Finally, the district governments would be responsible for comprehensively handling this matter. The matter was subsequently resolved according to these decisions, and no more complaints have since been filed.

Personal viewpoint

In the transition from a planned to a market economy, we have to make certain painful decisions. We have many legal documents and we may say we even have a complete system of legal documents, but we cannot claim that ours is a society under the rule of law. We have yet to establish a sound legal system. In this process, we feel helpless in the face of many problems. First, in dealing with the ordinary public, the government cannot entirely act according to the law. To ensure social stability, a case-by-case approach is sometimes indispensable. Second, in the course of transition, society is not a truly legal society under the rule of law and therefore the government cannot govern properly under the rule of law. How such a government requests its civil servants to dedicate themselves and fulfil their responsibilities of serving the people and their country remains an issue that we have to face and continue to explore.

Written in 2006

Part IV

Resources and the ecological environment

16 Analysis of the ban on crop stubble burning

Yang Shuping

In northern China, most peasant farmers manage their crop stubble by burning. In the summer and autumn harvest seasons, smoke and fire can be seen everywhere in crop fields. They come from the burning of crop stubble and spoil the landscape. They seriously affect the environment, production, life, human health and public security; they impede traffic flow and reduce visibility, forcing airports and expressways to close and interrupting traffic. They pollute the air, causing respiratory problems for nearby residents, and adversely affect their normal life; they trigger fire disasters, destroy communications and power-supply lines and cause life and property losses. Crop stubble burning has become bad practice and also a public hazard. Various strata of society have been complaining for some time and urging the government to ban it. In order to ban crop stubble burning, the relevant government departments have introduced regulations in recent years, and the regional governments have also adopted many measures and made great efforts to resolve the situation, but to little avail. Banning crop stubble burning has become a thorny problem for the grassroots Party committees and governments.

The city of Jiaozuo lies in the northwestern area of Henan Province. With the Taihang mountains in the north and the Yellow river in the south, the city has been noted for its agricultural development. It is one of the three major, high-yield, grain-producing regions in China. As the people's living conditions improve and the state's industrial policy adjusts, crop stubble burning has become increasingly hazardous. With a total cultivated area of 2.72 million mu and a total crop-sown area of 4.4 million mu, the city produces 2.32 million tons of crop stubble a year, of which 1.12 million tons or 48.4 per cent is burnt in the open air. The issue of crop stubble burning is an extremely serious problem and has provoked widespread public anger. As instructed by the central and Henan provincial governments, the Jiaozuo municipal Party committee and government believed after conscientious investigations that a ban on crop stubble burning would help protect the environment and resources and would serve the interests of both the country and the people. It was an inevitable move for the city to take. In 2000, the city officials decided to launch a campaign against crop stubble burning, with a view to a total ban within 3 years.

Before the start of the summer harvest in 2000, a city-wide conference was held calling for a ban of the burning of crop stubble. Guided by the principle of forceful methods and strict prevention, leading groups were set up at various levels, with the chief administrative officials serving as group leaders. Meanwhile, strict supervisory measures were worked out, and responsibility systems introduced for the county, township and village leaders. In addition, suggestions were unveiled on how to turn crop stubble into silage and compost. This meeting represented the beginning of a campaign to ban crop stubble burning. Three main measures were taken.

Intensive publicity and extensive mobilization. Media institutions were mobilized to guide public opinion. In keeping with the principle that intensive media publicity was conducted within a limited period to increase pressure, a powerful publicity campaign was launched. A total of more than 150 articles were published, more than 30,000 copies of the ban on stubble burning were printed and distributed, more than 100,000 slogans were posted, over 3,000 banners were hung, and publicity vehicles were used in 5,000 events. The massive public campaign created an aggressive social atmosphere.

Meticulous planning and unified organization. The city government dispatched seven supervisory groups led by chief county officials comprising more than thirty people. The groups visited every county, city and district to supervise the enforcement of the ban. The counties, cities and districts also acted likewise by sending their own working groups to various towns and townships, and the towns and townships sent their officials to meet with village leaders in the crop fields. The supervisory groups and working groups were requested to live at the grassroots level and to maintain a high profile. They were not permitted to return to their units before the end of the summer harvest.

Improved measures and strict rewards and punishments. Standards for rewards and punishments were set, according to which every fire would be investigated and the perpetrator punished. For each area of crop stubble that was burned, the county, city or district would be subject to a 10,000-yuan fine; and the counties, cities or districts where there were no incidences of stubble burning would receive a 100,000-yuan reward. During that period, vehicles equipped with loudspeakers toured the countryside, flags were hoisted, and Jiaozuo's vast territory was patrolled constantly. Posters bearing slogans such as 'Whoever burns will be punished' were posted everywhere, and patrolmen in camouflage uniforms and armed with fire extinguishers guarded fields and roads 24 hours a day. When the autumn harvest arrived, there was more crop stubble, and the ban became increasingly difficult to enforce. Jiaozuo again mobilized more people and put in more material resources to enforce the ban.

However, the municipal Party committee and government found after the 2000 fanfare was over that the results were not as good as expected. While crop stubble burning was not totally banned, the waste of human, material and financial resources mobilized to enforce the ban was considerable. In the summer and autumn harvest seasons, ninety-eight stubble-burning cases were discovered, with nearly 1,000 tons of crop stubble being burned. More than 100 villages in more than twenty towns and townships across the city were involved. While as much as 5 million yuan was spent on enforcing the ban, the officials and especially the grassroots officials worked for nearly 3 months in the fields, which had a serious impact on their normal work. After a year, nearly all the counties, cities, districts, towns and townships had been penalized, though to varying degrees. While the relevant counties, cities and districts paid 6.97 million yuan in financial fines, more than twenty leading officials at the town and township levels or more than one-tenth of the city's total received administrative punishments, with five of them being dismissed. Still more village officials were also punished. In addition, a few villagers deliberately set fire in reprisal incidents, causing village officials to be dismissed. Most officials and the public held different views on the ban. Many grassroots officials believed the ban was a difficult task to enforce and had strained their relations with the public. The peasant farmers argued that, after harvests, large amounts of crop stubble remained in the fields. If the stubble was not burned, this would impede seed sowing. Burning was easy and energy- and cost-effective, and could increase the potash content of the soil and kill certain pests. Some rural deputies to the people's congresses and the People's Political Consultative Council reflected that, while the ban helped protect the environment, the huge amount of crop stubble in the fields impeded sowing. If the stubble was deeply embedded in the soil, the costs would be too high. A complete ban was not in the interests of the peasants.

What went wrong? How to ban crop stubble burning?

The Jiaozuo officials began to reflect on how to enforce the ban on burning crop stubble.

As a farm product resource, crop stubble should be utilized. The peasants set fire to crop stubble mainly because they do not have the ways and means to convert and use the stubble due to the constraints of knowledge, technology, market, traditional farming practice and other factors. Exploring conversion channels, increasing processing capacities and extending industrial chains constitute a natural choice for using crop stubble and other farm product resources. The peasants' act of burning the crop stubble is a reflection that their capacity to process and convert farm products is weak and the level of agricultural industrialization low. Therefore, the issue of crop stubble burning cannot be treated in isolation.

In discussing how to ban crop stubble burning, one cannot just talk about a ban. Instead, the discussion should focus on how to cure both symptoms and root causes and how to combine resource protection with resource utilization. Once symptoms and root causes are tackled, the issue of crop stubble burning will be solved in a scientific and systematic way. Therefore, the discussion should not focus on how to 'ban'. It should focus on how to find an efficient way for peasant farmers to deal with crop stubble. 'Blocking' alone cannot solve the problem. 'Blocking' should be combined with 'dredging'. Without 'dredging', 'blocking' will be impossible. The practice of W county in Jiaozuo also proved this view. The county had 68,000 mu of rice-growing areas. The peasants in the rice-growing region grow two crops a year: wheat and rice. Rice planting is done manually and requires a great deal of labour. Prior to the ban on crop stubble burning, the peasants generally burned the wheat stubble in order to have the rice planted in time. After they had been ploughed twice with rotavators, the fields were flooded and rice planted. After the ban was introduced, two additional processes were needed. The crop stubble had to be chopped up and buried in the soil using high-powered tractors. As this method not only increased input but also affected sowing period and output, the peasants were not in favour of the practice. This was why the ban on crop stubble burning became a thorny issue for Jiaozuo. For a while, the peasant farmers even returned to their old practice of burning crop stubble. To find a fundamental solution, the leading officials of the city and W county visited the rice-growing region several times to talk to the peasants and hear their views. They concluded that the best solution was to 'return the stubble to the fields and utilize it in an integrated way'. Therefore, they proposed a method that integrated the operations of three kinds of farm machinery: the harvester, the stalk chopper and the rotavator should operate in coordination at a ratio of 1:2:2 during the summer harvest. With this method, the crop stubble would be returned to the fields and increase the organic matter in the soil. At the same time, the issue of crop stubble burning was solved.

In 2001, the city of Jiaozuo began changing its way of thinking. 'Strict blocking' was replaced by 'dredging'. On the one hand, continuous efforts were made to intensify the enforcement of the ban on crop stubble burning. On the other, efforts were made to convert and utilize crop stubble in conjunction with agricultural restructuring and agricultural industrialization. After years of effort, more than 95 per cent of the crop stubble in the city had been utilized.

To develop intensive dairy farming with silage made from crop stubble and to fully convert stubble into compost. The governments at all levels began to promote dairy farming as an effective way to convert and use crop stubble, restructure and optimize agriculture and increase peasant income. The municipal government introduced a series of preferential policies for this purpose, such as preferential treatment for land use and to subsidize silage pit construction. In addition, the municipal government allocated over 5 million yuan as discount loans for silage cattle farming. In the autumn of 2003, more than 600,000 mu of land was devoted to cultivating stubble for silage. The rural enterprises built more than ten dairy farms. As a result, the numbers of cattle increased from 200,000 in 2000 to 340,000 in 2003. Dairy farming alone consumed nearly 500,000 tons of crop stubble or 20 per cent of the total amount generated. Dairy farming also helped restructure and optimize the livestock industry, which became one of the main ways to increase peasant income.

To energetically popularize agricultural mechanization and return more crop stubble to the fields. In keeping with the principle of 'filling the gap and increasing the amount' and 'promoting popularization in key regions', the task of popularizing agricultural mechanization was divided and subdivided at all levels and, finally, to townships and villages. In the meantime, preferential policies were introduced to provide subsidies to purchase machinery. Since 2000, the municipal, county and township governments have contributed a total of 6 million yuan to developing combines and to upgrading and popularizing large and medium-sized tractors, stalk choppers and auxiliary machines. Over the 3 years, the city has added 540 large and medium-sized tractors, 614 combines, 1,899 corn stalk choppers, 2,784 corn sowing machines and 3,792 silage machines. As a result, the city has become a leader in the province in upgrading farm machinery and improving mechanization.

To accelerate research and development to find new methods of integrated crop stubble utilization. A fund has been established for integrated crop stubble utilization, from which more than 10 million yuan was given to twenty key projects on integrated crop stalk utilization. Intensified research and development, experiment, demonstration and popularization produced remarkable results. All the counties, cities and districts also adopted measures to encourage the peasants to launch their own projects. In addition to dairy farming and returning stubble to the fields, progress was also made in using crop stubble to produce edible fungi. In particular, more than ten towns and townships in three counties and two districts established their own experiment and demonstration centres for the production of edible fungi. More than 100,000 tons of materials were used for this purpose, and the output value was 200 million yuan higher than in the early days of banning stubble burning. Edible fungus production became a new growth point of the rural economy. In addition, they also established four plants to produce compressed stubble fodder and organic ecological feeds, and one plant to produce building materials. As a result, more ways were found to make integrated use of crop stubble.

To actively train peasant brokers to expand channels for crop stubble conversion. Close attention was paid to training peasant brokers and encouraging them to buy and sell crop stubble. All the counties, cities and districts introduced preferential policies on stubble transport, land use and small loans during the stubble-burning ban and offered quality services and financial support. So far, about 200 peasant brokers have been trained to engage exclusively in wheat stubble trading, and they have been active in the rural areas. Each year, a total of 1.1 million tons of crop stubble or nearly 50 per cent of the total are sold through peasant brokers. On average, each broker can earn 20,000 yuan a year. In summer, in particular, all wheat stubble is sold and stockpiled at designated places, benefiting the peasant farmers, enterprises and society.

To intensify publicity and service to create conditions for banning the burning of crop stubble. The Party committees and governments at all levels adjusted their way of thinking and combined publicity and management to provide all-embracing services. This move won the support of the peasant farmers and vigorously pushed forward the enforcement of the ban on crop stubble burning. In the meantime, the farm product marketing system, the system for technological extension, education and training, the information service system, the financial service system and other rural service systems were established and improved. Strong support was also given to the management system, institutional set-up and funding input. The opening of the agri-culture-related service hotlines and the introduction of the peasant farmer reception day system enabled peasant farmers across the city to be able to receive all services, including weather reports, improved seeds, management and pest control and, in particular, information on the stubble-burning ban, dairy farming, methods for returning stubble to fields and soil improvement. In the critical periods of the summer and autumn harvests and silage pro-duction, the city organized professional and technical personnel specialized in agriculture, farm machinery and animal husbandry to visit the peasants and offer face-to-face technical guidance and training. In order to reduce the impact on agricultural production of the SARS epidemic in summer and floods in autumn, the municipal Party committee and government in 2003 combined SARS control with the stubble-burning ban and support pro-gramme, and mobilized more than 5,000 officials across the city to help the peasant farmers. This ensured victory in controlling the SARS epidemic and in banning the burning of crop stubble in the two seasons. In addition, the move further improved relations between officials and the public.

Once the way of thinking had changed, more solutions could be found. Thanks to a 3-year investigation, Jiaozuo became the first city in the pro-vince to completely ban the burning of crop stubble. According to the Meteorological Bureau, while crop stubble burning occurred in seventeen of the eighteen cities in the province in the summer and autumn of 2003, none occurred in Jiaozuo. In the city, the air pollutant total suspended particulate (TSP) dropped 35 per cent and the air quality was visibly better than in 2000. Over the 2 years, no one in Jiaozuo was penalized for burning crop stubble.

In the summer harvest in 2004, the stubble burning ban was quietly enforced in Jiaozuo. The municipal authorities only mobilized a skeleton staff of six inspection groups to go to the grassroots level to oversee progress. The channels for wheat stubble purchase were effective, the quality of mechanized operations was high and government services were efficient. In particular, banning crop stubble burning was closely combined with offering services, such as dispatching machinery, training machine operators, repairing machines, helping households with problems, separating the harvest of wheat seeds and strong gluten wheat, and providing technical guidance for summer sowing. All these efforts ensured a bumper wheat crop and a bumper wheat harvest. The summer ban on crop stubble burning lasted for less than 20 days and proceeded in the normal way.

Great efforts brought about great results. Thanks to the determination of the Jiaozuo municipal Party committee and government to ban crop stubble burning and promote animal husbandry and the achievements made in these areas, and because of the preferential policies they offered to attract investment, the Mengniu Dairy Industry in Inner Mongolia laid the foundation stone for its Jiaozuo subsidiary on 22 June 2003, under which Mengniu would formally have a presence in Jiaozuo. The first phase of the project would require an investment of 400 million yuan to build twelve Tetra Pak Hoyer ice cream production lines and fifteen production lines for liquid milk. Once completed, the project would process 219,000 tons of fresh milk, with its sale revenues totalling 1.41 billion yuan and tax being 143.61 million yuan. In addition, it would boost dairy farming by 40,000 head of cattle and consume 400,000 tons of crop stubble. The adoption of a scientific approach has turned crop stubble from being a public nuisance into a 'rare' resource.

Practice proves that all our work should proceed from practical conditions and should be people oriented. A broad vision and use of scientific methods are crucial in ensuring that good things can be effectively achieved.

Personal feelings

Through the ban on crop stubble burning, I realize that if we want to do a good job, we must first of all change our approach to government and improve our working methods. The 'administrative government' should become a 'service-oriented government', and administrative intervention should be replaced by service provision. Otherwise, relying solely on administrative means cannot produce ideal results as happened in the early days of banning crop stubble burning.

Next, we must safeguard the people's interests and engage their trust. Without their support and participation, a good thing can turn bad no matter what its intentions. Third, we must proceed from a practical viewpoint and tackle the principal contradictions. The fundamental reason for the initial failure in banning crop stubble burning was that no alternative was offered. Combining 'blocking' with 'dredging' can help solve the problem.

Finally, we must analyse issues in a dialectic way and broaden our vision. Crop stubble is a resource. If it can be converted and used, burning can be avoided and alternative solutions found. Analysing issues from a different angle and adopting a new way of thinking can bring about a breakthrough in the stubble burning ban and give birth to a new industry.

Written in 2004

17 Should government-supported projects causing pollution be permitted if civilians are not allowed to be involved in those projects?

Chen Zhongbo

Introduction

In the gold and silver mineral area of Yizhang County, Chenzhou City, Hunan Province of China, spontaneous mining activities by civilians have caused severe pollution to the environment. In order to eliminate this uncontrolled mining phenomenon, local government contracted a company – Chenzhou Yixin Industrial Co. Ltd – to develop mining under legal authorization. However, this also led to pollution. Civilians cannot help but ask: 'If civilians are not allowed to be involved in those projects, should government-supported projects causing pollution be permitted?' Senior government officials determined to stop all such projects. However, the company believed that local government should fulfil its written promise to allow mining activities.

Under the supervision of the media and through the intervention of provincial and city governments, mining activities ceased in 2002. As the value of minerals increased, economic interest's motivation led to legal regulation of mining activities in 2006. Subsequently, the companies obtained related licences and resumed production.

The pollution problem has never been thoroughly resolved. Meanwhile, many officials involved in corruption have been apprehended and prosecuted.

Public administration of the government is in a dilemma.

On 15 May 2002 in the gold and silver mineral area of Yizhang County, Chenzhou City, Hunan Province of China, the 'Century Walk of Sanxiang Environmental Protection' news-gathering group discovered piles of mining equipment in the middle of the mountains despite the fact that the mining engineering project had been abandoned.

Although it is not apparent from the map, this village is famous for its rich resources of metal, such as gold, silver, tungsten and lead. However, this brings both prosperity and severe pollution to the neighbouring environment. Green vegetation has now become scarce, and waste residues, broken branches and dead trees litter the area.

Besides registering surprise, people cannot help but ask: 'Why not stop these activities? Why do these mining projects start again and again even when they are expressly forbidden?' To answer the above questions, we have to review the following scenarios.

Scenario 1: The government says civilians should not cause pollution

Jinzhu Ridge, Xinwu villiage, Changce village of Yizhang County is a place rich in gold and silver minerals. It is about 50 kilometres away from Yizhang County and about 2.5 kilometres from Provincial Express S324. It is located on the edge of Yaogangxian tungsten mine. Because it has convenient transportation, water and electricity facilities, it is a mature mining environment. It is a multi-metal mine and is estimated to contain some 237,000 tonnes of ore, comprising 508 kilograms of gold, 84 tons of silver and 60,000 tons of No. 4 mai tungsten minerals.

At local government level, between 1999 and 2000, a 'gold rush' was created by private project owners and farmers in Changce village and its neighbouring area. Some illegal mining points subsequently became active; it is likely that more than sixty points and more than 100 private projects were involved. Most use a traditional method to pick gold. This method produces a great deal of waste water full of noxious sodium cyanide while providing miners with huge profits. On one hand, natural resources provide wealth for human beings; on the other hand, pollution caused by uncontrolled mining destroys the living environment. In one interview, a local resident told a journalist that the polluted water was undrinkable – 'you feel uncomfortable after drinking that water' – so that they have to travel some distance to collect clean drinking water.

There are more than 13,000 villagers in the 87.1-square-kilometre area of Changce village. After learning of the threat to normal life and health, some villagers appealed to local government to take action. In May 2000, in an effort to safeguard civilians' health and the environment, Yizhang County Committee and government decided to halt the uncontrolled mining activities. County government organized the Public Security Office, inspection, justice, geology and mineral and environmental protection departments to take action to bomb parts of the illegal mines and mining equipment, and to destroy illegal mining and picking factories. Therefore, the mining area has been cleaned up to a certain extent.

Scenario 2: Civilians say that government-supported projects should not be permitted to cause pollution either

In order to eliminate the illegal mining activities in Changce village, the Yizhang County and Changce village government offices set up a company – Chenzhou Yixin Industrial Co. Ltd ('The Company') – in February 2001 to invest RMB 3,000,000 yuan building Changce silver mine in Jinzhulong and Jiaolong districts of Changce. To attract investment, the village government assured companies a smooth implementation of all the necessary procedures.

Local government hoped to support legal mining companies in order to permanently solve the conflict between economic development and environmental protection. By agreement, The Company would invest in labour and construction equipment. In mid-May 2001, The Company carried out experimental activities without applying for EIA (environment impact assessment) or the necessary environmental protection establishments, and drained waste water directly into Ceshui river.

However, owing to the lack of environmental protection established by the county and village government offices and The Company, the waste water was not appropriately treated and therefore polluted the river. At that time, no environmental protection facilities had been installed. This again provoked local residents' anger, particularly the private businessmen who were rectificated in Stage 1. Residents were asking: 'Could government projects be permitted to generate pollution while civilians are forbidden?' This controversy became an element of instability.

In the case of this 'three-pronged (design, construct and produce at the same time)' project violating engineering environment protection standards, the senior environmental office checked it out in July 2001. The Yizhang County environmental protection bureau demanded that it stop production and apply EIA and application procedures.

From this standpoint, as mentioned at the outset, this has caused a dilemma: The Company wanted to continue its production while the government decided to stop it immediately. Should the engineering project continue?

Scenario 3: Enterprises ask whether the government's promise is reliable

In consideration of the economic development of Yizhang County government, when inviting The Company, the government made a written promise that it would help to obtain the relevant approval for applications, such as EIA, so that The Company could invest in equipment and start construction in advance. The Company invested RMB 3,000,000 yuan and began construction and production without EIA. Currently, because senior environment officials have forbidden production, local government cannot fulfil its promise. A problem arises: 'Who is going to take responsibility for The Company's losses?'

In order to relieve a tense situation, Yizhang County government made three written promises to the Provincial Environment Bureau: (1) The Company is the only entity with a legal qualification to develop Jinlong Silver mine in Changce, and the government will continue to support it; (2) uncontrolled mining is strictly forbidden; (3) the County government will continue to monitor environmental protection of the mining area and ensure that business owners take the necessary environmental measures according to national regulations.

In order to proceed, investors and local government both wanted continuing production following the normal environment assessment procedures.

However, with the issuance of 'regulation of water resource protection of Dongjiang Lake in Hunan Province', this mining area has been included in the protection zone and no mining activities are allowed, especially gold or silver mining. In a response to the village government's announcement of 'non-waste water draining through recyclable use', general engineer Xu of the Provincial Protection Bureau pointed out that 'it is impossible, and so far there is no technology to obtain it', and asked: 'Where could you build a waste aventurine dam? What they built would not be appropriate for containing such a large amount of waste aventurine in the future'.

Owing to lack of consideration for local realistic situations and environmental protection requirements, this project is recognized by the 'Century Walk of Sanxiang Environmental Protection' experts as the wrong project happening in the wrong place. Since July 2001, and according to the news gathering team's confirmation in May 2002, this project is still due for closure. The government and investors are in a dilemma, as RMB 3,000,000 yuan has already been invested.

Scenario 4: Every side has its point on who is right or wrong

Why did the project owner not receive approval for EIA? General engineer Xu said in an interview: 'According to the regulation of water resource protection of Dongjiang Lake in Hunan Province, Jinzhulong belongs to Dongjiang Lake protection zone and therefore no entity or individual should be involved in traditional arsenic mining, gold or tungsten cleaning'. Jinzhulong is connected with Ceshui river and is only 10 kilometres away from Dongjiang Lake so that industrial waste water or domestic waste water will definitely pollute Dongjiang Lake. Waste residue containing noxious elements will cause severe pollution of the neighbouring environment. Under the circumstances, Jinzhulong mining zone is not suitable for development. On this point, Chenzhou City government came up with an explicit opinion in No. 21 (2001) document that Yizhang County government should do their jobs on the closure of the mines and prohibit illegal mining activities. It also arranged for the National Land Resources Department to be in charge of the monitoring work and to conduct the closures before December 2001, and the recovering ecological work before December 2002.

The project owners of The Company had their own opinion on the prohibition issue:

> We agreed to undertake the project because of local governments' promise. When we mentioned environment protection, officials said they could assist to solve any problems. Moreover, inviting a large company rather than small-scale mining enterprises could facilitate applications for regulation as well as stop uncontrolled mining activities or wasting resources. We don't know how to proceed with the current environmental protection concerns.

Why was the investor allowed to begin construction at that time? Officials from Changce village government replied: 'The situation is that the necessary procedures were applied for while construction went ahead. We communicated with the environmental offices and submitted an EIA, but no approval was received'. The journalist then asked what the solution was if no approval was received. The official responded: 'We could only wait for approval. Senior offices would make the decision'.

It is well known that the project aims to turn resource advantage into economic advantage, to facilitate county development as well as to avoid destroying the ecological environment as a result of civilians' uncontrolled mining activities. Thus local government holds high expectations and gives strong support to the project. However, based on the standpoint of protecting Dongjiang Lake water resource and ecological environment, Chenzhou city government does not support the project. Mr Lei –, deputy mayor of Chenzhou city – commented: 'No project should be started without EIA approval, so how could the county government make such a promise? Everyone should respect the law; the project is a violation of the regulations protecting Dongjiang Lake'.

As is well known, it is common in some places for engineering projects violating national environment regulations to follow a procedure of 'boarding the bus first without paying, then buying the ticket when necessary'. This is probably not same as the dilemma faced by Changce and Yizhang government in inviting companies to invest, however. Without issuing a regulation of water resource protection of 'Dongjiang Lake in Hunan Province', Yizhang County and Changce village government could make the mining activity legal by 'buying the EIA ticket'. The point is that environmental pressure will not be changed whether the regulation exists or not. Some projects without EIA approval have led to negative impacts upon the environment, although the impact is not severe enough to attract officials' attention.

Changce village is located in Chenzhou City and is rich in mineral resources. For historical reasons, the minerals development layout is not appropriate. Resources are overdeveloped. Besides, it can lead to pressure on a gradually depleted ecological environment and loss of resource advantage and, ultimately, becomes financially inefficient. According to statistics from 2001, waste water generated by mining accounts for 20 to 30 per cent of the city's industrial waste water; however, only 4 per cent of waste water has been treated. Most of the waste water has been drained directly into neighbouring rivers, thereby causing severe pollution. Eighty per cent of industrial solid residues are also generated by mines. These residues not only occupy land, but also lead to serious pollution to soils and water resources. Deterioration of the ecological environment around mines also activates a series of problems such as water resource crisis, land collapse and so on.

In July 2002, when starting to write up this case, the author commented:

The Changce gold and silver mine case might come to an end or just be suspended for a while. Many underlying questions make people think about: (1) Local government – people always hope to make use of the available resources to facilitate economic development; however, is it worth transferring it with the risk of environmental destruction and, if it is possible to transfer, how to do so without damaging the ecological system? (2) The government and private entrepreneurs always want to exploit more mines, earn more profits and more incomes. The GDP and revenue indicators are the political achievements of government, but are the environment and ecology independent of government political achievements? (3) The government always does its best to attract investment and projects, but the long-term regulations and services are often ignored. Why? (4) The government always thinks it is omnipotent and enterprises always ask the government to fulfil the promise fairly, so who broke the rules? (5) Why do so many people regard environmental protection as a great undertaking of lasting importance but not as an urgent matter? (6) Why do people not believe that the problems are serious and turn a blind eye until the special examinations and investigations are completed?'

New scenario: Action speaks louder than words, time will justify anything

Time passed and, in August 2006, I revised this case again according to the demands of the Chinese Development Research Foundation. When reviewing the beginning and end of the Changce gold and silver mine issue, I am reassured. Events began to progress in a new direction and to arouse people's conscience, although matters became complicated. Four years on, when the Chinese government confirmed sustainable development and environmental protection as the national development strategy, the Changce gold and silver mine case has become the prevailing trend. When economic development is based on environmental destruction, no more comments are helpful when facing the facts.

In July 2006, the Southern Hunan Province encountered severe rainstorms and flooding as a result of typhoon Bilis and typhoon Kaemi. Chenzhou City, including eleven counties and districts, was the worst affected area in these two disasters. The flooding caused 346 deaths and eighty-nine losses in Hunan Province, and 197 deaths and sixty-nine losses in Zixing County, Chenzhou City. The ensuing accidents led some scholars to reflect on the events. When analysing the causes of the disasters, the officer director of Hunan Provincial Drought and Flood Prevention Headquarters said:

> The geological structure of the counties and villages of Chenzhou City mainly consist of granite, low-grade metamorphic rock and other rocks. In severe rainstorms, the particular geological conditions may cause

mountain slide or debris flow. Most of the houses are built next to the hillsides and rivulets and are adversely affected by flooding, thereby causing personal injury. The severe rainstorms led to mountain slide and debris flow which were found in more than 8,000 places in Chenzhou City.

According to the opinions of experts such as Professor Chen, Professor Huang and Professor Liu from the China University of Geosciences and Hunan Provincial Bureau of Geo-minerals Exploration and Development, the ecological problems derived from mining behaviour mainly include environmental destruction of the earth's surface, air environmental destruction, water environmental destruction and secondary geological hazards. The thesis written by Hu, Cao and Miao shows that natural hazards reflect the hidden environmental risk troubles in Chenzhou City (*Chinese Environmental Newspaper*, 31 July 2006). The long-term ecological destruction in Chenzhou City during the past years, the illogical layout of enterprises, ignorance of environmental protection and an absence of necessary recognition and measures for hidden environmental risk trouble prevention have led to severe ecological destruction, even the environmental safety problem. Several enterprises have taken action to restore the vegetation after mine exploitation, but these measures cannot protect the hills effectively in the event of severe rainstorms because of the shallow root system and tree species singularity. Local government and enterprises lack the necessary emergency salvation measures, many residue fields of important pollution prevention and containment enterprises are swept away by flooding, causing wide-scale pollution. According to the statistics of Yongxing County Environmental Protection Bureau, the severe flooding in July 2006 caused tons of raw materials to fall into a branch of the Xiangjiang river. The raw materials included antimony powder, zinc powder, caustic soda, cathode soil, lead and zinc powder and poisonous debris.

In fact, governments attach more importance to safety production measures and environmental protection these days, and have put several necessary and even uncompromising measures into effect.

After listening to a report about the safety production situation compiled by Chenzhou City government in 2005 entitled '10,000 Mile March for National Safety Production', an interview delegate commented: 'Whatever, according to the ratio of total population to accidental *death-toll* or GDP to accidental death-toll, Chenzhou City is higher than the national average level, i.e. the life cost is too high.' (NB: During January to May 2005, there were fifteen accidents and fifty-one people killed in the 556 coal mines in Chenzhou City, the ratio increasing by 25 per cent and 75.8 per cent respectively.) On 15 April 2005, according to the inspection and law execution results, the Hunan Provincial Safety Production Committee announced illegal mine exploitation and production practices in Chenzhou City. The announcement shows that, from 1 January to 10 April 2005, there were twelve accidents in which forty-three people were killed in the city's coal mines, including four serious accidents resulting in thirty-three deaths. On average, an accident was occurring every 8 days and a serious accident was occurring every 25 days. In total, 399 coal mines were examined under the execution of centralized law, of which 199 were being exploited illegally – almost 49.9 per cent of the total; eighty-seven graphite mines were examined, of which fifty-six were being exploited illegally, almost 64.4 per cent of the total. In addition, there were fifty-nine illegally exploited mines in Yizhang County. The announcement also pointed to the causes: the government and related departments had not taken sufficiently strong action to prevent illegal mine production and did not prosecute the illegal mine owners. The execution of the law over conspiracy between government officers and mining business-men was too lax, as it allowed the resumption of illegal coal-mining activities and the perpetrators had to be punished and their practices annihilated.

Chengzhou City was also implicated in the illicit practice of officials withdrawing shares from mining companies. In the first half of 2005, at the onset of the crackdown on such corrupt practices perpetrated by officials and mining businessmen, thirty-eight officials had been apprehended in Chengzhou City, the highest rate in China. Among them were three city-level governors and nineteen bureau-level officials. In Changce village of Yizhang County, many officials have since been punished and relieved of office. For example, the former vice chairman Xiao of Changce township has been suspended from duties and was asked to make self-examination; the former chairman Ni, the former chairman Yang (Discipline Inspection Commission) and vice chairman (Security Production Bureau) Wu have all been investigated.

To our surprise, the corruption cases in Chengzhou City over the past 2 years were all related to mining activities, namely the conflict between public justice and private benefit as well as between environmental protection and pollution. One example is Lei's case. He abused his powers for personal gain from mining projects in various aspects of work arrangements, favourable policies and so on while he was in charge of the construction of infra-structures in Chengzhou City. According to statistics, he accepted bribes totalling RMB¥ 9,490,000 from thirty-nine people and defrauded RMB ¥ 26,500,000. This case is currently under review by the Changsha mid-level court. Another corruption case implicated Li (former secretary in Chengzhou City) and Yang (former secretary in the Chengzhou Land and Mine Management Bureau), and some 158 people were involved in this case. Thus, it is true to say that, in relation to the 'fight' for 'resources or benefits', the 'cost' will not only be paid by the public but also by those in power.

However, what we expected never happens, while the unexpected has happened already.

According to the investigation in August 2006, the project introduced by the Changce government of Yizhang County in Chengzhou City (with registration capital of RMB¥ 500,000) has already obtained a mining licence

(Certification No. 4310000534514) and is valid from March 2005 to March 2008. The production capacity is set at 12,500 tons per year and covers an area of 2.16 square kilometres. The Company has already invested RMB¥ 3 million to dig three mines and purchase sixteen cleaning tables. Currently, two mines have been excavated to depths of 150 metres and 80 metres respectively. Wu (The Company's manager) said they will invest at least another RMB¥ 2 million in The Company and another RMB¥ 3 million to build an advanced mineral separation plant which is located in Yangtan village in the same county.

In order to maintain a good production environment in the area of excavation, at the beginning of 2007, the local government of Changce distributed 3,000 copies of promotional materials and posted 200 announcements concerning the maintenance of a good production environment in the silver mine at Changce around each community. The local Party committee and government considered that what they did were new measures to implement the optimization of economic development environment.

Similarly, with the price of scheelite minerals increasing from RMB¥ 18,000 per ton in 2000 to RMB¥ 100,000 per ton in 2005, many illegal mines resumed activities under the economic upturn. Particularly in Yaogangxian, illegal excavations along the boundary of Yizhang County and Zixing City caused serious pollution such as the destruction of forests, separation pools located everywhere and cracks in the hills. What is worse, if it rains heavily, the cracks cause coast and mud rock flow, as the accidents in July 2006 demonstrate. According to confirmation by the Hunan Coal Security and Supervision Bureau, nine miners died and two went missing during that time, which did not include farmers coming from other provinces such as Hunan, Jiangxi and Guangxi who also died in the floods.

Comments on the case in August 2006

This case highlights the dichotomies between life and excessive profit, between ecology and pollution, between companies and civilians, between state council and local government, and between the current situation and sustainable development. I anticipated that the case of the Changce gold and silver mine would end in environmental and ecological success. To our disappointment, things have changed over time, and the positive achievements made by all levels of government and the media are only a distant memory, while the efforts made by each government and supervision sector have been to no avail. Especially in some areas of Chengzhou City, there have been many accidents and disasters due to illegal mining which have caused huge losses. When I review this case study, I feel sad and blame myself for not being able to do better. According to an old Chinese saying, 'If heaven sends down calamities, there is hope of weathering them; but if man brings them upon himself, there is no hope of escape'. I believe that time will justify everything.

The author's own thoughts on the case

I have my own principles of working: to appreciate what I did, learn how to do better and to try to do the best I can. I worked in the Science and Technology Administration Department for more than 10 years, and what I believed and practised was that respect for science is a supportive concept for administrative capability. This is in conformity with the Eight Honours and Eight Disgraces proposed by Chairman Hu jingtao in the socialist concept of honour and disgrace. Each official should uphold scientific ideology to observe phenomena and use scientific measures and knowledge to solve problems. With regard to the opposite, 'ignorance', we should not only be wary of the completely ignorant, but also the 'educated ignorant', namely those people who are educated but who lack administrative capability or are not able to apply scientific ideology to analyse and solve problems. What is more important, we should keep a watchful eye on the 'greedy ignorant', namely those who have been educated and possess good administrative capabilities, but who always prioritize profits and make decisions without conforming to rules or moral standards.

As Li Ruihuan (chairman of the National Committee of the Chinese People's Political Consultative Conference) said in a book entitled *Learn and Apply Philosophy*: the worst thing is those leaders who have a 'lack of knowledge, in the power position, in favour of subjective decisions'; if a leader lacks sufficient knowledge, it does not matter, he can try to learn; if a leader is lacking in knowledge and is in favour of subjective decisions, it does not matter, because he is not in a position of power and cannot make the final decision which will be widely implemented. On the other hand, if a leader is lacking in knowledge, in favour of subjective decisions and in a position of power, this is what is known as a 'trinity'. This is the worst-case scenario, because the possible consequences of this kind of person's decisions will be disastrous and impossible to put right.

Originated in 2002 and revised in 2006

18 How ground subsidence was solved in southern Jiangsu Province

Zhang Lei

As industrialization quickened and water consumption increased, many sectors and enterprises began extracting and using groundwater. Excess groundwater extraction can cause ground subsidence and groundwater pollution. The southern Jiangsu region is the fastest developing region in Jiangsu Province and one of the fastest developing regions in the Yangtze river delta, and even in the entire Chinese mainland. With the acceleration of economic development, this region has encountered water shortages and has thus begun extracting and using groundwater. In the course of groundwater extraction and use, the region has witnessed ground subsidence and pollution. The ability to properly handle the relations between development and the prevention of geological disasters has become an important issue for regional governments.

The provincial People's congress and the provincial government have paid close attention to the issue of excess groundwater extraction and use. In keeping with the principles of fundamentally solving the issue, monitoring the costs and changing the government's way of thinking in handling public affairs, they have adopted a series of effective measures and made some remarkable achievements.

Origin and impact of the issue

As industrialization and urbanization in the southern Jiangsu region have gained momentum, most surface water bodies have been polluted since the 1980s, although to varying degrees. Many units began drilling deep wells to extract groundwater (groundwater refers to the water deep under the ground, namely the water contained in the second confined aquifer[1] and below. It does not include the shallow groundwater. The deep well refers to the well drilled to extract the deep groundwater). As groundwater extraction increased annually in the southern Jiangsu region, the groundwater level declined dramatically, causing serious geological disasters.

First, ground subsidence is severe. Since 1991, a narrow subsidence funnel has formed along the Shanghai–Nanjing Railway in the region. By the end of 2000, areas totalling more than 5,000 square kilometres or accounting for

42 per cent of the whole southern Jiangsu plains had seen their ground subsidence exceed more than 200 millimetres. The areas east of the city of Changzhou and north of the city of Wuxi and the urban areas of Suzhou all saw their ground subsidence exceed 1,000 millimetres. The areas where ground subsidence was most severe were mainly where towns and townships were closely located and in particular places such as the Xixi region that were far away from the groundwater supply points. In 1999, the Jiangsu Institute of Surveying and Mapping of Geology conducted a special investigation into the topographic changes in the Xixi region and found that the maximum ground subsidence was up to 2.8 metres. The institute estimated that a low land with its elevation[2] below sea level had appeared in the region.

Second, economic loss is serious. The disasters of ground subsidence and ground fissure in the southern Jiangsu region have caused huge economic loss to the region. Preliminary estimates claimed that, by the end of 2002, the ground subsidence in the region had caused a loss of 2,969 billion cubic metres of earth and 35,849 billion yuan in direct economic loss. If the direct economic loss of about 1.28 billion yuan arising from ground fissure disasters is added, the total economic loss was 37.129 billion yuan. If the natural and geographic conditions of the southern Jiangsu region, the damage arising from the disasters of ground subsidence and ground fissure, and the region's locational advantage and economic development are taken into consideration, the region has become one of China's worst regions to suffer from the disasters of ground subsidence and ground fissure.

Third, what has happened in the southern Jiangsu region is by no means an exception. Similar cases exist elsewhere. A report from the geological and mineral investigation departments in Jiangsu, Shanghai and Zhejiang indicated that ground subsidence had caused a 350-billion-yuan loss to the central region of the Yangtze river delta. The report, entitled 'Investigation and Evaluation of the Groundwater Resources and Geological Disasters in the Region of the Yangtze River Delta', was the result of 5 years of investigations by these departments. Geological disasters of regional ground subsidence and ground fissure existed in a 100,000-square-kilometre area of the Yangtze river delta (south of the Yangtze river). In particular, the urban areas of Shanghai, the southern region of Jiangsu and the Hang-Jia-Hu region of Zhejiang had become three regional subsidence centres. Their maximum subsidence was 2.63 metres, 1.08 metres and 0.82 metres respectively. In addition, ground subsidence in the region of the Yangtze river delta tended to merge.

Fourth, the social impact is inestimable. Water use involves millions of families and millions of enterprises. Excess groundwater extraction and use cause ground subsidence. In addition, when the subsidence reaches a certain level, it will not only affect the production and operation of these enterprises, but it will also affect the normal lives of the people. More importantly, it can cause social panic. In the long run, it will also affect the investment environment of the southern Jiangsu region. Currently, it is a thorny issue to properly handle the contradiction between the water demand of the people and enterprises and the control over groundwater extraction and use.

Government measures

As groundwater is widely extracted and used, administrative measures alone are inadequate for a fundamental solution to this problem. Therefore, the Jiangsu Provincial People's Congress enacted the *Decisions on Banning Groundwater Extraction within a Time Limit in the Southern Jiangsu Region* (hereinafter the Decisions) in August 2000. The Decisions provided that groundwater extraction would be banned before 31 December 2003 in those places where groundwater had been overextracted and would be completely banned before 31 December 2005 in the southern Jiangsu region. The Decisions demanded that the approval of well drilling would be stopped and the drilling of deep wells prohibited as from the date when the Decisions came into force. Before the ban on groundwater extraction was enforced, the provincial government would reduce the total amount of groundwater extraction in the southern Jiangsu region and designate groundwater extraction quotas on an annual basis. The units and individuals extracting and using groundwater must measure their water use and pay royalties for groundwater resources. In addition, the construction of the projects designed to supply surface water would be speeded up and a regional water supply connected. The introduction of the Decisions signalled that groundwater extraction and use had entered a stage of exercising water administration according to the law.

Specific methods

As they were responsible for the natural environment and sustainable development, the governments in the southern Jiangsu region paid close attention to this work and strictly enforced the Decisions. In light of the local practical conditions, they adopted the following effective measures.

1 *Conducting extensive publicity.* Taking full advantage of the media, the governments in the region carried out publicity activities in various forms, at various levels and from various angles. In addition to television reports, newspaper articles and radio interviews, they organized field publicity in the central areas of the cities to increase public awareness of the necessity for the ban on groundwater extraction and the capping of wells, which has created a good social atmosphere.

2 *Investigating the actual situation.* After the Decisions were promulgated, the governments in the region immediately stopped approving the drilling of deep wells and cancelled the approval of undrilled wells. In the meantime, they swiftly organized forces to conduct detailed investigations

of the deep wells throughout the region and to work out well-capping plans on the basis of these investigations. According to investigations, the ban on groundwater extraction in the southern Jiangsu region involved twenty-one counties (cities and districts), 263 towns and townships, 3,481 villages and 3,892 enterprises and units. Excess groundwater extraction covered 3,935 square kilometres or one-third of the southern Jiangsu plains. Records showed that the largest annual groundwater extraction was 450 million cubic metres in 1995.

3   *Defining working procedures.* The governments in the southern Jiangsu region worked out a plan for capping wells in phases in light of the regional water supply plan and the water use of the enterprises. The plan highlighted 'five first steps and five later steps'. First, the deep wells within the water supply networks would be capped first and those in the extended areas of the water supply networks would be capped later in keeping with the priority principle. Second, the deep wells used for industrial purposes would be capped first and those for domestic purposes would be capped later in keeping with the principle of life first and production second. Third, the deep wells owned by Chinese-invested enterprises would be capped first and those owned by foreign-invested enterprises would be capped later in keeping with the principle of creating a healthy investment environment. Fourth, the deep wells used for general purposes would be capped first and those for special purposes would be capped later in keeping with the differentiation principle. Fifth, the suspended, standby and dead wells would be capped first and the extraction wells would be capped later in keeping with the principle of doing easy things first and difficult things second. Meanwhile, the necessary time would be provided for the water-using units to transform their water supply facilities and to ensure that both well capping and economic development would not be affected.

4   *Organizing professional teams.* In order to ensure that no new pollution and damage would occur to the groundwater environment after wells were capped, the regional governments instructed those water control technical extension stations with more professionals and technicians and advanced construction equipment to form professional well-capping teams to enforce the ban on groundwater extraction and execute the technical requirements of well capping. First, the deep wells with poor water quality, minimal quantity and poor value were permanently filled in with clean earth, while those with good water quality, high water volume and of reserve and observational value were capped with cover plates. Second, unified cover plates cast with warning signs were made for well capping so as to prevent the well mouths from being reopened. Third, the cover plates had an observation hole in the centre that could be opened and closed as necessary.

5   *Introducing supporting policies.* After making scientific calculations, the governments decided that municipal finance would provide 4,000 yuan

of financial support for the capping of each deep well. In the meantime, the governments also introduced a host of supporting policies to promote water transformation and conservation and to encourage well capping. First, regional water supply projects would be constructed, the transformation of the water use networks in various regions would be speeded up, and support would be given to the regions that were experiencing difficulties. Second, the substitution of water resources would be expedited. New water plants for industrial purposes would be built to provide purified surface water to the photoelectric subzones of the development zones and to reduce their demand for groundwater and urban running water. Third, the groundwater royalties would be raised repeatedly in light of the spirit of the relevant documents of the provincial price bureau so that price leverage would fully play its role in promoting the ban on groundwater extraction. Fourth, the governments would allocate special funds for the construction of water supply networks to make up the deficiencies arising from the ban on groundwater extraction.

6   *Establishing files.* All the regional governments established files for each of the capped deep wells. The files contained information about the water level, water quality, extraction volume and geographic location of each well over the years. These files, which are stored in a database and managed by computers, will provide detailed basic data for future groundwater management. More importantly, these files can help prevent future land development, municipal construction, urbanization and other uncertain factors from causing unfavourable impacts on the capped deep wells and can effectively protect the fruits of the well-capping efforts.

We can see that the governments in the southern Jiangsu region have handled the well-capping issue with careful consideration, good preparation and effective measures. They made meticulous arrangements for each link in their work on the basis of conducting in-depth investigations and having full information. In this way, not only was the well-capping task fulfilled both quantitatively and qualitatively, but also economic development was not seriously affected. While pressure from the government was strong, the practical interests of the water-using units were fully taken into account. The macro-arrangements were well conceived and the execution details elaborate.

Results and follow-up measures

By the end of October 2005, the southern Jiangsu region had capped 4,831 wells (except the eighty-six wells to be preserved with the approval of the provincial government), thus comprehensively fulfilling the goal of banning groundwater extraction within 3 years for the areas with excess extraction and within 5 years for the areas without excess extraction. The move produced a positive impact on the country as a whole. In summary, they completed three main projects.

1 The well-capping project

Over the 5 years, the southern Jiangsu region capped a total of 4,831 wells, of which 2,798 wells were in Suzhou, 1,100 wells in Wuxi and 933 wells in Changzhou (see Table 18.1). Total investment was about 50 million yuan.

2 The regional water supply project

Over the 5 years, the southern Jiangsu region invested more than 10 billion yuan in regional water supply projects. The capacities of the water plants built totalled 3.02 million tons, and 2,012.07 kilometres of trunk pipelines were laid to reach the towns, thus ensuring water supply to 244 towns and townships. While the people in the areas where groundwater extraction is banned can have safe drinking water, a water supply for urban and rural life and production is basically guaranteed.

3 The ground subsidence warning project

After 3 years of hard work, a topographic change monitoring network covering 12,000 square kilometres was established with an investment of 30 million yuan.

Since the provincial people's congress promulgated the Decisions in 2000, the southern Jiangsu region has made remarkable achievements in banning groundwater extraction. Monitoring data indicate that the scope of the regional groundwater funnel has gradually shrunk. By the end of 2004, the 40-metre water table[3] contour has regressed by 38 per cent, from 3,950 square kilometres at the end of 2000 to 2,445 square kilometres. From 2000 to the end of 2004, the three central cities of Suzhou, Wuxi and Changzhou saw the average water tables of their second confined aquifers rise by between 4 and 18 metres. The groundwater table rose further in 2005. The water tables in the Suzhou region all returned to the 30-metre safety line or above. As a result, groundwater resources and the environment have been visibly restored and improved.

The ground subsidence monitoring data for the same period also indicate that the subsidence velocity in the region has continued to slow down. In 2004, the annual subsidence velocity ranged between 10 and 25 millimetres.

Table 18.1 Well capping in the southern Jiangsu region over 5 years.

Region	2001	2002	2003	2004	2005	Wells preserved	Subtotal
Suzhou	841	709	792	188	219	49	2,798
Wuxi	267	354	385	37	36	21	1,100
Changzhou	287	260	292	62	16	16	933
Total	1,359	1,323	1,469	287	271	86	4,831

Throughout the region, no place posted an annual subsidence velocity larger than 35 millimetres. A global positioning system (GPS) survey indicates that the maximum subsidence velocity in the region was 31.5 millimetres (Wuxi's Yuqi satellite village). The area with an accumulated subsidence larger than 200 millimetres has stabilized at 6,000 square kilometres in the past 2 years.

Thanks to the deepening of the ban on groundwater extraction in the southern Jiangsu region, groundwater extraction dropped sharply from 288 million cubic metres in 2000 to 40 million cubic metres in 2004. Currently, groundwater extraction is zero. As a result, the region's share of total groundwater extraction in the Yangtze river delta has gradually reduced. Compared with neighbouring provinces, the ground subsidence velocity has also reduced.

On the basis of these preliminary achievements, the governments in the southern Jiangsu region adopted relevant follow-up measures.

First, to continue to publicize the importance of protecting groundwater resources. The continuous extensive and intensive publicity helped further increase public awareness of the importance of managing and protecting groundwater resources, and to mobilize various forces to monitor and support the ban on groundwater extraction.

Second, to continue to supervise and inspect the deep wells preserved for special industries and strictly execute the annual quotas for groundwater extraction assigned by the provincial authorities.

Third, to continue to improve the enforcement inspections of the capped wells to prevent illegal well drilling and reopening, and to consolidate the results of the well-capping efforts.

Fourth, to continue to conduct groundwater dynamic monitoring to accumulate the basic data for the management of groundwater resources.

Fifth, to conduct studies on using groundwater as emergency water resources so as to enhance water security capacities when unexpected water pollution, poisoning, terrorist attack and other unexpected events occur.

Conclusions

Thanks to 5 years of effort, ground subsidence arising from excess groundwater extraction and use in the southern Jiangsu region has been effectively controlled, and the water table in the region has been steadily rising. More importantly, a mandatory mechanism for controlling groundwater extraction and use has been established, which will provide an effective guarantee for the region's sustainable development.

As indicated by this case study, excess groundwater extraction and use has serious wide-ranging implications. If not properly handled, the issue can cause unimaginable consequences. The Jiangsu Provincial People's Congress and Provincial People's Government turned from retrospective rectification to active prevention and from passive response to active effort, and have achieved relative success. This is a striking feature of this case study. The government's traditional approach to public affairs is to offer direct relief, which is a passive and responsive action. Accordingly, this approach focuses on what can be done once an event has occurred. However, the most effective approach is to prevent a public event from happening and to use as little money as possible to prevent such an event from occurring instead of using lots of money to conduct rectification. Therefore, in handling public events, a modern government should emphasize active prevention and take decisive measures to remove the inducing factors of the public event before substantial damage is done.

Another feature of this case study is that the working method for handling public events is to emphasize legislation and administration according to the law instead of relying only on administrative means.

The government's traditional approach to public events emphasizes that swift administrative measures are used to cope with emergencies. For example, the traditional approach normally emphasizes the establishment of interim leading groups, full social mobilization and the adoption of the human wave strategy. With this approach, there are no well-defined provisions on the institutions set by the government to deal with public events, the functions, status, powers, responsibilities and fund sources of the government and its coordinating departments, and the rights and obligations of citizens. When a modern government handles public events, all necessary measures must be carried out within the constitutional and legal framework, namely exercising administration according to the law. The governments in the southern Jiangsu region took the Decisions of the Provincial People's Congress as the legal basis for their work, and further defined their working rules in light of local practical conditions, which provided a solid system guarantee for all-round orderly monitoring of groundwater extraction and use.

Written in 2006

Notes

1 The deep groundwater in the southern Jiangsu region is mainly located in the first, second and third confined aquifers, with the water levels being between 10 and 20 metres, 60 and 100 metres and 100 to 170 metres respectively. In particular, the groundwater in the second aquifer is noted for its wide distribution, large quantity and good quality, and is therefore the main source of groundwater extraction. The groundwater in the first aquifer is less extracted and supplied faster.
2 The elevation of a place refers to the absolute height between the ground surface and sea level. The base point of China's sea level refers to the mean sea level of the Yellow Sea worked out on the basis of the results of 18 years of observations conducted at the Qingdao Tide Observation Station.
3 The distance between the groundwater ceiling and the ground surface is also called the relative height. According to the relevant technical specifications, the area with a relative height exceeding 40 metres is a warning area, the area with a relative height ranging between 30 and 40 metres is an alert area and the area with a relative height of less than 30 metres is a safe area.

19 On selecting a location for the Nanxi River Water Conservancy Project

Zhang Miaogen

In 2000, the Yongjia County Government (YJCG), Wenzhou Municipality, Zhejiang Province, began to plan the construction of the Nanxi River Water Conservancy Project (NRWCP), which was considered to greatly benefit social, economic and environmental areas. The proposed NRWCP included Baojiang reservoir and Yongle Water Diversion Works. It was proposed that the former be located within the buffer reserve area for the famous Nanxi River Scenic Spot, which was named the National Tourist Scenic Spot by the State Council in 1988, and that the latter be located just inside the area of the Scenic Spot. According to the national laws and regulations for the review and approval of construction projects within scenery and cultural heritage areas, the project could not be recognized until the feasibility of its siting had been demonstrated by the specialists in scenery and cultural heritage conservation. However, the comments from the specialists were that the location selected for the proposed project was both unsuitable and unreasonable because it would impact on the ecosystem and destroy the resources of natural scenery and cultural heritage. In order to resolve the conflicts between development and conservation, the Wenzhou Municipal Government held meetings to hear comments and suggestions from specialists and relevant agencies.

Comments from investors

The YJCG believed that the priorities of NRWCP were to control floods and supply water. The construction of the project was the fundamental method to deal with problems of livelihood and development for people living in the areas along the section of the river within Yongjia County and Liuhong Plain within Leqing City. First of all, flood disasters occur frequently in the valley of the Nanxi river. Since Liberation in 1949, there have been twenty-three flood disasters, which resulted in major losses. Therefore, it was necessary and urgent to construct the water control works in the river's upper reach. Second, the area along the river bank within Yongjia County is its political, economic and cultural centre. The population and gross production value of industry and agriculture accounted for a quarter and two-thirds of the county total respectively. However, the people living in the area along the river bank suffered from lack of fresh water due to the limitations of natural conditions. Nanxi River Diversion Works (constructed in 1997) had resolved many water problems for the people in the area and had also supplied water to the Wenzhou power plant. However, the capacity of the water supply was limited to 100,00 cubic metres/day in the dry season because there was no special reservoir in the upper reach area and a sluice gate was located in the lower reach at the intake point. The average volume of water supply was 70,000 cubic metres/day in 2001. If the increase rate year on year was 10 per cent, the amount of water demand was over 100,000 cubic metres/day. Therefore, it was necessary and urgent to build a special reservoir. In addition, Hongliu Plain in Leqing City with its high population density and developed economy was severely short of water, which had further restricted economic and social development. Particularly in the Liushi area, the amount of water supplied could only satisfy demand in 2004, even if all possible capacity was included. If Baojiang reservoir was built, it would be a multi-year regulating reservoir with a capacity of 507 million cubic metres, which would fulfil in the long term production and domestic demands in the area along the river bank in Yongjia County, including the Wenzhou power plant. Therefore, the water problem in Hongliu Plain within Leqing City would be completely resolved. Third, water could be used to generate electricity as well as for flood control and water supply. The installation capacity of the hydropower station is 64,000 kW, while the average power production for multi-years is 127 million kW/h. With a greater capacity, the reservoir could be used for adjusting peak flow and in case of accidents occurring within the Wenzhou electrical power network system. Fourth, it would facilitate the improvement of the water environment of the Nanxi river. According to the data from the hydrometric station, water flow in the flood season was over 6,000 times that in the dry season, and the results from both flood and dry seasons had impacted on tourism in the Nanxi River Scenic Spot. The water in the reservoir was introduced by gravity through the Nanxi river into the channel of the diversion works, then directed towards Leqing City. The regulation of the reservoir would reduce the flow gaps between the flood and dry seasons and a balanced water level would be maintained; therefore, no more flood or drought disasters would occur. In addition, the water would be available for flushing sewage and assimilation in the dry season. Fifth, it would enlarge the area of the Scenic Spot. The reservoir would form a water surface area of 15.4 million square metres, similar to a large lake in the highlands, which would offer new vistas for sightseeing, holidays, recreation and summer resorts. In addition, the dam, at over 100 metres high, would provide a significant view. Sixth, it would assist in poverty reduction through relocation and urbanization promotion. Those people affected by the reservoir construction would be largely resettled in areas where the economy had been developed comparatively in Yongjia County and Leqing City. Such relocations would improve people's living standards and would also facilitate the areas' urbanization. At the same time, resettlement would reduce pollution sources, which in turn would improve water resources and ecosystems within the Nanxi river valley.

According to the above comments, it was necessary and reasonable to construct the NRWCP on the basis of the social, economic and ecological benefits of the project.

Comments from objectors

The location selected for the proposed project caught the attention of all those specialists renowned in the country for scenery and cultural heritage conservation. The opposition, represented by Xie Ninggao, senior adviser in scenery and cultural heritage from the Ministry of Construction, director of the China World Heritage Centre, as well as a professor at Beijing University, raised the following objections.

First, the Nanxi River Scenic Spot is famous for its beautiful lakes, exotic rocks, waterfalls, old villages, enchanting fish and forests. The village hamlets possess their special characteristics of promoting 'the culture of farming and reading'. With the perfect harmony of the culture of farming and reading with the natural scenery of beautiful lakes and mountains, it is an out-standing reflection of ancient Chinese agricultural civilization society. The ancient village hamlets have been nominated for the World Heritage List, thanks to their well-preserved and unique characteristics which are of high historic and cultural value. If the project were implemented, the impacts of engineering construction on the scenery and cultural heritage spots would be disastrous, and it would also break the promise made by the central government to the world to preserve the site. Second, the project would severely impact on the ecosystem, the core of the Nanxi River Scenic Spot. The reservoir, with a dam 120 metres high, would inundate an area of 15 square kilometres in the upper reach along with all the vegetation, old trees and precious plants as well as some natural views such as waterfalls. In the lower reach, the water diversion works would bar the way for some aquatic migrating animals to return to the sea, which would kill them. Third, in the upper reach of the river, the proposed reservoir would destroy much of the natural landscape, in which Yubei and Xikou are both typical ancient villages famous for their historical cultural characteristics. Yubei village is the birthplace of a major scholar (a title conferred on the candidate who came first in the highest imperial examination) in the Southern Song Dynasty named Wang, who was later appointed a minister of the Ministry of Personnel in feudal China and a member of the imperial academy. The village is home to thirty-five generations of his family. Over a period of 800 years, one person was number one scholar, eight people were successful candidates in the highest imperial examination, and ten people were successful candidates in the second highest imperial examination. The motto of the Wang family was 'Be rich by farming and be glorious by reading'. Yubei village is typical of 'the culture of farming and reading' in the Nanxi river reaches. The great ancestral hall of the Wang family, built in the Song Dynasty, still exists and was constructed according to the design concepts and the principle of 'wu xing ping hen' ('wu xing' means the five elements – metal, wood, water, fire and earth) held by the ancients to compose the physical universe and was later used in other fields, such as traditional Chinese medicine, to explain various physiological and pathological phenomena ('ping he' means balance). In the village, there are some 500 households and the ancient buildings account for 90 per cent of these, mostly in the styles of the Ming and Qing Dynasties. Each ancient building has its own distinguished name. Many bear honorific boards, arches, tablets and plaques, which reflect the characteristics of the farming and reading culture. Since Liberation, the village has been home to many future college students, senior engineers, professors and doctoral supervisors. In Xikou village, one family boasted six successful candidates in the highest imperial examination in four generations. There are many stories such as this and many ancient buildings, such as Xishui Pavilion, Jinshi Tomb, Shuangjian Palace, as well as the remains of an armed uprising during the Liberation War.

Fourth, the Nanxijang River Scenic Spot and the ancient village hamlets with their rich cultural characteristics and beautiful natural scenery are attracting more and more domestic and overseas tourists. In addition, national and international specialists and scholars are taking an increasing interest in them. In the summer of 2001, Zhao Qunli, a photographer and vice director of Hong Kong Phoenix Television, was killed in an accident when he was on a mission to film a bird's-eye view of the Nanxi river and ancient village hamlets in order to promote the unique scenery of beautiful mountains and lakes to the outside world. All aspects of the media drew the attention of the tourist industry to the ancient village hamlets and the Nanxi river. Fifth, the natural flow of water is the life blood of the Nanxi river. The proposed project would intercept the water in the 70-kilometre-long section of the upper reach of the river. Particularly in the case of low rainfall, the lack of water running into the river would be catastrophic. The river would dry up, even sections of the middle and lower reaches, and the scenic spots of lakes and beautiful mountains would be destroyed. In summary, the proposed project could never be implemented if the above factors are taken into consideration.

At the same time, those opposing the proposal were residents of about ten villages situated along the river bank who wrote repeatedly to the authorities at all levels to express their objections to the proposed project. They believed that the developing tourist industry on the Nanxi river had brought significant economic benefits. At the same time, economic agriculture in the peripheral mountainous areas had been developed. The proposed project would destroy the scenery and cultural heritage, and would severely impact on tourism. Subsequently, it would impact directly on the incomes of local people. When the working teams for the proposed project sent by the county government arrived in the villages, the residents expressed strong resentment towards the teams and claimed that the project was being promoted for political ends by unscrupulous officials using outdated powers. Therefore, they applied for interviews with the higher authorities at various levels of government or non-government organs to appeal for help to halt the proposed project and to protect the river.

A heated discussion ensued based on the differing viewpoints linked with protection and development as well as the useful or harmful aspects of the project. The discussion also attracted the attention and concern of the Zhejiang provincial government. Several leaders from the relevant departments at the provincial level visited the sites and demanded that Wenzhou Municipal Government and the relevant departments be responsible for demonstrating and appraising the advantages and disadvantages of the proposed project.

Initial decision

Through the demonstration and appraisal exercise conducted by the Wenzhou Municipal Government and relevant specialists, the following comments were made for the siting of the NRWCP. The proposed project was approved, but the conflicting interests with the scenic spots were to be resolved and the water conservancy departments put in charge of developing the engineering technical programme. According to the decision, the water conservancy departments proposed the following measures.

First, the two ancient village hamlets affected by the reservoir within the upper reach of the river would be relocated by the principle of duplication, which would maintain the original planning, layout and construction style. Second, it would be necessary to make holes in the dam in order to ensure daily runoff of the river. Third, a moveable rubber dam at the river mouth would be needed. The necessary water flow in the lower reach of the dam would then be met through adjusting the height of the weir. Several meetings were held, attended only by the people from the water conservancy departments, but no specialists in scenery and cultural heritage took part. As a result, no other comments from them were forthcoming.

In June 2001, YJCG submitted the report concerning the location selection and project proposal to Zhejiang Provincial Construction Bureau, which is responsible for the administration of scenery and cultural heritage spots. Upon receiving the report, the Provincial Construction Bureau asked several specialists in scenery and cultural heritage to demonstrate and appraise the feasibility of the proposal. The participants reached an agreement and stated that the protection of the ancient village hamlets should focus on their authenticity and complete uniqueness. It would not be possible to retain the authentic and original style of the old buildings through relocation. Second, a large number of residents lived in the two ancient village hamlets, which also contained many well-preserved historic buildings. It would be very difficult to arrange resettlement and relocation, particularly as no special funds were available to finance the work. Third, making holes in the dam to allow the release of water meant throwing away investors' money. If no effective measures were adopted, it would be impossible to make the method of water release effective. Fourth, the rubber dam method seemed a good way of maintaining water flow in the Nanxi river. However, such man-made adjustments would change the natural features and functions of the rivers, landforms and wild life, finally causing the original ecosystem to deteriorate.

Comments from responsible departments

After arranging site visits and conducting several meetings at the sites, as well as taking the different comments into consideration, the Provincial Construction Bureau finally made the decision that the proposed project should not be located in the area of the Nanxi River Scenic Spot. The reasons were given as follows. First, in terms of resources, it was obvious that the proposed project would impact on the ecosystem in the area of the Nanxi river valley and destroy the resources of scenery and cultural heritage, particularly those within the ancient village hamlets. Second, with regard to administration, the proposed project would be located within the area of national level Scenic Spots, but this had not been reflected in the Nanxi River Master Plan approved by the State Council. Therefore, there was no legal basis for the proposed project. Third, in terms of scale, the proposed project would take at least 5 years to complete. In addition, resettlement would be difficult. According to investigations, there were 21,000 people living in the area. Living there from generation to generation, they loved their homes. In particular, the tourism industry had brought benefits to the area, and few people were in favour of resettlement. Thus it could be estimated that the large scale of the project would bring great challenges in the form of financial issues, such as construction costs, funds for resettlement as well as loss of income from tourism. Yongjia County was not rich enough to finance such a project. Finally, the proposed functions of the project would be addressed as follows.

To ease flooding, the forest that had been planted on the river side in the 1950s and 1960s would act as an effective means of control. According to the causes of disasters, each disaster was almost always caused by mountain landslide and destruction by tide water wrecking unlicensed buildings within the areas where construction was forbidden. The way to resolve the flooding problems of the Nanxi river could be to build a 'green reservoir' by planting large areas of forest and consolidating a flood protection dyke in the lower river outside the Nanxi River Scenic Spot.

The problem of generating electricity could be resolved through the electric grid. The target of the first stage of the Three Gorges Hydropower Project is to serve Jiangsu and Zhejiang Provinces and Shanghai Municipality. Therefore, it would be unnecessary to build a hydropower station.

It was deemed unnecessary to regulate the water flow. The average annual rainfall in the area of the Nanxi river was over 1,800 millimetres, and even in a very dry season – a rare occurrence – the river had never dried up. Bamboo rafts would be available year round; therefore, there would be no adverse impact on tourism. Moreover, the dry season is also a slack period for tourism.

The issue of supplying water to Leqing City could be resolved without building dams, by drawing water from the section of the river downstream outside the Nanxi River Scenic Spot. There was another way; namely to build a reservoir in the mountain area in Leqing to regulate water supply, on the basis of drawing more in rainy seasons and less in dry seasons, in order to fulfil the city's needs.

Dilemma of the Wenzhou government

As the organizer for the project, the Wenzhou Municipal Government faced a dilemma. On one hand, the proposed project needed to be developed in the short term according to the NRWCP approved by the Wenzhou Municipal Government, and the master plan for the Oujiang river valley approved by the provincial government. The proposed project had also been listed in the municipal and provincial Tenth Five-year Plans. The proposed project would not only address the water supply issues for Leqing City and Yongjia County but also draw significant income from power generation. It was a good deed that the government should do for its people. In addition, the preparation work was nearly completed, such as topographical surveys, geological prospecting and earthquake resistance tests, which had cost in total RMB 10.6 million yuan. If the proposed project could not be implemented, all the money spent would be wasted. On the other hand, the proposed project would be located within the area of the National Scenic Spot, which was opposed by specialists, local people and the departments responsible for the administration of the Scenic Spot. If the suggestions raised by them were adopted, the natural resources as well as tourist resources would be well maintained, which would be of great benefit to the local people. It was also a good deed that the government could do for its people.

The question was: How to make the decision on the proposed project linked with how to deal with the conflicts between development and protection? Wenzhou Municipal Government faced the challenge of making a win–win decision for both development and protection.

Conclusion

With care and assistance from the Ministry of Construction and Zhejiang provincial government, Zhejiang Provincial Construction Bureau rejected the report advocating approval of NRWCP and its design proposal in April 2002, which meant protection of the unique natural resources and historic heritage of the Nanxi River Scenic Spot. At the same time, Zhejiang Provincial Construction Bureau put forward suggestions for domestic water supply to Leqing City.

Although the story of siting for the NRWCP has reached its conclusion, the conflicts between development and protection will continue in all areas, particularly in developing countries. In order to deal with them effectively, full consideration of all the issues is necessary. If NRWCP were implemented in a hurry, what would happen to the beautiful Nanxi river as well as the famous Nanxi River Scenic Spot?

In the past, I have been responsible for construction, environment, transportation and science technology at county and municipal level. Currently, I am commissioner of the Provincial Construction Bureau. Our responsibilities include accelerating urban and rural development, supplying the public with more products and services, and promoting economic and social development quickly and smoothly. Furthermore, we are committed to strengthening the protection of resources and the environment, to maintaining the harmony of human beings with nature and to realizing sustainable development in the face of the restriction of resources and environment conditions. In the course of my daily work, I often meet the problems demonstrated in this case study, such as the conflicts between protection of scenery and historical resources, and utilization and development, the protection of our historic heritage and the renovation of old cities, as well as urban enlargement and the capacity of the ecosystem. On the one hand are the issues of modern life. On the other hand, it is my historical mission to resolve such issues through wisdom and skill. I strongly believe that, in order to carry out the general requirements of the strategy of scientific development, to establish a harmonious society promulgated by the Central Committee of the Chinese Communist Party, to implement 'the 8–8 Strategies' to build a 'Safe Zhejiang', accelerate the construction of a grand cultural province and to actively build a 'Zhejiang Ruled by Law', which comprise the strategic plan combined for economy, politics, culture and society, we should lay more emphasis on the concept of a human-oriented view and the harmony of human beings with nature and scientific development. We should give full rein to the leading functions of such public policies as urban and rural planning in the construction field and to the function of organizing public resources so that we can retain our beautiful nature with its clean waters and green mountains for future generations.

Written in 2002

20 Sixiao Highway: from difficulty to success

Zhao Jin

Construction and environmental protection are one of the contradictions of modern society. However, the Sixiao Highway project demonstrates a good combination of tropical rainforest, modern science and national customs, and is a successful example of local government. This highway implemented scientific theory and the sustainable capacity of human beings and nature, and realized economic progress through environmental protection. Hu Jintao, the general secretary of the CPC Central Committee, praised this highway in his inspection of Yunnan Province in May 2006.

A golden passageway in nature reserves at national level

Sixiao Highway is also known as Simao–Xiao Mengyang Highway. Its overall length is 97.75 kilometres, and it is based on a national fourth-class road constructed in the 1950s. The construction was completed and opened on 6 April 2006. This highway is located in Xishuangbanna, a well-known tourist area. It is the only modern highway passing through natural reserves of tropical rainforest at a national level.

- *Golden passageway.* The Sixiao Highway is an important section of the Kunming–Bangkok Highway, which is an exit route from Yunnan Province and a trunk road from Yunnan to southeast Asia and south Asia. It is also a key route of the province in international regional cooperation and benefits Yunnan's participation in the construction of the Sino-ASEAN free trade zone. So far, the section of the Kunming–Bangkok Highway in Thailand has been completed, and the section in Laos is under construction. After the completion of the last section of the Xiao Mengyang–Mohang Highway in China in 2007, it will take only 20 hours to drive from Kunming to Bangkok in Thailand. A report by the Asian Development Bank (2005) said that, according to the Economic Cooperation Plan of the Mekong River subregion, the 2000-kilometre-long Kunming–Bangkok highway is being upgraded. If there is a highway network from Bangkok to Singapore and Kunming and then on to Beijing, it will ease transportation costs between Beijing and the

Malaysian Peninsula and offer more convenient travel for people, vehicles and goods, as well as promote trade between China and the Mekong River region and the more remote areas. This is known as the North–South Economic Gallery. It is the trunk road for Yunnan's transportation in central and southern areas, including the Kunming-Yuxi-Simao-Xishuangbanna Highways. A total of eleven counties and cities will benefit from this highway. The highway runs through areas with dense population and abundant products, as well as a production base for tobacco, cane sugar, salt, tea, rubber and grain. Moreover, it is a world-renowned tourist area and has great potential for economic development.

- *Passageway of helping the poor.* Yunnan Province is located on the southwest border of China. It is a western border area and a province of minority nationalities, mountainous terrain and poverty. Minority nationalities of Dai, Lagu and Bulang live along the Sixiao Highway, and their lives are very hard. This highway will help to develop the local economy and improve people's lives.
- *Strategic target.* Yunnan Province plans to develop the province by highlighting its unique characteristics of beautiful countryside, economic prosperity and national culture, and to enable a passageway between China and southeast Asia and south Asia during the development of western China. Sixiao Highway will no doubt form an important part of this strategy and will greatly contribute to the economic development of the province.

Project proposal

Research into the feasibility of the construction of the Sixiao Highway was begun by the highway construction department in February 1995 and completed in February 1997. The provincial government set up an expert group in May 2000 to study and discuss this project according to the Development of the West China Strategy. The group was headed by the provincial communications office and included provincial departments of the planning committee, environmental protection, communications, forestry, land, Simao Municipal Government, Xishuangbanna government and leaders and experts from the relevant departments. The head of the communications office was in charge of the group, the highway plan and design; the director of the Environmental Protection Bureau assumed responsibility for environmental protection, and other departments cooperated with them according to each function. After much deliberation, a report was submitted to Yunnan Provincial Government, which emphasized the following.

Currently, there is a national fourth-class highway that was constructed in the 1950s, namely the Simao–Xiao Mengyang Highway. This highway has seriously restricted the regional economic development of southeast Yunnan due to traffic jams, speed limits, accidents and low profits since the rise in traffic volume. Thus the renovation of this highway is essential to economic construction, opening up to the outside world and cooperating with southeast Asian countries. It needs to be renovated as soon as possible.

Contradiction: the golden passageway and the natural environment

The highway is an important symbol of modern society. However, it is likely to impact on the natural environment during construction and to damage the environment.

The tropical rainforest region enjoys most biological categories of the world, especially in Xishuangbanna, one of the world's top three large tropical rainforest regions and known as the kingdom of plants and animals, as well as a gene base of species. It is listed in the Top 10 Natural Reserves and International Biological Rim Protection Network by UNESCO. Xishuangbanna has more than 5,000 species of plants, 341 of which are rare and fifty-eight of which are nearly extinct. It not only belongs to Yunnan and China, but also to the world. It has attracted the attention of world governments, non-governmental organizations and experts and media circles because of its well-protected tropical rainforest system and rich variety of species.

There is one very difficult question concerning highway construction: the Sixiao Highway would pass through Xishuangbanna Natural Reserves, the only national tropical rainforest protection region. What effect will this large-scale highway construction have on the ecological environment?

There is an urgent need to construct the Sixiao Highway to further develop the economy of southeast Yunnan and to protect this unique tropical rainforest region during construction. No one would dare to damage this ecological system. How does one deal with this contradiction of highway reconstruction and environmental protection?

Many difficulties were encountered during the construction of the Sixiao Highway. The feasibility study took 5 years to prepare and offered three different routings: positive routing, D routing and C routing. Positive routing has obvious advantages of range, landform, engineering amount and cost, and was accepted in principle. However, a serious question was posed by the Yunnan Environmental Science Institute (YESI) during evaluating the routings in November 1997 when it was discovered that the structure of the natural reserves and the tropical rainforest would be damaged, and construction would harm the rare plants and Asian elephants. So, they suggested altering the routing.

The director of the ecological office at YESI, also an expert, participated in the evaluation and pointed out that China has few Asian elephants; they live mainly in the Mengyang region in Xishuangbanna. In the 1950s, the construction of No. 213 national highway divided the natural reserves into two parts. If the positive or the D routings were adopted, the natural reserves would be divided into three parts, and this would further impact on the living environment of the Asian elephant and other wild animals.

After comparing the substitute plan on natural reserves led by the provincial environmental protection bureau, a group of experts confirmed the C routing, which is near the former No. 213 national highway and would avoid splitting up the nature reserves. However, this routing would increase costs, the volume of work and the amount of time taken to complete the project.

There have been many comments from different sides on the routings which have resulted in heated argument:

- To construct a highway and improve transportation is the most important thing.
- Highway construction must come first, then ecological recovery; economic construction is the most urgent issue.
- The C routing will increase costs and amount of work and take more time.
- Any plan would result in damage to the ecological environment; for instance, tunnelling through mountains is now common in road construction.
- Which is more important: protecting the elephants or improving the lives of poor minority nationalities?
- Both the economy and ecology are important; we must protect the completeness and species of the tropical rainforest region.

A hard decision: C routing is determined at last

Yunnan Provincial Government paid close attention to the routing possibilities of Sixiao Highway and decided to take steps to maximize protection and recovery and minimize damage to the ecological region during construction. In May 2000, an expert group organized by the provincial government conducted a field investigation on the routing and environmental protection of the Sixiao Highway, and finally confirmed the routing after comparison and full discussion. Subsequently, they submitted the *Report of Routing and Environmental Protection of Natural Reserves during Construction of Simao-Xiao Mengyang Highway* to the Yunnan government.

The report pointed out that the C routing would pass through the natural reserves which are mainly secondary and economic forest, and this routing would minimize damage to the virgin forest. It would avoid the tropical rainforest and prevent a further division of natural reserves. Moreover, it would fully use the old road as a temporary area to store materials and processing machinery. The C routing was approved by the provincial government. The government also made a decision on additional investment in the highway. Investment in the C routing was increased to 3.95 billion yuan by the Ministry of Communications from 3 billion yuan in 1998; the numbers of bridges increased to 352 from fifty-four; tunnels increased to thirty from two; and the length of bridges and tunnels accounted for 26.4 per cent of the total highway. At Wild Elephant Valley, more than 70 per cent of the route comprised bridges and tunnels, an uncommon occurrence worldwide.

Establishing a strict management system for the project

In order to guarantee ecological environmental protection during construction, the Yunnan government established a responsibility hierarchy, and the Highway Construction Command Post (HCCP) formulated the Management Method on Water and Environmental Protection of Sixiao Highway, which offered effective protection for the ecological environment.

Yunnan provincial communications office set up an environmental protection committee of Sixiao Highway construction, and the office director served as chairman and two deputy directors served as vice chairmen. An office under the committee was in charge of environmental protection affairs. The committee strengthened environmental evaluation on project design and environmental supervision during construction. It strictly implemented a synchronic measure on ecological protection, environmental protection facilities and key project environmental protection, as well as combining environmental management with the construction management system. Contracted units had to undergo appropriate training before entering the construction field. The supervision unit was charged with compiling a supervision plan for each project according to the requirements of the Ministry of Communications and State Environmental Protection Administration of China, and each environmental protection project would be signed separately.

Yunnan Environmental Protection Agency (YEPA) and each relevant local environmental administration along the highway supervised the construction in strict accordance with the principle of the 'three synchronism'. YEPA continually examined ecological protection over a period of 3 years with forestry and hydraulic departments, as well as assisting the People's congress and political consultative conference on law enforcement inspection.

HCCP adopted simple and small section construction in accordance with the *Report of Environmental Protection Evaluation*. Every tree and shrub along the highway was protected as far as possible. Trees under bridges and near roadbeds were chopped down under strict supervision. The large trees were pruned appropriately. All rare plants growing along the route were labelled, and some were moved.

The Environmental Protection Office of Xishuangbanna was in charge of surveying and designating temporary roads for thirteen contracted construction sites. It designated seventy temporary roads, which both avoided forested areas and offered convenient transport for construction teams and equipment.

Environmental protection was taken very seriously during the construction process, with each tree and bush being well protected by builders. In one instance, the constructors widened a pilot road with an additional investment of more than 300,000 yuan to protect a 270-year-old ancient tree north of Wild Elephant Valley. Where a large banyan tree stood in the Red Sand River area, its branches extending to the highway, builders used a wire cable to hold the branches back from the highway. When construction began at Wild Elephant Valley, more than 30,000 builders worked as quietly as possible to protect the wild animals from noise pollution. When they saw an elephant, they would stop working, evacuate the area and assign someone to protect the animal. As a result of this protection, the elephants became very friendly with the builders. They often came to the nearby river and forest, sometimes even staying close by. There was no damage done on either side.

One day in November 2003, a group of wild elephants came to the warehouse near the bridge of Wild Elephant Valley and stayed there for the whole night and the following day. The keeper of the warehouse discovered that a female elephant was giving birth while the other elephants clustered around it. This situation lasted for one day and two nights before the baby elephant was born.

However, some illegal events did occur, such as when a construction unit cut down trees along the highway without permission, and the government, as well as reprimanding the person in charge, fined the company 5.86 million yuan.

Realizing a win–win situation on development and protection

The Sixiao Highway was completed and came into effect on 6 April 2006. It is an excellent construction project combining natural protection with modernization. The tropical rainforest has been effectively protected. When passing through this ecological highway, people will experience a beautiful environment, ancient forest, landscapes and local customs. People can see treetops, wide fields, valleys and mountains. One veteran driver said he had been driving on the Kunming–Xishuangbanna route for more than 20 years, but 'Sixiao Highway is the most comfortable highway for drivers, it's fantastic'.

The construction of the Sixiao Highway has claimed attention and recognition from relevant people and media both at home and abroad. According to the director of the Highway Management Office, they have received more than ten groups of visitors from home and six foreign consuls from Myanmar, Laos and southeast Asian countries.

The Sixiao Highway project won high praise from both sides, including people who had different viewpoints on the project, hardworking builders and local minority nationalities. Although the investment, construction and schedule exceeded the original forecast, it is a successful project. The ancient tropical rainforest of Xishuangbanna has been protected, which is the most important issue. It is the legacy of the Chinese people and government to later generations. On 21 July 2006, Xu Zuyuan, vice minister of the Ministry of Communications, made a special visit to Yunnan, where he strongly commended the construction theory of Sixiao Highway and pledged further support to highway construction in Yunnan.

Human beings and nature in perfect harmony

People experience serious disasters, such as mud rock flow, floods, drought, sandstorms and earthquakes, which are probably due to overcutting forests, steel-making and other ecological damage. If they violate natural law, people will be punished by nature. Today, we are facing a population explosion and resource shortages. What should we do: fight nature or respect the natural environment? Taking the Sixiao Highway as an example, we implemented harmonious theory at every step of the project, from project setting and routing designation through to construction. Thanks to the C routing plan, our tropical rainforest has been well protected.

The director of Yunnan Communications Office said the success of the Sixiao Highway indicates that we can realize a win–win situation on highway construction and environmental protection. With the development of people's lives, highway construction cannot be limited to infrastructure; it is not only a construction project, but also a comprehensive project of environmentally friendly policies, safety, comfort and economy, in which environmental protection comes first.

The head of YEPA also said that the Sixiao Highway construction project demonstrates that in order to implement scientific development and construct a harmonious society, we must rely on environmental protection. The synchronism of development and protection is not only necessary but achievable. The Sixiao Highway extends to the mountains but also enters our practice in the development of science, civilization and sustainability. It benefits the whole society through caring for nature, protecting ecology and assuming responsibility for the environment.

The success of the Sixiao Highway also demonstrates that the harmonious development of human beings and nature is the requirement of science, and we should not go against it. During economic development, there will always be a contradiction between human beings and nature, environment and resources, development and protection, which can sometimes be quite serious. If we handle the environment well, later generations will benefit from rather than suffer the consequences. A crucial issue is to transfer the theory of fighting nature to working with nature. Local government will be tested on strategic thinking, leading capacity and performance through implementing scientific development theory, key construction projects and decisions.

The construction of Sixiao Highway is a good example of harmony between resources and the environment, development and protection, as well as human beings and nature.

Written in 2006

Part V
Education and public health

21 Event of 'Immigrants for NCEE'

Xu Jun

In the course of constructing a socialist harmonious society, how to properly reconcile serious social conflicts and deal with emergencies poses a significant test for administrating organizations regarding their public administration capabilities. The event of 'Immigrants for NCEE (National College Entrance Examination)', which occurred in Hainan Province around 2005 is a case in point for us to study the making of public policies that deal with social issues and problems. Full of twists and turns, the event involved complicated conflicts of interests, reflecting a number of problems worthy of consideration.

Introduction

At 6:00 a.m. on Saturday, 18 May 2002, director H of the education department of Hainan Province was woken by a telephone call from the Haikou Municipal Education Bureau reporting that several hundred Grade 3 students from the senior high schools of Haifu district in Hainan Province were gathering in the Evergreen Garden of Haikou City. They were holding up banners asking the government to take measures to prohibit transient students from other provinces from entering Hainan unlawfully to apply for the NCEE.

Upon hearing the news, director H immediately hurried to the Evergreen Gardens, coordinating the administrating departments of education, school authorities and parents to intervene to prevent the matter from escalating. Gradually, over a period of 24 hours, the students began to disperse. This was the so-called 'May 18 Evergreen Garden Gathering Event', which shook the educational circle of Hainan. From then on, the problem of 'Immigrants for NCEE' began to surface.

Origins of the event

As China's youngest island province, Hainan Island's history dates back only 18 years, and it has a population of about 8,180,000 people. Taking the relatively undeveloped local economy and basic education into consideration, the Ministry of Education granted Hainan Province a preferential NCEE admission policy similar to that of such undeveloped regions as Tibet and Ningxia, i.e. higher admission rates for more low-grade students. The implementation of this policy played a positive role in the cultivation of local talent in Hainan, but at the same time caused an influx of 'Immigrants for NCEE'.

'Immigrants for NCEE' is a popular slogan (the accurate label should be 'transient students from other provinces'), specifically referring to those students who, in order to enjoy the preferential policy granted by the Ministry of Education to specific provinces or regions, transfer their permanent residence registration to those regions through abnormal channels and apply for the NCEE locally. As those students come from educationally developed regions, they often enjoy relatively obvious advantages over local students in NCEE. The possibilities for them to enter better colleges increase, thus unlawfully occupying local students' admission quotas.

Although 'Immigrants for NCEE' emerged in Hainan in an early period as in other remote provinces or regions, the numbers were small. The maximum number of such students in a year would not normally exceed 200, so its impact on local students remained minor. Therefore, at that time, Hainan's educational authorities implemented the policies of the Ministry of Education, in that students with Hainan permanent residence registration may apply for NCEE, and implemented no restrictions on transient students from other provinces.

In the early 1990s, Hainan, after being established as a province, suffered a serious real estate bubble. The burst of the bubble left in its wake overstocked commercial residential houses worth more than 80 billion yuan and numerous unfinished buildings. In order to optimize the real estate market and restore economic vigour, the Hainan Provincial Government decided to encourage people from outside the island to buy houses in Hainan through the policy of 'buying houses and obtaining permanent residence'. On 29 September 1999, the Hainan Provincial Government promulgated the 'Notice Regarding Certain Problems on Accelerating the Circulation of Overstocked Real Estate', prescribing that 'units or individuals who purchased 20- to 25-square-metre commercial residential houses may obtain permanent residence for one person. Students shall enjoy equal treatment with local people in NECC admission'.

The promulgation of the policy really enhanced the sale of Hainan real estate during a certain period of time, but the link between 'purchasing houses' and NCEE admission treatment left a loophole for 'Immigrants for NCEE'.

As expected, students from other provinces rapidly discovered this preferential policy and travelled to Hainan in large numbers to take part in NCEE. In 2000, the first year in which Hainan implemented the policy of 'buying commercial residential houses and obtaining permanent residence', the number of 'Immigrants for NCEE' skyrocketed from less than 200 in the past to 1,300, to 1,500 in 2001 and to 2,032 in 2002. The dramatic increase in 'Immigrants for NCEE' caused serious problems for local Hainan students, resulting in the demonstration by local Grade 3 students from the senior high schools in Evergreen Garden on 18 May 2002.

Taking measures to deal with the situation

Great importance has been attached to the events of 18 May by Hainan's local authorities. Consequently, in response to the requirements of the provincial government and the students concerned, the Education Department of Hainan Province carried out a special investigation into related problems and tried to come up with corrective measures. In December 2002, the Education Department made a 'Temporary Regulation on Requirements for Students to Attend College Entrance Exam in Hainan'. They decided to adjust application policies for NECC and to hold a public consultation meeting.

On 24 February 2003, the Hainan Provincial Government officially issued a 'Temporary Regulation on Requirements for Students to Attend College Entrance Exam in Hainan'. This placed special restrictions on students from other provinces participating in NCEE in Hainan and stipulated that

> those students may apply for regular institutions of higher education: the student and his/her legal guardian is entitled to permanent residence of Hainan. The student must take part in a senior high school for the last two years in Hainan. The student must be a graduate from a primary or junior high school in Hainan and his/her permanent residence registration must be in Hainan when he/she graduates. The student is entitled to permanent residence in the province if his/her legal guardian is in active service in Hainan or among outstanding talents introduced by provincial personnel departments. Those students with permanent residence registration in Hainan but not satisfying the above conditions may only apply for the second batch of regular colleges and technical academies.

However, the regulation failed to prevent 'Immigrants for NCEE' from travelling to Hainan. The number of 'Immigrants for NCEE' in 2003 was 2,165, while the number increased rapidly and reached 2,875 in 2004 (Table 21.1).

The reasons lie in the fact that, on the one hand, the qualifications for application and admission to NCEE were adjusted in light of the 'Temporary Regulation on Requirements for Students to Attend College Entrance Exam in Hainan', which restricts immigrating students from applying for colleges other than the second batch and below of regular colleges and universities. But the second batch of regular colleges and universities remains a considerable attraction for most 'Immigrants for NCEE' whose academic achievements rank at the middle to lower levels in their original provinces. The NCEE admission score line in Hainan was lower

Table 21.1 List of external students in Hainan Province from 2004 to 2005.

Year	Students in the province		Local students		External students		Ratio (%)
	Number	Increase (%)	Number	Increase (%)	Number	Increase (%)	
2002	26,936	—	24,904	—	2,032	—	7.5
2003	30,079	11.67	27,914	12.1	2,165	6.54	7.2
2004	35,167	16.92	32,292	15.68	2,875	32.79	8.2
2005	44,916	27.76	35,123	8.8	9,793	240.63	21.8

than in many inland provinces by 50 to 100 points, while the admission ratio was nearly 30 per cent higher. In addition, the policy of 'purchasing houses and obtaining permanent residence' was still being carried out, which made entry for students from other provinces more convenient. On the other hand, during the process of dealing with overstocked commercial residential houses, the implementation of the 'purchasing houses and obtaining permanent residence' policy caused large quantities of permanent resident 'quotas' simply calculated by the area of purchased houses. By utilizing those quotas and selling them to inland students in a public or semi-public way, some unscrupulous estate agents and developers added fuel to the fire by facilitating the so-called 'Immigrants for NCEE', resulting in more students from other provinces travelling to Hainan. And later on, even the entire-class immigration phenomenon has emerged.

The rapid influx of 'Immigrants for NCEE' unlawfully filled the admission quota for Hainan's local students. According to the education department of Hainan Province, the admission ratios of 'Immigrants for NCEE' from 2002 to 2004 were higher than those of local students. Especially for regular colleges and universities, the admission ratio of 'Immigrants for NCEE' was 75.4 per cent (over an average of 3 years), nearly double that of 39.5 per cent, the admission ratio of students from the province. From 2002 to 2004, a total of 6,255 'Immigrants for NCEE' passed the examination and entered colleges or universities in Hainan, which meant that 6,255 local students failed to win places in colleges and universities that should have belonged to them. In addition, as a result of the impact of 'Immigrants for NCEE', many local students had to accept places in the third batch of regular colleges or universities or even vocational schools who should have been able to win a place in the second batch of regular colleges or universities.

Sudden emergence of a crisis

Hainan students were detailed to apply for the NCEE from 20 to 30 March 2005. Before the application process closed, rumours about a dramatic increase in 'Immigrants for NCEE' spread like wildfire. It was stated on the Internet that the number of 'Immigrants for NCEE' amounted to 20,000. In addition, a representative of the local Hainan students began collecting signatures on the Internet, claiming to refuse to participate in the examination collectively to protest against 'Immigrants for NCEE' in Hainan.

Meanwhile, staff members of the Examination Bureau of Hainan Province experienced an unusually dramatic increase in the number of students from other provinces during the process of applying for NCEE, and reported this to the education department of Hainan Province.

Such provincial departments as the education department, the supervision department and the letters and calls bureau received many letters of complaint from local students and parents. Some people even appealed to higher authorities for help. They complained that 'Immigrants for NCEE' seriously jeopardized the chances of local Hainan students applying for college places, and that some people profited illegally from it. They strongly urged the authorities to penalize these illegal and undisciplined activities, thus maintaining the rights of the local students from Hainan.

In a letter entitled 'The Heartfelt Wishes of the Ordinary People', a local student's parent said that the phenomenon of 'Immigrants for NCEE' was getting worse. The seriousness of the situation worried not only the students in Grade 3 of the senior high schools and their parents, but also put the students in Grade 2, and even Grade 1, on tenterhooks. The parents and school authorities had done much to put the students' minds at ease. On the one hand, they told the students that the government would certainly take forceful measures to inhibit the tide of 'Immigrants for NCEE'. On the other hand, they tried to shield the news from the students to prevent them from becoming worried. However, this event impacted greatly on the students' future. They were paying close attention to the attitude of the government while at the same time wishing to express their concerns.

On 28 March, the leaders of the Hainan Provincial Government directed the education department to put forward countermeasures to the provincial government as soon as possible. By doing this, the authorities would be able to deal with the problem of 'Immigrants for NCEE' properly and uphold the rights and benefits of the local students of Hainan, as well as maintain social stability.

The application process for NCEE closed on 30 March. A total of 44,916 students applied to participate in NCEE, among whom 9,793 were 'Immigrants for NCEE', accounting for 21.8 per cent of the total, an increase of 6,918 over that of 2004.

Governmental decisions

With his extensive administration and management experiences, director H of the education department, who had been in charge of education affairs for many years, immediately realized the seriousness of the situation. Recently, he had been pondering the problem of 'Immigrants for NCEE' and the responsive measures necessary to solve the problem.

He faced a difficult problem: for the more than 9,000 students from inland provinces whose permanent residence registrations were transferred to Hainan, there was a legal obstacle if the authorities did not allow them to participate in the NCEE in Hainan in light of the Ministry of Education's principle of application in students' permanent residence registration region. That is to say, the provincial education department can only review the qualifications of the applicants. If related qualifications, including a graduation certificate and recognized status as a student, are eligible, the authorities cannot cancel the qualification of 'Immigrants for NCEE', as they do not contravene the law.

He believed that the most urgent task was to reassure the local students of Hainan by guaranteeing the stable performance of NCEE admissions work. He would spare no effort to overcome the difficulties this year.

Director H hosted a directors' routine meeting. He pointed out that, currently, staff members of the education department and the Examination Bureau must focus on three issues during the period of NCEE: first, to strictly review the qualifications of student applications from other provinces to reduce their numbers; second, to reassure the local students and so avoid an explosive situation; third, to employ all available means to increase NCEE admission quotas to reduce the pressure caused by the dramatic increase in 'Immigrants for NCEE'.

After several days of research, the education department reported a 'Request for Directions Regarding Related Issues of Properly Dealing with Temporary Students From Other Provinces In Our Province' to the Hainan Provincial Government on 5 April. Once approved by the government, the department immediately carried out the measures in all fields. The primary measures taken included:

1   A special review of the permanent residence registration and recognized status as transient students. First, to send letters detailing all the transient students' application information to twenty-one provincial public security departments and admission and examination departments of the original residence registration and residence regions, asking them to assist in reviewing whether or not those immigrant students were violating the regulations by keeping residence registration in two regions or applying for NCEE in two places; second, dispatching qualified representatives to six provinces with relatively more 'Immigrants for NCEE' including Henan, Hebei, Hunan, Hubei, Anhui and Jiangxi, to investigate the recognized status materials of transient students (Table 21.2).

2   Transferring some colleges and universities originally in the second batch of regular admission to the first batch of admission.

3   Dispatching representatives to the Ministry of Education to report on the rapid increase in 'Immigrants for NCEE' in Hainan, while at the same time trying to obtain more admission quotas from the Ministry of Education. They would also send official letters to all the colleges and

Table 21.2 List of home provinces of 'Immigrants for NCEE' who travelled to Hainan Province from 2003 to 2005.

2003		2004		2005	
Home province of immigrants for NCEE	Number of immigrants for NCEE	Home province of immigrants for NCEE	Number of immigrants for NCEE	Home province of immigrants for NCEE	Number of immigrants for NCEE
Hubei	533	Hubei	617	Henan	3,535
Hunan	507	Henan	583	Hubei	1,545
Henan	223	Hunan	507	Jiangxi	1,150
Anhui	215	Anhui	269	Hunan	1,025
Guangdong	153	Jiangxi	231	Anhui	774
Jiangxi	149	Guangdong	158	Hebei	528
Inner Mongolia	112	Hebei	132	Inner Mongolia	287
Hebei	108	Zhejiang	117	Zhejiang Shandong	186
In total	2,000	In total	2,614	In total	9,141
Percentage of migrants	81.1	Percentage of migrants	90.9	Percentage of migrants	92.9

universities with admission plans in Hainan, asking them to add admission quotas. Reporting and requesting the provincial government to amend the related policies of 'purchasing houses and obtaining permanent residence' and adjusting the 'Temporary Regulation on Requirements for Students to Attend College Entrance Exam in Hainan' to tighten up conditions for students applying from other provinces.

4 Sending official letters to the Public Security Department of Hainan to alert permanent residence registration management and to intensify their fight against such illegal activities as purchasing or selling permanent residence quotas.

5 Implementing news releasing systems, publishing statistics and latest policies in the media, and holding news conferences regularly to guide public opinion.

6 Consolidating ideological work and the letters and calls from the public to maintain social stability. First, to dispatch representatives to all the cities and counties to host meetings with students and their parents to convey to them the information that the provincial government stood firm to protect the interests of local students; second, to hold meetings in which directors of education bureaus of all the cities and counties and principals of middle schools directly under the provincial education department would participate, asking them to reassure local students; third, the Hainan Provincial Examination Bureau set up a 'Window for Letters and Calls from People' to answer questions from the students.

7   To form 'Emergency Planning for the Period of NCEE in Hainan Province in 2005' to establish a rapid response system for emergencies.

After formulating the above measures, director H heaved a sigh of relief. However, it was not the local students who launched an attack first as they expected, but the 'Immigrants for NCEE'.

First 'earthquake'

On 17 May 2005, according to the actual situation verified by the investigation team organized by the education department of Hainan Province, the office calculated that 340 students from seven provinces such as Hubei Province and Hebei Province were registered in their home town as well as in Hainan Province to attend the College Entrance Exam. This contravened the Ministry of Education's rule that no one is allowed to register in two places, so the education department of Hainan Province decided to deprive them of the qualifications to register in Hainan Province.

Upon hearing the news, these 340 students and their parents acted swiftly. Appealing to the education department of Hainan Province, to the governments and educational sectors of the cities where their residences were registered, even to the Ministry of Educational Administration through different channels, they asked to resume their qualifications to attend the exam. In addition, they related the news to the major domestic media. On the morning of 31 May, more than thirty parents demonstrated angrily at the gate of the Provincial Government, armed with a banner claiming 'Children should attend the Exam'.

The parents admitted that they had registered their children in two places, but also pointed out that some objective factors had led to the problem. They insisted that their children's permanent residences and educational archives were in Hainan, so the children should be registered in Hainan Province according to the related regulations from the Ministry of Education. If Hainan Province removed the children's qualifications for the exam, they could not also be registered in their home town.

As the exam was approaching, the reasons proposed by the parents could not be investigated and verified in time, Hainan College Entrance Exam Meeting, chaired by director H, made a final decision after discussion on the morning of 31 May that these 340 students could sit the exam in Hainan Province and their cases would be looked at individually. The measures taken to deal with these problems were as follows: first, if the students did not have two permanent residences whose original residence document had not been transferred to Hainan from their home town in time, then Hainan Province would accept their qualifications for the exam. Second, if the students had two residences or they had a genuine Hainan residence but did not have valid local certificates and study cards, they would be told to attend the exam in their home town. Third, Hainan Province demanded that students bring their ID cards and a guarantee before 4 June to register for the exam. The students would only be allowed to attend the exam in Hainan if the guarantee promised that the above-mentioned problems would not happen. Following the exam, if their guarantees were disproven, the students would be disqualified.

Second 'earthquake'

On the afternoon of 8 June, when the College Entrance Exam had finished, more than 500 examinees and parents appealed collectively to the Provincial Government that the education department of Hainan Province had awarded some quotas of the second batch colleges to the first batch colleges.

That evening, director H convened another College Entrance Exam Meeting to give a second consideration to complaints from the students and parents. The participants concluded that the Hainan Recruitment Committee had a full legal foundation and had abided by the related regulations set by the Ministry of Education.

On the morning of 9 June, director H met with representatives of the parents, explained the policy reform to them and announced the conclusions of the meeting of the previous night to the media. On the afternoon of that day, the parents dispersed. This event is known as the second 'earthquake' after the 31 May event during the 2005 college entrance exam in Hainan Province.

On 20 June 2005, the Hainan Provincial Government held an executive meeting in which a 'Temporary Regulation on Requirements for Students to Attend College Entrance Exam in Hainan (Revised Version)' submitted by the education department was reviewed and passed. The clauses about obtaining permanent residence through purchasing local houses, which was stipulated in the Hainan Governmental Office's 'Notice about Related Issues to Accelerate the Circulation of Overstocked Houses', had been adjusted to the regulation that Hainan's permanent resident policy should follow that of China's common policy. Meanwhile, in order to facilitate follow-up measures once the Interim Regulation was issued, the Provincial Police Department suspended the offer of permanent residence to house-buyers outside Hainan Province.

On 23 June, the Hainan Provincial Government officially issued a 'Temporary Regulation on Requirements for Students to Attend College Entrance Exam in Hainan (Revised Version)'. Based on the regulations for 2003, the Regulation added further requirements for registration. The first was to prolong students' study time in Hainan Province. The new policy stipulates that only those students who spend the full 3 years in Hainan senior high school are qualified to apply for the colleges in any batch. If they are not in residence for the full 3 years, they cannot apply for the colleges in the first and second batches. The second was to prolong students' residence time in Hainan Province. The new policy stipulates that students and their legal supervisors must have permanent residence in Hainan Province for at least

3 years by the end of the date of registration. The third is that students should have regular residence in Hainan Province. The fourth is to limit the scope of applicants more strictly. Since 2006, if the students do not stay in Hainan Province for two school years until the date of registration or they do not study in senior higher schools in Hainan Province, they can be registered in Hainan but can only apply for the third batch of undergraduate colleges, professional schools or senior training schools.

Top student cannot enter Tsinghua University

On 14 July, Li Yang, a student from Hubei who came top in Hainan's College Entrance Exam for science course students in 2005, was deprived of the qualification to apply for Tsinghua, a college in the first batch, by the education department of Hainan Province because he did not abide by the requirements stipulated in the 'Temporary Regulation on Requirements for Students to Attend College Entrance Exam in Hainan'; namely his study in Hainan was still 1 month short of 2 years. At the same time, another twenty-seven students like Li Yang were also denied the chance to apply to the colleges in the first batch. All came from other provinces before they entered Haitian Middle School in Haikou City.

This event drew widespread criticism. People started asking whether the College Entrance Exam system was fair. The issue of 'Immigrants for NCEE in Hainan' and related policies attracted people's attention once again.

In mid-September 2005, Hainan completed its enrolment procedure, enrolling 38,472 students in total. There were 29,427 local students and 9,045 external students who accounted for 23.5 per cent of the total number. Some 18,696 students were enrolled to enter undergraduate college courses (including those in the first, second and third batches), of which 6,969 were external students (37.2 per cent of the total).

During enrolment in 2005, the education department of Hainan Province transferred thirty-eight external colleges and four provincial colleges that had been in the second batch in 2004 to the first batch. Some 2,227 students were involved, including 1,128 from external colleges and 1,099 from provincial colleges. The colleges in the first batch could enrol 6,392 students from the original 4,165.

The Ministry of Education and related colleges also gave Hainan an additional quota of 6,585 places, including 5,157 for undergraduate course students and 1,428 for professional school students. This promoted Hainan's enrolment rate from the planned 76.6 per cent to 85.7 per cent, 30.7 per cent higher than the national average rate (Table 21.3).

After the 2005 College Entrance Exam, the education department of Hainan Province made full use of various domestic media to publicize the 'Temporary Regulation on Requirements for Students to Attend College Entrance Exam in Hainan', especially in provinces such as Hubei and Henan where there were more 'Immigrants for NCEE'.

Table 21.3 List of college entrance exam enrolment from 2002 to 2005.

Year	Number of enrolled students						Number of all enrolled students		
	Undergraduate (including colleges in the first, second and third batch)			Professional school					
	Entire Hainan Province	Among which		Entire Hainan Province	Among which		Entire Hainan Province	Among which	
		Local students	External students		Local students	External students		Local students	External students
2002	11,518	9,912	1,606	9,752	9,623	129	21,270	19,535	1,735
2003	12,447	10,850	1,597	12,051	11,735	316	24,498	22,585	1,913
2004	14,937	12,825	2,112	15,589	15,094	495	30,526	27,919	2,607
2005	18,696	11,827	6,969	19,776	17,700	2,076	38,472	29,427	9,045

Postscript

By 30 March 2006 when the registration for the College Entrance Exam in Hainan was over, 1,500 external students were enrolled, accounting for 3.7 per cent of the total, some 8,000 fewer than in 2005. A source from the Hainan Exam Bureau said in an interview that most 'Immigrants for NCEE' in 2006 could only apply for colleges in the third batch and professional schools and, as the quota for this batch was large, there would be no great impact on local students.

Moreover, since 2004, Hainan has become of one of four chosen provinces that carry out teaching reform in senior high schools across China. Since 2007, the College Entrance Exam will test students with new content after teaching reform, which will no doubt deter many 'Immigrants for NCEE'. On the other hand, many media within and outside the province have noticed that, in recent years, Hainan has promoted preliminary education construction at an unprecedented pace.

On 19 November 2003, as the leader of the Rural Education Investigation Team including eleven branches, province governor W carried out investigations into rural education in five state-level and six province-level poor counties.

In 2004, Hainan Province implemented a 10-year Plan to Develop Education in Hainan's rural area and decided to invest 100 million yuan for three consecutive years to support education.

In 2005, Hainan Province took the lead in exempting the tuition fee in compulsory education, offering free books to students in rural areas and poor students in towns, and subsidizing minority boarders.

From 2000 to 2005, Hainan Province invested 489 million yuan in total specifically to reconstruct dilapidated middle school and primary school buildings. The floor area of newly built and reconstructed school buildings covered 908,000 square metres. In 2006, Hainan Province took the lead in abolishing all D-level dilapidated buildings in middle schools and primary schools.

According to Hainan's 11th Five-year Plan, the province will build a good-quality junior middle school in every administrative town during the period and a good-quality senior middle school in every administrative county and city. These schools will employ good teachers from throughout China.

It is conceivable that, with the Hainan Provincial Government adjusting reasonably related policies and rapidly strengthening its preliminary education, the conflict between local students and 'Immigrants for NCEE' will soon cool down and be solved satisfactorily, and the students in Hainan will sit a fair, just and harmonious college entrance exam.

Written in 2006

22 College graduates 'go to mountains and villages' – idealistic or realistic?

Lu Gang

Prologue

Thirty years ago, millions of Chinese young people 'went to mountains and villages', a government-launched movement to send graduates of colleges and high schools to rural, mountainous and border areas. People of that generation devoted their most productive years to social progress and economic development. Viewing this from purely public governance, regardless of any political background, one can see the objective effect in both easing employment pressures and avoiding social crisis. If considering this from human capital theory, one can also see that those people gained valuable experience while society stored many well-educated people in its grassroots.

At the beginning of the new century, the Chinese government set a series of strategic goals for the nation to achieve by the year 2020, such as overall well-being, scientific development, a harmonious society, new rural construction and so on. In the meantime, China has been in a transition period. Great challenges appear one after another. On the one hand, cities face enormous employment pressures; on the other, qualified professionals are badly needed in rural areas; on the one hand, increasing numbers of college graduates call for more channels of employment to be explored; on the other, social development in the countryside requires qualified and talented personnel. In the market economy of socialism, how does one realize a meaningful allocation of human resources? This is an ideal in sociology but a challenge in economics. The question is: can governments turn this ideal into reality?

Challenge: who is going to teach English?

Hubei province has over 500,000 teachers in primary and middle schools, 70 per cent in rural areas. Among its seventy-three agricultural counties, twenty-nine are classified as 'poor counties' by national or provincial standards. In September 2003, the State Council decided that rural area schooling should be a priority on governments' agenda of education. Hence, the Provincial Department of Education (PDoE) sent several teams to investigate.

J County is nationally well known for its grain production. It is said that, at one time, the grain store could provide half a kilogram of grain for everyone in the whole country. A schoolmaster at a middle school in that county said: 'Last year, three English teachers left the school; we had to hire a bookshop keeper to teach English'. The investigation team found that students in local schools are almost all exposed to a kind of dialectal pronunciation in English classes.

T County is located in a provincial mountainous area where, 80 years ago, Chinese revolutionary veterans launched a famous rebellion and established one of the first military bases for the Red Army. When the students at a local middle school responded to the question: 'What are the highest mountain and the longest river in China?', it was astonishing that the answer, from the whole class, was a hill and a stream in the county! The investigation team was shocked. The problem of the quantity and quality of teachers in those rural areas was far worse than imagined.

Z County is also a 'poor county' by national standards. It is in the northwest mountainous area of the province. Nine-year compulsory education was successfully introduced to cover the whole region in 1999. As a result, a national medal from the central government was awarded to the county government for its excellence in education. Each year, 500 local high school graduates pass the national entrance examination for colleges and go on to pursue higher education. However, less than 1 per cent return to work in their county. 'To make things even worse, the teachers leaving for cities are at least twice those coming in. There was no single bachelor degree holder in all the 18 middle schools of all our 15 towns and townships of the county', said Wang, the director of the County Bureau of Education: 'we can't solve this problem on our own under the new situation of the market economy'.

The results of the investigation show that, although great progress in education has been achieved in the rural areas in the province in recent years, many serious problems still exist. There are some structural and distributional teaching imbalances in the schools: the allocations of teachers are over-resourced in urban schools but under-resourced in rural schools; there are many teachers in primary schools but few in middle schools; there are many administrative staff but few teaching staff; there are many traditional subjects but few newly introduced subjects. Most of the teachers are aged over 50 and few are below the age of 30. The majority of the teachers are not bachelor degree holders; instead, they are only graduates of teachers' schools which are below college level in the Chinese education system.

A reporter from the Xinhua News Agency writes: 'The gap between demand and supply of teachers in townships of rural areas is so large that it has already created outstanding problems of structural and distributional imbalances. A great shortage of qualified teachers has occurred in the countryside'.

The PDoE should respond to the challenge. What is the solution?

Another challenge follows: where are the jobs for college graduates?

In May 2004, an official document from the central government was conveyed to the PDoE from the provincial governing committee. 'The number of college graduates amounts to 2.8 million this year, 680,000 more than last year'. Facing the serious employment situation, the document advocated guiding and encouraging college graduates to work in areas of 'grassroots' and hardship.

Higher education is one of the comparatively strong industries in Hubei Province in terms of its reputation and number of students. In 2003, there were 133,000 college graduates, 48,000 more than in the previous year, an increase of 56.6 per cent, 10 per cent higher than the national average. An employment survey revealed that about 70 per cent of graduates choose to work in corporations or to pursue postgraduate study, and 80 per cent go to the more developed southeast coastal areas or large cities such as provincial capitals. No graduate has yet been found to choose to work as a teacher in a rural township school.

Going to the grassroots for employment certainly creates public value and is no doubt a right thing to do. However, a right thing does not necessarily become realistic in practice.

On the one hand, schools in rural areas are in urgent need of qualified teachers, while at the same time many college graduates desperately need jobs. 'To discover a certain relation between different sources of information is called "cross-referencing" in academic terms'. The cross-referencing of these two challenges confronts the leader of the PDoE: 'It is possible to mobilize some graduates to work in the countryside to enable the "go to mountains and villages" movement to happen again in the new era of market economy conditions'.

On 2 June 2004, the leader of the PDoE instructed its related divisions to take action in 'drafting a proposal in two days, which should take into account the following issues: teacher shortages in rural schools, reform of the current school personnel policies, government subsidy of college student loan compensation, and creation of job opportunities for graduates'.

On 4 June, a draft of the 'Supporting Action Plan for Rural Teachers' (SAPRT) was dispatched for internal review within PDoE. Four meetings for discussion among the relevant divisions, local education authorities, several college presidents and some experts were held before the modified version was formally submitted to the decision-making board of the PDoE on 11 June. The board unanimously approved SAPRT together with its working agenda for 2004.

On 14 June, two policy documents were issued by the PDoE. SAPRT was initiated in the province of Hubei.

The action plan provides a package of six new policies favourable to participating college graduates involved: an annual reward of RMB 5,000 yuan for each participant on the basis of academic year-end assessment, the money to go towards clearing the student's outstanding loan debt; there will be no probation period which, in normal circumstances, usually takes 1 year for newly employed teachers before formal confirmation of appointment; the salary will be included in the local government budget and the salary standard will be in accordance with the national policy; in cases where a participant is eligible for Master's degree study without any entrance test requirement, registration for a degree course can be held over for a period of 3 years; the participants can be selected as candidates for the programme of Master of Education based on end-of-term assessment; the participants' personal records and registrations can be kept, with their agreement, either in their colleges or in the Graduate Employment Centre of the PDoE at no charge, or even in counties where they are employed; for those participants graduating from non-teacher-training programmes, free training for the Certificate of Professional Qualification will be provided and all related costs will be paid by the PDoE.

'A new form of "go to mountains and villages" has re-emerged in Hubei Province', read the headlines in the *People's Daily*, the number one influential national newspaper, a year later.

The new thinking is very effective, but more challenges are emerging.

Enforcement is more important than new thinking

Most of the college graduates of 2004 had already signed their employment contracts by mid-June and hence were not available to participate in SAPRT!

Xiong Tingting, a graduate from the English department of a provincial university in 2004, is the only daughter in her family. She has lived in an urban city from childhood. Before hearing about SAPRT, she had already turned down an offer from a famous high school and was considering accepting a position in a university.

Ma Haitao, a graduate from a science and technology university under the Ministry of Education (MoE), comes from Xinjiang Autonomous Region. Because of his excellent qualifications, he had been offered a position in a state-owned enterprise in the provincial capital in May.

'It seems that every door had already been shut even before we had started'. The PDoE leader responsible for organizing this task felt that the government authorities were helpless in the face of market forces. 'Meetings and discussions do not work any more; we have to learn the marketing approach to attract students of excellence. But what should we do to attract college students nowadays?'

The PDoE decided to advertise for the first time in its history!

Ma Haitao said:

'*Experience of three years brings you treasures for life*'.

These words were to change my life. On the morning of 16 June 2004, for the first time I heard about SAPRT from the university broadcasting service. The words *Experience of three years brings you treasures for life* moved me deeply. It reminded me of the hard times of my early days' schooling back in Xinjiang. I thought of my teachers with their unsung work. It was their teaching that brought me to university. Now my life has changed, what can I do for those children similar to my own childhood? What can I do to repay those people who have helped me?

Jia Yanhui from Beijing is a graduate of the English department from one of the top national key universities under Ministry of Education jurisdiction. She said:

My parents have found a job for me in Beijing, but I am not content with that, feeling that if I go back to Beijing that way, there seems to lack of something in my youth time. On hearing about SAPRT, the words *Experience of three years brings you treasures for life* made me very excited. Isn't this what I have been looking for all along? I don't believe I cannot prove my value of life in small and poor places.

However, for those counties willing to receive these graduates, it was a major issue. It involved several core departments that were not easy to deal with. Furthermore, the necessary acceptance procedures could not be gone through in such a short time under normal circumstances. County bureaus of education felt helpless and unable to cope with the situation.

PDoE leaders talked with the government heads from the twenty-nine poor counties. To give the receiving counties incentives, the PDoE offered financial assistance for certain SAPRT projects. In this way, the acceptance issue was finally resolved.

On 9 July 2004, 306 selected college graduates officially signed service agreements to volunteer to teach in rural townships. Fan Xianlong, a graduate from a national finance and law university, chose to teach in the forest area: 'I am very thankful to the PDoE for giving me this opportunity. Now that I have chosen my path, I will go forward'.

On 26 July 2004, the last pre-service training day for volunteer teachers, the provincial government held a moving ceremony. The deputy secretary of the provincial governing committee, who himself joined the 'go to mountains and villages' movement in 1968, spoke of his own experience to encourage the graduates to adopt an optimistic attitude towards the approaching difficulties, to develop themselves in overcoming challenges and, finally, to become leaders of the profession through accumulating practical experience.

The first year completed, what happened next?

Soft power is more powerful than hard power

On 17 January 2005, President Hu Jintao of the People's Republic of China, speaking at a national convention, called for more efforts to be made to improve college students' ethical consciousness. He asked college leaders, teaching staff and education administrators to focus on the state-of-the-art approaches in conducting education so that a sound effect could be achieved.

Ethical education is a soft task. However, the right approach could greatly increase its soft power.

'Would those volunteer teachers with their heads full of dreams and ideals be frustrated in face of the reality of hardship after their passion has faded?', asked one sceptical journalist from the national Xinhua News Agency when he visited the campuses. He interviewed five representatives of volunteer teachers who were on a tour, organized by the PDoE, of twenty-six universities and seven cities to deliver a series of speeches sharing their own experiences with college students. They narrated their stories of how passion changed to doubt, and finally being stirred up again through practical action. Over 20,000 students attended to listen to the speeches.

'I haven't heard such terrific speeches for a long time; my eyes were full of tears', said the journalist. Fan Xianlong said: 'I am a college student from the countryside. Hearing your speech, I didn't calm down for a long time, feeling that nothing will stop my determination to go back to the countryside. ... I want to join "the Action Plan" to help those similar to myself by using what I have learned'.

The director of the Student Affairs Office in C University recorded forty-eight rounds of applause in his notebook. Some lasted for more than a minute.

'Who brought tears to the campuses?', A journalist from the Xinhua Agency asked.

In that year, 2,200 college graduates applied to join the action plan and, on 17 May 2005, 1,029 signed agreements with county education bureaus.

Soft power comes from the support of government leaders

The deputy minister of the Ministry of Education paid a special visit to some volunteer teachers to hear about their work and life in rural areas. Leaders of the provincial committee, the state council and other relevant ministries spoke highly of the project, calling for expansion of the successful experience to broaden areas such as personnel policy reform, employment and construction of teachers' teams nationally. The central committee of the Nine–Three Party, one of the governing participating democratic parties, made a proposal to the National Committee of the Chinese Political Consultative Conference that the government, by adopting the mode of SAPRT, purchase temporary service positions to attract college graduates to teach in rural areas. On 30 July 2005, the head of the Provincial Governing Committee met the recruited volunteer teachers of the year. He recounted his personal stories of working at grassroots level following graduation, and encouraged the young generation to learn more about the real side of society through working in rural areas and contributing to the progress of the country.

Soft power also comes from the media

Thanks to the coverage of the major media from both national and local agencies, news of the volunteers and their good works soon spread to the whole society. They made the headlines for quite some time.

But how are these youngsters really coping in the countryside?

First teacher of bachelor degree in history

Lin Xiaoping from Hunan Province graduated from a university of agriculture. When she came to the central school of Xinhua township in a forest area, she discovered that, astonishingly, she was the first teacher with a bachelor degree to teach history there. Today, there are fourteen volunteer teachers in the whole forest area. All are bachelor graduates.

The reality of the remote rural and mountainous areas far exceeded her expectations.

> On those nights I stayed in our school by myself, I felt lonely, and missed home very much. Travelling here is quite inconvenient, the mountain road is dangerous, a landslide happens from time to time. Mum called me and worried about my safety. I told mum, I have already grown up. Here I am quite capable of taking good care of myself; moreover I have learned to love my students.

The work of a teacher in the countryside involves far more than teaching.

> I have a student, she is blue, and her grades are poor. Her father died from a mining accident in Shaanxi Province, her mother remarried when she was five. She was entrusted for fosterage in her uncle's family. But her uncle already has four children, and has no more spare time to take care of her. One day, after helping with her homework, I was ready to leave, but she caught my hand and cried: 'I want mum, I don't want you to go, I just don't want you to go, I need mum'.

The volunteer teachers are more than schoolteachers.

Zhang Lin graduated from a university of Chinese traditional medicine. He came to Huangtugang central school in M County. The English grades of his three classes were always among the best in the school, therefore he was granted an excellent teacher award from the county. As he was so popular in the whole county area due to his expertise in traditional Chinese medicine, he was asked not only to be responsible for the hygiene of over 3,000 teachers and students in the school, but also to carry out preventive work against bird flu for the whole county during the anti-bird flu campaign. His massage skills released many people from body pain and rewarded him with the widespread trust of the parents of his students. He is greatly admired by his students who are becoming increasingly active and cooperative, and their class grades are continuously improving.

Jia Yanhui from Beijing organized her students to investigate why the river close to their school had no fish or shrimp. They found that the families along the river bank built their cattle and pig sheds beside the river, and all waste was emitted directly into the river, which became polluted by the long-term build-up of waste matter. This action attracted the attention of local government, and even generated an environmental protection movement that spread to all the villages in the whole township. 'My child doesn't even allow me to wash clothes in the river', said some parents.

Volunteer teachers are local resources with outside connections.

Xie Yongqiang graduated from a university of science and technology. Her school has only one well 3 metres deep to provide drinking water for all the students and teachers in the school. Even after deposition, there are large quantities of mud and sand in the water. The tank containing boiled water is covered in mud and has to be cleaned every few days. The parents of students say that, even though the water looks clear, if you drink too much, your whole body will itch. Xie Yongqiang wrote to the leader of PDoE about the matter and, as a result, a special fund was set up for the school. All the villagers and students now have clean and safe drinking water.

Fan Xianlong relocated his personal resident file to the forest area, but he also chose to leave it in his municipality. President Chen of his university visited him and donated books, culture and sports articles valued at RMB 5,000 to the school, and signed an agreement with the local education bureau, promising to donate RMB 20,000 every year to help poor students. Teachers and students of his mother university voluntarily donated 120 packages of cloth to the school he works in. After the media unveiled his story, people from all over the country promised to subsidise twenty-two poor students from the school to finish their studies from middle school all the way through to university.

'The government purchases staging positions of service for graduates to provide an initial phase of employment'. This was the original goal of PDoE.

Epilogue: a national movement

In 2006, SAPRT completed its third year. In that year, 2,310 college graduates went to the townships. In 3 years, some 3,645 graduates from over sixty colleges and universities teach in more than 430 township schools in seventy counties in Hubei Province.

On 19 April 2006, some volunteer teachers were invited to Beijing to appear in the news press of the Ministry of Education. They told their stories to the media in the capital. Hundreds of reports again hit the headlines and attracted the attention of the whole society once more and in even greater depth.

The head of the provincial committee asked the local government leader to visit Ms Chen Jingdao, a volunteer teacher who had taken her handicapped father with her to teach in a rural school. The leaders thanked her for her diligent work and zealous service, again acknowledging SAPRT. The Provincial Organization Department, Finance Department and Personnel Affairs Department have also issued new policies to support these volunteer teachers.

Three new policies have been issued by the provincial departments: buying basic medical insurance and accident insurance for the volunteer teachers, providing a yearly transportation allowance of RMB 400 yuan to each of the volunteer teachers, allocating a special working fund of RMB 5,000 yuan per volunteer teacher to the receiving county by the Provincial Finance Department; and a special programme is initiated for those volunteer teachers to be sent abroad to study for Master's degrees if they are still willing to stay and teach in the township schools after 3 years' service.

The Provincial Personnel Affairs Department announced that the future recruitment of public servants should include volunteer teachers as prior candidates.

In May 2006, the central government implemented a 'Special Position Plan for Compulsory Education Teachers in Rural Areas'. This plan was designed for the western part of China. The central government's Ministry of Finance would provide RMB 15,000 yuan annually for each teaching position in the continuous 3 years. Furthermore, the central government would also pay off those graduates' college loans.

This project assigned 1,000 positions to Hubei Province, which is not one of the western provinces. This resulted in 1,118 rural school positions being filled by college graduates.

A new wave of the 'go to the mountains and villages' movement has been activated throughout the country.

The PDoE of Hubei Province believes that more challenges are on the way.

Written in 2006

23 Analysis and practice of financial assistance to poor students in higher education institutions

Wang Chunqiu

Tuition fee collecting system in higher education institutions

China adopted a free education system in higher education under the long-term planning economy system. The central government began to push vigorously for the reform of the tuition fee collecting system in higher education institutions step by step from 1994, and this was completed in 1997. Thus, a new system of raising funding for education was formed, with government appropriation as the main financial support and many other channels providing additional financial assistance. Consequently, an increasing number of students have to pay their tuition fees themselves. Statistics show that the average tuition fees in higher education soared from RMB 800 in 1995 to RMB 4,000 in 2004. In 2005, the Ministry of Education issued a regulation for tuition fee collection in higher education institutions specifying that the maximum tuition fee per student per year for common specialties was RMB 6,000. In only 10 years, the tuition fee has quintupled. Similarly, accommodation fees rocketed from RMB 270 in 1995 to RMB 1,000 per student per year in 2004. If expenditure for meals, clothes and other living necessities were included, the average annual fee for each student would be 10,000 yuan. It is reported that the cost of financing a college student is equal to 4.2 years' net income of an urban resident and 13.6 years' net income of a farmer.

The reform of the tuition fee collection system in higher education institutions led to an enrolment increase, which inevitably resulted in a greater number of poor undergraduates. This worsened the situation of the settlement of defaulting students' tuition fees in higher education institutions (Figure 23.1).

An overview of poor students in higher education institutions

The population of college students has been increasing enormously with the expansion of college enrolment and scales. Accordingly, the number of poor students has also multiplied. Statistics show that enrolment has increased by 47 per cent since 1999, the first year of enrolment expansion, and reached

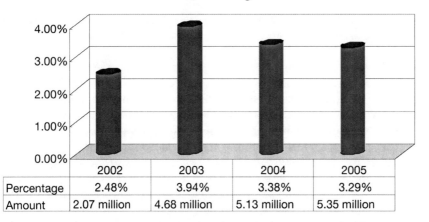

	2002	2003	2004	2005
Percentage	2.48%	3.94%	3.38%	3.29%
Amount	2.07 million	4.68 million	5.13 million	5.35 million

Figure 23.1 A survey conducted in S university, which shows the defaulting students from 2002–2005.

5,044,600 with a total number of college students of 15,617,800 by the end of 2005. Within the 2,400,000 poor students, approximately 20 per cent of the total population of college students, there are 60,000 to 1,200,000 extremely poor students, accounting for 5 to 10 per cent of the total population of college students, based on a survey conducted among Chinese higher education institutions in 2004.

Higher education institutions differ greatly in the number and percentage of poor students because they come from different regions and the consumption level varies from one region to another. For example, S University is a key comprehensive university in Shandong province with approximately 30,000 students. In this university, poor students are defined according to their monthly expenses. Those who spend less than RMB 200 on their living expenses are categorized as poor students and less than RMB 150 as extremely poor students. According to a survey conducted in the university, 9,074 students are poor and 2,822 are extremely poor, amounting to 30.25 per cent and 9.41 per cent of the student population, respectively, which is higher than the national average.

Existing policy of financial assistance to poor students

Central government attaches great importance to students from poor families. With more than 10 years of painstaking exploration and with the endeavours of the Ministry of Education, Ministry of Finance, the People's Bank of China, the China Banking Regulatory Commission and other relevant departments, a new policy has been promulgated, which involves a multi-system of financial assistance to poor students with scholarships, national student loans, work-for-study, special subsidies, tuition fee reduction and exemption as the main channels, based on the principle 'Try every means to assist poor students to solve their difficulties and spare no effort to prevent poor students from dropping out due to financial difficulties'.

- *Establish scholarships to encourage students to work hard.* Various scholarships have been established, such as the National Subsidy Scholarship, Excellent Student Scholarship, Professional Scholarship, scholarships set up by universities and special scholarships set up by social organizations or individuals to finance poor students or attract talent.
- *Strengthen cooperation between higher education institutions and banks, and help poor students obtain national student loans.* National student loans function as an important measure taken by the central government to strengthen financial support to poor students through financial means under the socialist market economy system. It is also the core of the policy of the financial support system in higher education institutions. In order to ensure that national student loans are carried out successfully, a trial was conducted in eight cities including Beijing, Shanghai, Tianjin, Chongqing, Wuhan, Shenyang, Xi'an and Nanjing in 1999. Since 1 September 2000, it has been carried out nationwide, and every college or university can help students apply for a national student loan. Achievements have been made since its overall promotion. However, some defects have also occurred in the policy design and operational mechanism. Consequently, most banks terminated their business cooperation with higher education institutions and discontinued national student loans in September 2003. In 2004, the Ministry of Education, Ministry of Finance and other departments of finance drafted a document, 'Suggestions on National Student Loan Improvement', based on their repeated investigations, careful study, comprehensive analysis and summary of existing problems, and issued it upon the approval of the State Department. This document made major changes and improvements to the national student loan policy, operational mechanism, risk and prevention, organization and leadership, and formulated a new policy and mechanism centring on the mechanism of risk compensation.
- *Set up a work-for-study foundation and create work-for-study opportunities.* According to the regulations of the Ministry of Education and Ministry of Finance, universities and colleges can take out 10 per cent of the total tuition fee, which falls under the work-for-study foundation's responsibility to fund the work-for-study students and provide financial support to other poor students.
- *Provide special subsidies to poor students in extremely difficult situations.* The governments at different levels and universities or colleges shall provide a temporary and one-off subsidy without repayment to poor students in case of special and emergency situations of difficulty.
- *Reduction in and exemption from tuition fees.* Universities and colleges should reduce the tuition fees of extremely poor students or exempt them altogether from the tuition fee, especially handicapped and orphaned

students, minority students, martyr's children and children from families with special needs.

- *Open Green Passage to new students from poor families.* In 2000, higher education institutions one after the other established a Green Passage System to ensure the successful entrance of all new college students from poor families. New college students from poor families should be allowed to go through the admission procedures followed by different measures of financial assistance according to different family backgrounds.

Defects and problems in the existing system of financial assistance to poor students

In the existing system of financial assistance to poor students, the national student loan plays a much more important role than any other means of collecting tuition fees from poor students. The reason is that it is easy to solve living difficulties through other methods, but it is impossible for them to cover tuition.

The national student loan failed to meet the needs of most poor students for a loan. Thus many poor students cannot pay their tuition fees in full. They began to show dissatisfaction with their colleges or universities, and society as well, due to the limitations on the amount of the national student loan and practical operational difficulties. They were tortured by the idea as to whether they could complete their studies successfully. Poor students from the local province and from other provinces complain that it is difficult for them to obtain a national student loan. According to the former, although they can apply for a national student loan, it is not so easy to obtain such a loan due to the rigid requirements and complicated procedures as well as the availability of a guarantor with a secure job and income. According to the latter, they cannot apply for a national student loan to pay for their tuition because such a business is not open to students from other provinces. Parents have to resort to as many relatives and friends as possible for financial assistance so that they can pay the tuition fees for their children. However, even in this way, they are still unable to raise the money to pay the tuition fees. One parent said with a sigh: 'I feel sad to see my children at a loss. I hate myself for being so incompetent'. With so many poor students failing to pay their tuition fees, higher education institutions have no alternative but to take such measures as discontinuation of monthly living subsidy, no registration for the following term, no participation in examinations, no issuance of graduation certificates and class advisers' constant pressure on students for tuition fees, which hurts the self-esteem of students from poor families and leads to confrontations between the class advisers and students.

Colleges and universities are educational entities in which students play a vital part. They shoulder the grand responsibilities of imparting knowledge, educating people and nurturing talent to ensure that students from poor families do not drop out for financial reasons. In the meantime, they have to collect tuition fees to meet the basic requirements of the teachers and students, and to maintain normal operations. Colleges and universities are in a dilemma.

Despite the fact that much work has been done, many students, still in financial difficulties, have a lot of complaints; the huge population of poor students makes the student loan available to only a small fraction, according to the director of the Student Affairs Department in S University, who takes charge of poor student assistance. The director of the Academic Affairs Department in S University is responsible for the management of student registration. In his words, according to the regulations of student management, students are not allowed to register for the next term before they pay the tuition fees. They cannot take the examinations without registration. Even if they take the examinations, they cannot get credit. Although regulations are regulations, it is hard to carry them out for the sake of maintaining stability because many students from poor families cannot pay all their tuition fees. A class adviser in S University may have more complaints. Poor students belong to a disadvantaged group. While advisers have to urge students to pay tuition fees as required by the university, they need to find a good explanation in order to prevent them from psychological obstruction and other problems caused by arrears in tuition fees. Improper solutions may affect the stability and development of the university. However, it is difficult to know the family background of all the students. Thus, those who can afford the tuition fees may exploit this advantage and refuse to pay the fees deliberately, which worsens the campus atmosphere.

A final solution worked out by the university

There are two causes for the existence of poor students: one is that the students cannot afford the tuition fees; the other is that they can barely cover their living expenses. The major solution to the tuition fee issue, a kernel issue in offering financial assistance to students, is to strengthen the cooperation between banks and universities and promote a national student loan system. Formulas such as work-for-study, scholarships and special subsidy can be adopted to cover basic expenses at college. The final solution, a result of the joint efforts of all relevant parties, is to increase the accessibility of the national student loan to students. That means universities and banks should strengthen cooperation and sign agreements to make sure that national student loans can be made available to every poor student in addition to the fulfilment of auxiliary measures for providing financial assistance to poor students.

Feasible plans

- *Strengthen bank–university cooperation to achieve a win–win re*sult. Guided by the national student loan policy, the university chooses to cooperate with a bank with quality service and a good reputation. The university sets up an account at the bank and deposits the tuition fees into the account while the bank provides student loans to the poor students at the university. By adhering to a principle of mutual reciprocity, mutual benefit and sharing risks, a win–win result can be achieved on the basis of this mutually restrictive mechanism.

- *Sign agreements with the bank for a collective transaction for the national student loan.* First, the university and the provincial financial department allocate risk-proof capital, amounting to 8 per cent of the actually released loans in the same year, to the bank on a 50–50 basis. Second, the university opens a deposit account in the bank that cooperates with it and pays deposits into the account, with the deposit equivalent to 2 per cent of the actually released loans in the same year. Once the students cannot return the principal and interest of the loan, the bank withdraws the same amount of money from the university's deposit account. Thus the risks can be substantially reduced for the bank to release loans.

- *Promote honesty and credit education among students, set up credit archives for students and increase students' awareness of honesty and credit so as to relieve the worries and reduce the risks of the bank in releasing loans.* First, the university sets up credit archives for the students and places on the file the history of their receipt and repayment of loans. The university keeps a current record of the students' study, life and other relevant information and gives feedback to the partner bank. Second, the university promotes the delivery of honesty and credit education, publicizes the individual credit system, increases the students' awareness of honesty and credit, and encourages students to act in accordance with the socialist concepts of honour and disgrace. Third, students settle the formalities for the confirmation of a loan repayment schedule before graduation. The university collects information concerning the students who have received loans and incorporates it into the national individual credit system. The names, ID numbers and other relevant information of those students who have defective records, such as severe breach of contract and intentional default of loan, will be made public. All banks share the information and set limitations for those students in housing loans, mortgage, company registration and so on.

Bank–university cooperation to provide loans for poor students is a major approach for assisting students in the fulfilment of their formal education. In addition, S University tries every possible way to seek out more approaches for the purpose of offering financial aid to poor students. For instance, the university develops cooperative relationships with enterprises; it sets up scholarships to pay the tuition fees for students who promise to work for the enterprises after graduation; it signs agreements with enterprises for the joint education of students and includes it in the enrolment plan every year. The enterprises allocate capital for the recruitment of students from poor families and train them for their own use. An integrated implementation of all the above approaches could guarantee that poor students will complete their formal education successfully.

Interest analysis of relevant parties

- *Bank* – First, with each transaction being only a small sum of money, the student loan involves complicated formalities, high operating costs and a large body of staff. Second, with an imperfect credit system in China, banks take great risks when making loans to students, as there is a high rate of breach of contract among students. Third, banks need to spend a lot of money in pressing the students for repayment of the loan and managing the follow-up records of the students. However, the large population of students gives the banks some enthusiasm to seize the huge student market and develop future potential clients.
- *University* – First, as education entities, universities take great risks in the operation of the student loan as they have to pay compensation to banks if students break their contracts. Second, there are a large number of poor students who cannot pay the tuition fees in full, which affects the financial budget and operating order of the university. But universities have a greater enthusiasm and initiative than banks to develop the student loan; because they are under pressure to 'ensure students from poor families don't drop out due to financial difficulties', universities have worked out an approach, namely assisting students by loaning money to them, to make sure that the students can fulfil their education without interruption.
- *Student* – With an easily available student loan, students from poor families are able to pay their tuition fees in full. This helps reduce economic pressures from their families and prevent the occurrence of intentional default of loans, and has been warmly welcomed by the students.

In a word, the poor student group is a big concern of society. It is of great importance to take steps to help them with their actual difficulties, which fully displays the advantages of the socialist system and mutual care among people. As poor students only account for a minority of the population, it is totally within the capacity of the universities, banks and people from all walks of life to help them. The student loan policy has been warmly welcomed and won wide support from students, parents and universities. Banks also have considerable enthusiasm for it. S University has already signed agreements with the bank to commence the operation of a student loan in the coming half-year.

In the past few years, S University has made efforts to explore and experiment with ways of providing financial aid to poor students. Having developed several effective approaches, S University is preparing for the experiment and assessment of some other methods in practice. The existence of poor college students has become a social phenomenon that is worthy of public attention from the whole of society. To resolve the problem, the university needs support from all social sectors in addition to its own capacity. The successful solution of the poor student issue will not only contribute to social stability but also create favourable conditions for the growth of students. The exploration of this issue is also of great significance to the establishment of a harmonious society.

Written in 2006

24 The dilemma of government student loans

Kang Ning

In 2000, the Chinese government implemented its student loan scheme throughout all tertiary institutions in China. Unlike commercial bank loans (secured loans taken from commercial banks by individuals), eligibility for the above scheme is restricted to the families of students who are facing financial difficulties. Fifty per cent of the loan interest will be subsidized by the government, while the other 50 per cent will only have to be repaid annually after graduation. This policy indicated an increased government emphasis on the welfare of the lower income strata of the population, and has been very popular with the people.

However, for the past 2 years since the scheme was implemented, results have been dismal. The Ministry of Education classifies students with a family income of less than 200 yuan a month as facing 'financial hardship', while students with a family income of less than RMB 120 a month are classified as facing 'extreme financial hardship'. According to Ministry projections, 30 per cent of all tertiary education students nationwide fall under the first category, while 15 per cent of the students are classified as facing 'extreme financial hardship'. This works out at an astronomical sum of 10 billion yuan of student loans annually. Figures from the China National Centre for Student Assistance indicate that, as of December 2001, student loan agreements between tertiary education institutions and banks amounted to 2.43 billion, a mere 35.4 per cent of the total student loans that had been applied for. Only 272,000 students, or 31.7 per cent of the total number of applicants, have successfully signed contracts for student loans. In addition, although the government has set aside 266 million yuan in subsidies for the loan interest, only 13.95 million yuan of actual subsidies (5.24 per cent of the total amount) have been distributed.

On one hand, the government faced problems with distributing the subsidies, while on the other hand, 70 per cent of families who were facing financial difficulties were unable to apply for student loans. It begs the question why this well-intentioned and initially well-received scheme is in its current state.

Background information on tuition reforms and the education funding framework

Reforms in tertiary education tuition began in 1989 (previously known as the Education Cost-sharing Plan), and experimental reforms were implemented in thirty-seven tertiary institutions in 1994. In 1997, after making adjustments to the initial reforms, they were implemented nationwide. Considered to be one of the biggest reforms in the Chinese tertiary education system since the opening up of the market economy, the primary goal was to create a system whereby the cost of education would be reasonably shared among the government, society, tertiary education institutions and the individual. As a result, cost sharing has created more than 20 billion of income for tertiary education institutions, which equates to 22.2 per cent on all student expenditure and 27.7 per cent on all recurrent expenditure (Table 24.1). Not only has this changed how capital is invested in the tertiary institutions and made up for the lack of investment from the government, it has also made the expansion of tertiary education a real possibility.

In the past, because of a system that advocated low wages and equal welfare, the incomes of the urban population were generally very low, while the rural population practised a point-based rationing system, which only managed to provide the most basic necessities. Although the government provided free education at the primary, secondary and tertiary levels, the scale of the education system on the whole was small. After 20 years of market reforms, the Chinese gross national product (GNP) is growing at the rate of 9.5 per cent a year and the income per capita has also risen dramatically. This has led to the progressive implementation of tertiary education tuition as a viable policy. Throughout the process of tuition reforms, the government has placed emphasis on three key points: first, compulsory basic education will be free; second, schools at the non-compulsory stage are free to collect reasonably priced fees according to their operational needs; and third, the pace of tuition reforms needs to be conservative and fees should not be too high.

Tertiary education is an impure public good and is not considered part of compulsory education. The returns received by the individual are higher

Table 24.1 Expenditure breakdown of a college student (given in yuan).

Year	1995	1998	1999	2000
Total expenses	8,280	13,991	15,231	15,974
Recurrent expenses	6,541	11,020	11,854	12,815
Tuition revenue	1,114	1,974	2,769	3,550
Percentage of tuition fees in total expenditures	13.5	14.1	18.0	22.2
Percentage of tuition fees in recurrent expenditures	17.0	17.9	23.4	27.7

Source: Shanghai Education Service Industry Research Group, October 2001.

and, therefore, the collection of tuition fees by tertiary institutions is widely accepted by the public. When the experimental reforms were introduced in 1989, the tuition fees of the tertiary institutions rarely exceeded 100 yuan, but have been rising gradually every year. In 2001, the government recommended tuition fees to be at around 25 per cent of a student's total expenses. Most tertiary institutions now have tuition fees in the range of 4,000 to 5,000 yuan. Dormitories in these institutions also charge 800–1,200 yuan in addition to tuition fees. In recent years, many tertiary institutions have turned to tuition fees as an important source of income.

Objectively speaking, the tuition fees currently charged by tertiary institutions are not considered high and only make up a small fraction of the cost of education. The majority of the funds today either come from the government or are privately raised by the tertiary institutions themselves. However, China is still a developing country where economic progress has been unequal nationwide. Income levels are generally lower and 30 million Chinese still live in extreme poverty. Out of a population of 1.3 billion people, 800 million Chinese are farmers, and such expenditure far exceeds their annual per capita income (see Table 24.2). In recent years, economic structural changes in the cities have led to a rise in the number of students who are classified as facing financial hardship. There have been many instances of students who have been accepted by the tertiary institutions but who fail to turn up for registration because of financial difficulties. The government cannot turn a blind eye to such cases. Government leaders have emphasized the need to provide other forms of support to academically outstanding students who are unable to pursue higher education, as well as the role of tertiary institutions in retaining all students who have been accepted, despite their financial circumstances.

This is an issue of ensuring social equity and stability, as well as keeping the tuition reforms on track. Since 1994, the central government has spent the premier reserve funds annually (945 million yuan as of 2000) to aid students with financial difficulties from the 300 tertiary institutions that come under the direct administration of the central government. After the floods

Table 24.2 Income gap between urban and rural populations (given in yuan).

Year	Average income per capita		
	Urban	Rural	Urban/rural (%)
1995	3,893	1,578	2.47
1996	4,377	1,926	2.27
1997	5,160	2,090	2.46
1998	5,425	2,160	2.51
1999	—	—	—
2000	6,280	2,253	2.79
2001	—	—	—

Source: China Statistical Yearbook 1998.

in 1998, the central government once again distributed financial aid to needy students who came from the disaster-affected zones. At the same time, the Ministry of Education, the Ministry of Finance, local governments and other related agencies have strived to build a sound policy framework to support students who require financial assistance. Currently, this system is only in its initial stages, and its objectives are primarily achieved through the following five aspects: awards and scholarships, work assistance, subsidies, tuition reductions and study loans.

Awards and scholarships are targeted at academically outstanding students with financial difficulties, as well as students who major in special subjects such as agriculture, education, physical education and culture. Work assistance refers to providing simple employment opportunities on campus to needy students in areas such as teaching, research and administration, in order for them to earn an income based on their own efforts. Subsidies are given out by central and local governments every year to students who require them. Apart from this, the tertiary institutions are required by the government to set aside about 10 per cent of their income obtained from tuition fees to provide assistance to financially underprivileged students. Such students can benefit from reduced tuition fees or have their tuition fees waived. Currently, the government has made education free for students majoring in the above-mentioned special subjects, while recommending the reduction or waiving of tuition fees for financially underprivileged students. Lastly, loans refer to the various loans taken out by students from financial institutions, which largely comprise secured commercial loans.

At the same time, to ensure that these students successfully complete their tertiary education, the Ministry of Education has requested that all tertiary institutions set up a 'green passage' to expedite their university registration process. After validating their actual financial status, the five channels of assistance could be used to keep this group of students in the education system. (According to 2001 statistics, 150,000 students have benefited from such a plan during the registration process.) Furthermore, the government has made use of the mass media to mobilize the general public to provide various kinds of assistance to these college students.

Systems and policies in other countries

Student loans refer to loans taken by students from the government or other financial institutions to pay for tuition fees or daily expenses during their tertiary education years. These loans will have to be repaid within a specified period of time upon graduation. In general, tertiary institutions in other countries receive tuition fees from students. Even in countries that provide free tertiary education such as Germany, financial assistance is given to needy students in the form of bursaries. Denmark, on the other hand, provides government guarantees to the banks when students take out loans, and also subsidizes part of the interest that students have to pay. As we can see from Table 24.3, universities in other parts of the world take the same approaches to student loans. Before the Chinese government set up the student loan scheme for tertiary students, it carried out considerable research into the policies of various countries (see Table 24.3). In other words, the student loan scheme in China is not a new innovation, but rather a product of the experience of others.

Background to the student loan scheme

The year 1999 was important for tertiary education in China because the central government made a major policy decision to increase the number of students admitted to the tertiary institutions. In that year, the number of students admitted to undergraduate and associate degree courses jumped by 42.9 per cent, while the total number of tertiary students increased from 6.231 million in 1998 to 7.189 million. In the following 2 years, tertiary education continued to expand. Taking into consideration adult education in tertiary institutions and self-study examination students, the number of students enrolled in all tertiary institutions amounted to 13 million, of which 7.58 million were enrolled in colleges. The tertiary education admission rate increased by almost 4 per cent, from 9.8 per cent in 1998 to 13.2 per cent in

Table 24.3 System of student loans in other countries.

Loaning agency	Autonomous government agency (UK) Government-appointed public banks (Brazil) Government-appointed private banks (USA)
Loan status	With interest, for the duration of study
Start of scheme	Denmark (1913), Sweden (1918), USA (1942)
Scale of scheme	Popular during the 1970s and 1980s. Currently implemented in over fifty countries and regions
Type of loan	Unconditional loans – no special restrictions on eligibility (Brazil) Conditional loans – only available to students who meet family income, academic criteria (Sweden)
Purpose of loan	Tuition or living expenses
Loan assistance	Government acts as guarantor or subsidizes the loan (USA)
Repayment	By instalments, to be completed within a specific period of time (USA) Using a proportion of annual or monthly income upon graduation, which will be deducted together with income tax (Australia) From the employers of the graduate, who pay an amount proportionate to the employees' (Ghana)

Source: Zhao Zhongjian. 'Student Loan in Other Countries'. Beijing: China Education Newspaper, 2 January 1995, 2nd edn.

2001. This expansion in tertiary education arose from the need to meet demands for a higher skilled workforce by the developing socialist market economy, as well as from demands for higher education by the population. This was widely covered in the mass media and was well received by the public.

As the number of students increased, the number of students from financially underprivileged backgrounds also went up. According to preliminary surveys conducted by the Ministry of Education, 20 per cent of students are currently classified as facing financial hardship. In certain tertiary institutions, such as institutes of agriculture, the proportion may be as high as 30 per cent, of which 10 per cent are classified as facing extreme financial hardship. In light of such demographic changes, the previous strategies of awards and scholarships, work assistance, subsidies, tuition reductions and loans (normal commercial bank loans) would not be adequate. As such, much can be learned from foreign experiences. Through the induction of financial institutions, the scope and effectiveness of aid offered to the financially underprivileged can be greatly improved.

In view of the aforementioned need, in June 1999, the central government approved the policy paper 'Regarding Legislation for the Government Student Loan Scheme', which was jointly drawn up by the People's Bank of China, the Ministry of Education and the Ministry of Finance. Starting from 1 September 1999, the government student loan scheme would be implemented in eight cities with high concentrations of tertiary institutions (Beijing, Shanghai, Tianjin, Chongqing, Wuhan, Shenyang, Xian and Nanjing). According to the legislation, financially underprivileged students would not only be able to enjoy government aid from the five channels of assistance, but could also apply for student loans from the Industrial and Commercial Bank of China (ICBC) for their tuition fees as well as their basic daily expenses. The amount of the loan that can be taken by each eligible student is limited to RMB 6,000 per annum. Fifty per cent of the interest would be subsidized by the government, while the rest of the loan would need to be repaid within 4 years after graduation.

It should be pointed out that the ICBC was chosen to give out student loans because, of the four wholly state-owned commercial banks in China (ICBC, Agricultural Bank of China, China Construction Bank and Bank of China), the ICBC had the best financial status and also had the greatest number of branches.

In accordance with the previously mentioned policy paper, ICBC drafted another paper entitled 'The ICBC – Government Student Loans Scheme Experimental Implementation', while the Ministry of Education drafted a paper entitled 'Regulations for Government Student Loan Scheme (experimental)'. These two papers outlined the way in which the policy would be implemented and how the system would be regulated respectively. Upon approval of 9-million-yuan subsidies for loan interest by the Ministry of Finance, the Ministry of Education issued 870 million lines of credit to 138 colleges in eight cities. An inter-ministry committee was formed by the Ministry of Education, Ministry of Finance and the People's Bank of China to coordinate the efforts of the individual agencies, while the Ministry of Education set up the China National Centre for Student Assistance to oversee the administration of the government student loan scheme.

The People's Bank of China has stated that, although there have been problems in the initial stages of the student loan scheme, the effects of the policy are clear. Most students and teaching staff agree that the policy has been heading in the right direction and this will alleviate much of the burden from financially underprivileged students. Commercial banks also see the potential in such a market.

The problem with secured loans

However, when school reopened in September that same year, the government student loan scheme was unexpectedly given the cold shoulder in many tertiary institutions. Demand for the loans from eligible students was low.

From reports submitted by tertiary institutions to the China National Centre for Student Assistance, the Ministry of Education identified five main reasons why the scheme was poorly received in practice, which were discussed by the inter-ministry committee: first, the ICBC offered only three types of secured loans – guarantee security, collateral security and mortgage guarantee – which many students were unable to afford, and this was the biggest problem with the scheme; second, the ICBC branches insisted that the tertiary institutions act as guarantors in order to share the risk, but the institutions had refused to do so because they could not be responsible for students who had graduated, nor could they be liable for the loans taken out by these students; third, the application process at the ICBC was too complicated for students; fourth, students see these loans, which have to be repaid within 4 years after graduation, as too great a burden, and would prefer not to be in debt when they join the workforce. This is especially important for students who plan to pursue a postgraduate degree, which would further limit their ability to pay off their loan regularly.

First policy amendment

The banks were largely responsible for the undesirable outcome of the push on loans. As private entities, banks are responsible for their own profits and losses, and hence are apparently reluctant to undertake too many risks for this government policy. However, under the coordination of the Office in the State Department and the People's Bank of China (PBC), the ICBC relented and agreed with the Chinese people. The banks, Ministry of Education and Ministry of Finance then drafted a new bursary loan bill.

In February 2000, the amended 'Opinions on Student Loans' was officially introduced. In this paper, the following aspects were addressed:

1 Ways to promote credit-based student loans – students can borrow after signing the appropriate application forms and getting recommenders and witnesses to attest to their credibility.
2 If the student loan borrower experiences difficulties in repayment after graduation, the repayment period may be extended accordingly.
3 Banks are to simplify the paperwork for borrowing.
4 To revoke the joint responsibility of the school and the Student Loan Management Centre for unpaid loans, which was formally stipulated in the 'Regulations for Government Student Loan Scheme (experimental)'.
5 To allow financial institutions to continue offering commercial student loans.

Policy changes resisted

The introduction of the amendment relieved the colleges of their repayment responsibilities; the new guarantee system made it easier for students to borrow but, evidently, the banks bore higher loan-associated risks. In June 2000, under the leadership of the deputy director of the Office of the State Leading Group of Science, Technology and Education, the research team consisting of members from the Office in the State Department, Ministry of Education, PBC and ICBC conducted experimental surveys in three cities, namely Beijing, Tianjin and Nanjing. From the survey, one can tell that the amendments to the policy had, to a significant extent, solved the loan guarantee problem in the workings of the national student loan system. This is especially true for the provision of commercial student loans, which made it easier for students to apply for loans. In principle, this adjustment should be well received by colleges and students. In reality, to the surprise of the research team, during the 4 months after the implementation of the policy, the national student loans granted by the ICBC in the eight experimental cities were all guaranteed loans, and the credit-based student loan system was not activated at all!

There are thirty-eight ministry-owned colleges in Beijing, of which half had signed the National Student Loan Cooperation Agreement. The other colleges that did not comply with the agreement had different interpretations of the 'recommenders' and 'witnesses' in the credit-based lending system and, in particular, were unable to accept the additional measures implemented by the ICBC. Only 518 students secured student loans with the ICBC, and this is clearly disproportionate to the student population of over 200,000.

The situation in nearby Tianjin seemed better. All four colleges signed the cooperation agreement, and 667 loan applications were received. However, only 175 applicants were successful, and the loans amounted to 1.56 million yuan, which means that an average student borrows less than 10,000 yuan.

There are fifteen colleges in Nanjing, of which six had signed the cooperation agreement. Seventy applications were received, of which forty failed to meet the guarantee requirement. The remaining thirty applications were still being processed in the other cities; hence, not one student managed to claim any national student loan.

Summing up the statistical data from all eight cities, one can see that a total of seventy-nine ministry-owned colleges had signed the cooperation agreement, 53 per cent of all the colleges involved in this pioneer project. The banks received 5,365 applications altogether, but only lent to 1,729 applicants, and loans amounted to 19.52 million yuan. This means that only 32 per cent of the applicants were successful. It is essential to note that the credit-based student loan system had not been activated in three of the eight experimental cities, namely Chongqing, Nanjing and Shenyang.

Significantly, the interest-subsidized national student loans attracted only a small number of applicants, and the applications approved by the banks were even fewer. However, the commercial student loans were becoming more popular. To the date of the survey, the ICBC, the Agricultural Bank of China, the Bank of China, the China Construction Bank, Pudong Development Bank, City Bank, China Merchants Bank and credit coopera-tives had introduced commercial student lending in all eight experimental cities. There were 3,336 lending transactions and 35.64 million yuan were lent, which is almost twice the amount of national student loans.

Apparently, even though changes were made to the policy, it was still resisted during its implementation. The banks did not place an emphasis on national student loans, but were more inclined towards commercial lending targeted at students who are not impoverished. The responses of the colleges and students were also not as enthusiastic as expected.

Searching for reasons

The research team conducted the following analysis in the report submitted to the statesmen.

ICBC's worry about loan-associated risks

Because the new policy freed colleges and the student loan management centre from the responsibility of loan repayments, the ICBC was concerned that it would have to undertake the loan-associated risks by itself. This explains why the ICBC came up with 'Additional Regulations for the Experimental Government Student Loan Scheme' and added some clauses regarding witnesses. For instance, 'the witness must submit his recent receipt of his paycheck, his water bills, electricity bills and gas bills'. Moreover, the ICBC indicated in the standard text edition of the 'Student Loan Cooperation Agreement' that if 'the Sponsor [college] breaches the agree-ment, hence resulting in the Lender's loss of loan interest, the school will be responsible for compensation'. It was also stipulated in the standard text edition that the witness must bear a certain amount of responsibility for the full repayment of the student loan and interest. These additional clauses contradicted the tenet of the amendment, and showed that the bank lacked the motivation to promote student loans.

The concerns of ICBC handling personnel

There are stringent procedures and responsibilities involved when it comes to lending. According to the relevant regulations stipulated by the general rule for bank loans, the responsibility and objective of credit management is to keep the bad debt percentage of personal loans under 0.3 per cent, and this is achieved through the assessment of overdue loans, stagnant accounts and bad debt write-offs. On one hand, ICBC personnel are disturbed by the great mobility of students who are financially challenged, as that brings bigger loan-associated risks. On the other hand, the bank will not able to apply the principle for commercial loans, which eradicates loan-associated risks (through mortgages, collateral and so on) to student loans. As the handling personnel will not be getting extra returns, and instead will have to undertake greater risks, one can see why they lack motivation.

Even though the colleges and teachers are free from repayment responsibilities, the system still calls for concern on recommenders' and witnesses' parts. The policy paper does not give an accurate description of the role and responsibility of the witness. A good example will be that the witness 'should keep in contact with the Borrower after graduation'. Because witnesses cannot promise that they will still be able to keep in touch with students several years after graduation, teachers are dubious about taking up the responsibility. Teachers are also worried that if they fail to fulfil their duties, 'the names of the witnesses and recommenders will be published and publicized', hence inadvertently tarnishing the reputation of the school and themselves. For the above reasons, colleges are reluctant to provide recommenders for credit-based loans, and teachers are not willing to be witnesses. The additional clauses written by the ICBC are also deemed unacceptable by the schools and teachers, thus affecting the impetus for schools to promote the national student loan scheme.

Lack of understanding towards impoverished students

The poorer the student, the harder it is for him to find a guarantor, but can we say for sure that the poorer a student is, the worse his credit is? The banks seem to think that way, and so insist that these students provide guarantors or witnesses. Undergraduates who fail to find guarantors or witnesses usually have no choice but to forfeit their applications.

Second amendment

The report was submitted to the deputy premier in charge of the scheme, who was not impressed by the progress of the student loan scheme. He ordered that 'PBC, along with ICBC, Ministry of Education, Ministry of Finance and other relevant institutions analyse and solve the existing problems'.

Thus, the inter-ministerial coordination team members sat down together again to devise a solution to the problems. In August 2000, a paper entitled 'Additional Comments on the Management of the Student Loans' was introduced.

In this paper, some changes were made to the terms of the original policy, which elucidate the teachers' understanding of the responsibility of witnesses and took into consideration the banks' concern regarding loan-associated risks.

The paper gave a clear definition of the witnesses' responsibility: 'Witness refers to a natural person who shares a close relationship to the Borrower; he need not provide guarantee for the Borrower. His duty is to help the recommender and the lending banks to understand the circumstances of the Borrower'. The directive in the original policy, which says, 'the names of the witnesses and recommenders will be published and publicized', was also removed.

'If bad debts occur as a result of student loans, after being audited and certified by the headquarters, the actual loan before tax deduction will be written off as stipulated'. In this paper, the most implausible and the most sensational clause is the territorial expansion of student loans. The results of the experiment in the eight experimental cities were not ideal, and yet the territorial range of student loans would be extended from schools in the eight cities to cover all tertiary institutions in the country. Student loans would also be provided by ABC, Bank of China and CCB, in addition to the original ICBC. The pool of borrowers had also been expanded to include graduate students, instead of targeting only undergraduates and diploma students. Perhaps policy-makers pinned high hopes on the prospects of this policy.

Policy-makers hope that, after a year of experimentation, this privileged student loan policy will benefit all indigent students. But to dismiss the problems without really resolving them, particularly at the start of a new college term in August, invites new problems that will persistently crop up in the future.

Solving the problem of asymmetric information

At the same time, another extremely thought-provoking issue for department heads was the problem of asymmetric information. The supervisors involved specifically ordered that all information relevant to the provision of financial aid to needy students (especially student loans), including the operating method, procedures, results and questions, and government requirements, is to be published in newspapers immediately in the form of question and answer sessions with journalists. Hence, following the expansion of the experimental pool, to ensure that more colleges and students had a better understanding of the national student loan policy, the supervisors allocated funds to print millions of copies of promotional brochures, which were to be distributed to some 3.5 million graduating high school seniors from all over China. They also requested that all tertiary institutions include an introductory note on national student loans when posting their admission offers; lastly, one of the directors in charge, who was from the Ministry of Education, penned a long article on the national student loan policy, invited the prominent chief editors from the press to the Ministry of Education and explained to them the importance of publishing this article. Many journalists were moved by the director's sincerity and tried to publish the full original text of the article despite the space constraint. A few days later, this director held a press conference personally to inform the press on what the government was doing for impoverished students, and he reiterated the scope and relevant contents of the policy. Publicity of the national student loan policy was suddenly at an all-time high.

Despite the painstaking efforts of the director, a lot of colleges and banks responded that the documents needed for the nationwide launch of the student loan experimentation were distributed in late August, and the policy would go into force when the new academic term commenced on 1 September. The organizers were unable to digest, strategize and execute the policy in time, and time lags still exist.

Third setback

Since the introduction of 'Additional Comments' at the start of the new term, up until the end of the January semester in 2001, the Ministry of Education National Student Loan Management Centre had been receiving feedback on student loans from various colleges. From the response, one could see that, although the number of student loan applicants was increasing, the figure was still far from expectations. The Ministry of Education and the participating banks held six coordination meetings on the implementation of the national student loan scheme. Meanwhile, the Ministry of Education, together with PBC, Ministry of Finance, ICBC and ABC, did a project survey in different provinces and realized that they cannot be too optimistic about the situation.

In February, the departments of education and ministry-owned schools submitted urgent reports on national student loans upon the request of the Ministry of Education. After computation, there were 514,000 student loan applicants, and the applied loans amounted to 3,230 million yuan; the number of students who signed loan agreements totalled 111,000, and the amount loaned was 1,260 million yuan; the interest deduction set aside by different levels of administration amounted to 13.75 million yuan, and the total interest paid was 9.3418 million yuan. From the statistics, we can see that there were a lot of applicants, but only a minority were successful in their applications. The implementation was more successful in central ministry colleges in Beijing, Shanghai and Chongqing, but it faced more difficulties in other provincial colleges. There are two provinces without concrete implementation of the national student loan policy, and nine provinces without arrangements for interest deductions. The Ministry of Education tried to investigate the reasons for failure through seminars with the schools, but even the school administrations could not fathom why. Was it not agreed upon that the bad debts occurring as a result of student loans would be written off? Why were banks still afraid of undertaking risks and did not have enough confidence and coordination in credit-based student loans to the extent of setting stringent borrowing conditions in the actual implementation and transferring the risks to colleges?

Banks have their own explanations. Bankers say that, if schools are not confident that the students they educate are credible, and are unwilling to bear any loan-associated risks, why should banks, who do not know the students, undertake such risks? Even though the regulation that the full sum of bad debt can be written off is included in the 'Additional Comments', the maximum amount is not specified. In addition, as the assessment from the grassroots uses the incorporated account system as well as the bonded assessment, once late payments or bad debts occur in student loans, the organizer will inevitably be penalized by his superiors, even though the debt can be written off. Furthermore, colleges are enrolling students in large numbers, resulting in the employment prospects of college students becoming poorer. Their repayment ability has now become questionable. In addition, risks and benefits should be in equal proportions. However, the small amount of a single student loan involves many parties that do not bring scale efficiency (compared with the same amount of loans being made to businesses, which will yield higher positive returns). This requires the procedure of evaluation, investigation and collection. Nevertheless, banks do not get any tax concessions or profits. In such circumstances, how is it possible to motivate banks to issue student loans? Apart from that, the practice of handling government student loans is a one-to-one deal, whereby an education institution is asked to receive loans from a specific bank. As different banks provide different services, commercial banks with early study loan set-up have relatively more loan transactions to deal with, resulting in a longer time delay and inconvenience to students. Commercial banks with late introduction of the student loan system basically do not receive any sign-ups from colleges, thus prompting them not to offer the loan service.

Conduct a national work conference on government student loans

Once the core of the problem was identified, members of the inter-ministerial coordination group got together to work out a new solution. On 22 June 2001, the Government Student Loan Work Conference was held in Beijing. This was the first time since the establishment of student loans that ministries and banks converged in a meeting. Deputy directors from the Office of

Education in each province and the vice presidents of provincial branches of the four major commercial banks also attended the meeting. Other than requesting education institutions and banks to implement the various policies of government student loans, three new requirements were also introduced.

1 To reject the original plan of a one school–one bank relationship and replace it with one school being able to deal with more than one bank.
2 To create a separate ledger, separate subject appraisals and a separate accounting system. Once approval is given after the occurrence of bad debts, a full tax write-off is permitted.
3 Business tax exemption on government student loans.

The above new regulations raised during the meeting solved the aforementioned problem. When an education institution is given more choices to deal with many banks, this will increase competitiveness among the four chosen banks. Separate ledgers make it easier for officers to handle their work, and business tax exemption gives the opportunity for banks to create revenue for themselves, no matter how small the profit might be. Hopefully, the student loan system can now go on to fast track.

Unexpectedly and yet frustratingly, by the end of the year, the statistical data showed the outcome we did not wish to see, as mentioned earlier.

In February 2002, when ministries and banks launched the specialized management plan (the four selections – school, scale, sum of loan and scheduled banks; and the three appraisals – monthly review of the number of candidates who apply and loan applications, monthly review of the number of qualified candidates and approved loans, monthly review of issuance of loans from banks) and fully implemented the loan scheme through a national video and telephone conference, there was not much improvement. There is a phenomenon whereby banks are more willing to issue study loans to students from the local city which has good financial status and employment prospects. Banks are, however, reluctant to offer loans to non-local students in poor financial circumstances and with unpromising employment prospects, such as students from the arts stream.

Anhui Province reflected on this matter and had this to say to the attitudes of banks:

> The targets of bank loans are mainly from prestigious and well-known schools, while vocational schools and non-reputable schools stand very little chance in getting the bank loans; the amount of loans given to city schools are larger, accounting for 70 per cent of the total sum, and the remaining 30 per cent is rural schools. {.. .} Although banks generally consider college graduates to be potential quality clients, with the current situation in the country where students are not guaranteed a job, graduates from certain schools and academic majors find it hard to secure a job, or may be receiving low income, therefore making it

difficult for them to repay the principal and interest on a study loan. Second, higher student mobility nowadays makes it difficult for banks to trace the whereabouts of students who have already graduated, giving it a certain amount of credit risk.

Is there any basis for banks to worry about student credit loans?

The problems exposed by media reports

As the schools and banks make efforts to reduce loan-associated risks, in spring 2002, the media coincidentally published continuous reports on the risks brought about by student loans, intensifying the panic behind the cooperation between banks and schools.

For example, as one newspaper reported, during May and June 2002, a provincial ICBC main branch conducted a survey of the 10,887 graduated student loan borrowers from twelve different branches. It was found that up to 45 per cent of borrowers breached the contract and did not repay their loans on time, and 90 per cent of these cases can be ascribed to subjective factors. This will naturally make the banks more apprehensive. The publication of such loan-associated risks in the press further aggravated the worries that the banks had always had.

The China Economic Times article on 16 March 2002 entitled 'Credibility Crisis Plagues School, Student Loans Get Thorny – Banks Suffer when Undergraduates Fail to Repay their Loans' reported an interview with several bankers on credit-based loans:

> The journalist finds it hard to believe that the credibility crisis is spreading in the tertiary institutions. These are some shocking statistics: in the main state-owned commercial banks, the percentage of bad debts that occur because of student loans is on average higher than 10 per cent, and some banks even have to face the problem of not being able to track down 45 per cent of the student loan borrowers when the repayment period is due.
>
> The supervisor of the Finance Division of a CCB branch told a reporter: because there is no required guarantee for credit-based national student loans, the bank only has a photocopy of the borrower's identification. When students graduate and find their jobs in other cities, there is no way to contact them, much less to press for repayment. Sending letters to the students is like throwing stones into the sea, and the banks cannot possibly order someone to go down to the borrower's place personally, not to mention that we do not have that much manpower. Furthermore, the costs of travelling are too high, and we may not necessarily be able to get the repayment successfully.
>
> According to the supervisor of the Finance Division of an ICBC branch: ICBC had signed student loan agreements worth 4,300 million

yuan with 43 colleges in a city, and 1,800 million yuan had been loaned. Since 20 December last year, the repayment period had started for some 1,250 students, but to date there are more than 110 borrowers that have not repaid their loans, and they make up almost 10 per cent. He says if other undergraduates do the same thing, then the losses incurred by ICBC will be huge. The inexplicable thing is, as compared to undergraduates, the percentage of other consumer loan borrowers that failed to repay their loans is less than 0.1 per cent.

The situation in the Bank of China is better. The Public Relations and Publicity Department of the bank said: the Bank of China only lends to MBA students in Peking University, Tsinghua University and People's University, because these borrowers usually have a certain degree of career foundation, and their economic endurance and credibility are higher. The bad-debt percentage is usually kept under 2 per cent. As for the general student loans, the banks who started earlier can handle them.

The journalist also found out that: lots of banks are considering jointly exposing the students who fail to repay their loans. When the time comes, the names of the schools will follow the scrolls of 'black lists'. To the teachers and students of the school, just imagine the pain inflicted.

People in the banking profession think that the national student loan scheme was destined to be a failure since the start of its creation. The so-called 'black lists', pressing for payments in other cities, joint exposure and so on do not serve much purpose. If we resort to that, then won't the cost of societal credit establishment be too big? A supervisor from a relevant department in CCB commented munificently, CCB is willing to support the national bursary policy. As long as it can contribute to the building of a credible society, it is willing to incur any amount of losses, but most importantly, we as a part of the society should believe in fulfilling our promises.

The following has been adapted from the *China Industrial Economic News* of 2 April 2001:

Someone from the Fuzhou Department of Education told the reporter, it's best not to report. Because if you make it sound good, or report too much, students and schools will comment – why is it that we always fail to borrow; if you do not report enough, there will be resistance, the banks will be displeased, and it stymies business negotiation. The best is to do it and not talk about it.

In Nanjing, the reporter requested an interview with the four commercial bank managers of the student loan scheme, but coincidentally they turned down the reporter by either saying that they are outstationed, or they are not in town. The other bank personnel said, 'We cannot talk irresponsibly, the main branch will explain', 'we are a commercial bank. As to whether there is commercial value behind this scheme, god knows'.

The person in charge of a bank branch in Shanxi told the journalist, regarding student loans, that in principle they do not publicize nor accept interviews. As bankers, risk awareness should be a top priority. Students' mobility is high, and there are many variable factors involved. To locate someone in a talent market that moves both ways is no different from finding a needle in the sea, the cost is very high. And, the banks are not confident of getting the interest subsidy from the government. Take Shanxi, for instance; public finance is already tight as it is, how it will provide 50 per cent interest subsidy remains unknown. Although the policy paper had stipulated the writing off of bad debts, no concrete measures were taken by any banks to finalize on the maximum amount of bad debt that would be written off, so how can we decide on this amount? Nobody knows for sure. High academic qualifications do not equate high credibility. Based on the current economic development, it is not easy for a typical graduate to repay ten thousands of loans within four years of joining the workforce. I feel that the banks will naturally have their own reservations towards credit-based loans.

Taking into consideration the difficulties that the banks face, the Department of Education in Jiangsu Province agreed a major compromise: the maximum amount that a person can borrow every year is lowered from 8,000 yuan to 5,000 yuan. Even then, it does not eliminate the apprehensions of the banks: even though there is 50 per cent interest subsidy and the guarantee that bad debts will be written off, the lending banks will still have to bear two-thirds of the losses. They reckon that even in the US, where the credit system is established, they still see 10 per cent of bad debts occurring from student loans. The credit system in China is not developed yet, and by performing this service, banks will definitely incur losses.

An ICBC branch in Sichuan province has a more 'ingenious' way of handling student loans; to the date of the interview, that branch had only handled one student loan borrowed by an indigent student.

The progress in Zhejiang province is not ideal. It has been reported that the Department of Finance and Department of Education had set aside 10 million yuan for interest-subsidized loans in September last year, but up until the end of last year, only 2.858 million yuan had been loaned out, and until now 7.142 million yuan had yet to be borrowed.

The interest-subsidized loans in Zhejiang province follow the 5.85 per cent loan interest rate, and the provincial Department of Finance bears 50 per cent of the loan interest, which greatly reduces the burden on students, but why is this good deal seeing such slow progress?

The person in charge of a Bank of China branch in Hangzhou asserted during the interview that some schools and students misunderstand that 'there is no risk involved in student bursary loans' and 'student loans are part of the education welfare policy'.

Commercial banks think that bursary loans are also a type of loan, and should be managed according to the fundamental laws of the workings of credit and capital, whereas some colleges and students see the scheme as an important measure taken by the government to educate and prosper, and this scheme is an education welfare policy carrying government subsidies. This difference in understanding is another factor that affects the progress of the national student loan policy.

Adapted from *Huaxi City News* on 20 December 2001: 'Banks complain, schools air grievances while wanting student defaulters on SWUFE online' (Note: SWUFE stands for Southwest University of Finance and Economics).

Recently, 'lists of students who default on bank payments' have been appearing on the intranets and notice boards of several universities in Chengdu, causing uproar in the school – the widely applauded student loan scheme has encountered 'lack of credibility' from borrowers in Chengdu.

Previously, the list of graduated student defaulters belonging to the 1996 and 1997 cohorts had been promulgated. It had been reported that the five people on the list were one of the first few in Chengdu to have received national student bursary loans. Even though the amount involved was small, the students disappeared into thin air after leaving the school. According to an ABC branch in Chengdu, about 5 per cent of student borrowers do not repay their loans. While looking at the 'black list', the person in charge lamented that he had no choice but to resort to such means!

From what the journalist found out, national student loans are not just unprofitable for the banks, they also carry heavy risks. A particular school applied for close to 10 million yuan of loans and, in the end, the bank only approved 6 million yuan.

Right now, loans are approved and given out to schools, and so whether or not students fulfil the criteria will depend on the proof provided by the school, but the school does not bear guarantee responsibilities. The school obviously hopes to see more impoverished students receiving financial aid, but when faced with such student defaulters, the school feels 'it has been wronged'.

One university teacher supervising student loans commented that, without a good system of supervision for personal credibility, and being dependent on only schools and banks, the ability to handle such a scheme will not surprisingly fall short of expectations.

Although the five SWUFE graduates in the 1996 and 1997 cohorts, as mentioned above, had provided various forms of contact as guarantees, following graduation, either they had moved address or they were no longer at their original workplace. It appeared that such people had evaporated into thin air, and naturally there was no follow-up on interest and loan payments.

A teacher from the student affairs department of SWUFE told the journalist, 'The students obviously have not realized the importance of credit in society in the future'.

The 'Matthew effect' arising from this series of reports on the 'absence of credibility' is disturbing and, after official investigation, it was found that the students involved in the cases of 'defaulted loan repayments' had mostly taken out commercial loans. Judging from the time, the repayment period for national student loans was not yet due. Therefore, within a period of 4 months, the Ministry of Education held an urgent press conference, where the director in charge gave a two-hour talk on the general public's opinion that loans are not 'unpaid', but 'not borrowed'. He asked the media to report the positive effects of the student loan scheme and to emphasize the amount of assistance rendered to impoverished students instead of over-stating the risks involved. Perhaps the sincerity of the director persuaded the press, as we have not seen reports of 'unpaid loans' since.

However, subsequently, an inherent and strange phenomenon in the credit-based loan system surfaced and caught the director off-guard.

The following is adapted from the *China Industrial Economic News* of 2 April 2001.

The extension and essence of 'school loans' for undergraduates are experiencing a series of changes; the 'bursary loans' intended to offer timely support for impoverished students are now proffering new consumption and management uses for some college students in Shanghai.

A fourth-year student, Yu, applied for a student loan of 2,700 yuan to purchase a cell phone and office wear. 'In order to help myself get a good job, I need to invest and package myself, but I do not wish to add to my family's burden because of this'. It is common for Shanghainese college students to use bursary loans to 'package themselves'. Liu, from another university, also applied for a 2,000 yuan loan from the school. He planned to attend graduate school and he hoped to earn more money during these few months so as to afford the expensive tuition for his graduate course. For many Chinese students who want to stay in Shanghai after graduation, settling down in Shanghai involves an arduous transition period. They need money to look for jobs and to afford accommodation and other living expenses, and so they turn to student loans. An undergraduate said that these few thousand yuan helped him to settle down in Shanghai in advance. 'Can I use the student loan to buy a computer or buy a pager?' The journalist found out in his investigation that many students use the student loan for diverse purposes.

In response to this phenomenon, the supervisor of the financial management division in a Shanghainese university said that, in principle, schools provide loans to students in the hope of allowing impoverished students to attend school. As for the students who misuse the student loans for other purposes, the school strongly opposes their actions, but if the students really did do that, there was nothing anyone could do about it. The school only serves as an intermediary to help students apply for student loans from the banks and does not have any powers over how the money is spent. Regarding how to correctly handle the student loan, this awaits further coordination between the school and the students.

Commercial banks believe that bursary loans are used primarily to cover the living and tuition expenses of destitute students. As for the other applications made by students whose families are not that hard up, be it for purchasing computers, communication tools or other items, commercial banks think they should be processed as commercial loans.

Conclusion

The government student loan scheme was originally intended to support around 1.2 million students and amount to tens of billions of yuan. However, as of June 2002, of the loans that would have been applied for, only 31.18 per cent had been approved by the banks (31.7 per cent at the end of 2001) (applicants numbered 1,124,514, while the number of loans approved numbered 350,624). Local tertiary institutions had an approval rate of 23.50 per cent, while ministry-owned colleges had a rate of 58.08 per cent. The bank had approved loan contracts amounting to 3.0317 billion yuan, which made up 36.75 per cent of the total amount of loans applied for (35.4 per cent at the end of 2001); the total sum of loans applied for amounted to 8.17234 billion yuan, of which local tertiary institutions had an approval rate of 24.72 per cent, while ministry-owned colleges had a rate of 64.64 per cent. The actual figures for the student loan scheme are as follows: (1) The students who received the loans numbered 326,688, which was 29.05 per cent of the total number of applicants; of these, local tertiary institutions had an approval rate of 21.29 per cent, while ministry-owned colleges had a rate of 56.25 per cent. (2) The actual sum of money given out amounted to 1.68614 billion yuan, which was 20.63 per cent of the total amount applied for (local tertiary institutions 15.04 per cent, ministry-owned colleges 33.28 per cent) and 56.15 per cent of the approved amount (local tertiary institutions 61.60 per cent, ministry-owned colleges 51.48 per cent). The amount of subsidies set aside by the Ministry of Finance amounted to 451.28 million yuan (266 million yuan at the end of 2001), but the actual amount of subsidies given out amounted to 33.63 million yuan (13.95 million yuan at end 2001), which was 7.45 per cent of the total amount set aside (5.24 per cent at the end of 2001), of which local tertiary institutions were at 9.90 per cent and ministry-owned colleges at 6.45 per cent. These figures indicate that the efforts of the government have not paid off and the expectations have not been met.

The matter ultimately boils down to a single issue – creditworthiness. The tertiary institutions have sought to instil financial credibility into their students in various ways, making this a key education priority. For instance, 250 graduates from Zhongnan University who had taken out student loans put down their signatures on a 10-metre-long banner, which proclaimed 'Credibility starts from me'. The *People's Daily* also reviewed the issue with an article entitled 'Peking University started Forum on Personal Credit Education for College Students'. Wuhan University also started a forum entitled 'Loss of credibility for one, Shame for the rest' to instil credibility in students. However, despite such education measures, internal safeguards in the system are still lacking. At the same time, with regard to credibility from the point of view of the bank, although student loans can be treated as bad debt and can be written off completely, too much bad debt will ultimately harm the bank's image as a commercial entity. Furthermore, it would be difficult to determine whether the bad debts were a result of incompetence on the part of the bank managers, and instructions to absolve them of all responsibilities for the bad debts may not go down well with these managers.

Banks and tertiary institutions know that to avoid loans is a shared goal. If the avoidance of responsibility by one party increases the risk taken by the other party, the tug of responsibilities between the two parties would be ongoing. Consequently, the government student loan scheme would not be implemented successfully. Therefore, both parties hope that a personal credit history database and a personal credit framework can be established as soon as possible.

The Ministry of Education has done much research and preparation for the establishment of a personal credit history database for student loans. According to the plan, all tertiary institutions were to complete their collection of information by July 2002. The figures were to be compiled at the national level and put online by August and, by 1 September, the website was to be functional for the utility of the banks. However, those responsible for the system noticed a problem with it because, in the long run, it would not be able to keep track of students after they graduated. The most that could be done was to keep track of students into their first jobs, after which information could not be obtained. Therefore, only with the development of such a database can the problem be solved.

From the establishment of the first private credit institution to the development of a national personal credit database in the early 1980s, the building of a well-run credit framework in the United States took approximately 100 years. It is this system that provided a sound foundation for the American system of personal loans. On the other hand, the credit framework in China has only been established recently. In 1999, the People's Bank of China approved the experimental collection of personal credit history data in Shanghai. To date, the credit history data of 1.1 million people have been collected. The commercial banks in Shanghai have linked up with the database and have been granted restricted access to the credit histories.

During the National Convention for Student Loans, the People's Bank of China indicated that a nationwide credit history database would be set up based upon the database in Shanghai. The banking credit registration and consulting system, the bank's personal credit information system, monitoring system for payment and bank account management system would be merged so that resources could be shared.

However, the establishment of such a database would need to come together with the introduction of second-generation identification cards by the Chinese public security departments. Initially, the authorities had planned to completely solve the problem of credit history information in 2002 when tertiary students around the country replaced their identification cards. Two outstanding issues have made this a distant possibility: first, the issue of legislation. The second-generation identification cards would include the thumbprints of the card owners, which would require legislation approval from the National People's Congress. At the moment, the 'Citizen Identification Card Bill' still remains a draft. Second, there is a technical issue involved. The responsible agencies believe that the identification cards should use domestically engineered, domestically manufactured chips, but the technology involved still remains at the experimental stage and will require some time before mass production is possible.

It seems that all the bank and tertiary institutions can do now is to wait. Similarly, the authorities responsible for the scheme, despite their urgency, can only wait.

The current situation regarding the government study loan scheme (GSLS)

As the example above demonstrates, problems plaguing the GSLS as a scheme to help the poor and needy have invariably been the following: unsupportive bank response, unsuitability for students and loan delinquency. All these problems have hampered the implementation of effective policies. There are two reasons for this situation: first, there is little government subsidy given, thereby causing commercial banks to shy away from taking on such a big risk. Second, students tend to extend the period of the loan beyond the stipulated 4 years, resulting in substantial losses on the part of the banks. During June 2004, in order to improve the situation, the Ministry of Education, in conjunction with the Ministry of Finance, the Bank of China and the China Banking Regulatory Commission (CBRC), made adjustments to improve the implementation of the GSLS (see Table 24.4).

At a press conference organized by the State Department, the aforementioned four bodies made much of the newly improved GSLS. According to this new policy, the chances that banks giving out loans will be appointed by the government will be less; instead, the policy will allow for bidding by loan agencies state and nationwide depending on geography and other factors. During the bidding process for the 116 state-owned colleges nationwide, the Bank of China was the only bank to win a tender. According to the new policy, the Finance Ministry and a high school do not contribute equally to the compensation fund, but now do so according to how much they contravene the contract. In other words, the more a student contravenes what is

Table 24.4 Comparison between the new and old government student loan schemes.

	Interest subsidies by the Finance Ministry	Deadlines for repayment	Processing banks	Risk compensation
New policy	Full subsidy coverage while in school, to be fully undertaken by the student upon graduation	Depending on employment, the student starts repayment 1~2 years after graduation and is to repay the loan within the next 6 years	Decided by tender	The Finance Ministry and the school put equal capital into a risk compensation fund, through which they remunerate the bank according to the compensation rates as agreed during the tender
Old policy	50 per cent subsidy throughout the period of loan	Within 4 years after graduation	Appointed by government	Nil

Source: Lu Rong and Zhang Yong. 'The Start-up for New National Student Loan Policy'. Guangdong: Nanfang Weekend, 9 September 2004.

stated in his or her contract, the more his or her school will have to pay towards the 'risk fund'. As assistant bank president Wu Xiaoling put it: 'This will function as a positive stimulus'. Therefore, the compensation fund mechanism greatly reduces the worry that banks have by reducing the possibility of bad debt from students and also allowing them the possibility of gaining from the fund. An aide of the Finance Minister, Zhang Shaochun, came up with the following calculation: if a bank loans 10 billion yuan based on a 10 per cent rate of compensation, the compensation risk fund will subsidize the bank by 1 billion yuan; this subsidy is in excess of the interest that the Finance Ministry pays. If the bank does well and the loss on the loan is less than 10 per cent, the bank will profit; conversely, the bank will have to shoulder part of the risk.

On 6 September 2004, at a Senate-held television-cum-telephone conference to discuss subsidies for students from underprivileged families, it was made public that many state college student loans offices require the help of local governments to set them up. However, in the central and western parts of the country where there is a scarcity of financial resources, the central government will employ the carrot-and-stick approach towards them during the setting up of their respective branches.

In the end, the new GSLS not only makes use of the market mechanism, it also increases the size of government subsidy. It is a new system of market mechanism and government policy and is borne of practicality – this is an outstanding feature of the GSLS.

Despite all this, experts claim that the most persistent problem of the GSLS – the question of the reliability of the person taking out the loan – still cannot be solved totally. The four agencies listed above only brought up the following five points: the National Financial Management Agency should build an infrastructure that speeds access to personal information to improve risk-preventing mechanisms; second, banks giving out the loan should charge customers who contravene the contract interest as punishment, and at the same time enter their names on a common database of such people and not provide any financial services for them in the future. Third, there should be periodic disclosure of the names, citizenship number, graduating school, specific breach of contract and related information of people who continuously default on loan payments for a year or more and do not actively contact the corresponding bank to the China National Centre for Student Assistance; fourth, to make known on the Internet the academic background of nationwide graduating students who default on loan payment, in addition to the names of those people already named in the press. Fifth, the police should collaborate with the banks that provide such loans to investigate thoroughly the identity of these student loan defaulters when exchanging second-generation identity passes for normal college students. In fact, these requests have already been brought forward since the inception of the national student loan in 1999, but it was discovered that these measures lacked the appropriate impact.

Since June 2004 until the end of June 2006, during which time the new national student loan mechanism was implemented, the number of loan applications throughout the nation stood at 2.111 million, bank-approved loans were 1.543 million, while educational aid loans were 17.18 billion yuan and bank-approved loans totalled 13.17 billion yuan. Compared with 2005, the number of approved loans and loaned amount total 339,000 and 2.91 billion yuan respectively.

With the advent of summer 2006 signalling the end of another round of college entrance exams, there are again a number of underprivileged students who face problems even paying for university tuition and, once again, news of how this large-scale default on payment is causing banks major headaches is being splashed all over the media. In an article entitled 'Underprivileged Students Not Able To Obtain Graduation Certificate', the *Southern Weekly* reports that: 'according to Chen Xiaoyang, president of a university located in the south, in the year 2006, the number of year 2, 3 and 4 undergraduate students defaulting on loan repayments was 20 per cent, the sum of their debts amounting to a staggering 49.7 million yuan, the equivalent of a year's salary of university staff'. On top of that, a substantial proportion of these students either did not take a GSLS or did not take enough off the loan; and this phenomenon is also more prevalent in the following locations: in 2005, the collective tuition that Guizhou University students owed amounted to 30 million yuan, and students who did not pay, or defaulted when the time for payment came, constituted 35 per cent. Also in 2005, the amount of tuition fees for students from the Heilongjiang Province colleges reached 0.5 billion yuan.

Despite the controversy around the issue of student loans every year, there are also positive examples of what can happen. Lu Gang, head of the educational branch of Hunan Province, and colleagues are trying a new method of solving the problem that these underprivileged students have when it comes to difficulty in repaying loans and credit reliability by replacing compensation monies. They are urging university graduates to teach in rural villages for a period of 3 years, and each year translates to a reduction of 500 yuan in their debt – in other words, the state government will help these students repay their loans at the end of 3 years. Since the employment of this new method, more than 3,000 college students have taught in villages. This has not only solved the twin problems of employment and loan difficulty, it has also served to educate the students on this programme to understand villagers and their environment, and also to train both their minds and physiques. What this teaches us is that solutions are always more than problems.

The constant revisions made to the government study loan scheme send out an important signal: any policy put in place faces restrictions on many different levels due to environmental changes. Policies always subject to change prove more rational when adapting to market conditions and, coupled with the continual strengthening of the arm of the law in the marketplace, the aforementioned problems will finally be resolved. The media should try their best in their reports to reflect useful thoughts and actions made at the grassroots level; the government on the other hand should stop avoiding conflicts, objectively sort out the myriad new problems and encourage innovation in relevant areas so as to add more effective tools to the problem-solving toolbox that is policy.

Originated in 2002 and revised in 2006

25 Franchise rights and the interested parties

Yu Xinrong

People take it for granted that they can eat meat every day, but they may not realize that the sources of meat supplied in the market can still lead to many problems. To reorganize the unhealthy trends in the slaughter markets, the government has decided to carry out the franchise rights of fixed-point slaughters, but this will definitely influence the interests of some individual slaughter dealers. It is a contradiction faced by the government, namely to ensure that its citizens can eat healthy meat and at the same time help the individual slaughter dealers find new ways out of the problem.

On 18 June 2004, apart from the supermarkets, no fresh pork was supplied in the city district of Shaoyang. The pork retailers began to go on strike, which the municipal government had foreseen. Although 223 live pigs were slaughtered in the slaughterhouses, which represented half the normal supply, most pork was hung in the premises of the wholesalers. Many retailers visited the wholesalers to find out what had happened. Even worse, the retailers gathered and beat up law enforcement officers at one of the wholesale premises. The situation did not improve until the municipal government sent in the police who arrested the ringleader. On 19 June, some retailers began to sell pork, but the price rose from 15 yuan to 17 yuan per kilogram. One lady who bought half a kilogram thought the price was too high and went to the municipal government offices to confront the mayor. On 20 June, the pork supply returned to normal, and a leader of the provincial government called to ask about the pork price and was told it had risen to 20 yuan per kilogram in Shaoyang markets according to a report from the Hunan Provincial Committee of CPC (actually, it had been kept at 17 yuan per kilogram all the time). Up until 22 June, the supply in the markets was normal and the price fell slightly. A reform that had fermented for a year, involving more than 1,000 slaughter dealers and retailers and influencing the lives of all the city residents, gradually came on track.

The source of fixed-point slaughter

Shaoyang City is located in the southwest of Hunan Province and is divided into three parts by the Zijiang and Shaoshui rivers. It has a population of nearly 500,000 in the city district, most of whom are, first, Han, and second, Hui nationality (about 11,000 people). The food supply for the urban residents is what most concerns the municipal government. To ensure that people eat healthy meat is the common wish of both the government and the residents, and fixed-point slaughter is the main way of solving the problem.

At the beginning of the 1980s, the wave of reform and opening up to the outside world hit Shaoyang's citizens, and a small business economy began to develop. Some labourers who had little money and some businessmen who came from the rural areas decided to go into the business of slaughtering pigs. At the time, pigs in the urban district were slaughtered, and the pork was packaged by the state-owned meat liaison packaging factories and then sold to the markets. Individual slaughter dealers, recognizing the disadvantages of the state-owned enterprises, quickly plugged the gaps in the market, then gradually took it over.

The competitive advantages of individual slaughter dealers are, first, their low costs. All they need is usually one pot, one knife and one hob, which cost only about 200 yuan. The second advantage is the flexibility of their operations. There is basically one person – the individual slaughter dealer – who buys the live pigs and sells the meat, so the response to the markets is flexible. The pigs are killed at around 4:00 a.m., and the meat can be in the markets by dawn so that it is relatively fresh. Third, the dealers escape taxes, which exceed 50 yuan per person. Fourth, they inject water into the meat and sell the sick and dead pigs to gain high profits. As a result, the state-owned meat liaison packaging factories had closed down within a few years, while the individual slaughterhouses increased to more than forty, and the number of individual slaughter dealers reached nearly 100, so the market was in disarray.

As for the above-mentioned problems, there were many responses from various circles of society, but because the individual and individual-owned economy needed to be developed and there were no clear provisions in the laws at that time, the government put the emphasis on surveillance and management of the markets to examine whether the sick and dead pigs were sold, which was very difficult to prohibit.

In 1998, *The Rules of Fixed-point Slaughter of Live Pigs* began to be carried out by the State Council, which included the following stipulations: first, the country should carry out the system of fixed-point slaughter, centralized quarantine, unified tax payments and dispersed management of live pigs. Second, the municipal and county people's government should organize the commodities circulation administrative management, farming and animal husbandry, and other relevant departments to examine and determine the fixed-point slaughterhouses, then promulgate the universal signs according to the establishment plans and conditions stipulated by 'the Rule'. Third, the fixed-point slaughterhouses must conform to the state standards concerning technique, quality, health and environment protection. Subsequently, 'the operation methods' of the provincial government require the cities directly under the jurisdiction of the province to decide on the location of the fixed-point slaughterhouses, which will number between one and three.

As the fresh meat supplied to the markets is a special commodity that affects people's basic living standards, in order to ensure its quality security, fixed-point slaughter will become the government's franchise right. On the other hand, fresh meat is a basic necessity and has a relatively large commercial value and stability in management, so it becomes a goal of many businessmen. After 'the Rule' was issued by the State Council, the municipal government organized many large-scale reorganization activities and reduced the individual slaughter dealers to seventeen by means of mixing administrative interference with voluntary mergers so as to solve the problem of their small size and widespread locations. From April 2002 to June 2004, the municipal government largely standardized the quality, taxes and fees of the fixed-point slaughter of live pigs. The government also took strong measures to comprehensively regulate the slaughter markets and established the Fixed Point Slaughter Affairs' Office of the municipal government, which is responsible for coordinating the relevant departments, carrying out a one-ticket system in taxes and fees, severely penalizing the sale of sick and dead pigs and reducing the individual slaughterhouses to six fixed-point slaughterhouses (which cover seven slaughter points).

The requirement of local economic development

Shaoyang is a city where agriculture is given priority, and the specific gravity of agriculture occupies 30 per cent of gross domestic volume. Grains, pigs and oranges have been important sources of farmers' income. However, the recession in grain markets, the low prices and low demand for oranges have for some time limited farmers' ability to increase their income. At the same time, the state-owned meat joint packaging factories stopped production, so the channels for packaging and selling live pigs decreased. Most live pigs were sold to Guangdong by the businessmen and the packaging volume decreased, which meant that tax resources flowed out of the city. In the past, the annual slaughter of live pigs amounted to 7,000,000 if they were slaughtered in the city, and taxes would exceed RMB 100,000,000 yuan, which was a crucial issue for the financially deficient government.

A particularly serious issue is that some meat packaging factories in the neighbourhood need to find and enlarge their markets. In order to support the agricultural products packaging enterprises and break the regional blockade, the provincial government issued a document in which it required that enterprises whose annual output is above 300,000 pigs be permitted to sell their products in the province. That is to say, if Shaoyang cannot expand its own meat packaging enterprises, not only will its financial income decrease, but its urban residents will have to eat imported meat or 'the domestic sales of commodities originally produced for export'. This will seriously hit the farmers in the city and affect economic development.

At the time, the reform of state-owned enterprises was being carried out. Both the leaders of the factories and the staff agreed to reform the meat packaging methods, and an individually owned enterprise was keen to participate; therefore, the enterprise changed from a state-owned to an individually owned company, and the Baoqing Meat Joint Company was established. The owner promoted a new plan for development, which included exploiting the Hong Kong and Russian markets, consolidating the Guangdong and Hainan markets, ensuring the native market, combining breeding with packaging and pledging that the product volume would surpass 10,000,000 yuan within 2 years. In order to realize these aims, the enterprise required the government to set it up as the only fixed-point slaughter enterprise. It became an implicit aim to establish a leading enterprise for agricultural products to drive the development of livestock breeding and to increase fiscal income by encouraging large tax-paying families. It became a recessive aim to drive the development of livestock breeding by establishing an agricultural products leading enterprise and to increase income by cultivating large tax-paying family. At the same time, the provincial government held several meetings requiring the fixed-point slaughterhouse to establish production lines for slaughtering, which became a dominant aim.

The basic situation of the slaughterhouses

The six fixed-point slaughterhouses (at seven points) were located in three districts, two of which owned three points separately and a third which owned one point. Among them, the Jiujiang Village slaughterhouse and Wulipai slaughterhouse belonged to the village collectively and was located on the outskirts. Both the Meats and Aquatic Products Company (two points were set in Xiwaijie and Tianjiang which actually stopped production) and the Iron Shot Factory Slaughterhouse belonged to the state-owned enterprises that were close to bankruptcy. The Xiangnan and the Meat Joint Factory (which rented the site of the original Meat Joint Factory) belonged to the individual and stock-holding enterprises. None of the six fixed-point slaughterhouses conformed completely to the conditions issued by the state on technology, quality, sanitation, environmental protection and mechanized slaughtering. Basically, their production conditions were primitive and included a row of sheds, a pot and a collection of hobs. According to the information collected by the Municipal Fixed Point Slaughter Affairs' Office, all of them had employed illegal practices such as tax evasion and tax dodging, injecting water into meat and so on because only 400 to 500 live pigs were consumed in a normal day, and only 12 yuan was charged as a packaging fee per pig, the total income was less than 6,000 yuan. Thus, the profit of every slaughterhouse could not exceed 1,000 yuan. They would not make any money if there was no malfeasance and if the costs of water and electric supply were included. However, currently, the six slaughterhouses are running very smoothly. As there is a large number of slaughterhouses and none of them can reach a big enough scale, they are not willing to increase investment to buy new equipment. If the government does not take sufficient measures, none of the six slaughterhouses will be competitive and will only make a living through the hundreds of live pigs on the market.

The decisive project of the municipal government

In March 2004, the municipal government held the first meeting for the owners of the slaughterhouses, studied the related laws and regulations and put forward the advantages and disadvantages of appointing one to three slaughterhouses and soliciting their suggestions, and then adjourned the meeting to consider the issues involved. The municipal government subsequently held a meeting for the leaders of the three districts' government in the urban areas and relevant municipal departments to solicit suggestions. In April, the municipal government held a second meeting for the owners of the slaughterhouses. At this meeting, the programme was put forward that between one and three companies should be fixed-point slaughterhouses. As the individuals who rented the Meat Joint Factory had the stock share of the new Baoqing Meat Joint Company, the Baoqing Meat Joint Company actually became one of the owners. Amid fierce opposition, the owners put forward the suggestion of appointing one slaughterhouse, and asked the government to consider giving the other slaughterhouses an alternative role. After that, the government held a meeting for the relevant municipal departments, and told the leaders who took charge of the enterprises in the three districts about the suggestions of the owners to solicit their ideas. The leaders of the three districts sympathized with the municipal government's position, but said they would have to think matters over. On the basis of discussing and soliciting suggestions, the municipal government formulated an initial plan that live pigs, cattle and sheep were to be taken to one slaughterhouse, while the other five slaughterhouses (actually four) would be turned into sales companies. The plan was discussed by the administrative meeting of the municipal government and agreement was reached. At the beginning of June, the municipal government held a joint meeting for the three districts' governments and the municipal departments to announce the government's decision.

The municipal government focused on the following three points in making the decision from beginning to end. First, the legal administrative approval rights for fixed-point slaughters belonged to the municipal government, and the government must administrate according to the law. Second, reappointing the slaughterhouses actually adjusted interests, so the various interests of breeders, slaughter businessmen, salesmen and consumers had to be taken into consideration. Third, restrictions would only be temporary, while market measures would not take effect for some time. Therefore, contradictions had to be addressed as soon as possible at present, and convergence with the market must be done over a long period. Actually, while these programmes were being formulated, the municipal government made many comparisons. One was to apply the market economy method; that is, whoever conformed to the conditions would be approved and, from the government's point of view, this method was the best one, but the programme was difficult to implement. According to current conditions, only the reformed Baoqing Meat Joint Company had the necessary premises and equipment and sewage-handling capacity. If the Baoqing Meat Joint Company was appointed, the other four slaughterhouses would have to buy new equipment and refurbish their premises; otherwise, they would comprise an alliance of interests to tangle with the government. The government would probably need to set up a compensation fund because the four slaughterhouses had been approved and given licences to trade. Another way would be to sell to management outright, whose task it would be to solve the compensation problems of those owners who had withdrawn from the slaughter profession. But whether and how long the franchise rights of the profession could be sold and how much the compensation would be were also major problems. If the compensation was too little, those owners who had withdrawn would not accept it; if it was too much, no one could afford it. In this case, even if someone could buy the franchise rights at a high price, they would pass the burden on to the consumers so that the meat price would rise. The third way would be for the enterprises to operate under government guidelines. The government would determine one fixed-point slaughterhouse for pigs and one slaughterhouse for cattle and sheep according to current conditions, and the remaining owners could still engage in live pig sales. Either four wholesale departments would be set up or one company would be formed. In this way, the aim of excellence would be achieved and would conform to the reality that only one live pig slaughterhouse can meet basic conditions. At the same time, the future of the other slaughterhouses would be guaranteed

The programme encounters difficulties in its operation

When the meeting was convened, more than 100 residents of Jiujiang Village attended to oppose closing the slaughterhouse in their village. Their reason was that the slaughterhouse in their village had been approved by the municipal government and more than 90 per cent of the land in their village had been collectivized, so the villagers lacked living resources. The living expenses of all the old people in the village came from the fees collected from the slaughterhouse. After the villagers had lodged their complaints with the municipal government, they went to the municipal committee of the CPC. The municipal committee of the CPC notified the secretary of the district committee of the CPC to give assurances to the villagers and required the municipal government to give assurances to the residents of the district, the countryside and villages; otherwise, the programme would not be able to be carried out. Following this, the slaughterhouse owners and some villagers went to the provincial government. The municipal government reported to the Provincial Inner Trade Office first, so they were persuaded to return home.

Meanwhile, the four slaughterhouses convened meetings among themselves. Because of their varying profits and poor quality of management, they were unable to reach agreement as to whether the four slaughterhouses should operate independently and compete with one other or whether they should form a joint consortium. The government's attitude was that management was the enterprises' own responsibility, so it only offered them guidance and did not interfere. At last, the four owners agreed that they would form a united sales company, which coincided with the previous idea of the municipal government.

To unify the slaughter of cattle and pigs involved the interests of Hui slaughter dealers. Before that, most of Hui's slaughtering was finished off by Ayan, and the Municipal Islamic Association received a 3-yuan management fee per cow. The collective slaughtering inevitably involved the problem of taxes and fees. If the slaughtering of cattle and sheep were tax free, it would not only lead to the tax revenue being lost, but it would also cause the fixed-point slaughter of live pigs to fluctuate. If different tax standards were carried out between the Han and Hui slaughterers, Han's cattle price would be higher and the beef would not be sold, which would influence the interests of Han's slaughterhouses. Thus, the programme devised by the municipal government was to ensure that the Islamic Association would receive a 5-yuan surveillance and management fee per cow. It was tax free for the Hui slaughterers within 1 month and subject to a 50 per cent tax reduction within 3 months. The municipal government had numerous discussions with the Municipal Minorities Affairs' Committee and the Municipal Islamic Association but, when they convened a meeting with the Hui representatives, the latter were strongly against it. The reasons they gave were as follows. First, the Communist Party of China and the central government of the People's Republic of China had always given the minority preferential treatment and had not collected taxes before, but now they were taxed so they could not agree. Second, they said Hui's customs must be respected, so the Hui slaughterhouse must be managed by Hui themselves and Han should not be permitted to enter the premises. Following the meeting, the Hui slaughterhouse owners went on strike secretly so there was no Islamic beef sold in the markets during the following 3 days. The provincial director of the Islamic Association conducted an investigation in the city for 1 day and concluded that the municipal government was correct in its policy of fixed-point slaughter and that it was wrong for the Hui to go on strike. At the same time, they asked the municipal government to reduce the standard in packaging fees but the Hui slaughterhouse owners did not agree to this.

A new round of fixed-point slaughter starts at last

In August 2003, the State Commercial Ministry, the Food and Medicine Surveillance Bureau and five other departments held a joint television and telephone conference on collective reorganization of the live pig slaughter markets. The management of live pig slaughtering was required to be strengthened to ensure the meat's security. In April 2004, the State Commercial Ministry issued *The Notice on National Special Inspection on Live Pig Slaughtering*. In the strong east wind, through 1 year of consultation and cooperation, the municipal government held a further standing meeting to discuss and pass the revised programme on fixed-point slaughter. Its main points were: first, the decision remained unchanged that only one slaughterhouse – Baoqing Meats Liaison Company – be appointed. Second, the Municipal Islamic Association would be responsible for the preparation of the fixed-point slaughterhouses for cattle and sheep, which are licensed to go into business after the Municipal Fixed Point Slaughter Affairs' Office had organized the departments to examine and meet the necessary standards. Third, the Xiangnan slaughterhouse, which was formerly confirmed as the fixed-point slaughterhouse for cattle and sheep, should be allowed to set up a mechanized slaughter packaging line, mainly packaging frozen meats and at the same time should be used as an emergency facility. Fourth, the four slaughterhouses due for closure are allowed to form a stock meat sale company and the wholesale price gap would be carried out by the Municipal Price Bureau and market sales dispersed to the slaughter dealers. The principle was called 'One knife to slaughter, one level to wholesale, one line for emergency and one big area for sale'. Various circles believed this to be the only way forward, so the municipal government reported to the Municipal Committee of the CPC and the Municipal People's Congress Standing Committee and notified the Municipal Political Consultative Conference in order to form a consensus opinion in the leadership. Speeches were televised and answers to reporters' questions were published in newspapers so that a positive atmosphere of public opinion was created.

Originated in 2004 and revised in 2006

26 Where is the solution to the farmers' problem of seeing a doctor?

Dong Yong'an

In order to construct a well-off and harmonious society, we have to solve the problems relating to the countryside, agriculture and farmers. One of the most important reasons for these problems is the poor supply of public services in the countryside. Now both central and local governments have pledged to develop rural medical care and sanitation and to solve the farmers' problem of seeing a doctor. As a main body providing countryside public health products, township hospitals have been lagging behind because of insufficient investment. Thus, these hospitals are unable to perform their social functions effectively, and the farmers' problem of seeing a doctor becomes a hot potato for society. The city of Anyang has been exploring the restructuring potential of some urban hospitals and transferring excessively centralized urban health resources to the rural area. Such an endeavour has succeeded to some extent, but some new problems have since emerged.

A news report

Anyang Daily reported that a journalist saw a Mr Zhang, who appeared, exhausted and indifferent, at the gates of the county hospital in Anyang. He had spent nearly a day trying to get his sick mother treated and, owing to the inefficiency of the township hospital, his mother died at the gates of the county hospital. Zhang said sadly:

> We are only 2.5 km away from the township hospital, but more than 25 km from the county hospital. However, the township hospital has only one X-ray machine which is out of use. My mother suffered from acute gastric perforation; if diagnosed and operated on by the township hospital in time, she wouldn't have died.

The difficulty in seeing a doctor has always been one of the problems that farmers complain about, and this problem is directly related to the conditions in the township hospitals. As for the situation of seeing a doctor in China, in 2002, there were 2.1 million outpatients, of whom 1.2 million chose to go to the township hospitals.

The situation of the township hospitals of Anyang

In 2002, Anyang Public Health Bureau carried out an investigation of the ninety-two township hospitals in the city, and the results showed that the conditions of the township hospitals were not optimistic. Generally, they were struggling for survival among the harsh competition of comprehensive hospitals, private clinics and all kinds of pharmacies. The first reason for such a condition is the serious lack of investment. Some township hospitals still have obsolete equipment, such as stethoscopes, clinical thermometers and sphygmomanometers. Among the township hospitals being investigated, 40 per cent were built before the 1980s. The wards were dirty and chaotic, the windows and doors were damaged, and wallpaper was peeling off. For some township hospitals, the dangerous wards exceeded 60 per cent.

The second reason is the deficiency in skilled staff. For various reasons, doctors and nurses were paid low salaries, and talented professionals were not willing to stay. For 30 per cent of the hospitals, there was not even one qualified medium-level professional doctor, which was far from meeting farmers' demands for medical care. The third reason was poor management. The management mode of the township hospitals cannot adapt to the development of the market economy, which results in inefficient hospitals and low managing benefits.

Currently, in such conditions, the township hospitals are not only unable to provide farmers with basic medical care, but they are also unable to perform public health services, such as epidemic prevention and maternal and child health care. This is one important reason why farmers with illness are poor or return to poverty.

What to do?

Changing the status quo of the township hospitals has become urgent. But how to do it? Obviously the input should be increased. Provided that the government's input is insufficient, then on the one hand, the medical care facilities cannot be increased, and the medical care conditions cannot be improved; on the other hand, staff are paid low salaries, doctors' and nurses' thoughts are unstable, their initiative cannot be brought into full play, and the service quality becomes increasingly lower. Serious diseases fail to be diagnosed and ailments cannot be cured. Gradually, the rural patients will go to the village clinics when they are ill, and to county hospitals when they are seriously sick, because few people want to go to the township hospitals. As the number of patients decreases, the hospitals get a lower income; this will make them unable to develop further. Therefore, increased input is the key point to improving the situation of the township hospitals. As the township hospitals perform the function of providing a rural public health service, the government should bear the main costs involved.

Therefore, the mayor of Anyang instructed the Public Health Bureau to propose a fundraising scheme to rebuild the township hospitals' infrastructure as well as improve the facilities within 3–5 years. After conducting numerous studies, the Public Health Bureau proposed two sets of fundraising schemes.

- *Scheme 1*: Sponsored entirely by government finance, or the governments of the city and the town each bearing half the costs.
- *Scheme 2*: Choosing the city's two or three public hospitals of medium scale and level, and implementing joint-stock system reform or private-owned system reform. Then allocating a proportion of the capital obtained from the hospitals' system reform as input capital for the township hospitals.

Views of various circles

The mayor of Anyang held an executive meeting and an expert conference to discuss the fundraising scheme. In addition, he conducted an investigation into the hospitals and listened to others' comments.

Regarding Scheme 1, the development and reform committee as well as the Finance Bureau said that, temporarily, the government was unable to afford the whole construction input for the township hospitals; however, they could overcome difficulties to fund 50 per cent of the input. In view of the fact that the majority of Anyang's counties rely totally on government finance, they would be unable to bear the remaining 50 per cent co-funding. Thus, this scheme had to be set aside. The fundraising scheme in which government finance would support most of the input has not yet been passed.

After Scheme 1 was rejected, Scheme 2 became the focus of the controversy.

Views of the government officials

Some believed that the hospital property rights system reform was an effective way for the government to transform facilities and enhance working efficiency. Following system reform, the hospitals would be able to act on their own more freely, and would carry out self-management and self-development more efficiently. The government would set aside more energy resources, lay down regulations, strengthen supervision and oversee the reform measures, thus providing society with better widespread, basic medical care and public services. Others believed that, after system reform, the government might lose control over supervising medical care funding and service quality that would possibly harm citizens' interests.

Views of the experts

Some believe that hospitals should have been privatized and operate according to the market economy rules. In our nation, various phenomena exist in the current medical care service field, such as overexpensive low service levels, and the shortage of high-quality medical care services in the rural area results from the government's monopoly. Some believe that, although public health belongs to public products, the ways and main bodies that provide health care could be multi-faceted. In addition to the medical care institutions that provide basic medical care services, other medical care institutions should enter the market and be operated according to the market's rules; thus a competitive system would be introduced to the field of medical care services which would help to improve the standard and quality of the medical care services of the whole society. Others argue that the government performs the function of providing social public products, and public health is purely a public commodity, so it should be provided totally by the government. This is the only way that efficiency and fairness can be ensured.

Views of the hospitals' presidents

Some believe that, after the system reform, there will be fewer 'mothers-in-law' and wider autonomy. There will be more flexibility in the fields of inspiring staff and managing directions, and there will be a wider space and broader future for the hospitals' development. Some believe that the hospital property system reform cannot solve the problem of modernized management for hospitals. The government's reform of the systems of some low-benefit hospitals is actually to throw away burdens. Some believe that the hospitals should be operated by the government, but not be privatized. If left to their own devices without any government input, some hospitals would face difficulties in surviving. Some people are against system reform, worrying that presidents will be elected by the major shareholders after system reform, and thus their own future would no longer be guaranteed.

Views of the hospitals' staff

Some people think that only by system reform can the unfair practice of 'eating from the same big pot' be broken and a competitive system set up, which would revitalize hospital staff and improve services. Some consider that after system reform the hospitals will enter the market, and they will have to face the market risks, so the most important thing in the process of system reform is to choose a president who is good at operating and management. Some worry that: first, system reform may harm their own interests, including whether they are able to keep their identification, salaries, professional titles, pensions and so on; second, system reform may lead to laying staff off and possible loss of jobs.

Views of the citizens

Some think that, after system reform, major hospitals will increase input, invite talented people and purchase up-to-date equipment, the medical care conditions and service quality of the hospitals will be improved, and they will benefit as a result. Some think that, after system reform, the government's public health department and the hospitals will not be like families as before. So when conflicts occur between the hospitals and the patients, the public health department will deal with the problems in an objective and just way. Some worry that, for the privatized hospitals, their public character would be weakened and they may pursue economic profit excessively; consequently, the costs of medical care will rise. Not only will this not solve the problem of not being able to see a doctor quickly, but it will also make the problem of expensive medical consultations increasingly serious.

Thus, the mayor of Anyang is facing three options: (1) postpone action and wait until more funds are available; (2) act positively and adopt Scheme 2; (3) take no action.

Mayor's decision

The mayor of Anyang altered his thinking. The farmers' difficulty in getting a doctor's appointment is a serious social problem; it concerns every family far and wide, and it impacts directly on social harmony and stability. Therefore, the problem must be treated seriously and solved quickly. Carrying out the policy of new village cooperative medical care in the rural area is an important measure in solving the problem of seeing a doctor for farmers. The policy of new village cooperative medical care mainly depends on the township hospitals. Whether the policy will be carried out successfully is related to whether or not the township hospitals undergo reconstruction. Therefore, to solve the farmers' problem of seeing a doctor, we must change the current conditions in the township hospitals.

However, all six third-level hospitals that have advanced facilities and technologies are in the urban area. There is an oversupply of medical care institutions, staff and facilities in the urban area. From the viewpoint of funding, expenditure on health takes 8–9 per cent of the entire budget. Of the total expenditure on health, 70 per cent is allocated for the urban area and 30 per cent for the rural area; yet 70 per cent of the city's population lives in the rural area; that is to say, 30 per cent of the population takes 70 per cent of the available health resources. The division of health resources between the urban and rural areas is seriously flawed.

If we continue with the old system and finance expenditure method, the current conditions in the township hospitals will remain unchanged. The expenditure on public health products for the rural area will still be seriously deficient, and the division of public health resources in the whole of society will become increasingly unfair. To change the current situation, we must break with the conventional method and reform the current division system of health resources so that more people may benefit from it.

Therefore, Scheme 2 should be a feasible choice. We should displace the too concentrated health resources in the urban area through hospital reform.

We should then transfer the displaced resources to the less developed rural area as public capital, spending the money on purchasing facilities for township hospitals, attracting talented people and importing basic facilities. We will then be able to achieve a reasonable division so as to change the situation of a serious imbalance of health resources.

The mayor of Anyang, together with some of the relevant government, visited other cities to conduct an investigation, do a survey of the hospitals and organize an expert demonstration in order to make the scheme more scientific and more feasible and to reduce the reform costs as far as possible. On this basis, the government held an executive meeting to research the capital-raising scheme, and in particular to improve Scheme 2.

First of all, in order to ensure the supply of public health and basic medical care services, the government focused on Anyang People's Hospital, Anyang Traditional Chinese Medicine Hospital, Anyang Maternal and Child Health Hospital, Anyang Hospital of Infectious Diseases, Anyang Psychiatric Hospital, Anyang Blood Station and Medical Emergency Centre as well as some community health service centres that are non-profit-making public hospitals; these hospitals perform the public service functions of medical teaching research and social security.

Second, in order to ensure that the rights and interests of the majority of the staff of the reformed hospitals will not be harmed, and to allow better use of public health resources, the government of Anyang has made the measures of 'the Four Unc`hanged' and 'the Three Untransferrable': after reform, the identifications of the hospitals' staff will remain the same, the files and salaries will not be changed, nor will professional titles or the ways of adjusting salary and winning promotion and pension rights; the hospitals' names, land-use rights and staff accommodation will not be affected.

Third, the new presidents of privately owned hospitals will need to improve the rules and regulations. They will not be permitted to dismiss staff at the old hospitals at will, but should follow the principle of 'old rules for old staff, new rules for new staff'.

Carrying out the scheme

After perfecting the fundraising scheme, Anyang has founded 'the leadership organ for system reform' and worked out a specific method for hospital system reform. The first point is to issue the system reform proclamation a month beforehand, and to hold a staff meeting; the second point is to let a qualified organization estimate the state of the property, prepare a report and then for the state-owned assets supervision departments to approve it; the third point is to check the fixed assets, floating assets and speciality assets of the hospital; the fourth point is, following system reform, that both sides concerned in the assets made over should visit the Bureau of Land Resources to go through the legal formalities on the hospital's land-using rights; the fifth point is to regulate the spending of capital arising from the property rights made over. The capital should be deposited in one account and used for special purposes. The capital will mainly be invested in the less developed rural areas as public capital according to the plan, and it will be spent on the establishment of township hospitals to effect the reasonable division of health resources, so as to rectify the seriously flawed situation of the allocation of funding.

After 2 years of practice and exploration, we should say that the medical system reform in Anyang, which is focused on the system of property rights, is on the whole successful. The reform raises resource efficiency and encourages the initiative of doctors and nurses. The industry of medical care services in Anyang has changed dramatically since the reform of the hospital system began. First, the capital input of hospitals has increased following system reform. The initiative of the presidents of the hospitals has been raised by the reform; they try every means to improve services. One of these hospitals has increased capital input by 10 million yuan in 1 year compared with the previous year. Second, the unfair practice of 'eating from the same big pot, stable jobs' ceased following system reform, and the attitude and quality of the doctors and nurses has improved enormously. Third, the competition system has been introduced to the city's industry of medical care and is gradually improving the quality of services. Fourth, the government has used over 40 million yuan of the capital raised from hospital system reform to establish thirty central hospitals, four first-level township hospitals and five county-level disease control centres. Currently, among Anyang's ninety-two township hospitals, seventy-six have been reconstructed using this capital, and the reconstructing percentage has achieved 81.7 per cent. The conditions in township hospitals have changed dramatically, and the problem of establishing new village cooperative medical care stations has been solved. This has improved the establishment of the security system of new village cooperative medical care greatly. Over 2 years, the experimental counties for the new cooperative medical care services have expanded from one to four. The percentage of people with the new village cooperative medical care insurance has increased from 71 per cent to 82 per cent, and also the number of farmers in the scheme has increased to 2,590,000. This virtually meets farmers' need for medical care. They can be treated nearby if they get sick; therefore the farmers' problem of seeing a doctor has been largely resolved.

New problems raised

However, every coin has two sides. Some new problems have emerged during the process of system reform.

If the farmers of Anyang get sick, they no longer need to travel miles to the major hospitals, and they no longer need to worry about the problem of seeing a doctor. The problem of poor farmers becoming ill has been largely resolved.

The first problem raised concerns system transformation. Some township hospitals' systems have not been transformed sufficiently. The situation of 'eating from the same big pot' has not changed in every case; talented people still refuse to work at these hospitals and valuable staff are not willing to stay; although the input is increasing for township hospitals, the technical level is low and farmers' needs cannot always be met, so the number of patients fails to increase. Soon, the hospitals will be unable to make ends meet.

The second problem is the lack of a complete set of policies. The system reform of hospitals is related to the problems of revenue, state-owned property, the personnel system of the government-sponsored institutions and so on. It is sometimes hard to put the reform into practice because of the lack of a complete set of policies concerned with system reform.

The third problem is about supervision. Following system reform, the hospitals became financially independent corporations and are able to act on their own more freely. Therefore, the government's supervision mode for hospitals should also be changed. However, the kinds of activities that should be supervised are not clear. In some areas, the phenomenon of 'four disorders', such as inspecting disorderly, charging disorderly, etc., still exists.

The fourth problem is about the thoroughness of the reform. Anyang has carried forward the system reform step by step in order to smooth the system reform's path. As the reform deepens, the measures of 'the Four Unchanged' and 'the Three Untransferrable', etc., which reassured people in the early phases of reform, for example, became barriers, which restricted the further development of the hospitals.

Afterthoughts

We are still in the early stages of an affluent society, and the government's ability to fund improved health care is limited. The situation of multi-faceted hospitals will help the government to concentrate people, resources and capital to improve basic medical care, to invest the limited funds where they are needed most. Through system reform, we are able to accelerate the process of the reasonable interflow and division of health resources, and to improve rational competition among hospitals to encourage them to raise management and service standards. Following system reform, hospitals are competing with each other equally, and this helps to increase vigour at all levels, improve the management standards of medical care services, as well as offering efficiency and benefits. The public will be the ones who ultimately benefit from system reform. During the process of the system reform of hospitals, the government will also establish more public hospitals, including the most powerful regional Comprehensive Hospital and Hospital of Infectious Diseases, the Psychiatric Hospital, the Maternal and Child Health Hospital, the Blood Station, Medical Emergency Centre and so on to ensure the basic needs for medical care, as well as to improve the fairness of the medical care services. The final judgement criterion of system reform should be whether it contributes to improving the health of the poor and people with middle and low-level incomes, whether it solves people's problem of seeing a doctor and so on. The system reform will be complicated due to the influence of the old system, people's traditional ideas and so on. However, if it helps to improve the whole medical care system as well as providing society with better medical care services, then system reform does not depart from its initial intentions.

Written in 2005

27 Experiment on a new rural cooperative medical system in Ezhou City in Hubei Province

Xu Songnan

How to solve the peasants' difficulty of getting to see doctors, how to ensure that they can afford to visit doctors, how to prevent their minor diseases from evolving into serious diseases and how to ensure that they will not fall into poverty as a result of disease has become one of the top issues for the Party committees and governments at various levels. To allow the new rural cooperative medical system to play greater roles and benefit more peasant farmers, the city of Ezhou in Hubei Province conducted its own experiment on building a new rural cooperative medical system. It has made some progress but also encountered some problems.

A peasant farmer's misfortune

A peasant farmer in Ezhou suffered superficial gastritis in the early 1990s when he was aged 30. Curing the disease would cost only a few hundred yuan, but he did not visit a doctor because his family was poor. In the mid-1990s, he felt that the disease was getting serious. Diagnosis indicated that he was suffering from deep erosive gastric ulcers. The doctors advised that he should be hospitalized to have the ulcer tissue removed. This would cost about 3,000 yuan. But the peasant farmer could not afford to pay, so he bought some medicines and returned home. At the end of 2004, the disease became even more serious and he grew extremely thin. When he went to hospital, he was diagnosed as suffering from gastric cancer. He was hospitalized, had his whole stomach and adjacent lymphatic tissue removed and received carbon ion radiation therapy. To pay his medical expenses totalling more than 20,000 yuan, he had to sell his water buffalo and pigs and borrow money from relatives and friends. While his family lived in abject poverty, he also lost the ability to work and had only a few years to live.

Introduction of a new rural cooperative medical system

What happened to this peasant is not unusual in China's rural areas. Many rural families cannot afford to see a doctor or are unwilling to spend too much on medical treatment. As a result, minor diseases evolve into major ones and major diseases evolve into incurable ones. This is a common phe-nomenon in China's rural areas and especially in the central and western regions. Therefore, one of the priority tasks for the Party committees and governments at various levels is to establish and improve the country's social security system, solve the peasants' difficulties in visiting doctors, guarantee the peasants' rights to life and health and promote economic and social development in the rural areas. In 2002, the State Council issued the *Decisions on Further Strengthening the Rural Medical Work*, which explicitly provided that a new rural cooperative medical system should be gradually established. In 2003, the State Council transmitted the *Opinions on Establishing a New Rural Cooperative Medical System* worked out by the Ministry of Health in conjunction with other ministries and commissions. After that, experiments were carried out throughout the country on how to establish such a new rural cooperative medical system.

A new rural cooperative medical system is a self-help medical system for peasant farmers. It is organized, guided and supported by the governments and voluntarily joined by the peasant farmers. Individuals, collectives and governments contribute funds to the medical pool, which covers the expenses of major diseases. We should say that this new system is a fairly ideal medical system for China's countryside.

The new medical system now under experiment has the following features. First, in terms of the beneficiaries, the new medical system covers all rural residents, while the traditional cooperative medical system only covered peasant farmers. Second, in terms of the fundraising mechanism, the gov-ernments have the economic responsibility to raise funds and should be the main fund contributors, while the traditional medical system relied on indi-vidual peasants and collectives to contribute funds. Third, in terms of the fundraising policy, the fact that peasant farmers participate in a cooperative medical service and perform the fee payment obligation in order to ward off disease risks cannot be regarded as an increase in their financial burden, while the traditional medical system had no such provisions. Fourth, in terms of the management mechanism, the counties (cities) should be the fundraising units, while the traditional medical system was run and managed by villages. Fifth, in terms of the insurance mechanism, current insurance mainly covers 'major diseases'. In other words, it covers the large amount of medical expenses arising from major diseases, in order to prevent peasant farmers from falling into poverty as a result of either disease or both poverty and disease. Although insurance is against major diseases, minor medical allowances are also accommodated. Thus, the new system can not only boost the risk resistance ability of the peasant farmers but also benefit them to some extent.

Experiment in Hubei Province

Hubei Province lies in the central part of China. The provincial Party com-mittee and government have paid close attention to establishing a new rural cooperative medical system. They held several special conferences to discuss how to conduct the experiment, established a coordinating and leading group for this purpose and selected eight counties (cities) as the first group of units for the experiment. They also set the basic principles for selecting the pilot units: (1) The units must be voluntary, which means the regions must have an active demand for participating in the experiment. (2) The units must contribute counterpart funds, which means that regional finance must be able to pay counterpart funds fully and in time as required by the central authorities. (3) The units must be representative, which means that the selected regions must have the topographic features of mountains, hills and plains, and the peasant farmers must be selected from those earning high, middle and low incomes. The provincial authorities worked out a unified plan for the experiment and specified the principles and overall requirements for the organizational management, fundraising mechanism, fund management, compensation coverage, medical services and supervisory management for the establishment of the new rural cooperative medical system.

The experiment formally began in April 2003. All the pilot counties (cities) conducted baseline investigations (including the incidence of disease, medical treatment and willingness to participate) and worked out their implementing plans. The principles were that participation must be voluntary and the funds must be contributed by various parties, that spending must be based on revenue and the security must be appropriate, and that management must be scientific and with strict supervision. Compensation would cover major diseases and subsidize minor diseases, with the emphasis being placed on major diseases. The participation rate for that year was 53.1 per cent.

In early 2004, the provincial government decided that, in light of the progress in the experiment and in order to strengthen fund management, the township (town) cooperative medical institutions should be separated from the township health centres and subject to vertical administration. This move helped streamline the township (town) cooperative medical management system. In light of their experiment in 2003, the pilot counties (cities) properly adjusted their implementing plans. They introduced the systems for subsidy classification, major disease subsidy and minimum subsidy, lowered the threshold line for claim reimbursement and raised subsidy ratios. These measures helped increase the confidence of the peasant farmers and mobilized their enthusiasm to participate. In order to cope with the fast growth in medical expenses and to ensure real benefits to participants, these regions strictly complied with the catalogue of basic drugs for cooperative medical care and contained any unreasonable increase in medical expenses.

Statistics indicated that, from 1 January to 31 December 2004, the eight pilot counties (cities) had 2.362 million peasant farmer participants, raised 70.86 million yuan in funds, posted a participation rate of 63.44 per cent and treated 2.281 million patients. Specifically, 2.1925 million outpatients were treated, 15.3187 million yuan was subsidized, 88,600 people were hospitalized and 44.2978 million yuan was subsidized, which was 499.98 yuan per person and accounted for 25.35 per cent (excluding the relief for major diseases) of the total hospitalization expenses of all the participating peasant farmers. In 2005, the participation rate was 68.32 per cent (by March).

In general, the experiment was successful. (1) A management and operating mechanism for the new rural cooperative medical system began to take shape. (2) The medical care of the participating peasant farmers in the pilot regions improved somewhat, their economic burden arising from diseases becoming significantly lighter and whether they fell into or returned to poverty due to disease was somewhat improved. (3) The service conditions of the rural medical institutions improved somewhat, as did the qualifications of the medical personnel. (4) Relations between the Party and the people and between the officials and the public became closer, which promoted rural development.

However, the experiment also encountered some pressing problems. The primary problem was the difficulty in raising funds and that safe operation lacked effective guarantees. The funds for a cooperative medical service were jointly contributed by the central, provincial and regional finances and by individual peasant farmers. While the funds from the central and provincial finances were contributed fully and in time through transfer payments, the regional government found it difficult to provide counterpart funds and the peasant farmers found it difficult to pay their personal contributions. For this reason, the participation rate rose only slowly and even declined in some places. The risk resistance ability of the funds was not strong. Next, the operating and management costs were rather high. As the new rural cooperative medical system involved complex and difficult work that affected tens of thousands of families, publicity and mobilization in the initial stage required considerable fund input. Originally, the expenses of the pilot counties (cities) were paid by the health departments. After the reform of the management system, the operating institutions had a major shortfall in their working funds.

Third, some of the specific methods in the plan were not sufficiently mature and, to a certain degree, dampened the confidence and enthusiasm of the peasant farmers to participate in the new rural cooperative medical system. (1) The ratio of hospitalization subsidy in the pilot counties (cities) varied widely. In places where the ratio of hospitalization subsidy was highest, hospitalization funds were overdrawn. In places where the ratio of hospitalization subsidy was relatively low, hospitalization funds showed considerable surpluses. Although most of these surplus funds were subsidized to the participating peasant farmers through major disease relief, the fairly low ratio of hospitalization subsidy brought less or no benefit to the majority of the peasant farmers, which inevitably dampened their confidence and enthusiasm to participate and affected the sustained development of a cooperative medical service. (2) The utilization rate of the funds for outpatients and medical examination in some pilot counties (cities) was relatively low. As the outpatient fund accounted for only 30 per cent of the total amount of the cooperative medical fund, the subsidy for outpatient expenses had to be low. As this was where the peasants benefited least, this was also where the peasants were most dissatisfied with the cooperative medical service. The health examination fund cost only 1–3 yuan per person. Therefore, examination had to be limited to conventional methods such as inspecting, knocking, touching and hearing, which had no appeal for the peasant farmers, who felt that health examinations needed to provide some medical treatment facilities to examine patients suffering from chronic diseases, women and old people. (3) The designated medical institutions needed to strengthen their management, improve their medical facilities, enhance the quality of their services and control their expenses. (4) Equity was a problem. Because of the differences in ideology, medical knowledge and economic ability, those who benefited most could be those with relatively high incomes, instead of the low-income peasant farmers who needed protection most.

Ezhou's attempt

Ezhou is an emerging city in the eastern part of Hubei Province. Although it was not included in the province's pilot regions, the municipal Party committee and government decided after investigation and evaluation that it would select some regions for a small-scale experiment on a new rural cooperative medical system. They based their decisions on the following points.

- Ezhou possessed a certain ability to establish a new rural cooperative medical system.
- The city possessed certain economic features. Being in the southeastern part of Hubei Province, Ezhou had three county-level districts under its jurisdiction. It had 1.05 million people, of which 70 per cent lived in rural areas. In 2004, its GDP was 14.2 billion yuan, its per capita urban disposable income was 7,500 yuan, its per capita rural disposable income was 3,300 yuan, and its fiscal revenue was more than 1 billion yuan. According to the existing fund contribution standards for cooperative medical service, the city's finances at two levels could basically afford the fund contributions that would be paid by the regional finances.
- The city had a relatively sound three-tier rural epidemic prevention and health care network. The city had twenty-one administrative townships (towns), and each township had a public health centre. In all, the city had more than 1,900 medical personnel. Each township health centre had an epidemic prevention and health care station, which was responsible for the tasks of epidemic prevention and health care in the township. The city had 310 villages and 280 village clinics, of which 90 per cent reached the

standard for a class A clinic. In all, the city had 450 rural doctors. The administrative villages with no village clinics were mostly the seats of the township health centres. In recent years, the city has strengthened administration over the township health centres and increased funding for them.

- The city had the basis for a cooperative medical service. The city vigorously developed a rural cooperative medical service from the 1960s to the 1980s and introduced a cooperative medical service for all administrative villages (production brigades). The cooperative medical service was one of the basic rural health systems. The cooperative medical system was in the doldrums after economic restructuring began in the 1980s, but the administrative villages where economic conditions were good still maintained this rural medical security system. From a historical perspective, the former cooperative medical system laid the foundations for the establishment of a new rural cooperative medical system. From a practical perspective, the peasant farmers were quite familiar with this type of system and were supportive of it.

- The city had a fairly sound rural financial service system, thus providing a technical guarantee for the new rural cooperative medical system in the areas of fund collection, transfer and closed and safe fund operations.

- The experiments across the country and the province provided valuable experience, methods and models.

- The establishment of the rural medical relief system provided support for the poor rural population groups to participate in the new rural cooperative medical system. To ensure that the extremely poor rural people could visit doctors when they were sick, the city had established a rural medical relief system. Under this system, households enjoy the 'five guarantees': the extremely poor rural households and the individuals receiving special care and preferential treatment did not have to pay their medical fund contributions when they participated in the cooperative medical system. All their funds were paid from the transfer payment for tax and fee reform, the medical relief fund and the fund for giving special care and preferential treatment. This move provided support for the rural people to participate in the new rural cooperative medical system.

- The rural people had a strong will and certain financial abilities. In view of the existing conditions of the rural health undertakings, they strongly demanded and urgently needed to rebuild the rural cooperative medical system. Since the beginning of reform and opening up, especially over the past 2 years, the peasants' cash incomes increased considerably thanks to the introduction of a series of preferential policies by the central authorities. This provided certain economic conditions for the peasants to receive medical care locally. The idea of mutual help began to take shape, and the concept of medical consumption was also changing. As each person only had to pay 10 yuan each year and each peasant family on average only had to pay about 50 yuan, most peasant farmers could afford and were willing to participate.

Ezhou's basic guidelines for the experiment

In working out its plan for the experiment, the city of Ezhou gave full consideration to the experience and lessons of the pilot counties (cities) in the province. The experiments in the pilot counties (cities) revealed the difficulties in fund operation. On the one hand, the peasant farmers were not enthusiastic about participation, and hence the participation rate was low. On the other, medical expenses rose rapidly and the fund could not sustain them. Some people attributed this problem to the fact that the value preference and goal definition of the cooperative medical system were unable to effectively stimulate peasant farmers' enthusiasm to participate and had underestimated their medical needs.

In terms of the insurance mechanism, the new rural cooperative medical system explicitly emphasizes protection against 'major diseases'. The system reflects the strong desire for the sharing of experiences and gives due consideration to the minor diseases of outpatients. Claim reimbursements in 2004 indicated that 2.1925 million outpatients were treated at a cost of 6.99 yuan per person per time. Also that year, 88,600 patients were hospitalized at a cost of 499.98 yuan per person per time. The expenses were mainly for those patients who were hospitalized for major diseases and, as a result, a few people enjoyed a fairly high standard of medical services. Accordingly, the relevant people in Ezhou held that, currently, the rural cooperative medical system should provide low-level and extensive coverage and should emphasize basic services. This definition was somewhat different from that defined by the higher authorities. Simply put, the emphasis should shift from solving the issue of 'becoming poor due to major diseases' to solving the issue of 'minor diseases evolving into major diseases', and from the principle of 'hospitalization subsidy first and outpatient subsidy second' to the principle of 'emphasizing outpatient subsidy and giving due consideration to hospitalization subsidy'. This could allow more participating peasants to benefit from cooperative medical services.

Why should the coverage be low level? We can compare some of the city's data about urban medical insurance in 2004 (see Table 27.1).

The comparison indicates that the personal contributions and government subsidies cannot fully meet the medical needs of the peasant farmers. Once the peasant farmers participate in a cooperative medical service, their

Table 27.1 Comparison of urban and rural medical insurance in 2004.

	Per capita fund contribution (yuan)	Per capita fund possession (yuan)	Per capita medical expense (yuan)
Urban areas	110	678	563
Rural areas in pilot counties	10	30	25.24

medical needs, previously suppressed by poverty, will be released and personal expectations will be far higher than originally forecast. As the regional bodies are unlikely to increase their inputs in the near future, the current level of medical security has to be relatively low, so as to conform with the level of economic and social development.

Why should the coverage be extensive? The hospitalized patients were few in number, but most of the funds were spent on them. The fact that only a limited number of people benefited from a cooperative medical service was the main reason why the peasant farmers were not so enthusiastic about participation. Peasant farmers' needs had a unique feature: their income and affordability were low but they expected to receive timely and higher returns from their contributions. In other words, they had a high return consciousness but a low risk consciousness. They lacked the awareness of health investment: when the peasant farmers were not rich, they looked to the cooperative medical service to solve part of their difficulties; but they had a 'try-your-luck' mentality towards medical consumption and lacked the awareness of regular investment in such consumption. There were two examples. Some peasant farmers had not been hospitalized for a year. Owing to their narrow petty peasant consciousness, they believed they had not benefited from the cooperative medical service and their fund contributions had been spent by other people. Several dozen yuan a year was very important to a peasant farmer, and so he might choose not to participate. Some peasant farmers were hospitalized in the first year and refused to participate in the second, because they believed that they would not be so unlucky as to fall sick again the following year, and so had no need to pay for other people. For this reason, the participation rate dropped in some places after the first year of operation. Therefore, in view of this unique feature of peasant farmer demand, the coverage of the cooperative medical service should be extensive and benefit more people.

Why are the basic services so important? Emphasizing the provision of basic services means that preferential treatment should be given to basic medical treatment and preventive health care. This is because: (1) both the cost and the funding pressures are low; (2) the majority of the participants can benefit; (3) the efficiency of medical input is high and basic medical treatment can prevent minor illnesses from developing into major diseases. One yuan spent on preventive health care can be as efficient as 70 yuan spent on medical treatment. This can, from the 'upstream', prevent rural people from becoming sick as a result of poverty.

Some possible issues

Financial affordability

As Ezhou was not a provincially designated place for experiment, it could not receive a financial subsidy from the higher authorities. Instead, it had to raise funds by itself.

1   The city's financial revenue was uneven. Municipal finance was fairly healthy but the district and township finances were stretched. As cooperative medical services took districts as the implementing units, the district and township finances had considerable difficulty paying cooperative medical expenses.

2   Currently, reform is in a crucial period and interest adjustment involves cost payments. Governments at all levels have many problems to solve and many things to do, all of which require financial resources and increase pressure on financial expenditure. Therefore, they have to choose the right direction for their financial inputs.

3   Once a decision is made to introduce a cooperative medical service, governments at all levels must include it in their annual budgets, and this budget outlay will continue to grow. Therefore, government financial spending will increase. If a cooperative medical service is interrupted because of financial unaffordability, the move will produce a wide negative social impact and political loss. Therefore, government funding support is rigid.

The new rural cooperative medical fund would face huge pressures. The city decided that the service would have as wide coverage as possible in order to benefit as many people as possible, and claim reimbursements would be proportionally high. But the fund is relatively small and the per capita fund possession is also small and far smaller than medical insurance in the urban areas. Currently, even though urban medical insurance has a very strict control over claim reimbursement, the fund still faces tremendous pressures. We can therefore imagine how great the pressure will be for the city's new rural cooperative medical fund.

As the value preference and system design of the city's new rural cooperative medical service were different from those foreseen by the higher authorities, they did not conform to the policies set by the higher authorities and could form a policy vacuum. In the long run, it remained questionable whether it could receive policy and financial support from the higher authorities.

The city's cooperative medical service was defined as having low-level and extensive coverage and emphasizing basic services; the major disease relief programme now implemented for the extremely poor population group was targeted at this group and to combat major diseases, while commercial medical insurance was targeted at the rich population. As a result, there was no proper solution to the incidence of major diseases among the middle-class peasant classes. How the policies on a cooperative medical service could be integrated with other policies to solve the problems that peasant farmers encountered or fell back into poverty due to major diseases required further study and exploration.

The peasant farmers should be guided to form the concept of mutual help and problem sharing so that they can both fully enjoy the benefits of a cooperative medical service and cherish the limited medical and health resources available to allow them to produce maximum efficiency. While the peasants should be encouraged to actively participate, rational policies and methods must be worked out to control unreasonable and uneconomical expenditure and to prevent the fund from running the risk of drying up. How to guide the peasant farmers to rethink their concepts still requires exploration.

The fund's risk resistance ability also requires evaluation (other pilot regions also have this problem).

Currently, the city's experiment with a new rural cooperative medical system is proceeding steadily.

Conclusion

The above was written in August 2005. The author investigated the experiment conducted by the city of Ezhou on a new rural cooperative medical system. In 2006, its experiment was not included in the scope of the provincial experiment for various reasons. Therefore, the city had to explore such a system at its own expense. As the experiment was self-financed and the plan design was different from that of the higher authorities in some respects, the city's exploratory work was limited in scale.

This case study tells us that plan design is very important to a project. If a project is differently oriented, it will adjust the interest relations between different population groups and will have impacts on the weight of the value, ability and support of the 'three-cycle theory' for public administration and on the size of their common areas.

Originated in 2005 and revised in 2006

28 Thoughts on the wheat flour issue

Zhang Jianjin

Located alongside the Bohai, China, Tianjin City is a metropolitan area with a population of nearly 10 million. The various leading news media exposed on 14 June 2006 that, upon sampling and inspection, 60 per cent of wheat flour in Tianjin market contained potassium bromide (PB), a kind of carcinogenic chemical additive. This news shocked the citizens, who are used to regular lives. A battle gradually emerged concerning the contaminated wheat flour.

The emergence of the 'toxic' flour

At the end of 2005, the State Food and Drug Administration (SFDA) organized a comprehensive review of the Trusted Food Project initiated in thirty-one cities countrywide. In the sampling inspection of wheat flour on Tianjin market, it was discovered that only 35.48 per cent passed. It was a very serious problem.

In the first half year of 2006, the Tianjin Food and Drug Administration (TFDA) organized the relative departments, namely the industrial and commerce bureau and the quality supervision bureau, to inspect and supervise the wheat flour circulated in Tianjin market. This was the first inspection and supervision exercise by TFDA since the government set up the organization to enforce comprehensive standards on food and to coordinate various functions. The inspection involved twenty varieties of wheat flour, which covered about 20 per cent of the total varieties on the market. The inspection mainly involves two indexes. The first is PB, which should not be detected; the second is benzoic peroxide (BOP), which should be less than 0.06 milligrams per kilogram, according to national standards.

On 10 June 2006, the inspection results indicated that, in twenty varieties inspected, involving twenty manufacturers, the BP contents were as follows: eight samples from six manufacturers passed, while twelve samples did not pass; thus the pass rate was 40 per cent. The BOP contents in all twenty samples were below national standards and thus passed.

PB is a kind of chemical additive, which can increase the strength of flour gluten and whiten flour, and can also cause bread made from inferior flour to swell and become dense. As it is reasonably priced, PB is commonly used in the flour industry. However, it was found in recent studies that PB is a type of carcinogenic agent that could result in diseases such as renal cancer. The related international cancer research institute listed PB as a carcinogenic agent, and the World Health Organization (WHO) proposed to forbid the use of PB in previous years. In 2005, the State Quality Administration, China, and the State Standardization Committee, China, issued a notice that, from 1 July 2005, PB was forbidden to be used as a food additive in food manufacturing industries. Thus, PB has now been totally banned.

However, nearly a year since the state banned its use as a food additive, PB was detected in wheat flour in Tianjin market. How to settle this issue became a problem for TFDA. Generally, if contaminated wheat flour is detected, they will only penalize the manufacturers. However, the wheat flour inspected this time accounted for 20 per cent of the total marketed in Tianjin. If only the manufacturers were penalized, it would greatly threaten the food safety of the public. However, if this was publicized, would the public accept it? If the public asked questions and apportioned blame, they would target the government. In reviewing the dilemma, TFDA believed the results proved that they were not qualified; they should not allow citizens to eat contaminated wheat flour by mistake, and should publicize this fact to remind them to purchase uncontaminated flour.

On 13 June, TFDA held a press conference with the relative departments to publicize the issue of contaminated wheat flour by sampling inspection, revealed the twelve enterprises manufacturing the flour to various media and also announced that all contaminated wheat flour would be withdrawn from the market. The industrial and commercial departments would inspect the contaminated flour and penalize the relevant enterprises.

On 14 June, various major media all carried reports of the conference, and thus the news spread rapidly. The citizens applauded the settlement and thought the government had acted correctly. The Tianjin Association of Grain and Oil and other major wheat flour manufacturers sent letters to the government to thank them for their prompt decision on market standardization and correction, thus maintaining the food safety interests of citizens.

Exposure by the media led a collective group to visit the government

On 15 June, the day after the exposure of the issue by the media, TFDA received an emergency call from the Complaint Letters and Requests Handling Office, the Tianjin Municipal Government, saying that there were over twenty people at the gates of the government building demanding to meet the mayor. This group claimed that the report exposing the contaminated wheat flour issue was not true. The call requested TFDA to send someone to settle the issue. Although TFDA had made some preparations for the aftermath of the media exposure, they had not anticipated that the manufacturers of the contaminated wheat flour would collectively visit the government unexpectedly, which made the issue more serious.

The exposed manufacturers of contaminated flour considered that TFDA had no qualifications to organize the inspection, and the method of sampling and testing was also not in accordance with relevant stipulations.

On 14 June, the exposed manufacturers of contaminated flour stormed the Tianjin Bureau of Industry and Commerce and the Tianjin Bureau of Quality Supervision, requesting them to deny the validity of TFDA's sampling inspection.

On 15 June, the district- and county-level sub-bureaus of TFDA called TFDA, asking whether or not to implement the inspection of contaminated wheat flour, as some supermarkets were abiding by the ruling of taking wheat flour off the shelves. In a short time, complaints were heard everywhere, and most people thought that TFDA was doing other people's business.

In the afternoon of 16 June, TFDA held a meeting with the relevant enterprises, listened to their thoughts and gave them the relevant information about the inspection by TFDA. But the two sides insisted that both were right and failed to reach a compromise. The enterprises visiting the government pointed out that, if TFDA did not withdraw the decision, they would bring a lawsuit against TFDA in Beijing.

On 19 June, TFDA received a letter from unit A in Beijing requesting SFDA to help the related enterprises investigate the issue to find out the facts, and copied TFDA in. Unit A claimed in their letter that the ten leading wheat flour manufacturers claimed jointly that in no case had PB been added to their products; TFDA had possibly sampled false products, or perhaps there had been some errors in the testing method and the wrong results obtained. Nor had TFDA informed the relative enterprises or paid any attention to the enterprises' requests.

Unit A also pointed out in the letter that, if it turned out to be the enterprises' offence, they should be severely penalized and ordered to tighten up their procedures; but if it was not the enterprises' offence, this should be corrected immediately and the enterprises should be absolved of all blame. Unit A also suggested to SFDA that:

1   SFDA should entrust an authoritative organization to reinspect products from the same batch of the above enterprises, the samples should be confirmed by the enterprises, and the test method of ion exchange chromatography should be used.
2   Before the issue was clarified, SFDA should not penalize the relative enterprises for the moment, and not enlarge the publicity and disseminate the influence.

It was reflected at the same time that unit A was prepared to reorganize an inspection of the wheat flour in Tianjin market.

The situation took a sudden unexpected turn when the relevant departments in Tianjin also began to doubt the inspection and exposure of contaminated wheat flour.

The inspection and sampling of wheat flour was organized by TFDA with the relative departments, such as the industrial and commercial bureaus and quality supervision bureau, by sampling and purchasing from the market but not informing the relevant enterprises, and the testing organ was a legal food inspection institute. The enterprises pointed out that this did not conform with the procedural requirements of legal sampling and inspection, because:

1 Such inspections should not be organized by TFDA. The previous inspections were done by the industrial and commercial bureaus.
2 The inspection results at previous times were passed on to the relevant enterprises, which would propose a retest of the contaminated flour, while in this instance, the results were settled before any retests were conducted, which did not conform with the legal requirement of such procedures.

Another disputed issue was that the testing method used did not accord with the requirement of relevant stipulations. This inspection used the titration method, also called the qualitative method. On 1 June 2006, the State Quality Administration and the State Standardization Committee promulgated jointly that, since 1 June 2006, the PB tests on wheat flour should use ion exchange chromatography, also called the instrument method. The titration method mainly uses experimental facilities, such as a glass blender, beaker, Whitman filter paper, burette and so on, with reagents such as zinc sulphate and sodium hydroxide; while the instrument method mainly extracts PB in the samples with pure water, removes the disturbance of chloride ion in the extracted liquid by a column of argentums and hydrogen, removes water-soluble large molecules in the extracted liquid by ultra filtering and tests the liquid by anion exchange chromatography – an electro-conductive detector. This method of testing by instruments is more accurate than the titration method.

TFDA had no common opinion on who was right through coordinating the relevant departments. If the situation continued, TFDA would be placed in an embarrassing situation. Now there were only two ways open to TFDA: withdraw the decision and acknowledge the enterprises' requests, or insist on its own decision and compete with the enterprises.

Final results

TFDA convened the relevant responsible personnel to achieve a unified opinion. As wheat flour is the main food in people's daily lives, especially in northern China, and there is a population of over 10 million in Tianjin, making the everyday consumption of wheat flour around several hundred tons, if they do not withdraw the contaminated wheat flour, many people would eat the 'toxic' food, thereby threatening people's lives. No matter which department was involved in this issue, they should focus on the food safety of the public, so the contaminated wheat flour should not continue to be marketed. This opinion was unanimously recognized by the various departments. At the same time, the participating parties analysed the current sampling procedure and testing method. TFDA conducted the sampling inspection according to its remit, which conformed with the investigation and settlement procedure of serious accidents according to the relative stipulations of the *Tianjin Preliminary Proposal of Emergency Case of Food Safety*. This inspection was approved by the Tianjin government and applied for a specific outlay of sampling and inspection. TFDA organized the relevant departments to conduct the inspection jointly. In the sampling inspection, the sampling personnel purchased the samples themselves without informing the relevant enterprises, which, impersonally, could truly reflect the quality of wheat flour in the market of Tianjin. All samples were tested by a legal inspection institute; the preliminary results were rechecked and were found to be accurate. In addition, as for the testing method, the state had previously promulgated the new instrument method when the inspection institutes in Tianjin did not possess the correct type of instruments. We had no reason not to inspect and sample the wheat flour on the market just because we did not have these instruments. But the industrial and commerce bureaus and the quality supervision bureau also pointed out that such a procedure of sampling, information and announcement did vary in some characteristics from the related stipulations, and that the settlement method should be properly studied.

In the stalemate that ensued, TFDA decided to ask the Tiainjin government to insist on maintaining the qualification, procedure and results of this sampling inspection, and to further tighten up market supervision and management of the relevant departments. The leaders of Tianjin government decided, upon analysing the sampling and inspection methods, that: (1) they affirmed the settlement of the sampling and the results; (2) they agreed to tighten up supervision and management, and that the contaminated products should be withdrawn from the market; (3) the relevant departments should take charge of their own methods to conduct strict supervision, and to rectify the supervision of unqualified enterprises.

On 20 June, according to the direction of the government leaders, TFDA convened a coordinating meeting with the relevant departments and announced the settlement of the wheat flour issue. They deployed further enlarged sampling inspections of wheat flour in circulation according to the requirement of the government leaders.

On 22 June, TFDA also convened an announcement meeting which the twelve unqualified enterprises attended. At the meeting, TFDA explained the situation and the settlement opinion. The twelve enterprises all expressed the view that they were willing to withdraw the contaminated products from the market.

The issue of enterprises visiting the government triggered by the contaminated wheat flour issue in Tianjin was finally settled. However, this issue provided much food for thought.

Discussion

1 How to ensure that the public eats healthy food? The contaminated wheat flour was finally removed from shelves and withdrawn from the market in Tianjin. The public applauded the action, but the matter left TFDA with the problem of how to proceed in the future.
2 How to coordinate smoothly the system of food supervision and management? The supervision and management of food, from planting and growing to manufacturing, processing and distribution as well as to eating and sanitation, involves various supervising departments, while the outlays and personnel for them are separate, and there are no unified management and operating systems.
3 Although TFDA leads the organization, supervision and inspection, they have no material administrative power and lack legal guarantees and support, which causes practical difficulties.

Background

The Tianjin Municipal Committee of CPC and the Tianjin municipal government promulgated the stipulations of the functions of TFDA, which are:

- To execute the comprehensive supervision functions of food, health care products and cosmetics (FHC) of Tianjin City; organize and coordinate the relevant departments to undertake their safety supervision of FHC; organize and coordinate specific activities of enforcement and supervision of FHC according to the authorization of the government; initiate inspection and penalization of severe safety accidents of FHC in Tianjin; organize, coordinate and cooperate with relevant departments to conduct emergency and salvage operations of severe safety accidents of FHC.
- To generally coordinate safety inspections and review of FHC; co-prepare announcement methods of safety supervision information on FHC with relevant departments; integrate safety information on FHC of relevant departments and announce the findings to the public at regular intervals.
- To conduct preliminary inspections of the registration application of new drugs, generic drugs, traditional Chinese medicine (TCM) protected products, eliminated drugs, drug package materials and health care products; inspect import and export drugs, organize and implement the over-the-counter (OTC) system; oversee the review of drugs and supervision of drugs' adverse reactions.
- To supervise and enforce the implementation of manufacturing quality management practices and authentication systems of manufacturers,

distributors of drugs and medical devices, and medical units of preparations; issue licences to manufacturers and distributors of drugs and medical devices and medical units of preparations; examine and approve the advertisements of drugs and medical devices; examine and approve clinical trials of Class II medical devices.

- To supervise and enforce the implementation of the legal standard of medical devices; examine and approve registration of medical devices; oversee the review of medical devices and adverse reaction supervision.
- To oversee supervision and inspection of quality of drugs and medical devices, press announcements of quality of drugs and medical devices; inspect and punish illegal acts of manufacturing and selling false and inferior drugs and medical devices.
- To supervise and manage narcotic drugs, psychotropic drugs, medicinal toxic drugs, radioactive drugs and special drugs.

Written in 2006

29 How can a good thing be well done?

Chang Xiaochun

On the first working day after the long May Day holiday in 2004, deputy mayor Z, who was in charge of education and health at Songyuan City in the northeast province of Jilin, was surrounded in front of the government building by more than twenty students and parents who came to lodge their complaints over a food poisoning incident. During the New Year's Day and the May Day holidays, he had gone twice to Beijing to persuade the complainants to return to their homes. He tried repeatedly to explain to them how the municipal government would handle the issue. But they refused to listen, and the mayor became worn out both physically and mentally by the deadlock.

Poisoning incident

At 2:00 p.m. on 4 December 2003, the Municipal Health Bureau received a report from the city's central hospital that a poisoning incident had occurred involving some students of Changning Primary School in Songyuan City after they had eaten some soymilk biscuits. The report received close attention from the Municipal Party Committee and government. The mayor personally went to hospital to visit the victims and instructed the relevant departments and the district government to do all they could to save the students' lives.

It was understood later that, at about 6:00 p.m. on 3 December 2003, twenty-one students from Changning Primary School exhibited symptoms of fever, vomiting, diarrhoea, fatigue and sore throats. These students were sent to the city's central hospital for treatment on the morning of 4 December. The hospital suspected food poisoning. Over the next few days, some students from another three schools also exhibited the above symptoms. By 20 December, 177 people had fallen ill. While eighty-eight of them were cured and discharged, eighty-nine remained in hospital for observation.

The municipal government immediately set up a steering group to handle the incident with the mayor serving as its leader. At the same time, the government activated the *Contingency Plan for Unexpected Public Health Incident in Songyuan*.

The Municipal Health Bureau discovered in an epidemiological investigation that the twenty-one students demonstrated similar symptoms almost simultaneously, and that they had all eaten the same soymilk biscuits produced on 1 December 2003 by the Songyuan Lihua Industrial Company. This batch of soymilk biscuits was distributed to eight schools in 20,286 bags. The Municipal Health Bureau and the Education Bureau immediately organized for the retrieval of these biscuits. In all, 15,767 bags were retrieved, and the rest were eaten by the students. The company was ordered to stop production and delivery immediately, and its inventory and the related instruments, equipment and production sites were also sealed off.

The provincial and municipal disease prevention and control centres conducted joint tests of the soymilk biscuits, retrieved possible pathogenic factors and carried out nearly 100 laboratory tests. They excluded nineteen harmful elements including lead and arsenic, organic phosphate pesticide, rat bane, soybean anti-nutrition factors, pathogenic microorganisms, some food additives and other pathogenic factors.

After the provincial and municipal health departments failed to discover the specific pathogenic factors through multiple tests, the provincial health department requested the Ministry of Health to dispatch experts to Songyuan to supervise the work. Eight experts in food hygiene, epidemiology and poison control dispatched by the Chinese Centre for Disease Control and Prevention and the National Centre for Health Inspection and Supervision arrived in the city of Songyuan on 13 December and began further epidemiological investigations and analyses and the screening of the poisons and patient symptoms. On 17 December, the national, provincial and municipal experts held an appraisal meeting on the incident and made the following conclusions. (1) In light of the epidemiologic characteristics and clinical symptoms and in accordance with the *General Principles of Diagnostic Criteria and Technical Management of Food Poisoning*, this incident of food poisoning arose from consuming the soymilk biscuits produced on 1 December 2003 by the Songyuan Lihua Industrial Company. (2) As laboratory tests failed to discover explicit pathogenic factors, this incidence of food poisoning was recorded to have occurred for no known reason in accordance with the relevant state laws, regulations and procedures. (3) The laboratory tests on the suspected poisoning foodstuffs and the raw materials excluded some harmful elements and some common poisoning chemicals. (4) The hospitals participating in rescue and treatment had made an accurate diagnosis and administered appropriate treatment for the patients. Based on clinical symptoms and auxiliary examination, this food poisoning incident would have had a fair prognosis and no consequences. All the national, provincial and municipal experts accepted the conclusions.

However, the parents of the poisoned students refused to accept these conclusions. First, they argued that, as the expert group had failed to identify the pathogenic factors, they should not conclude that there would be no consequences. Second, they argued that, as issuing soymilk biscuits was part of government policy, the government must bear all the expenses and repercussions. Third, they argued that the relevant personnel should be prosecuted for legal liabilities. Afterwards, these students and their parents began putting forward all kinds of demands in an organized way at hospitals, schools and the office buildings of the municipal Party committee and government. They also lodged complaints to higher authorities, attacked government institutions, smashed up public property and verbally abused government personnel. At the same time, the Songyuan Lihua Industrial Company, as the producer of the biscuits, also felt that it had been unfairly treated. It argued that, as the pathogenic factors had not been identified, the enterprise should not be held fully responsible. The enterprise was also angry over the government's move to seal off the enterprise's production outlets and freeze its bank accounts. It also wanted to safeguard its own interests through legal channels once the storm over this incident had blown over.

Experiment on 'soymilk programme'

The 'soymilk programme' was designed to provide soymilk foodstuffs to primary and middle school students. It was a programme jointly introduced by the State Council and the governments of the three northeast provinces. The programme was designed to increase soybean production to restructure agricultural planting by expanding the soybean-growing acreage in northeast China, to promote the development of the soybean industry and the related industries through soybean processing, packing, transport and other links, and to improve the nutritional and health conditions of the primary and middle school students by providing soybean foodstuffs to them. This was a good thing that could bring about diverse benefits. The State Council instructed that the experiment on implementing this programme should be regarded as an important task of implementing the thoughts of 'three represents' and should be treated from the strategic perspectives of improving the quality of the Chinese nation and pushing forward agricultural restructuring.

To implement the instructions of the State Council, the Jilin provincial government issued a special document and worked out a plan for the experiment in the second half of 2002. The experimental plan requested that the producing enterprises of soymilk foodstuffs must be selected through bidding. In other words, tenders would be invited from the soymilk-producing enterprises in and outside the province that had passed corporate qualification evaluation and affirmation according to the six basic requirements of the ISO9000 quality certification. The six requirements were specified in the *Notice on the Evaluation and Affirmation of the Qualifications of the Pilot Enterprises for the 'Student Soymilk' Programme* jointly issued by the Ministry of Agriculture and the Ministry of Education. Those enterprises noted for higher quality, lower price and better service would be selected, and the responsibilities of the relevant parties would be specified in contracts. The provincial Economic and Trade Commission, the Agricultural

Committee, the Quality Supervision, Inspection and Quarantine Bureau, the Health Bureau, the Price Bureau and the Education Bureau would be in charge of the supervision, inspection and dynamic management of the production capacities of the designated enterprises, the dovetailing of the enterprises with the designated peasant farmers, and the quality, hygiene, price and service of the products respectively. The plan also requested strict compliance with the document *Implementing Rules of Jilin for Access Permit of Soymilk Products*, by which those enterprises without access permits were all prohibited from entering schools to sell their products and under which fake, inferior, expired, deteriorating and other unqualified products were prohibited from schools. Once the rules were violated, those who were responsible would be severely penalized and their leaders held accountable. If serious consequences occurred, the relevant personnel would be prosecuted under the law.

The experiment on the soymilk programme was conducted with the policy support, administrative expertise and consumption guidance of the government. The willingness of the students and their parents and their right to select consumption were respected. While no mandatory orders would be allowed, those without the correct conditions for the experiment would not be forced to participate. In addition, the experiment would be tilted towards rural students as far as possible. To ensure that students could afford to drink soymilk and the families of the students would not have an additional financial burden, the 'soymilk programme' also contained a subsidy policy. Each year, central finance would subsidize 50 million yuan and provincial finance would offer a counter subsidy of 25 million yuan. For those students willing to consume soymilk powder or biscuits, the daily subsidy would be 0.10 yuan for each urban student, 0.25 yuan for each rural student and 0.25 yuan for each poverty-stricken student (whose tuition and miscellaneous fees were exempted). The price of each bag (25 grams) of soymilk powder or biscuits would be more than 0.30 yuan. The subsidy would be higher for those students who chose to drink liquid soymilk.

The Municipal Education Bureau selected the schools for the experiment on the basis of full publicity. The experiment would cover one-third of the total number of primary and middle school students. The pilot schools would organize the students to drink one cup of soymilk each day. On holidays, the students would bring soymilk with them and drink it at home, and the schools would register and supervise them. The pilot schools and the designated enterprises filled up the Soymilk Purchase Order for Primary and Middle School Students in Jilin (purchase certificate), which would be used as vouchers for delivery and account settlement by the enterprises. The duplicates of the purchase order were held by the schools, the provincial, municipal and county educational authorities and the enterprises. The enterprises were responsible for delivering goods to schools according to the quality and quantity requirements specified in the contracts and for providing the relevant equipment.

The monitoring of the experiment on the 'soymilk programme' over the past 18 months indicates that the results were tangible. The programme has helped improve the nutritional and health conditions of the students in the pilot regions, mobilize the enthusiasm of the peasant farmers in certain regions to grow soybeans, increase the incomes of the peasant farmers, restructure agricultural planting and promote the development of the soybean industry and related industries.

Conflict of interests in an unexpected incident

Although the governments, the relevant authorities and the enterprises have all tried hard to do as required in policy support, implementation, production and processing, three poisoning incidents arising from eating soymilk foodstuffs still occurred in the course of implementing the experiment in the three northeast provinces. They happened in the cities of Anshan and Chaoyang in Liaoning Province and the city of G in Jilin. All these poisoning incidents triggered prolonged and fierce group opposition, and the regional government mobilized large amounts of human, financial and material resources to solve these incidents, which have not completely settled down, even today.

After the incident of 4 December occurred in the city of Songyuan, the municipal government introduced a series of clear-cut measures and effective solutions in the areas of offering timely medical treatment, sending the students back to school, offering reasonable compensation, prosecuting legal liabilities and stabilizing ideological fluctuations. Of the 177 poisoned students, most recovered rapidly, were discharged from hospital and resumed their normal life and study.

About fourteen students and their parents and relatives have refused to accept the solutions offered by the municipal government. Although some of their reasonable demands were met by the municipal government in a timely manner, they continued to put forward new demands. For example, they did not trust the hospitals designated by the provincial health authorities and demanded that the best doctors be found from the best hospitals in other provinces or in the country to treat the students. For 18 months, these parents accompanied their children to the large hospitals in the provincial capital or in the neighbouring provinces for diagnosis and treatment. They also visited some large hospitals in Beijing. But they were still dissatisfied with the treatment by all these hospitals. Whenever their children felt physically uncomfortable, they would suspect it was a consequence of poisoning. They also used this advantage to repeatedly treat the diseases their children had caught before the incident. In addition, they demanded that the municipal government assume unlimited liabilities and be responsible for the lifetime health of their children or pay a lump sum compensation of 200,000 yuan. They demanded that their children receive education while in hospital. This was because the municipal government offered a 50-yuan daily subsidy for absence from work for each of the parents who accompanied their children to hospital. Therefore, even if the children were fully recovered, their parents still refused to allow their children to leave hospital but wanted their children's education not to be affected. They even argued that the experts were government hired and therefore were not reliable, and that their conclusion that the pathogenic factors were unknown was designed to shirk responsibility.

The municipal government treated all the demands of the parents of the students seriously. It immediately solved the issues that could be solved and patiently explained the reasons why some of the issues could not be solved. For example, in selecting hospitals and medical treatment, the municipal government worked out the relevant principles on seeking medical treatment outside the city, allowed the students and their parents to seek treatment in any hospital in China either on their own or accompanied by government personnel and agreed to reimburse all the actual medical expenses. In addition, the government invited experts from the Ministry of Health three times for group consultation. In ensuring the students' education, the government mobilized teachers to go to the students' homes to coach them and suggested that those students who recovered should leave the hospitals and receive outpatient treatment before they returned to school as usual. In assuming responsibility and offering compensation, the government suggested that parents seek solutions through legal channels. The government also sent personnel to the cities of Anshan and Chaoyang to learn about handling poisoning cases. The provincial government closely followed the handling of the incident. The provincial governor and the responsible vice provincial governor personally went to the hospitals to visit the students and their parents.

Parents' distorted mentality

Most of the parents who refused the normal channels for communication and made repeated complaints were jobless people, noted for their lack of qualifications, unstable employment and low income. Their lives were relatively difficult. While they were concerned about the impact of the poisoning incident on the future health of their children, they also intended to take this opportunity to receive as much compensation as possible. Over the past 18 months, Xinhua News Agency and other media institutions carried follow-up reports on the student poisoning incidents in Liaoning Province and the city of G in Jilin Province. In particular, their critical questioning of the policy loopholes of the 'soymilk programme', the criticism of the poor coordination between the local government and the relevant departments in planning execution and the inefficient response to the incident, and especially the exposure and exaggeration of the haematosepsis and other harmful after-effects experienced by some students, all aggravated the mental burden of the parents and further increased their dissatisfaction. Coincidentally, social stability in the city of Songyuan was seriously affected by the mass complaints arising from corporate transformation, municipal resettlement and land disputes. The primary and middle school students were a highly sensitive and exceptional population group. The close attention paid by society to the student poisoning incident and the spread of certain emotive comments all further complicated the handling of this incident.

These parents believed that seeking a solution through legal action was not economically sensible. They did not have the money to fight a legal battle and the government was bound to intervene in court trials. Therefore, fighting a legal battle would not only cost them money and time, but the result was bound to be unfavourable to them. They felt that, at a time when the Party Central Committee and the State Council were pursuing a policy of 'ruling for the people' and the Party committees and governments at all levels emphasized social stability, the government would yield to pressure as long as they could allow the incident to spiral out of control. So they repeatedly resorted to radical approaches and went to the municipal Party committee and government to complain, and raised funds and organized more students and parents to go to Beijing to attack the Xinhua Gate, Tiananmen Square, the Central Commission for Discipline Inspection and other state organs. They even resorted to attacking the residences of the experts in Beijing who had come to the city of Songyuan for group consultation and appraisal. These irrational and abnormal group complaints and the repeated instructions of the State Bureau for Letters and Calls and the provincial government brought great pressure on the Songyuan municipal government. Since the incident of 4 December, the parents have pursued this approach. As the primary and middle school students involved were all minors, the municipal Party committee and government could not take mandatory control measures over their radical actions and the government's normal operations were affected from time to time. The personnel of the municipal government repeatedly told the complaining parents that their children were still young and should recuperate or go to school instead of being dragged along to lodge complaints. But the parents refused to listen and continued to bring their children along with them each time they lodged complaints. Some of the children even ran into government buildings and smashed up public property, shouting, 'We are minors, and the law cannot do anything to us'. These students, numbering a dozen or so, remained in hospital and refused to go to school. Looking at these children who indulged in hooliganism at the instigation of the evil elements and their parents, a primary school principal lamented, 'The children are innocent, the parents are too irresponsible, and the children will be ruined if they carry on like this'.

As the incident in Songyuan of 4 December could not be solved in a short time and in order to avoid the recurrence of similar incidents, the provincial government issued an internal notice 6 months after the incident that the experiment on the soymilk programme would be suspended throughout the province.

Afterword

There has been no definitive conclusion as to the causes of this poisoning incident. The same incident occurred in the city of Haicheng in Liaoning Province and subsequently in the city of Songyuan in Jilin Province. Immediately after the Haicheng incident, the Ministry of Health, the Ministry of Education, the Ministry of Agriculture, the Ministry of Public Security, the General Administration of Quality Supervision, Inspection and Quarantine and the State Administration of Industry and Commerce issued the *Notice on Drawing Lessons from the Soymilk Poisoning Incident in Haicheng and Further Strengthening the Hygiene and Safety of School Food.* The document requested all regions and all relevant departments to further tighten up administration measures over food safety. The poisoning incident in the city of Songyuan occurred after the document was issued. Despite the earnest efforts of governments at all levels, the enterprises and the educational authorities to implement this document, poisoning still occurred, and there has been no definitive conclusion as to whether the problem was to do with the raw materials, with the link of processing and production or with the link of transport or tests. As soymilk is a fresh food, it can go bad or get secondary pollution if it is not treated with great care in any of the links of raw materials, processing, storage and transport. And as the primary and middle school students are a special and sensitive population group, any problem occurring with them can cause social repercussions. Therefore, the introduction of the soymilk programme involves certain objective risks.

The municipal government's handling of the incident was successful in that it adopted a series of effective measures. In rescue and treatment, the municipal government invited medical expert groups from the Ministry of Health, the Provincial Health Department and the Harbin Medical University to hold eight group consultations for the poisoned students, and designated five provincial hospitals as the referral hospitals. The hospitals established medical files for the discharged students and promised that they would be accepted immediately and treated effectively if the symptoms recurred. As those students with mild symptoms had to receive treatment and continue their education, two hospitals set up a special outpatient area to ensure that the students would be treated by experts. The government immediately arranged economic compensation for those parents accompanying their children to hospital and set up and executed reasonable measures to handle medical expenses, compensation for absence from work, nursing care and nutrition advice. If students needed to be transferred to other hospitals and their families were in financial difficulties, they were offered compensation before they were transferred. In addition, they could claim reimbursements from the original treating hospitals with the relevant invoices every five or seven days. One-on-one special arrangements were made, under which teachers coached students to make up for missed lessons. To ease the anxiety and anger of the parents, the government held several meetings with them to brief them on the latest developments and answer questions. In addition, the municipal and district education authorities assigned teachers to have one-on-one exchanges with the students and their parents. The Jilin provincial government and the Songyuan municipal government also appointed press spokesmen to be responsible for communicating with media institutions and actively responding to their requirements, such as arranging interviews with the relevant officials and seeking relevant information. Thanks to the smooth operation of the communications mechanism, media reports were not as exaggerated as when they covered the Haicheng incident but were objective and even-handed. Social repercussions were very limited.

So far, all the 177 students affected in the Songyuan incident have fully recovered, left hospital and returned to school. They have reported no consequences and they have remained in good health. As the health of the students has stabilized, the complaints of their parents have gradually subsided. The whole incident is now over.

Written in 2004

30 The trust crisis caused by 'coconut face-changing'

Zeng Yu

Exposure of toxic coconuts on closed circuit television (CCTV)

At 12:30 p.m. on 6 June 2004, the *Weekly Quality Report*, a programme on CCTV which broadcasts to a wide audience, featured a special report, 'The Face-changing of Nata de Coco'. Families listened closely to the woman announcer's offscreen voice.

It was not easy for people living at some distance from Hainan to drink coconut milk. Now, through microbial fermentation, a new technology can transform coconut milk into Nata de coco, which is then sold in block form or in tins. Thus, people all over China can enjoy the local products of Hainan. But, recently, a letter claimed that two processing factories in Haikou were manufacturing Nata de coco in an abnormal way.

- Fresh coconut milk was being replaced with water. The reporter visited this coconut processing factory in Haikou in Hainan Province. It was quite a large factory and was headed by Wu Jiancai. Technicians working in the factory said that their output of Nata de coco was relatively large in terms of trade in the region, being up to 300 tons per month.

Fresh coconut milk is a raw material of Nata de coco. Thus, a factory with an annual production of about 4,000 tons should use a large amount of fresh coconut milk. However, after several days' continuous observation, the reporter had not seen workers add any fresh coconut milk to the pool of raw materials. Meanwhile, the tap by the pool disgorged water into the pool every day, and workers poured barrels of slices of newly harvested coconut into the water.

Workers told the reporter that, after several hours' soaking, the slices of coconut in the pool could turn 5 or 6 tons of water into coconut juice. In this case, the costs of production would be greatly reduced.

- Bleached coconut with industrial hydrogen peroxide solution. Subsequently, the water, which had turned the colour of a dark reddish yellow, was pumped to the workshop, where workers poured it into culture trays. After 7 days' fermentation, Nata de coco was the result. The reporter noticed that the Nata de coco that had been fermented recently was a yellowish brown colour, while that being sold was white and transparent and had an appetizing appearance. Wu Jiancai explained the reason: 'It is bleached with powder'.

Two days later, the reporter visited the factory again. Workers poured some colourless transparent liquid into the pool that was filled with Nata de coco. They told the reporter that it was hydrogen peroxide solution. 'It is not white at first. If you change the water it will become a little whiter, and if you press it with hydrogen peroxide solution, it will become much whiter'.

It is reported that industrial hydrogen peroxide solution is mainly used as a bleach in the papermaking and textile industries. China has prohibited its use in food processing by formal decree. If hydrogen peroxide solution gets on to one's hands, it will sting. Therefore, even the factory workers dared not eat this kind of coconut product.

- Tiantian Nata de Coco employed tricks to deal with the test. The reporter discovered that this was not the only enterprise that used hydrogen peroxide solution in processing Nata de coco. He also found the same practice in Hainan Limited Food Company of Tiantian Nata de Coco.

The superintendent of the factory told the reporter that, due to the rigorous investigations of the relevant departments, they were all careful not to be caught while using industrial hydrogen peroxide solution to bleach Nata de coco. Wu Xiaosheng, general manager of the company, said that owing to the high toxicity of industrial hydrogen peroxide solution, special methods were used for neutralization in the factory. Subsequently, while in the warehouse, the reporter noticed a worker scattering some base over the Nata de coco affected by the industrial hydrogen peroxide solution. Wu Xiaosheng said that the toxicity was counteracted in this way and cannot be tasted.

These products were provided for Changchun in Jilin, Xiaogan and Wuhan in Hebei, Quanzhou, Fuzhou and Jinjiang.

Hydrogen peroxide solution can cause deformities and gene mutation. It contains a large amount of organic and inorganic impurities. For example, it contains lead, arsenic and similar substances that are harmful to the human body. If consumers eat any food treated with industrial hydrogen peroxide solution, deformity and even potential dangers such as gene mutation may result.

- The responsible institutions were quick to respond. Meanwhile, the leaders and staff of the relevant departments in Hainan who were spending Sunday at home were shocked after having watched the special report on CCTV. The staff members of hygiene departments of the province, cities and regions were also quick to respond. Simultaneously, leaders of departments of industry and commerce, quality supervision, super-intendence of food and medicines immediately organized personnel to deal with the matter. At 2:00 p.m. on the day of the broadcast, they began separately to investigate and prosecute Wu Jiancai Nata de Coco Factory in the foreign industrial area of Guilin in Haikou, Qiongshan Food Factory of Cool Coconut, Chutian Food Factory of Nata de Coco in Qiongshan and Tiantian Shuang Food Factory of Nata de Coco. After an initial state of confusion, the numerous personnel in these departments found that these factories all used non-food-grade chemical raw materials such as hydrogen peroxide solution, sodium hydrosulphite, glacial acetic acid and so on in food production. The hygiene departments closed down two enterprises on the spot and took samples for examination and testing. The others were investigated and prosecuted by the departments of industry and commerce and that of quality supervision. The Office of Public Health of the province notified cities and counties such as Wenchang, Qionghai and Wanning at the same time to check the manufacturing enterprises of Nata de coco in all areas.

- The shocking scene. When the enforcers entered the Nata de coco factory in the foreign industrial area of Guilin in Haikou Province, a dense, sour stench greeted them. In the factory, more than thirty employees were working at several separate pools filled with Nata de coco. All the shelves in five or six large rooms were filled with slices of fermenting Nata de coco which were covered with newspapers.

The unnamed Nata de coco factory in the foreign industrial area of Guilin in the city of Haikou was headed by Wu Jiancai. Technicians from the factory admitted that their output of Nata de coco was relatively high in the trade of the region, being up to 300 tons in 1 month. In the face of the enforcers' inspection, Wu Jiancai became flustered, claiming they never used raw industrial materials to process food. However, the enforcers discovered a barrel of hydrogen peroxide solution weighing 25 kilograms in a corner room and poured it over a pile of slices of Nata de coco recently removed from a fermentation pool. A whiff of sour chemicals was immediately evident. Several minutes later, yellow slices of Nata de coco turned white. It was thus confirmed that the substance was definitely hydrogen peroxide solution. In the face of this fact, Wu Jiancai was left speechless. Subsequently, hygiene enforcers found chemical raw materials such as sodium hydroxide, industrial potassium dehydrogenize phosphate and a bottle of glyphosate with high efficiency and low toxicity. It was estimated that the factory had an output of 300 tons per month. Its industrial and commercial business licence and tax registration card had been issued by the former city of Qiongshan and had not been updated. In addition, it had no hygiene licence or production process chart.

In the Food Factory of Cool Coconut in Qiongshan, enforcers found that the factory used bleach from an illegal source, its hygiene licence was overdue and it had no testing standards. It only had one overdue hygiene licence (the term of validity was due for renewal on 22 April 2003) issued by the Hygiene Bureau of Qiongshan, which had been merged with the city of Haikou. The superintendent of the factory said that they purchased the semi-produced goods from the east suburb in Wenchang and continued the practice, not knowing whether it accorded with the enterprise's standards.

- The investigation and prosecution was a 'brilliant' success. For several days, more than 250 enforcers from the industry and commerce departments of Haikou, as well as the hygiene and quality supervision officers, checked fourteen processing factories producing Nata de coco, 262 units selling Nata de coco jelly, and placed ten cases on file against the fruit processing factory of Nata de coco, of which five possessed a valid business licence but no hygiene licence, four had no licences at all, and three were suspected of being involved in using raw materials harmful to the human body to process the Nata de coco. While inspecting the Tiantian Shuang processing factory of Nata de coco in Longtang town in Qiongshan district and the Chaomin Commercial Bank of Haikou, the industrial and commercial enforcers discovered and seized more than 30,000 trays of fermenting Nata de coco, thirty-eight barrels of semi-produced Nata de coco (100 kilograms/barrel), 607 cases of fermented Nata de coco (50 kilograms/case), more than 300 cases of Bacai puddings and fifty cases of Yeshun Nata de coco puddings and thousands of kilograms of raw materials such as white sugar, fermented fungi and so on. More seriously, while inspecting the Tiantian Shuang processing factory of Nata de coco, Wujiancai processing factory of Nata de coco and Yezhishuang food factory, they discovered large quantities of industrial raw materials containing industrial chemicals harmful to the human body as food additives, such as 4.5 packs of flaky hydrogen and oxidized sodium totalling 225 kilograms, two packs of phosphoric acid and two of hydrogen potassium totalling 100 kilograms, and eight barrels of hydrogen peroxide solution. After several days' inspection, they found conspicuous problems concerning the Nata de coco processing industry in Hainan: first, licences for some production units were not complete, such as production licences and workers' health certificates; second, there were no product standards; third, there was no authoritative testing; fourth, the underground processing units operating without licences were well disguised and continued production even after being banned.
- The toxic Nata de coco reaches distant places. After Bacai Nata de coco and Bacai fruit pineapple produced by Chaomin Bacai Food Limited Company in the bonded area of Haikou were exposed on CCTV, the relevant departments immediately organized undercover investigations of some of the large-scale markets and supermarkets in Haikou, but found that no Bacai jelly was on sale.

At 6:00 p.m., undercover investigators visited Nangong supermarket. The jellies were a feast for the eyes. Brand jellies such as 'Xizhilang', 'Qinqin', 'Jinwa' and 'Wangwang' were on the shelves, but not Bacai. They asked a shop assistant: 'Do you sell Bacai jelly?' She said: 'No'. Later, on Pearl Square, at the First Department Store, DC City, Wanfulong supermarket, they encountered the same answer.

It was reported that Bacai products are mainly sold to inland cities such as Nanchang, Hunan and Harbin, rather than in Haikou itself.

• The hidden danger of the market should not be ignored. Two days later, one insider who refused to give his name called to reveal to one newspaper agency that was trying to track down the toxic Nata de coco that, on Zhongshan Road in Haikou, there was a food additive shop that sold many kinds of industrial chemical raw materials and food additives, posing a potential safety hazard. 'The price gap is wide, from 20 to 30 yuan to over 100 yuan between the industrial chemicals and food additives containing the same substances. In order to reduce the cost, some illegal retailers usually buy industrial raw materials to serve as food additives. In addition, when the two substances are stored in the same area, this is liable to lead to food poisoning'. He added: 'The Nata de coco accident that has just happened is a very good example'. Under the guidance of the insider, one reporter went to Haikou Hao, a certain chemical industry company on Zhongshan Road, Haikou. At the entrance to the company building, he noticed various plastic bags containing industrial chemicals and food additives piled up in the entrance and covering about 10 square metres, as well as borax and ammonium, hydrogen of sulphuric acid and industrial carbonic acid hydrogen sodium and sodium bicarbonate (food sodium, hydrogen of carbonic acid). It was reported that borax is a toxic industrial chemical. The relevant departments had already stipulated clearly that this could not serve as a food additive. However, hydrogen ammonium sulphuric acid is a food additive used for neutralizing and is often used in the manufacture of stuffed buns and so on. In addition, the food additives such as citric acid and earthen bowl potassium sour sodium and carbonic acid magnesium (additives often used to produce coconut palm fruit) are mixed with various raw materials in industrial chemistry.

They then visited the Xiong industrial chemicals company on Changti Road in Haikou where, although the raw materials for industrial chemistry were stored separately from the food additives, they were still kept too close together. Where the food additives were stored, the plastic bags containing alum products of potassium were not labelled as food additives. According to the insider, the 'food additive hygiene management' regulations issued by the Chinese Health Ministry in 2002 ruled that 'food additives' had to be clearly labelled.

- The Judicial Department became involved and investigated the various findings. More than 1 month later, they had made fresh progress.
- The public security bureau placed the investigation on file. On 15 July, Wu Xiaosheng, supervisor of the processing factory of Chutian Nata de coco in Qiongshan and legal representative Zou Guihua, who were suspected of being involved in the production and sale of toxic and harmful foodstuffs, were arrested by a detachment of the public security bureau of Haikou and placed on file.

Wu Xiaosheng and his wife had registered Haikou Qiongshan Chutian Nata de coco processing factory with the industrial and commercial bureau on 8 March 2004, but had continued to operate without a hygiene licence. Before being caught by the provincial Quality Supervision Department, they had produced three batches of fruit products of Nata de coco – about 8 tons in total. They initially produced more than 3 tons, which had been sold to a Mr Wang in the Huangyanmeng Food Co. Ltd of Zhejiang at 1,800 yuan per ton.

In the course of manufacturing and processing the product, in order to make the Nata de coco look and taste appetizing, Wu Xiaosheng and Zou Guihua purchased industrial chemicals such as industrial hydrogen peroxide, flakes alkali, hydrochloric acid, magnesium sulphuric acid, phosphoric acid two hydrogen potassium and other substances to bleach, embrittle and neutralize the semi-produced goods of Nata de coco. In the enterprise run by the couple, the division of labour was clear. They were both responsible for the technological side of production. Wu Xiaosheng was mainly responsible for sales, and Zou Guihua for financial affairs.

The court held a hearing on the morning of 28 January, when Haikou people's procuratorate of Qiongshan district opened a court session to deal with the case of Wu Xiaosheng and Zou Guihua, who were accused of producing and selling toxic and harmful Nata de coco.

The public prosecution charged the couple that, in order to reduce the cost and to render the appearance attractive, they had mixed industrial chemicals such as oxidized hydrogen (hydrogen peroxide solution), hydrogen to oxidize sodium and industrial hydrochloric acid in the course of producing Nata de coco, which violated the relevant regulations of the national food hygiene laws. From March to June 2004, they had produced 7 tons of Nata de coco, of which 3 tons had already been sold to the market, and 4 tons had been seized and destroyed by the products quality technical supervision department in the province. When examined by the products quality supervision personnel of Hainan Province, the Nata de coco produced by the couple was found to contain arsenic, lead and mercury, all harmful to the human body.

Results of the court's investigation

In court, Wu Xiaosheng and Zhou Guihua did not dispute the charge, but they thought the accusation levelled by the public prosecution was untenable.

They gave three reasons. First, they did not use a mix of harmful industrial and chemical materials in production. Second, the quantities of arsenic, lead and mercury did not exceed the legal amount. Third, no one had been harmed. This case was not judged in the court.

• The following were verified by the officials of the court. On 8 March 2004, Wu Xiaosheng and Zou Guihua set up the Chutian Processing Factory of Nata de coco in Qiongshan, Haikou City, with the authority of the industry and commerce department. They rented around 300 square metres of workshops, which belonged to the leading factory of architectural materials in Qiongshan, Haikou City, to process Nata de coco. The factory's property was an individual business. During the process of producing Nata de coco, in order to reduce the manufacturing costs and to make Nata de coco more appetizing, they accidentally violated the relevant stipulations of the National Food Hygiene Law. They arbitrarily purchased some industrial and chemical materials, such as industrial sodium hydroxide and industrial hydrochloric acid, from Haikou's market, and added them in the manufacture of Nata de coco.

From March to June 2004, they produced a total of 7 tons of Nata de coco, of which the quality and technical supervision unit of Hainan Province seized and destroyed 4 tons. However, the other 3 tons had already gone on sale in the market.

• The legal basis of the public prosecution. The representative of the public prosecution proposed that the crime of producing and selling toxic and harmful foodstuffs refers to knowingly violating the national food hygiene management laws and regulations by mixing toxic and harmful non-foodstuffs in food production or selling the food mixed with toxic or harmful non-foodstuffs. What needed to be established was whether the person knowingly mixed toxic and harmful non-foodstuffs in food production, or sold the food mixed with toxic or harmful non-foodstuffs, even if there were no actual harmful effects. If such a process had caused harm, the crime of producing and selling toxic and harmful foodstuffs should be added. In this case, during the process of producing food from Nata de coco, the accused, namely Wu Xiaosheng and Zou Guihua, had known that raw industrial materials were harmful to people, yet they mixed them in Nata de coco foodstuffs which they then sold in large quantities. This fact seriously violated the country's food health control system and jeopardized citizens' health. Therefore it should be judged as a crime. According to the 144th criminal law (which comprises 150 clauses), whoever knowingly mixes the food to be manufactured or sold with toxic or harmful non-foodstuffs, or sells the food mixed with toxic or harmful non-foodstuffs, shall be sentenced to a fixed-term imprisonment of not more than 5 years of criminal detention, and concurrently or independently be ordered to pay a fine of not less than half the sum obtained through sale and not more than twice that sum. If the offence results in a serious food poisoning incident or disease caused by food-borne bacteria, thus seriously harming human health, the offender shall be sentenced to a fixed-term imprisonment of not less than 5 years and not more than 10 years, and will concurrently be ordered to pay a fine of not less than half the sum obtained through sale and not more than twice that sum. If the offence causes death to a person or serious harm to human health, the offender shall be sentenced to a fixed-term imprisonment of not less than 10 years, life imprisonment or death, and concurrently be ordered to pay a fine of not less than half the sum obtained through sale and not more than twice that sum, or confiscation of property. If a unit commits this crime, the unit shall be ordered to pay a fine, and those directly in charge and others directly responsible for the crime shall be punished according to the above articles.

- The decision by the court. After some days, the People's Court of Qiongshan Region, Haikou City, reconvened for the trial of the first case of producing and selling toxic and harmful foodstuffs in Hainan Province. As a result, Wu Xiaosheng and Zou Guihua were sentenced to a fixed-term imprisonment of 2 years, and each was ordered to pay a 5,000-yuan fine.

The chief judge of Qiongshan Court believed that, during the process of producing Nata de coco, Wu Xiaosheng and Zou Guihua used industrial materials. They knew that raw industrial materials are toxic and harmful, but they still produced and sold them. Their behaviour constituted the crime of producing and selling toxic and harmful food, so legally they should be punished.

After the first trial, the couple refused to accept the decision and announced that they were going to appeal to a higher court.

- The coconut fruit's expert, senior engineer Zhong Chunyan, the patent inventor of 'fermenting coconut' water into edible fibre and its manu-facture, explained that the full name of Nata de coco is 'high-fibre Nata de coco', which is a kind of natural food. The high-quality Nata de coco is produced by fermenting 100 per cent fresh coconut milk. It is a white or ivory-coloured gelatinous substance, which can be mixed with various fruits, jellies, soft drinks or tea and canned. The industry of Nata de coco has more than 100 years of development history overseas. It has only begun to develop in Hainan Province in recent years. During this period, the share of imported Nata de coco in the domestic market has slowly decreased. Hainan gradually became the main producing area of Nata de coco, selling semi-manufactured and manufactured products to inland provinces and cities. The processing industry of Nata de coco in Hainan mainly distributes in Haikou, Wenchang and Qionghai. Nata de coco is considered to be one of the best high-fibre foodstuffs. Therefore, it has a broad market. And Hainan has a natural advantage in this respect which other provinces cannot compete with.

As a rare expert of Nata de coco's industrial production, Zhong pointed out that, before 1997, the Nata de coco in the domestic food market was mainly imported from the Southeast Asian countries, the price of each ton exceeding 18,000 yuan. Since the development of Nata de coco's industry in Hainan, the price of Nata de coco has dropped rapidly, and the current price is a little over 1,000 yuan per ton. In Hainan, the annual output of Nata de coco is about 200 million tons, making up 99 per cent of the whole country's output. The production of Nata de coco is an expanding and profitable industry. The legal Nata de coco is a gelatinous substance, which is produced through fermenting fresh Nata de coco milk with micro-organisms. It is widely used in the canning of various fruits, jellies and soft drinks. As the production of fresh Nata de coco needs massive amounts of fresh Nata de coco milk, it is only Hainan, where coconuts are abundant, that can produce Nata de coco. However, in the whole process of producing toxic Nata de coco, which was exposed by the media, the illegal factories' staff soaked the fruit in running water, causing it constantly to seep out Nata de coco milk. They produced Nata de coco in this way (including a little Nata de coco milk) to replace the fresh Nata de coco milk. Because the juice produced in this way is tan-coloured, these factories used hydrogen peroxide to bleach it, making it appear clear and white. The hydrogen peroxide is an industrial chemical containing strong oxidizing and corrosive substances that are extremely harmful to the human body. The Nata de coco produced in this way is obviously a 'toxic coconut' product. Meanwhile, compared with the regular factories' higher price, the cost of producing 'toxic Nata de coco' is relatively low. Therefore, it has a wide sale in the marketplace. These factories not only supply the markets of Heilongjiang, Jilin, Changchun and Hubei, but also other places, such as Fuzhou, Quanzhou and Jinjiang. The products are sometimes used as materials to produce canned food of Nata de coco, containing mixed fruits, fruit jellies and soft drinks. Thus, using inferior and low-price Nata de coco is not only harmful to the human body, but also harmful to regular enterprises' brands and their image of quality. This will cause serious harm to the developing industry of Nata de coco in Hainan Province, and may even induce its total destruction.

• The industry of Nata de coco was facing a crisis of trust. Considering the sudden exposure of the incidence of toxic Nata de coco by the media, Zhong became both worried and puzzled. She was general manager of the Hainan Nata de coco Food Company, which is a regular manufacturing enterprise of Nata de coco. On the one hand, she supported the government in rigorously investigating the illegal production of counterfeit and inferior Nata de coco and called for investigation of the relevant individuals ' responsibility and to charge them according to the laws. On the other hand, she worried that the development of the Nata de coco industry in Hainan would be curtailed as a result. She believed that Hainan's Nata de coco industry actually represents China's Nata de coco industry. Accordingly, its main competitor is in Southeast Asia. The exposure of inferior Nata de coco would objectively give an opportunity to Southeast Asia. It is said that some organizations in Hong Kong had already informed residents that their Nata de coco products were imported from the Philippines. All these issues reflected the fact that Hainan's Nata de coco industry faced a crisis of trust, and Hainan's manufacture of Nata de coco was bound to suffer as a result.

She also pointed out that the media had exposed the fact that there were illegal factories using industrial raw materials to manufacture coconut products. This had attracted the general attention of the public. With the deepening of the investigation, the many problems inherent in these coconut processing factories were exposed and the underground processing factories eradicated. However, the negative influence and impact on the whole industry was far from over. She pointed out that the overall serious impact on the Hainan coconut industry was unavoidable. The government suggested establishing a long-term and effective management system for coconut food supervision as soon as possible in order to prevent a recurrence of these events. The permissions system for entering the market should be more stringent; for those with unsuitable conditions for production, the issuing of licences should also be rejected; hygiene quality standards in Hainan coconut producing and processing should be established as soon as possible; and a responsible investigation system should be put in place. Coconut enterprises must be managed locally. Departments of industry and commerce, quality supervision and hygiene should strengthen routine supervision in their administrative regions. The relevant leaders who were irresponsible or weak in implementing measures or in rectification would be investigated, and an emergency treatment system established. Zhong also reminded the canned fruit-producing factories of their responsibilities. For mixed canned fruit using coconut, there must be strict quality supervision, and the use of industrial coconut would be expressly forbidden; those that had already been manufactured must be destroyed; and where tainted products had already entered the market, action must be taken to remove them from the shelves and even, if necessary, to call in the products. Because the relevant departments are still investigating Nata de coco processing enterprises, those of canned fruit, jellies and drinks are not yet affected; thus, it is hoped that those enterprises will take precautions to avoid future major losses. Zhong also reminded the general public to choose products with a reputable brand name.

The government's measures

- The vice governor held a very clear stance. After CCTV exposed the incident of Hainan's 'Nata de coco face-changing', the Hainan government gave the issue its full attention.

At 5:00 p.m. on 6 July, an emergency meeting was held, and the chief director, vice governor Liu Qi, listened to reports by the departments of hygiene, industry and commerce, food and medicine supervision. Liu Qi reiterated that food safety was extremely important; all the relevant departments were to give it urgent attention and to conduct a thorough check of the coconut industry in Hainan. The unqualified enterprises should be eliminated and the illegal coconut processing enterprises suppressed.

- The mayor arranged all-round rectification. On the afternoon of 8 June 2004, Haikou city government held a city food safety rectification meeting with city leaders and relevant officials. The Municipal Party Committee Office issued the *2004 Haikou City Food Safety Market Rectification Programme* and formed a steering committee with the mayor as team leader. The team organized and led the rectification exercise on food safety and market order and arranged Haikou's food safety special rectification, the focus being people's daily food diet. The proposed measures were to strengthen the treatment of the resources of planting and breeding; encourage the food producing and processing enterprises to strengthen quality management and make sure the factories strictly followed the national and legal standards for food processing and production; investigate and penalize the actions of illegal production and processing of toxic and harmful food, as well as adulterated or misbranded foodstuffs; strengthen the management of appointed pig slaughter points; combat illegal food production and processing without licence and the actions of infringement, false advertising and so on; strengthen safety management on production for food in the agricultural market; taking the campus cafés as key points, to carry out a graded management system of food safety supervision and at the same time combat special products on the agricultural market; conduct a through investigation on enterprises selling pesticides; and regularize the agricultural market with the key focus on combating the actions of producing and selling adulterated and fake pesticides and pesticides eliminated by national decree.
- The vice mayor emphasized the system construction. Mayor Yuan Xiumei pointed out to the reporter that the food market in Haikou is safe in general; however, there are still some problems such as weak management, an incomplete market entrance system, an excess of pesticide residue and frequent occurrences of adulterated and fake goods. The relevant departments should fully recognize the problems concerning Haikou's food marketing, strengthen the sense of urgency and mission in rectification and take the exposure of the incident as an opportunity to examine all food-producing links. Meanwhile, pesticide residues should be appropriately treated, and the practice of selling pesticides containing high levels of toxins monitored. All vegetables sent for sale and those ready to enter the market should be quality checked, and those with excessive pesticide residues destroyed or rejected; efforts should also be made to

increase people's daily consumption of fish and meat. She also advocated the establishment of a system of food standards in the marketplace, a system of agricultural products checking, a system of food quality and safety management, building the long-term security system to ensure good food quality and safety standards. All the relevant departments and districts should work in coordination and make sure that prompt and effective action would be taken so as to protect the public's health. The rectification period would take place over 4 months and would be divided into four phases. Meanwhile, the mayor announced that the following systems would be established: a goods quality examination and registry system, significant goods being put on a records system, a quality random test system, a goods information open system, and a system of compelled and agreeable elimination of goods. These six systems would act to block any adulterated and fake goods entering the market.

- The supervising department holds a press conference. Liu Hongtao, in charge of provincial food comprehensive supervision, announced on 2 July that, in order to ensure food safety, Hainan government would establish a 'long-term food supervision system', a 'chief executive-responsible system' and a 'long-term prevention and alert system'. Their aim was to strengthen the routine supervision of food safety rather than to carry out spot checks only after the problem had been exposed. This should promote the sound development of the Hainan coconut processing industry by establishing a long-term supervision system. There were to be no more occurrences of simultaneous examinations by different functional departments.

- Establish a second-rate food safety coordinating committee. The speaker said that the recent exposure of 'poor-quality milk powder' in Fuyang, 'toxic rice wine' in Guangzhou and 'toxic coconuts' in Haikou had exacerbated the public's anxiety and attention to food safety. Regarding this concern, following the establishment of a provincial food and medicine safety project office last year, on 6 June 2007, Hainan established a food safety coordinating committee comprising sixteen members: the Provincial Food and Medicine Supervision Bureau, the Development and Reform Bureau, the Security Bureau, the Agricultural Bureau, the Hygiene Bureau, the Education Bureau, the Sea and Fishing Bureau, the National Estate Bureau, the Quality Supervision Bureau, the Industry and Commerce Bureau, the Grain Bureau, the Salt Business Bureau, Customs, State Administration for Entry–Exit Inspection and Quarantine, the Safe Production Bureau and the Tourism Bureau. The food safety committee of the province mainly coordinates the job of food safety and solves major food safety problems. At present, food safety committees are established in nineteen cities, counties and districts in the whole province, each shouldering the task of food safety supervision in its own administrative district. A food safety committee office for the province has been set up by the bureau of provincial food and medicine supervision and management, together with other relevant bodies, to coordinate food safety management.

- To establish a long-term prevention system and emergency treatment plan. It was pointed out that food safety is an issue that the public will pay most attention to. Following the current system, there are sixteen departments co-managing the issue, which will inevitably result in loopholes in the system that criminals will take advantage of. As a result, the relevant Hainan departments are establishing long-term food safety supervision systems, in particular taking measures to improve routine checks. Those who are irresponsible or weak in taking the necessary measures will be investigated accordingly. A long-term preventive system will also be established to carry out routine checks and reforms; to examine frequently the relatively crowded marketplaces; to prevent the possibility of food safety problems; and to prepare an emergency plan for major food safety incidents and, if such an accident occurs, to enable the plan to be implemented without delay.

- Food safety trust pilot systems will be set up. Liu Hongtao also announced in the latter half of 2004 that the Hainan government would strengthen the routine supervision of food safety, deepen the 'safe food programme' and tighten up checks on basic foodstuffs such as corn, vegetables, meat, fish products, fruit, dairy products and beans and pulses, as well as on all links from planting, breeding to production, floating and marketing, and conduct special management measures on food safety in the whole province, particularly in the fields of pesticide residues, seafood processing, group catering (especially cafés on campus), coconut processing and so on. In Hainan Province, a 'food protection war', which aims to protect meat, vegetables, fruit, dairy products, beans, seafood and all basic foodstuffs, has been instigated. The relevant departments in Hainan Province will take 6 months to combat illegal acts, which include the production and marketing of unqualified and fake food, and to initiate the food safety trust system, in order to keep an eye on food manufacturing and processing, to see if they meet the national and legal standards, as well as prosecute those factories illegally producing and processing harmful and even toxic food. In addition, in catering and school canteens, a classified management system has been implemented whereby any enterprise in which the credit is recognized as D will not be allowed to open or will be subject to regular checks.

- All the relevant departments should take their responsibilities seriously. After the establishment of the food safety committee, the following units were put in place: Hainan Food Safety Special Project Rectification Programme, Hainan Food Safety Supervision Coordination System, Hainan Information Statistics and Announcement System, Hainan Food Safety Supervision and Report System and Hainan Major Food Safety Accident Emergency Programme, which made food safety management increasingly systematic and standardized. All units in the food safety committee have rectified the food safety problems. The Provincial Administration of Industry and Commerce, Quality Supervision Bureau and Hygiene Bureau have also investigated and handled issues such as poor-quality milk, fresh juice processing and the dangers of the toxic day lily; as did the education administration concerning the canteen food-poisoning incidents; and departments of commercial administration made special checks on the practice of pig slaughter. Meanwhile, the Quality Supervision Bureau placed more emphasis on the formulation of the Nata de coco quality criterion to support and regulate the sound and rapid development of the Nata de coco industry.

- Finally, the *Coconut Hygiene Standards* were published. Wide attention was given to the toxic 'Nata de coco' in Hainan due to the CCTV exposure, but every coin has two sides; at least it prompted the publication of the *Coconut Hygiene Standards.*

On the morning of 27 January 2005, Hainan Quality Supervision Bureau held an auditors' meeting about local Nata de coco hygiene standards. During the meeting, nine specialists from the food and hygiene industries, management, teaching and research passed the audit of the *Coconut Hygiene Standards* in principle. The approved standards clearly defined Nata de coco's definition, sensory organ quota, physics and chemistry quota, microbe quota, testing methods and hygiene requirements on producing and processing when it was used for original material as well as on the packaging, labelling, transportation and storage of Nata de coco. Those in charge in the Quality Supervision Bureau pointed out that the criterion was based on the wide research and testing of the Nata de coco enterprise and its products in Hainan; they also took the reality of the Nata de coco industry into consideration, which is advantageous to the standardizing of the rapidly developing Nata de coco industry in Hainan.

It is known that there are currently sixty-two standard Nata de coco enterprises in Hainan, the majority of which are small or medium sized and have poor working conditions and old equipment. The large-scale enterprises can make their own standards, while others belong to the 'No standards' lists. The research on the Nata de coco hygiene standards in Hainan in June 2003 and the 'Nata de coco event' prompted the *Coconut Hygiene Standards* research and hastened the formulation of the Nata de coco hygiene standards draft and investigations, which were carried out over a 6-month period.

According to the specialists, the industrialized processing of Nata de coco products originated in the Philippines in the 1970s, but centralized standards were not established, so Nata de coco was produced using the by-products of coconut water in 1996 in Hainan. Nata de coco processing has decades of history, before which there were no standards implemented by government departments or standardized organizations, so all the enterprises had their own standards.

- Related material links to Nata de coco, based on the main raw materials such as coconut water or coconut juice: a fibre gel substance made from fermented wooden acetic acid bacillus, its local name is Nata de coco; it is also known as Nata in the Philippines and other Southeast Asian countries. People mistakenly believe that the Nata de coco is a palm tree fruit because of its name but actually they are different. Nata de coco mainly applies to the jellies, drinks and canned fruit in the food industry; it is very high in fibre and can be very healthy.

Research on Nata de coco has realized some significant achievements in the fields of medicine, new materials and so on. From this, we know that the outlook for the Nata de coco industry is bright.

Food additives are a type of chemical combination of natural resources, which aim to improve the quality, colour, flavour and taste of food, and are also based on the need to preserve and develop a craft.

The current food additive regulations and standards include the *Food Hygiene Law of the People's Republic of China*, *Food Additive Hygiene Management Regulations*, *Food Additive Producing Enterprises Hygiene Standards* (GB2760–1996), *Food Nutrition Intensifier Utilization Standards* (GB14880–1994), *Food Labels General Standards* (GB7718–1994), in all a total of eleven.

Written in 2005

Part VI

Economic reform and development

31 The hardship, pain and happiness of reform

Chen You'an

At 8:00 a.m. on 17 March 2003, when China was dominated by SARS, the day before the US army launched an attack on Iraq, a meeting was held in the Business Department of Gansu Province (BDG), involving some of the high officers from the government. At the meeting, an announcement was made about the assignment and dismissal of certain personnel. L was assigned as president of the commerce department of Gansu Province. Immediately after the meeting and the departure of the participants, more than 100 old cadres, workers and veterans from the provincial Export and Import Package Company, which is a subordinate company of the commerce department of Gansu Province, surrounded the entrance of the main building of the commerce department of Gansu Province. They held up banners and chanted angry slogans, demanding that the government pay their salaries, which they had not received for years, and settle their medical fees, which had also not been paid for years. They declared that, if their reasonable requirements were not met, they would continue their protest at the provincial government centre and at the centre of Gansu provincial committee, some even announcing that they would attempt suicide in case of the failure of their protest. More and more people turned up to watch the protest. Occasionally, some protesters lost patience and the situation spiralled almost out of control and had reached a critical point. Confronted with such an unexpected occurrence, the newly assigned president was deeply impressed and somewhat astonished. Although he had experience of different posts, he had never encountered such a situation, which by then was inevitable and had to be solved.

In the 6-hour-long talks with the representatives of the protesters, there were still angry slogans and exchanges of words. President L explained clearly and patiently the national and provincial policy and strategy concerning what the protesters demanded. He told the representatives that he would give them a satisfactory answer based on the factual investigations and the government's financial situation. Seeing the sincere attitude of the president, the representatives agreed to retreat and wait for a solution. The closed door of the BDG was open. The critical moment was over and everyone began to leave, but they declared that they would come again if their problems were not resolved.

What happened that very day when he was newly appointed gave L a big shock. He could not understand why there should be such a big movement involving so many miserable and pitiful workers. He began to ask himself how serious the problem was and whether it was an exceptional phenomenon or universal. A heavy burden was suddenly laid across his shoulders.

The process of L's investigation

The next day after the incident, on the morning of 18 March 2003, the president convened a meeting of all the leading staff members of the commerce department of Gansu Province to discuss the solution to the problem raised by the movement. Some members said that the reform in the field of business in Gansu Province was too slow in spite of the year-long reform policy; others argued that the main reason for the current difficulty was the non-division between government and enterprises because the non-division situation indicated that the workers would seek a solution from the government if the enterprises failed to solve their problems; there were yet other members who believed that there were too many leaders in the enterprises and too many workers of low quality. Because of the complicated reasons offered by the members, the president decided to conduct his own investigation in order to have first-hand and real information about the problem.

On 18 March, the president visited the former leaders of the commerce department of Gansu Province and some retired cadres and old Red Army soldiers; between 19 and 22 March, he conducted talks with eighty-nine officials working in the commerce department of Gansu Province; from 23 to 24 March, he visited and investigated the provincial Export and Import Package Company, the provincial Animal and Local Products Export and Import Company, the provincial Carpet Export and Import Company and other companies (a total of eight in all) that were experiencing severe financial problems and talked to the leaders of the companies and workers; from 25 to 26 March, he met eighteen leaders who were in charge of the eighteen main provincial foreign business companies; from 27 to 29 March, he conducted investigations in Lanzhou Aluminum Company and The Third Wool Manufacturing Group and another thirteen export and import companies which had more than $5 million in export businesses.

From 1 to 3 April, the president investigated and consulted the provincial Treasury Department, the National Tax and Revenue Bureau, the provincial Reform Office, the provincial Financial and Business Committee, the provincial State Property Committee, the provincial National Land Resources Department, the provincial Labour and Social Security Department, the Dongfang Property Managing Company, Bank of China, Lanzhou Customs and the provincial Medical Supervision on Commodities of Export and Import Bureau; from 5 to 9 April, he hosted two meetings involving the senior leaders of the commerce department of Gansu Province and announced the results of the investigation.

On 10 April, an anonymous poll was held about the reform problem involving all the members from the executive offices and general offices of the commerce department of Gansu Province; in addition, from 18 March to 15 April, the president visited some very poor families in the provincial Animal and Local Products Export and Import Company, the provincial Carpet Export and Import Company, the provincial Advertisement Company and the provincial Chemical Industry Export and Import Company. Most of these families could no longer afford the costs of water and electricity and food and medicines.

On the morning of 15 April, a general meeting was held in the commerce department of Gansu Province, and was attended by all the cadres. At the meeting, the president announced the results of the 1-month investigation, and asked all the cadres to take action to solve the difficulties and problems involved in the reform, which was also the starting point of their work.

According to the investigation, like all the other export and import companies in China, from 1949 to 1992, Gansu export and import companies suffered the experience of transferring from a 43-year-long planned economy to a market economy after 1993. In just half a century, the companies had their monopoly golden time, the recession period resulting from market competition and the very hard time of near bankruptcy.

In the highly planned economy period, when commodities were in great need but also suffering serious shortages, the national companies in export and import monopolized the business. The export and import companies of Gansu Province were under the direct charge of the Business Department and the Foreign Business and Trade Department, in which there was an integrated management style controlling the personnel and materials system. As a result, the Foreign Business and Trade Department issued various permission certificates and quotas of export and import to all their subordinate companies to generate profits. These government-based companies reaped huge profits from their special status and their control over these best-selling products. Then and there, those companies became the best and most competitive companies in society. Moreover, bank loans at the time of the planned economy were based on the mandate of the government. Banks had to grant the loan if the project was permitted by the government. In addition, there was no need for the export and import companies, which were dealing with the best-selling products at both home and abroad, to apply for loans. At the time, all the export and import companies in Gansu made profits ranging between hundreds and thousands and millions of dollars. The companies were collectively known as 'the gold phoenix'.

In 1993, *The Decisions on Some Problems in Establishing a Socialist Market Economy by the Central Chinese Communist Party* was issued, in which the government began to exercise control over the change in the export and import system by enlarging the domestic companies' rights in selecting, buying and selling products, and extending their right to enlarge their businesses. At the same time, major changes took place in the exchange rate, which had a profound influence on the export and import companies of Gansu Province. With the increasing productivity of manufacturers and the open policy of export and import business, these formerly prosperous companies began to lose most of their profits in the competitive market economy and forfeited their prestige in the public eye.

In the time of the planned economy, almost everyone agreed that the nature of socialism was the planned economy. Consequently, no one dared to put forward the idea of reforming the export and import business in China, let alone the implementation of reform. In 1994, the central government pronounced the reform of exports and imports, which was characterized by the diversity of export and import companies, the removal of state-owned companies' monopoly, the open system for export and import permission and incentives for more companies engaged in export and import. The exchange rate was changed from the governmental RMB 3.7 to $1 to RMB 8.7 to $1, which led to the depreciation of RMB but also made consistent the exchange rate between government and market. These reforms exerted an unprecedented influence on the export and import companies. Those companies that made profits mainly through import suddenly experienced a reversed trend in losing profits. Those companies that mainly dealt with exports still held the upper hand and continued to make huge profits. It was a valuable chance for the export and import companies to adapt to the reform situation. However, the export and import companies of Gansu Province lost their chance and did not take any action to reform. As a result, most of the export and import companies, especially those with debts from foreign loans, suddenly had a financial burden of double debt in one night.

The overall financial deficit for the export and import companies of Gansu Province began in 1994. In the following years, the debt and deficit situation began to snowball. What is worse, the financial institutions exercised stricter control over the application and granting of the loans to these companies, and even stopped loans to some companies. All this added up to a heavy burden for these companies.

Until April 2003, there were forty-six companies and enterprises under the immediate control of the Business Department, of which twenty-two dealt with export business and twenty-four with import business. The total number of employees working for these companies was 11,335, of whom 9,197 workers were registered in the personnel files including 4,046 workers had who left or furloughed and 2,138 retired workers (156 workers had left their posts early and 1,982 workers had retired). There were 3,240 Communist members among these workers (1,313 Communist members were still working, 1,074 were retired and 853 had left or furloughed). The total assets of the companies were RMB 2.43 billion yuan with a debt of RMB 4.13 billion yuan and the net assets totalled a negative RMB 1.7 billion yuan, the average debt percentage of 170 per cent. Of this, the export and import companies were in debt by 204 per cent, which was far above the average in-debt rate of 77 per cent for the whole export and import companies of China. The provincial Animal and Local Products Export and Import Company had an in-debt rate as high as 1,643 per cent. If the debt were distributed among all the documented workers of the commerce department of Gansu Province, each worker would be in debt to a sum of RMB 449,000 yuan, and the workers in export and import companies would be in debt to a sum of RMB 1.264 million yuan. Based on the loan rate of the time, the daily interest would be RMB 598,000 yuan and 6.92 yuan every second. The actual deficit was 1.88 billion yuan (1.69 billion belonged to the export and import companies alone) and the potential deficit was 1.09 billion yuan, which totalled 2.97 billion yuan deficit. If the deficit were distributed among the registered workers, the average deficit would be 323,000 yuan per person. Assuming that the commerce department of Gansu Province was set up at the same time as the People's Republic of China and the salary for workers was 500 yuan every month and 6,000 yuan a year, the total salary of all the workers would be 2.87 billion yuan and, compared with the total deficit, that would still be 100 million yuan less than the deficit. This was a ridiculous situation.

Forty-six enterprises basically followed the management pattern and management system of the planned economy, most of which had not set up a modern enterprise system. These enterprises adopted management administration bodies that were similar to the government's. The management staffs of the enterprises also had their executive position such as county level, assistant county level and investigator: 'Wait for, rely on and ask for help from the governments'. This kind of thinking from the planned economy was predominant. These enterprises adopted equalitarianism in income distribution. They relied on their directors instead of the market. Most of the legal representatives did not want to talk about the historical problems, and none was concerned about the losses in the decision-making and management administration activities. Losses resulting from the wrong decision being taken were shouldered by the country, while they reaped the benefits.

Forty-six enterprises were in debt to the tune of 4.12 billion yuan, and the amount in arrears to banks totalled 2.85 billion yuan, of which 2.018 billion yuan were divided into two parts to four major asset management companies (181 billion yuan for China Orient Asset Management Corporation, 148 million yuan for China Huarong Asset Management Corporation, 550 million yuan for China Cinda Asset Management Corporation and 50 million yuan for China Great Wall Asset Management Corporation), and 835 million yuan to China Commercial Bank could not be covered. Over 90 per cent of enterprises were litigated by different financial departments to various extents, and law enforcement departments sealed up assets and froze accounts and funds. Some of the enterprises were implicated in internal and external lawsuits and even beholden to the commercial departments of the government due to the loan guarantees. As the administrative department of these enterprises, the provincial commerce department's financial accounts were hidden for many years, and the expenses of the department's construction, daily financial costs and staff salaries were all in crisis. The provincial department was often accused because of the irrevocable guarantee certificates for the enterprises, such as the dispute with Longjiang Corporation and Longgang Corporation, which had a very bad impact on Gansu Province in and out of the country.

Until the end of March 2003, according to the status of twenty-six enterprises, these enterprises owed 4.34 million yuan to the laid-off workers, 10.66 million yuan to the workers, pensions amounting to 3.1 million yuan, unemployment insurance of 1.94 million yuan with the total amount of 20.04 million yuan. Eighteen enterprises were closed for 7 or 8 years without any production. Only a few of the forty-six enterprises were under normal management, but others could not even afford the salaries of the workers. Because the basic subsistence security allowances for workers and the 'reserve fund, pension and social insurance' could not be paid, the laid-off workers formed enterprises such as the Local Stock-breeding Import and Export Corporation of Gansu, Blanket Import and Export Corporation of Gansu, Advertisement Corporation of Gansu and Chemical Industry Import and Export Corporation, and often appealed to the commercial department and even the provincial government and the CPC provincial committee for help. These workers published letters referring to 'revolutionary comrades' and threatening that 'if you do not remove ** from his position, we will not stop appealing'. Some of the words they used were from the Cultural Revolution and some of the workers said that they would go to Beijing to appeal to the central government. According to the records, there were on average five appeals lodged with the commercial department every day, with reception of more than twenty workers and ten appealed letters. All this activity disturbed the normal work of the staff in governmental departments and had a very bad social effect.

The provincial commerce department was the only one that administrated the forty-six state-owned enterprises. The department not only had to execute micro-economic administration, but also handled the lawsuits of the personnel, labour and financial disputes, and more than 200 managers, deputy managers and secretaries of the CPC were referred to the provincial commerce department. The problems were all dealt with by the provincial commerce department. These enterprises handed in their bills monthly and yearly to the provincial commerce department while no one could see a way out of the financial problems. The role of the provincial commerce department had not been brought into full play, which did not meet the requests of the restructuring reform by the central government, the State Council and the provincial government, and restrained the marketing system construction.

The problems in the foreign trade enterprises and internal enterprises under the administration of the provincial commerce department were accumulating day by day, which had a very bad effect on social security. These problems were the result of an inevitable situation, but how could the president solve them?

The path of president L's reform

Forty-six enterprises under the administration of the provincial commerce department were in financial deficit, which was known to everyone. Workers faced financial difficulty and continued to appeal to the government. All these problems occurred more than 10 years ago; if effective measures had been adopted then, the situation would not be so bad now. The relevant departments had no clear requests and the enterprises were not willing to face these problems. The enterprises had made many contributions to the country, but now their problems had to be solved.

In nearly 1 month's survey and investigation, the legal representatives of all departments, units and enterprises generally believed that reform would be the only way out, but they expressed different attitudes and different views on reform.

The provincial government supported and approved the provincial commerce department's reform for enterprises. In order to prevent large-scale unrest and to implement the reform smoothly and gradually, the provincial government requested that the main problems be solved first followed by the more difficult ones and to adopt experimentation. Combined with the power of the reform, the speed of development and the social burden, it was necessary to promote the development of reform under a situation of social stability, to accelerate social stability through reform development and, at the same time, to accurately assess the complicated and formidable rules of reform.

Most departments of the provincial government supported the provincial commerce department's enterprises reform, but the provincial finance department, labour and social security departments pointed out that they could not provide the large funds needed by the enterprises for reform, while without money, reform could not be implemented.

The officials of the provincial commerce government voted for reform immediately; some believed that reform should have been implemented as early as 10 years before, while some doubted the department's claim to reform year after year without any improvement, and now that reform was put forward again, why should it be successful this time? Some thought reform was an inevitable step, and that early reform was the best way forward. Reform involves people: where should they go? Reform needs huge funds: where can they get the money?

Most of the civil servants under the sector chief level believed that reform should be implemented as soon as possible. Some believed that the provincial commerce department should continue to manage the enterprises. Some thought the reform had nothing to do with them but was the responsibility of the officials. Some were afraid of reform and its failure. Some thought that it was the enterprises themselves that lacked the confidence and courage to reform, and that the governments should not assign any managers to the enterprises.

Related banks and asset management corporations were not focusing on whether the enterprises reformed or not, but whether their claims would be protected, whether the crisis would increase or decrease, as they were worried about the increasing debt of non-performing loans.

The customs and the entry–exit inspection and quarantine bureau were not very concerned about the reform of the enterprises, but were concerned about the tariffs and fines some enterprises failed to pay. They were concerned that reform would cause the amount of imports and exports to decrease, which would have an effect on tariff income and could not be explained to the upper level.

The thinking of the managers of these enterprises was quite complex. They all believed that reform would be a stream trend and an inevitable road, and previous managers called for reform, but nothing was done; now that it was their turn, they still did not want to do anything. The enterprises that were not well managed were against reform because, without reform, those managers could still own cars and have money to spend. Those enterprises that were under good management had the ability to reform but were afraid of opposition from others. The average performing enterprises were waiting to see whether the reforms of other enterprises progressed well before proceeding. What concerned those managers was the fact that reform would necessitate a board of directors, and whether those directors would still hire them as managers. They were also worried about the large funds that reform needed and they did not wish to take on those responsibilities that had been accumulated by the ex-managers. Some retired cadres, ex-servicemen and workers advocated combining those small enterprises into one large group, because they were worried that their salaries would be reduced or that they would even lose their jobs.

All the cities, regions and people paid close attention to the provincial commerce department's reform of the enterprises; some supported it, some approved it, some doubted it and worried about it, some were against it. What they focused on and worried about was whether the governments' functions could be separated from the enterprises' management, whether the enterprises could be restructured, whether the delayed salaries and 'three insurances' could be paid to the workers, whether the workers could be replaced, where to obtain the large funds needed, how long the reform would take, where the 200 managers assigned by the government would be located, which units would be responsible for the management of the enterprises after reform and whether reform would have a bad effect on the foreign trade of the whole province.

Considering the benefits and disadvantages of more than 10,000 workers, facing the problem of a necessary reform fund and the increasing appeals of workers and the different attitudes towards reform, president L decided to begin fundamental reform of the management system and management policy of the forty-six enterprises.

On 28 April 2003, the provincial commerce department delivered a report on the enterprises' innovation at the seventh routine meeting of the provincial government. The meeting approved the principle of reform and agreed with the provincial commerce department to implement the separation of governmental functions from enterprise management, and to follow the request of 'easy first and difficult next, adopt experimentation, step by step, solve the main problems first'. The provincial commerce department restructured the relevant departments and set up a steering group headed by the provincial commerce department, the provincial economic and trade commission, the finance department, the provincial labour and social security departments, the provincial land resources department and the provincial system reform office. The leading group selected the Cereals Oils Import and Export Corporation, Provincial Hardware Chemical Corporation, Longfeng Food Corporation and Jinzonglu Corporation for reform.

On 9 June 2003, the provincial commerce department held the first system reform coordinated meeting. The meeting discussed and explored the complex and difficult problems such as labour contract termination, asset reorganization, property sharing, staff placement and, on the basis of a successful and effective result, arranged the reform work of the enterprises under the direct control of the provincial commercial department.

From 12 to 13 June, the provincial commercial department listened to twenty-six officials' views on the enterprises' reform work of internal and external trade corporations. All the vice directors asked for advice from the middle management staff and staff representatives, and most of them understood the need for reform.

On 17 June, the experimental enterprises and other enterprises introduced their measures and experiences.

On 19 June, the commerce department of Gansu Province held a meeting of civil servants and enterprise principals aimed at giving a mobilization talk on enterprise reform. This meeting stressed that reform could be speeded up and that enterprise reform should be the central task. Meanwhile, an enterprise reform leading group of the commerce department of Gansu Province was set up with the director as leader, a vice director was assigned to the position of office director of the enterprise reform leading group, and fifteen vice directors were put in charge of the reform of fifteen corporations. Each of twenty-two section chiefs was responsible for the reform of two corporations, and a connection and responsibility system between the enterprises and directors and section chiefs was set up to help the enterprises to work out a reform project. The Enterprises Reformation Office of the Bureau also drew up a syllabus of enterprises directly under the Bureau of Reform and Propaganda to build a good atmosphere for discussing reform at the meeting.

On 31 August 2003, all forty-six enterprises set up the reform project and reported to the commerce department of Gansu Province. These projects were established in accordance with the principle of 'regulate the process of the plan, clear and open operation, one measure for one enterprise, better replacement of workers, comprehensive and vigorous innovation, rapid and orderly withdrawal of governmental administration'. The commerce department of Gansu Province engaged in demonstration and reply on an enterprise reform project and staff settlement project in order successfully to fulfil the successive aims of reform. On the other hand, the China National Service Corporation for Chinese Personnel Working Abroad Gansu Branch and six other enterprises also carried out their reforms, and the commerce department of Gansu Province set up a demonstration of their reform projects.

On 1 September 2003, enterprise reform entered the enforcement stage, with each enterprise tackling the task according to the reform project and the request 'to stand up together to end the past, get re-employed and welcome a new future'. The heart of the reform was to quantify effective assets to workers according to the policy and to pay salaries to workers retroactively as well as compensation for cancelling the labour contract of ownership by the people. Those who were willing to be shareholders could buy shares and realize their dreams of owning companies and sharing property. The shareholders could elect a new board according to the Law of Enterprise so that the enterprise would be separate from the executive level and the enterprise could exercise self-determination. Once the state-owned enterprises had cancelled the labour contracts with their workers, the workers could choose to become shareholders; otherwise, workers could accept one-off economic compensation and become free workers after underwriting social insurance. Early retired workers and retired workers were appropriately installed by innovated enterprises in trusteeships.

More and more difficulties arose when enterprise reform entered the substantive stage. The historical and realistic problems were emerging in an endless stream. The commerce department of Gansu Province launched a real interest game with the enterprises under the Bureau of Commerce of Gansu Province's command. As the commander of enterprise reform, president L carried out a series of effective measures with the comrades of enterprises reform offices and all the officials of the commerce department of Gansu Province.

- The office assigned a working group to tighten up supervision and direction on Gansu Province Transportation and Storage Corporation, Gansu Province Department Store, Gansu Province Carpets Import and Export Corporation, Gansu Province Chemical Import and Export Corporation to accelerate reform.
- Developing policy consultation and explanation. In 2 months, the office received more than 600 visitors. More than ninety kinds of appeal and communications meetings, symposia of difficult and complex problems and policy discussions were held.
- Negotiations with assets institutions, such as Bank of China and Orient Assets Management Corporation, on the financial problems of the forty-six enterprises. According to the level of risks, re-identify and reconfirm the bad assets that are divested from corporations to those assets management companies and loans from banks. To discuss and set a debt

servicing ratio that was acceptable to both sides. To solve the historical problems and to settle most of the debts of the enterprises, and to find alternative solutions for the more difficult cases.

- To investigate these forty-six enterprises and to collate the advice of workers according to the basic set-up of the enterprises. To decide to start restructuring twenty-six enterprises and to bankrupt and close the other twenty enterprises.

- To obtain financial support from the provincial finance department and Ministry of Commerce. Gansu is an undeveloped province in western China so it is hard to obtain local financial support. After a long period of patient work, the provincial finance department applied for 31.2 million yuan. The Ministry of Commerce provided 29 million yuan for the reform of foreign and internal enterprises.

- Evaluation of the assets. To develop the assets evaluation work for these enterprises by applying to some high-level assets evaluation institutions to obtain an accurate number of assets, debts and workers. To announce the innovation plan and workers' replacement plan to all staff; after approval by the worker's congress and worker's conference, the plans were ready to be implemented. The total amount of the budget was 10.33 million yuan. Seventy-five workers were not on the list because of transfer, dismissal or death. Some 8,950 documents were found, and fifty innovation and replacement plans were posted on the noticeboard together with fifty-nine pieces of advice and fifteen problems.

- 'Six steps' that aim to strengthen 'one responsibility', namely to check 'a set of materials', to prepare 'an announcement', to sign 'a group agreement', to co-sign 'an application' and to implement 'a credit card'. To pay the salaries and compensation for every worker over time.

- The Party organization adopted a method of local administration. The Party organization department of the CPC provincial committee announced a 'notice of Party organization in the restructure of the enterprises under the administration of the provincial commerce department'. Following the restructure, the Party organization scheme of those enterprises would be transferred to the local legal registration office. The Party organization scheme of the retired workers in those bankrupted enterprises would be transferred to the community offices and Party organizations.

During the process of reform, many knotty problems occurred: the management theory, marketing means and management system of some enterprises were not transferred to a marketing system effectively, and innovation and competitive powers were very weak in adjusting to the change in market. Many problems remained that had to be solved resulting from operation transfer, land transfer, state-owned capital evaluation, reservation assets, cash settlement and documentation management of the retired cadres. The ex-managing members of these restructured enterprises relieved the employment relations. These managers had been devoting themselves to the enterprises and, following reform and closure of the enterprises, they got what they deserved. They would not be offered executive positions and, while they were still concerned about their political careers, some even expressed their dissatisfaction. All these problems needed to be discussed and solved.

On 25 March 2005, the enterprise reform was comprehensively launched, the majority of enterprises gaining marginal achievements. Meanwhile, the commerce department of Gansu Province issued 'the notice on carrying out separation of administration from management' to the enterprises directly under the commerce department of Gansu Province. After that, the commerce department of Gansu Province could no longer supervise enterprises directly, and the enterprises were no longer an adjunct to the commerce department of Gansu Province and operated independently in accordance with the law. On the basis of that, the separation of administration from management was at last realized.

On 10 June 2005, the reform of the overwhelming majority of enterprises was complete, and the commerce department of Gansu Province issued 'the notice on the end of reform of the enterprises directly under the Bureau of Commerce of Gansu Province' and officially announced that the enterprise reform was complete. It had taken 2 years, 3 months and 13 days to realize the strategic shift in the work focus.

On 8 December 2005, the commerce department of Gansu Province made a report to the 75th executive meeting of the Gansu provincial government on enterprise reform accomplishment conditions. The leaders of the Gansu provincial government awarded high marks on reform exploration and practice to the commerce department of Gansu Province and commented that the commerce department of Gansu Province had explored alternative ways for the whole province and accumulated a wealth of experience for the enterprises. The experience garnered by the commerce department of Gansu Province during the process of reform would be of benefit to the entire province.

The achievements of president L's reform

The forty-six domestic and foreign trade enterprises directly under the commerce department of Gansu Province employed 11,335 staff, 10,349 of whom were installed by the enterprises through reform, and accounted for 91 per cent of the total number of employees. Some 6,081 of the workers accepted a new job after cancelling their labour contracts, and 1,332 workers sought other jobs after cancelling their labour contracts, while 798 workers took early retirement and 2,138 workers retired. Although 986 workers have not received compensation for cancelling their labour contracts due to difficulties in realizing the stock assets into cash of some enterprises, this represented 9 per cent of the total number of employees.

There were twenty-six enterprises carrying out joint stock reform out of the forty-six enterprises. By installing 7,245 workers on the list by quantifying effective assets or changing the effective assets into cash totalling about 220 million yuan, 1,925 retired workers were taken on by reformed enterprises. In fact, 9,170 workers were reinstated. Another twenty enterprises experiencing extreme difficulties were made bankrupt with the provincial government's approval. Gansu Labour and Social Security Department and Gansu Provincial Finance Bureau approved the use of 53.3 million yuan (31.2 million yuan were supplied by Gansu provincial finance budget, and the rest was supplied by the Ministry of Commerce) to reinstate 1,179 workers. Some 842 workers severed employment relations, received economic compensation and were re-employed (72 per cent); those seeking early retirement numbered 124 (10 per cent), and retired staff numbered 213 (18 per cent). A fund of 31.64 million yuan was set up to pay for the reform. In addition, 21.66 million yuan were used to pay for living costs, old age and medical insurance. Eleven ex-managers received compensation after they lost their positions in the democratic vote. Up until now, the problems that had been accumulating for 50 years have all been solved.

The reform gave an impetus to development; the total imports and exports amount of foreign trade increased by 3.3 times within 4 years and realized a historic leap. The total imports and exports amount increased by 49.5 per cent in 2005; this was higher than the national average of 26 per cent and set a record for the first increase in the national import and export amounts. The retail amount of social consumables increased by 12.87 per cent and this increase achieved the national average level.

The fundamental reform of the domestic and foreign trade enterprises directly under the Bureau of Commerce of Gansu Province was conducted before the policy of trade circulation and enterprise reform was issued. This reform represented a bold experiment. Therefore, this reform not only benefited from the experience, but also encountered insurmountable difficulties and deficiencies that were brought about by environmental limitations.

Written in 2006

32 How to take advantage of resources

Bu Xiaolian

Background

Situated in an arid and ecologically fragile region in northwest China, Alashan is rich in mineral resources, which is its main advantage. There are eighty-six types of proven mineral resources under the ground of Alashan; moreover, the region is blessed with favourable geological conditions of mine formation and potential for large and productive mines. Along with the increasing 'bottleneck' restrictions of resources and energy, more and more people have begun to realize the advantages of the mineral resources in Alashan. Experts predict that the region will become an important option for capital transfer of resource-oriented enterprises. The advantage of Alashan lies in its resources; the potential for development lies in the industry; the promotion of regional prosperity based on resource advantages is the aim of those advocating local economic development.

For some time, Alashan has lagged behind in geological work; the reserves of resources have not been recognized and the mining industry has failed to expand on a large-scale basis. In order to expedite exploration and exploitation of mineral resources, the local government formulated the *Opinion on Speeding up Exploration and Exploitation of Mineral Resources* in 2000, adhering to the principle of 'explorer and developer benefit from the mine', encouraging various scientific and research agencies, geological exploration units, enterprises and individuals to explore and exploit mineral resources in various ways. Positive policy guidance and strong market demand have attracted many investors and benefited the local economy to some extent.

However, there has been no updated plan concerning the set-up of 'mining rights' in Alashan. Towns act in their own ways and accept investors as long as they bring funds to the area, with no thought for their individual strengths, scale and level of technology. Miscellaneous investors have different reasons to invest. Some possess the necessary expertise and regulatory operations; some only buy land to profit from resale rather than exploration; some substitute exploitation for exploration and open up more mines within one mine; thus integrated mines are often divided up intentionally. Most integrated and associated mines cannot be mined comprehensively because of restrictions of technologies and funds. Some profit-driven investors explore mines in an irresponsible and chaotic way, choose mineral-rich mines and abandon lean mines, carry out plunderous exploitation of resources and seek instant profits. The mining industry is plagued with the following problems: a disordered development market; low-level deep processing of developed resources; an extensive pattern of economic growth of enterprises where the resource advantages have not been brought into play. As a result, the ecological environment has been seriously and irrevocably damaged.

In order to utilize the resources effectively and facilitate the rational development of the economy, Alashan League decided to suspend the set-up of the rights of exploration and exploitation (hereinafter referred to as 'Two Rights') at the end of 2004. The purpose of the suspension was to rectify the situation of the mining market and create favourable conditions for enterprises with advanced technologies and comprehensive utilization capability to enter the mining market, thereby exploring and utilizing resources and protecting the environment more scientifically and reasonably. Alashan was the first and only league in Inner Mongolia to suspend the 'Two Rights' set-up, integrate resources and seek harmony and unification between resource exploitation and economic development at that time. Thus, the enactment of the above-mentioned measures has become our sole responsibility.

Advantages versus disadvantages

Suspension of the set-up of the 'Two Rights' has resulted in a series of disputes on the advantages and disadvantages of the measure.

The governments of leagues and towns

The integration of resources and implementation of large-scale development are not helpful as Alashan is backward geographically and poor in natural resources. When viewed from the vantage point of taxes paid, employment and so on, the economic and social benefits produced by small-scale development are more direct. Recently, although the development of resources has been plagued with many problems, the local economic indexes have increased rapidly and the locals have gained great profits. This development will be seriously affected in case of suspension of the 'Two Rights' and the adoption of measures of market rectification and resource integration.

The competent department of economy

It is hard to tell whether it would be favourable or unfavourable to suspend the set-up of the 'Two Rights'. The economy of Alashan relies mainly on the mining industry. Small enterprises have generated abundant funds and employment, and have maintained a steady momentum of growth, despite their huge numbers, low technical levels and unsatisfactory quality of development. We can continue a relatively rapid momentum of development if we maintain the status quo according to the current policy, as the immediate benefits are assured. Although the long-term benefits are promising, they are uncertain. Suspension of the 'Two Rights' set-up and integration of resources are favourable for resource allocation of some large projects in the future; however, the large-scale projects have not yet been guaranteed, and it is hard to estimate whether or when these major projects will be introduced into Alashan. It will certainly affect the completion of economic indexes for this year, even if increasing development in the future in the event of the suspension of the 'Two Rights' set-up and the adoption of measures of market rectification and resource integration.

The competent department of resources

Technically, geological prospecting is a kind of venture investment. We should find out detailed information about the resource reserves in Alashan as soon as possible. At present, prospecting activities in Alashan are very few. We should encourage and welcome those who intend to carry out prospecting activities in Alashan. Politically, the right of examination and approval is under the control of the government of the autonomous region while the procedures of application are carried out by the league. It is difficult for city-level governments to suspend the 'Two Rights' set-up without the support of a superior power and coordination from the grassroots. At present, fifty-nine mining licences and sixty-six prospecting licences have expired and need to be extended, and ten enterprises or individuals are applying for mining rights. These companies have already made heavy investments. How to pay compensation for losses incurred in case of the suspension of handling of the 'Two Rights'? We need to try our best to communicate with both the superior power and the grassroots.

The department of investment promotion

Alashan is in a disadvantageous position in terms of transport, and the commercial environment has not yet taken shape. Therefore, few investors would wish to invest in Alashan even if favourable policies have been adopted. Investment promotion will be influenced directly in case of the enhancement of the admittance threshold of exploration and exploitation of mineral resources. The loss outweighs the gain in the event of failure in the introduction of large-scale investors and enterprises while being a drain on small investors. In addition, the signed agreement of investment promotion involving mineral resources cannot be fully carried out owing to the suspension of the mining rights set-up and resource integration.

Geological and mining experts

Taking the long view, suspension of the 'Two Rights' set-up and regulation of administrative measures will surely have a positive effect on improvement in the mining industry, facilitate allocation of resources to advantageous enterprises and speed up economic and social development. However, most of the lands of the 270,000 square kilometres in Alashan remain 'blank' geologically and rely on very limited state-funded investment, so it is impossible to make large-scale breakthroughs in the short term. Moreover, the local economy relies heavily on the mineral resources and is pressing for urgent geological exploration; therefore, any investor who intends to make an investment in Alashan should be supported.

There are two opinions within the administrative office of the league. Some people believe that the technical level of exploitation of mineral resources in Alashan is relatively low at present and phenomena of destroying and wasting resources prevail, which will result in damaged resources and unsustainable development in case of failure in the adoption of rectifying measures, and blind pursuit of immediate economic growth. Therefore, the principle of 'laying equal stress on mining development and protection' shall be adhered to in the process of exploration and exploitation, and necessary resource integration will be implemented in order to allocate the resources to advantageous industries and key enterprises, extend the industry chain and enhance the comprehensive use of resources. Others consider that the natural conditions in Alashan are poor and cannot compare with those of other areas in terms of the hard environment. Enrichment of mineral resources is our only advantage; however, economic development is severely restricted by the low level of geological exploration. Thus, some investment will be redirected to other areas if excessive restrictions are imposed, thereby affecting the progress of geological exploration, current economic growth and even economic development in a future period. Therefore, we should develop the mining market freely initially and take regulating measures later. Except for economic factors, the absence of a political basis is the main obstacle. The 'Two Rights' set-up of mineral resources is under the control of the Department of Land and Resources vertically on a top-down basis. It is mainly examined and approved by the department concerned in the autonomous region. It is difficult to suspend the 'Two Rights' set-up and enforce measures of market rectification and resource integration without the recognition and support of the autonomous region. In addition, Alashan is the first league in Inner Mongolia to do so; if approved, it means partial power transfer of mineral resources to lower levels for the autonomous region in a certain sense, and other leagues will follow suit and make similar requests. Therefore, it is hard to tell whether we can obtain the recognition and support of the autonomous region.

Investors are very concerned about the suspension of the 'Two Rights' set-up. They visit the government office to seek information and to enquire whether the investment policy will change frequently. In addition, people continue to press for the handling of the set-up of the 'Two Rights', as the price of iron ore in the international market was soaring at the time and domestic coal continued to remain in short supply in the market. As for governmental suspension of the 'Two Rights' set-up and integration of resources, some enterprises consider that it is in favour of large-scale pro-specting, large-scale exploitation, centralized allocation of resources and enhancement of comprehensive utilization of resources. However, most companies consider that it is the best opportunity for resource-oriented enterprises to grow. It takes a long time to suspend the set-up of mining rights and conduct resource integration. This will surely delay the resource allocation of proposed projects and affect the development of enterprises.

In the face of various opinions, the administrative office of Alashan League has made the final decision: suspension of the set-up of exploration rights and mining rights and adoption of measures of market rectification and resource integration will surely affect current economic growth and investment attraction; in addition, they will have a certain impact on the mining market remaining at the start-up phase. The economy will maintain a relatively rapid growth rate in the short term if the status quo is maintained; however, growth is costly, unhealthy, inferior and unsustainable. Blind set-up of the 'Two Rights' will lead to the destruction and waste of resources if current economic growth and realization of economic indexes are taken into consideration in spite of the scale and technology, especially the man-made partition of integrated mines, whereby abundant resources are occupied by small enterprises who are incapable of exploitation while no resources are available for competent large enterprises. Therefore, we will lose the opportunity of exponential growth eventually as resources are not available for large projects. We can develop more quickly and efficiently using our existing resources because, to some extent, the economy in Alashan possesses a solid foundation. Therefore, we must deal efficiently with the relations between the present and the future, heighten the admittance threshold of the mining industry in terms of resource comprehensive utilization, environmental protection and safety production and so on, and deter the incidence of resource waste. Our long-term plan is to integrate advantageous mineral resources and create conditions for enterprises with the financial strength and technical capabilities to carry out large-scale exploration and comprehensive development of mineral resources. It is also a kind of contribution as long as we leave the well-protected resources to our offspring, even if we are incapable of developing the resources or fail to introduce large-scale investment in Alashan at present.

Measures

On 14 November 2004, the administrative office of the league decided to suspend the set-up of the 'Two Rights' of mineral resources within the league and report to the government of the Land and Resources Department of the autonomous region.

On 7 March 2005, the administrative office of the league publicized the *Implementing Opinions on Further Strengthening the Management of Rights of Exploration and Exploitation of Mineral Resources within the Whole League,* and put forward the main measures of strengthening the management of exploration and exploitation rights of mineral resources of the whole league.

- To speed up and improve the *Alashan Geological Prospecting Plan* and *Development and Utilization Plan of Mineral Resources in Alashan.*
- The new mining rights will be set up strictly in line with the plan; to increase the strength of marketing allocation of resources; stick to the principle of 'consistency between mine reserves and construction scale'; prohibit the phenomena of 'opening up more mines in one mine' and intentional partition of mines.

The new set-up of the 'Two Rights' must be initially studied and commented on by the standing board meeting of the governments of subordinate districts and counties and then reported to the standing board meeting of the administrative office of the league for decision-making, and finally reported to the registration and administrative departments for examination and approval.

We are entitled to ask the Office of Registration and Administration to revoke prospecting licences and to recall the resources to serve as governmental reserves in line with the law and procedures should one of the following circumstances occur:

- Those whose projects are incompetent for investment or fail in minimum prospecting investment; those who substitute exploitation for exploration, substitute enclosure for exploration and accept supervision and management; those whose projects are not approved by the registration and administrative departments; those who transfer rights of exploration and exploitation without authorization; those who explore and mine mineral resources without licence or beyond the permitted boundary.
- Registration formalities for extension of mining licences after the expiry date are prohibited should the exploitation scale fail to meet the required minimum design scale; the recalled resources shall be reserved by the government if the on-the-spot rate of coal resource falls short of 50 per cent.
- Integrated mining areas such as coal, iron and so on and mines suitable for scale exploitation and development should be prospected via governmental investment or government-dominated financing and allocated in accordance with the construction scale, investment scale, technology and technical transfer rate, thereby facilitating centralized allocation of advantageous resources to advantageous enterprises and industries.

Results

Suspension of the 'Two Rights' set-up of mineral resources in Alashan and adoption of measures of market rectification and resource integration have been enthusiastically received and recognized, and supported by governments and administrative departments at various levels.

Since the implementation of the special regulation of illegal exploitation, we have shut down eight enterprises violating the stipulations, blasted nearly sixty mineshafts without licence and integrated more than twenty small mines. Low-level and small-scale exploration and exploitation have been kept within limits, and the mining order has improved enormously as a consequence.

Geological prospecting has not been affected; however, it has made notable gains. At present, twenty-six geological teams from ten provinces and cities are working in Alashan. The Mining Industry Company, established jointly by Alashan League, enterprises and the Bureau of Geological Exploration of the autonomous region, is the first prospecting agency in the autonomous region jointly invested in by government, enterprise and geological departments. The three parties have brought their own advantages into play and achieved positive results in a very short period.

The government has strengthened the management and control of advantageous resources through resource integration, and has further laid foundations for allocation to advantageous industry and advantageous enterprises, buildup of total economic volume and enhancement of economic benefits.

A batch of new projects has been invested in successively as the government has been able to allocate resources to large enterprises due to integration of some resources. Relying on the resources of lake salt and coal, circular industrial bases of salt chemical industries and coal chemical industries in Alashan are being planned and are under construction. Financial agencies have increased credit support in accordance with the advantageous situation of the mineral economy. The construction of railways and highways running through the enrichment area of mineral resources has also begun ahead of schedule.

The management of mineral resources in the entire league has become more open, equitable, transparent and regulated; the development and health of the economy continue to grow; GDP of the whole league in 2005 increased by 21.6 per cent from that of 2004.

Postscript

Mineral resources are important strategic resources of the country. The government manages the resources on behalf of the country. Government officials perform their administrative duties strictly in accordance with the law. In the process of utilization of mineral resources, we not only act actively, but also scientifically and reasonably. We will focus on the relationship between present and future and the relationship between development and protection, emphasize energy saving and protection of the ecological environment, realize compensational utilization and high-efficiency development of mineral resources, and facilitate harmony between economic development, resources and the environment. The market admittance threshold of significant strategic integrated resources shall be heightened in terms of requirements such as sustainable development, state industry policy, environmental protection, safety production and so on. We shall increase the comprehensive utilization level of mineral resources to its maximum by means of the development of a circular economy and extension of the industry chain. Mineral resources are non-renewable; however, economic and social development cannot be completely divorced from mineral resources under existing scientific and technological conditions. Some important resources must be well protected if we are to utilize them comprehensively and efficiently in the present as well as in the future.

Written in 2005

33 'Entrance test' for a new official

Zhang Xiaolian

On 25 April 2005, after his first full month in his new post in Heilongjiang Province, Z was given a surprise. Around 100 teachers blocked the gates of the Sengong Group (Sengong is an abbreviation for the forest industry in Chinese) and demanded to see the official in charge of complaints and education. Some shouted through their home-made loudspeakers: 'We want higher pay, we want food, and we want to see Z'. Some said: 'He is an assistant to the provincial governor and represents the provincial government, and he is also head of the Sengong Group. We want to know whether he will implement the No. 9 document of the State Council and whether Sengong is still ruled by the Communist Party'.

Collective complaint against Sengong's failure to implement the No. 9 document

What these demonstrators had in their hands was the *Notice on Properly Solving the Pay and Benefit of the Retired Teachers of the Primary and Middle Schools Run by the State-owned Enterprises* issued in January 2004 by the State Council. To Z, this document was tantamount to an 'imperial sword'. As the serial number of the document was nine, the document was called the 'No. 9 document'. The document provided that, if the wages of the teachers and the basic pensions and allowances of the retired teachers of the enterprise-run primary and middle schools that had not been handed over to the regional governments for administration were lower than those of the personnel of the same categories of the government-run primary and middle schools, the enterprises should pay their wages, pensions and allowances according to the standards for the personnel of the same categories of the government-run primary and middle schools. The above spending by the enterprises would be included in their costs and deducted before income tax. If the money-losing enterprises found it truly difficult to pay the wages, pensions and subsidies according to the standards for the personnel of the same categories of the government-run primary and middle schools, the government finance department at the same level should provide proper subsidies. The document would be implemented as from 1 January 2004.

The No. 9 document reflected the concerns of the central government and leadership for the welfare of the teachers of the primary and middle schools run by the state-owned enterprises. However, the document only directed policy and requested the regional governments and enterprises to allocate real money for solving this issue. The central government did not allocate any financial resources. This was a typical case where 'the boss entertains the guests and the subordinate pays the bill'. In general, many problems in China are not difficult to solve as long as the central government has issued the relevant documents. But why could this people-oriented policy of central government not benefit the teachers of the schools run by the Sengong enterprises in Heilongjiang Province? Why did the provincial government and the Sengong enterprises fail to work together to turn the policy issued from Beijing into a benefit for the people's teachers?

In the face of the angry criticism and demands of the teachers, Z experienced great sadness and pressure. Driven by his strong sense of responsibility, this young official from Beijing could not sleep well at night and had no appetite for food. As a government official and the chief leader of an enterprise, failing to implement a document from the higher authorities was tantamount to failing to fulfil his duties assigned by the higher authorities and to take responsibility for the ordinary people. He was like a 'rat in the bellows' – pressurized from both sides yet having no place to complain.

So Z began to read files, listen to reports and consult with other officials for information and solutions. The investigation surprised him. In 2005, the annual average wage was 13,300 yuan for primary and middle school teachers across the country, 13,000 yuan for teachers in Heilongjiang Province and 16,800 yuan for teachers in the land reclamation enterprises. The annual average wage was only 5,000 yuan for teachers in the schools run by the Sengong enterprises, which was far lower than the national and provincial levels and the levels of some neighbouring units. The schools in some rural areas were even in the red. When he looked at the total amount, he was even more surprised to see that 536 million yuan would be required to bring the wages of the primary and middle school teachers in the Sengong region to the regional level. This funding shortfall would account for 80 per cent of the province's total fund. For a large province whose annual fiscal revenue was a little more than 30 billion yuan, this 'big hole' was impossible to fill. A glance at the work reports from the complaints office indicated that the complaints lodged with Z by the teachers were not meant for him alone. Other leaders also had their share. After the No. 9 document was issued in 2004, eight people went to Beijing to complain, eighty-seven people in five groups and sixty-eight people as individuals went to the provincial capital, and even more went to the head office to complain. In the first 4 months of 2005, complaints over teachers' wages were rising rapidly. Five people went to Beijing, eighty-nine people in five groups and thirty-two people as individuals went to the provincial capital, and visiting Sengong's head office was almost a daily occurrence. This was the knottiest issue Z had encountered since he began his political career. Seeing Z in real difficulties, some people attempted to comfort him: 'Don't worry, Zhang. It takes more than one cold day for the river to freeze one yard deep and it certainly takes more than one day for the ice to melt. The problem has accumulated day after day, and has to be solved day by day'. Others advised Z not to stir up a hornet's nest because, if the wage rise was not as high as they hoped, the teachers would continue to make trouble and might well cause a chain reaction: the workers whose wages were delayed might stir up bigger troubles. Others offered him a few suggestions, which could be classified into two categories: (1) As the document had been issued over a year ago and as they were unable to implement it even if they had wanted to, the higher authorities and the teachers could do nothing about it, but only play around. A dead pig was not supposed to be afraid of boiling water. Thus, the best approach was to play for time. (2) As the document was issued by the higher authorities, they should be the ones to solve the problem. It was true that, when the higher authorities entertained guests, the provincial government had to pay the bills. But the provincial government was experiencing financial difficulties, which was known even to the central authorities. The provincial government could ask the State Forestry Administration for help and, as Z was from Beijing, it was suggested that he might try to get some money from the central finance department and from the relevant ministries and commissions.

Very soon, Z knew the whole history about the implementation of the No. 9 document. In fact, ever since the day when the document was issued, all the relevant parties had been trying to overcome difficulties and create conditions for its implementation. Shortly after the document was issued, the provincial government adopted active measures and carried out a strategic restructuring of the 'organizational structure'. A special working group was set up, with the state-owned assets supervision and administration commission of the province as its leader and the provincial financial, labour and personnel departments as its members. The joint group was tasked with conducting investigation, evaluation, risk forecast and fundraising for the Sengong Group and other state-owned enterprises. After intensive hard work, the joint group concluded that meeting Sengong's shortfall would cost too much money. 'Tightening the belts of most people to feed a few well' was not an advisable approach.

The joint group had no alternative but to report the issue to the provincial government. The group suggested that Sengong be excluded when the province implemented the No. 9 document. But the provincial leaders said that no matter how serious the financial position of the provincial government was, some money should be given to allow the teachers of the schools run by the Sengong enterprises to share the care of the Party and government. The joint group had been serious and conscientious in their investigations, and knew that no body could bear such a heavy burden. Instead of wasting time in proving this, the group presented a proposal a few days later to the provincial authorities: the provincial finance department would provide proper subsidies for the implementation of the No. 9 document. In fact, the word 'proper' here had no concrete content; it was just an attitude. As different stakeholders had totally different interpretations of the word 'proper', several attempts to harmonize the differences ultimately failed. 'Proper' turned into 'inoperable'.

If the wages of the teachers of the Sengong enterprises were to be paid according to the standards specified in the No. 9 document, there would be a huge fund shortfall, which the strained provincial finance department was unable to cover. Therefore, repeated 'considerations' were needed. When the schools opened in the spring, the teachers became even more irritated when they saw that other people's wages had been increased.

In his capacity as an assistant to the provincial governor and a secretary of the Party committee, Z personally contacted the relevant departments of the provincial government and formed an alliance with them in prompting the provincial government to bring the issue back on to its agenda. Provincial governor Z paid great attention to the issue and designated the executive vice provincial governor to take command and enhanced the authority of the working team. Shortly thereafter, the team presented a new two-way strategy: solving the issue mainly by relying on its own efforts and at the same time seeking support from the higher authorities.

On 5 February 2006, the Heilongjiang provincial government submitted a report (Document No. H. ZH. F. 2006) to the State Council for instructions on how to solve the wage problems of the teachers of the primary and middle schools run by the Sengong enterprises in the province. On 23 March, the Ministry of Finance replied to the Heilongjiang provincial government in a document (Document No. C. N. H. 2006–9). Entitled *Opinions on How to Solve the Wages of the Teachers of the Primary and Middle Schools Run by the Sengong Enterprises in Heilongjiang Province*, the document read:

> The financial resources required by your province for solving the wage problems of the teachers of the primary and middle schools run by the Sengong enterprises should come from the provincial government instead of from the subsidy of the central finance department. Otherwise, policy inconsistencies may encourage other provinces to try to keep up with the Joneses.

This road was impassable. It seemed that this issue could only be solved by the province using its own resources.

Conducting basic analysis by employing three-circle theory and related tools (Table 33.1)

Public value analysis

When there is common ground over major issues and differences over minor issues, efforts should be made to seek common ground while reserving

Table 33.1 Analysis of stakeholders.

Stakeholder groups	Interests of various groups	Utilizable resources	Ability to mobilize resources	Position
Teachers and relatives; corporate officials and employees; Sengong Group and enterprises; central, provincial and regional departments of finance, education, labour and staffing; trade union and teachers congress; Hope Project	From top to bottom	Financial and material resources; obtainable and controllable information; social status; legality	Difficulty in resource mobilization	For or against

differences. While most stakeholders were supportive, the officials and employees of the forest region feared that, if the Sengong enterprises contributed too much money, their welfare would be affected. For this reason, they were against the proposal. However, they would also be indirect beneficiaries because, if the teachers received higher pay, there would be an influx of good teachers into the area, and their children would receive a better education. From the perspective of indirect beneficiaries, they could give tacit consent.

The government and all other stakeholders felt that awarding higher pay to the teachers was a good thing that would benefit both the country and the people, and should be implemented as soon as possible. They were supportive (Figure 33.1).

Ability analysis

The ability to pay was grossly inadequate. Both the regional governments and the Sengong Group did not have sufficient financial resources. As a result, the central policy would be beyond the reach of the teachers and their relatives in the forest region. The subsidy from the central finance department would be limited, while the regional finance department would not be able to afford any subsidy, the Sengong Group was unable to contribute funds, and other 'allies' could only offer solidarity instead of financial support (Figure 33.2).

Support analysis

Limited support and different views could turn into strong unity and full support. As a result of persuasion, interaction and communication, a strong

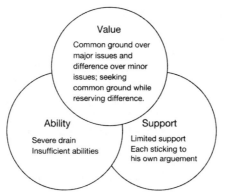

Figure 33.1 The 'three-circle-theory' model.

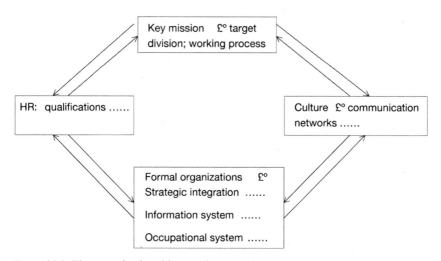

Figure 33.2 The organizational integration model.

political voice could be formed in the end. For example, the officials from the departments without resources could say: 'Go ahead! We shall speak for you'. The leader of the provincial financial department could say: 'As long as the provincial governor makes up his mind, I shall allocate money no matter how difficult it shall be!'

This was a difficult issue, with no ability and insufficient support for a solution. But as a result of our persistence and tactics and in particular as a result of our efforts to seek support, the process of seeking support became a process of enhancing ability, which was also a process of bringing the three circles closer so that the common ground would cover more than half the area. In the end, we passed the test of turning a 'gospel' into a 'blessing' (Figure 33.3).

Strategy–effective execution and regulation–expectations

Thanks to the efforts in various sectors, the provincial governor's working conference adopted a new policy: *Notice of the General Office of the Heilongjiang Provincial People's Government on Properly Solving the Pay and Benefits of the Retired Teachers of the Primary and Middle Schools Run by the State-owned Enterprises* (Document No. H. ZH. B. F. 2006–36). The document provided that, in light of the reality that the wages of the teachers of the primary and middle schools run by the Sengong enterprises in the province were too low, the provincial finance department would give proper subsidy and the Sengong's provincial head office and its enterprises would meet the resulting shortfall. The word 'proper' in this context was quite meaningful: 200 million yuan a year.

In accordance with the requirement of this document, the Sengong Group worked out its own specific rules for the schools run by its enterprises to implement the No. 9 document. Sengong contributed 60 million yuan as the counterpart fund to the 200-million-yuan annual transfer payment from the provincial finance department. By adding the two funds together, the wages of the teachers would double to about 900 yuan a month as from January 2006.

According to the principle that social undertakings would be separated from enterprises, the schools would eventually be handed over to the regional governments. For the transitional period of 3–5 years, the strategic targets were set and the supporting action plans formulated. (1) The central and provincial governments and the Sengong system would offer preferential policy treatment for the educational reform of the enterprise-run schools (educational resources would be integrated and school locations adjusted so as to cut the number of schools from 607 to 220). (2) Efforts would be made

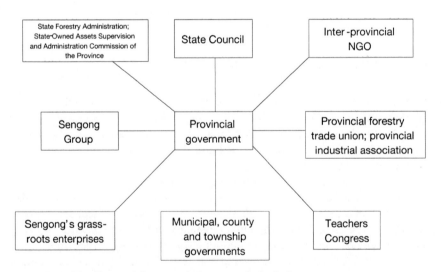

Figure 33.3 The 'Antony' framework for network analysis.

to promote the reform of the personnel and income systems of the schools and to rationally reassign the redundant school personnel as a result of optimization and competition (the teaching staff would be cut from the current 27,000 staff to 12,000).

Working tactics

To mobilize public participation

Informal meetings were held with the leaders of educational departments and enterprises; old school principals and high-level teachers were invited to voice their opinions; experts in education and labour policies were invited to work as consultants; public hearings and questionnaire surveys were conducted to appraise public opinion, tell the truth, disseminate information and control the developmental trend.

To launch a media campaign

Newspapers, radio stations, television stations and the Internet were mobilized to offer three-dimensional coverage, to interact with different population groups and to seek the understanding and support of the workers in the forest region for implementing the No. 9 document on the basis of ensuring the full exercise of their rights to know, to participate, to select and to supervise.

To promote cooperative production and increase re-employment

Currently, the employment rate of the forest region was only 49 per cent. While resources were integrated for industrial development, workers were encouraged to participate in reforming forest ownership, to become community workers and to accept flexible employment.

To conduct risk control

Feedback was sought in the course of policy execution. Complaints were administered according to law to maintain harmony and stability. Possible contradictions were nipped in the bud at the grassroots level, and no second wave of collective complaints bypassing the immediate leadership was allowed. Those receiving money were not allowed to complain. Efforts were made to prevent other population groups from lodging complaints due to mental disequilibrium.

Currently, the work of implementing the No. 9 document of the central government and the document of the provincial government is still going on. After the provincial document was issued, it was welcomed by the teachers of the Sengong enterprises. Some said that their problem was a knotty and longstanding one and that they were surprised to see results so soon. They applauded the determination of the provincial government and the Sengong Group to solve the problem. Some said that solving this problem required supporting reforms and that the primary and middle schools of the Sengong enterprises would have no future if they were not reformed. Others said that they saw hope in the documents and actions of the provincial government and the Sengong Group, and they were satisfied with the results because implementation would involve too many difficulties.

Written in 2006

Appendix

To ensure the effective implementation of the strategy of the provincial government, the Sengong Group worked out a package in cooperation with the relevant departments:

1   The Plan for Reforming the Personnel System of the Primary and Middle Schools
2   The Plan for Employing the Primary and Middle School Teachers
3   The Plan for Appointing the Primary and Middle School Principals
4   The Plan for the Institutional Set-up and Staffing of the Primary and Middle Schools
5   The Plan for the Institutional Set-up and Staffing of the Administrative Departments of Basic Education
6   The Rules for the Position Setting and Personnel Employment for the Administrative Personnel of Basic Education
7   The Plan for Reassigning the Administrative Personnel of Basic Education and the Teachers of the Primary and Middle Schools

34 The 'Green Bank' that supports farmers

Chen Weimin

In September 2004, Mr Y, director of an office in the forestry department of Jiangxi Province, received an order demanding that he be responsible for the recently established Office of Forestry Property Rights Reform. As a veteran cadre working in the forestry industry, Mr Y was quite familiar with the new job and knew Jiangxi's forestry better than anyone else. Located in the central part of China, Jiangxi Province is known as a key forestry region of the south, with a coverage rate of 60.05 per cent, ranking second in China. The area of forest in Jiangxi Province is 130 million mu, with a total standing crop of 350 million cubic metres. The people in the province vividly describe the features of the province as follows: '60 per cent of the total area is mountains, 20 per cent water, 10 per cent fields and 10 per cent roads and residential areas'. What is more, much of the forest contained in the overlapping mountains has become a precious natural resource which is vividly named 'Green Bank'. However, people in Jiangxi have derived no benefits from the wealth of the Green Bank but, instead, have suffered from extreme poverty since the establishment of the People's Republic of China. What has happened?

Three ups and three downs for the southern forest

Jiangxi is renowned as a town of fish and rice in China. Its residents have been living off the land ever since the Nan Song Dynasty. Therefore, it is true that the natural resources of Jiangxi, and forest resources in particular, are well preserved, and both the forest coverage rate and the storage volume are among the best of their kind throughout the nation. Director Y still remembers quite clearly that, when he was a small child, the mountains in his home town were covered in bamboo as big as a bowl in diameter, which was used for hanging out the washing and poling the boats. Bamboo cut down from the mountains was formed into rafts, and sometimes there was enough to completely cover the surface. Bamboo shoots and various kinds of wild fruits and delicacies could be found everywhere in the mountains.

In 1958, the central government organized land reclamation in order to solve the problem of food shortages. Jiangxi Province at that time was an important food production source as well as a key forestry base. In response to the summons, villagers chopped down a large quantity of trees to turn forests into cultivated land. Some mountains became completely bare with the constant sounds of axe and saw. However, the newly cultivated land was soon abandoned on account of its low productivity and its serious effects on soil erosion and environmental protection.

In 1981, the policy of reform and opening up was introduced in China. With regard to agriculture, the newly created system of contract production quotas to individual households, with the household contract responsibility system as its core, was successfully adopted. Being a key forest supplier, Jiangxi provincial government not only put into practice the new system of contract production quotas to individual households, but also implemented the policy of allotting forest resources to individual households in the light of the specific provincial conditions. But it turned out not to be as expected, because villagers adopted no measures to protect and rationally exploit the forest resources but instead acted illegally to chop down trees, sell on and use up the wood, once again bringing about severe damage to the rejuvenating forests. The then director Y in the Forestry Bureau of A county was designated by the forestry department of Jiangxi Province to go to the grassroots to look into the problem. Mr Huang in Xiaotang Village of A county told him:

> as an old saying goes, 'It takes ten years to grow trees, but a hundred to rear people'. It takes more than 20 years for a tree to grow from a young sapling into a big tree, but now we do not even have enough to eat. How would we be able to wait until the saplings grow up? It is surely better to chop the trees down and sell as many as possible. Anyhow, we could make some money.

Mr Li also agreed:

> The policy is sort of like the moon, which is always changeable. Who knows how long the policy of allotting forest resources to individual households will last? We believe it is better to get just some today than wait to get a lot tomorrow. Rather than waiting for the trees to grow, it would be better if we just sold them now to earn some money.

Thus, driven by short-term interests, farmers continued with deforestation. Having learned about this, director Y reported to the Jiangxi forestry department in a short space of time, listing the various disadvantages caused by the policy. Before long, a notice issued by the central government called a halt to the practice, whereas a certificate of forestry title had been granted to farmers in Jiangxi Province.

Later, Jiangxi provincial government drew lessons from its reform of forestry policy and organized experts to investigate and study its forestry policies. In the wake of survey and study, an idea was put forward that efforts should be made for an appropriate scale operation and collective forestry centres. The forestry department of Jiangxi Province adopted experts' opinion following careful study and consideration. According to the requirements of the provincial government, local governments at all levels took back the forest allotted to villagers and ran collective forestry centres. Meanwhile, a campaign to eliminate the deforested land was encouraged throughout the whole province, converting passive forests waiting for natural restoration to active afforestation, as a result of which forestry departments in Jiangxi Province soon gained great fame. However, on account of the early implementation of allotting forests to individual households, the government was worried about its prestige, which would be harmed by its changeable policies, and about the unnecessary trouble that would be brought about by villagers' unwillingness to return their allotted forests and their objections to the active policy of appropriate scale operation. In view of this, certificates of forestry title were not recalled from farmers. At last, a new phase came into being where property rights went to villagers and management went to the collective, which was jokingly referred to by the local residents as those who owned the forests were not in charge and those who did not own them were in charge.

With the gradual establishment of the system of a market-oriented economy, collective forestry centres encountered many problems after the appropriate scale operation had been executed for a period of time. The former administration mode was challenged and gradually became unfeasible, mainly characterized by serious problems of forestry tax and fees. A case in point was that residents no longer toed the line to plant trees compulsorily but regarded afforestation, forest rejuvenation and wasteland elimination as market-oriented behaviours, and as a result demanded money from the government.

Director Y had just been transferred to the forestry department of Jiangxi Province when a decision on hastening the development of forestry was issued by the Party Central Committee and the State Council. In order to have a complete understanding of the current states of Jiangxi's forests, director Y conducted a careful survey of its all-round forestry-related work. Both director Y and the head of the provincial forestry department were astonished by the result, which showed that over 80 per cent of Jiangxi's current forests belonged to the collective but forest property rights remained unspecifically stated for a long time. For example, the village community collectively ran a forestry farm for several years while the villagers held its property rights certificates issued by the government. The problem seemed inconspicuous when forests were not regarded as valuable resources; however, with the increasing appreciation of forest resources, some farmers began to lodge their complaints with the government by asking whether or not the property rights certificates were still valid. What was worse, local protectionism still existed in some areas, and their financial revenue strongly depended on arbitrary charges on forestry, causing widespread complaints from the public. Having undergone dramatic changes, the forestry work of Jiangxi Province was again in a predicament.

Hope appears through borrowing others' experience

Jiangxi's forestry policies have gone through many twists and turns over the past half century. But now, confronted with another grim situation, forestry departments found themselves in a dilemma and at a loss to know what to do. At the time, F Province, which is adjacent to Jiangxi Province, carried out a successful reform of the forest property rights system. Jiangxi forestry departments believed that the successful experience in F Province was likely to be the last chance to help its forestry industry get out of the deadlock. Besides, the neighbouring F Province shares a lot in common with Jiangxi Province, such as key forest suppliers, hilly terrain and abundant forest resources.

N City in F Province, separated from Jiangxi Province by a range of mountains, also prides itself as an important forest base and a key collective forestry area in the south, with its forest resources ranking first in F Province – 80 per cent of it is mountains, 10 per cent water and 10 per cent fields. At present, it has an annual commercial lumber capacity of 1.8 million cubic metres, accounting for one-third of F Province, and 5.26 million mu of bamboo, supplying 52 million pieces every year and making up one-tenth of the total in China. Local governments at all levels in F Province earn good money through the forestry industry, with the Forestry Bureau of N City alone owning a deposit of RMB 50 million.

Director Y told the Head of the Forestry Bureau of N City:

> We are honoured to come here to learn from you. According to our understanding, in the early 1980s, all forestry farms in the south carried out the policy of allotting mountains to individual households, but you were very resolute in your behaviours not to allot but to operate collectively. On the contrary, now you are taking the initiative in forestry reform and allocate all property rights to villagers. Why didn't you stick it out?

The head of the Forestry Bureau of N City said:

> That's because we couldn't stand it. First, wood is getting more and more valuable, thus civilians are attaching more importance to it, which is different from the situation in the 1980s. Second, our cadres of collective forestry farms are quite restricted in their operation and management. Things would be better if they were more competent; however, it could be very troublesome if they left. So it is better to rely on the mechanization than on people.
>
> Until the early 1990s, except for the fact that family plots and bamboo hills were by and large fulfilled to be allotted to individual households, most collective forestry farms were still under the system of village-based unified management, which caused a series of conspicuous problems such as indistinct property rights, inflexible operation systems, and irrational interest distribution. In addition, forest owners' rights of

production, operation and product disposal, as well as operational interests, could not be effectively guaranteed, giving rise to many difficulties in afforestation, forest rejuvenation, and the prevention of fire, disease and pests. Clearly, wood owners' enthusiasm was hampered. Output and benefits were decreased.

Director Y continued: 'Then how did you reform your previous operation mechanism to promote a sound forestry industry?'

The head of the Forestry Bureau of N City replied: 'Actually, the only way forward was to clarify property rights and allot mountain areas to individual households simultaneously accompanied by corresponding reform measures of forest property rights. Only in this way could forest owners' enthusiasm be completely engaged to activate rural economy cells and promote forestry development'.

These discussions gave director Y much food for thought. He immediately reported back to the forestry department of Jiangxi Province and wrote a feasibility study about the reform of the forestry property rights system, suggesting that discussions about the reform programme be conducted throughout all forestry departments in Jiangxi, and then for the programme to be implemented. Mr L, director of the forestry department of Jiangxi Province, organized a formal discussion about the reform with those responsible for forestry departments.

It turned out to be a hectic round of discussions triggered by the news, which resembled a bomb blasting through the whole forestry system. Objections were voiced unceasingly. Many local chiefs of forestry departments came immediately to the provincial capital, explicitly expressing their disagreement with the reform of the forestry system. In Jiangxi Province, the forest areas occupy two-thirds of the territory; therefore, the counties' revenue from the forestry industry is the major source of local government's income and about two-thirds of its population live in the mountainous areas. Owing to these factors, it would lead to the curtailment of the income of forestry departments, even of local governments, if the reform of the forestry system, namely clarifying property rights and prohibiting arbitrary charges, were to be carried out. Some top-ranking leaders at county level interceded with the provincial authorities in person, claiming that local governments would be paralysed on the day the reform began.

Director Y visited the finance department of Jiangxi Province and asked for a survey on forestry charges. The department prepared a paper about the survey on reform of the forestry tax and fees and its relevant policies and suggestions, its statistics indicating that total forest taxes and fees in Jiangxi in 2003 reached RMB 935 million, of which RMB 205 million came from log and bamboo and RMB 730 million came from forestry charges. The survey also suggested that the financial incomes of counties, especially key forestry counties, depended heavily on forestry taxes. Take a county in Jiangxi Province, for example. In 2003, its annual forestry expenditure reached RMB 17.35 million, RMB 445,000 allocated from the government, namely 2.56 per cent of its total, making the charge income 97.44 per cent of total expenditure. If they were not allowed to live off the mountain resources and were not offered some solutions, the local governments would probably become completely paralysed during the period of reform.

In addition, everyone still had memories of the last deforestation. Some even put forward the claim that the last unsuccessful experience had proved the reform of the forestry property rights system to be unworkable. What was the point of turning back? What would be done if there was yet another deforestation after the allotment?

Last but not least, it was still not known whether villagers' enthusiasm for afforestation would be accelerated. Since the period of wasteland elimination when a record of planting 5 million mu of trees per year was set, it had been over a period of 20 years and only a little more than 1 million mu of land had been planted. Only hewing could be seen, but no planting. If reform was to be carried out this time, the important criteria used to weigh its value would be whether or not farmers would acknowledge the government's superiority and whether or not the afforestation area would be increased.

Therefore, a dilemma was reached whereby the successful reform experience from the neighbouring province was on the left and the grim situation of its forestry on the right. This predicament could not be solved without forestry reform, but many risks lay ahead. The forestry departments of Jiangxi Province were once again faced with a difficult decision. What course should Jiangxi's forestry industry follow? How should the reform policy be carried out?

The twists and turns of forestry reform policy

Having gained the relevant information, director Y wrote an urgent report to the head of the provincial forestry department and the deputy secretary of the Provincial Party Committee, who were responsible for the forestry industry. Two proposals were put forward. First, support would not be offered to the long-existing disorderly charge by local governments at all levels and the wrong approach of subsidizing the financial gap with forestry charges. The problem of the financial gap following reform would be solved all together by the provincial government. Second, a survey and study by experts organized by the government would be prepared to ascertain whether or not another deforestation would be caused following the implementation of allotting forests to individual households and whether or not the afforestation area would be increased through the reform. A relatively rational policy would then be put forward.

In light of the deployment, the Provincial Government convened six units, namely the Department of Agricultural Work, Office of Policy Study, Provincial Finance Department, Office of Tax Reform, General Office of Provincial Government and Provincial Agriculture Department, and decided that three survey and study teams on forestry reform would be founded to go to the grassroots in order to look into the matter. It was director Y's job this time to accompany the deputy secretary of Jiangxi Provincial Party Committee, who was responsible for forestry, to lead a team to T County to carry out surveys and researches.

T County Committee attached great importance to the survey and convened the major members of its leading team and chief cadres working in the forestry industry. Considering the policy was still at the incubation stage, and concerned that farmers might make inappropriate comments, the committee did not arrange for any farmer delegates to participate in the meeting, at which a lot of incisive questions about the reform of the forestry property rights system were posed.

The general secretary of T County Party Committee spoke first:

The reform would not only greatly weaken the financial ability at two levels of a county and a town, but endanger the normal operation of their governments; that is to say, for local governments forestry reform equals self-destruction, which is too risky. As far as its benefits for the industry are concerned, it's too dangerous. I'm afraid I cannot agree to the reform.

The deputy secretary of the Provincial Party Committee replied:

If you say the reform would greatly weaken the financial ability at two levels of a county and a town, then what is the source of your revenue? Most of it comes from arbitrary charge. Would this not decrease the government's prestige? Even if we don't carry out the reform, it is clearly stipulated in some document issued by the state that arbitrary charge must be prohibited. You can no longer collect money that way. Then what difference does reform make? Besides, our forestry industry is facing a rather grim situation. So, the earlier we reform, the earlier we benefit; the later, we could reach an impasse.

The director of the Forestry Bureau asked:

Since the reform means allotting forests to individual households, will it be the same as last time to give deforestation a passport? The lower level cadres are in confusion, worrying that the reform will tighten up official regulations but connive at deforestation. In some places there exists such a concern that farmers will not plant any trees after allotment. If we ran out of resources, what would we leave for our next generations?

The deputy secretary responded:

The reason why farmers deforested at that time was mainly because, first, they had no confidence in the continuity of the policy, and second, their insufficient understanding of forestry resources made them think only of the money, believing that they had permanent resources. In order to resolve this problem, we need to, on the one hand, reassure the public that the policy of forestry reform is not in pursuit of some fashion but a long-term solution; on the other hand, we need to convince them of the massive value of forestry resources, translating permanent resources into short-term gain and dead capital into real income. This is not an insurmountable hurdle.

The head of T County put forward a suggestion:

> We've already experienced failure in forestry reform. And the reform worked out in the neighbouring province, which doesn't mean that we are sure to make it in Jiangxi Province or in my county. In my opinion we should be discreet. It's better to have some trial plots first and popularize it when we've got enough experience. In addition, we should be a little conservative, and not to allot forests completely but to implement a new scheme of allotting shares rather than whole forests; that is to say, villagers' property rights should be converted into shares, then handed over to the collective forestry farm in the form of share and operational revenue and should be distributed to villagers according to the proportion of their shares. In this way, we will not only win a transitional period but also facilitate our management. If it succeeds, we will then allot forests to them. If it doesn't, we take it back.

Following discussion, all agreed that this scheme made sense. The team filed a report to the Provincial Party Committee and the provincial government, clearly stating the programme of allotting only shares rather than whole forests, which was subsequently approved. The Provincial Party Committee and the provincial government also determined seven key forestry counties in Jiangxi Province as the first trial units, requiring them to give prompt publicity to the policy of forestry reform to farmers and to assure them and win their support.

Having received the relevant documents issued by the provincial government about forestry reform, Zhulin Village Committee of T County convened its farmer delegates to discuss the programme of allotting shares rather than whole forests, at which all the villagers burst into commotion.

One man, Liu, said:

> I don't think it's reasonable. What's the point of allotting shares rather than forests? Actually it remains the same in essence. We will still own no decision-making powers to operate with everything decided by the government and officials and they can do whatever they want. So, what's the difference?

Mr Huang also expressed his opinion:

> I felt something was wrong when last time leaders from the provincial capital came to investigate. How could we not be informed of such an

important issue? And how would the programme be reasonable by only listening to the officials without asking for our opinions?

Mr Zhao continued:

> I don't think the programme will work. As far as I'm concerned, either we introduce no forestry reform, or we take reform seriously, enforcing the policy of thorough allotment to individual households. Only if we pay our taxes on time could we plant whatever we like and sell however we like.

Mr Zhang also aired his views:

> The so-called reform will be just a repetition in vain. How would the share be calculated without clearly defining property rights? What will Mr Zhao and I do with the unsettled proprietorship issue of a mountain? And what will the government do with so many disputes about property rights in our village? If the problem of property rights is not resolved, people are sure to make trouble in my opinion. I'd like to make it clear first that I will not accept any forestry reform uncompromisingly unless there's a clear definition of property rights. Otherwise I will not be afraid of complaining even up to Provincial Party Committee level.

After fierce discussion, the villagers voted not to accept the programme. The result was soon transmitted by the Party secretary of the village, first to the Town Party Committee, then level upon level up to the provincial agriculture department. It was discovered that farmers in other villages enjoyed the same situation as those in Zhulin Village: unwilling to admit the programme but requiring a thorough allotment and a clear definition of forestry property rights and self-managing the forested areas independently.

Green Bank reinvigorated by forestry reform, like a phoenix

Villagers' viewpoints were promptly reported to the provincial government and startled all relevant officials. They soon realized that the previous management scheme of undertaking and considering everything on the public's behalf no longer accorded with the current development tendency and that this was a blind area when preparing the policy of allotting only shares rather than entire forests. Having given it further thought, the investigation team visited the town again. This time, honest villagers became the focus, and the team finally found the crux of the problem after carefully hearing the representatives.

To sum up and analyse the reason why the former policies failed, the team believed the crux lay in a correct understanding and solution of the relationship between dead capital and a current income, big money and small returns, long-term capital and short-term income. On the previous occasion, after allotting forests to individual households, the government thought it would be out of the question to do so in the absence of any follow-up management, thus causing villagers short-term monetary problems in the face of long-term gains. With regard to farmers' lack of enthusiasm for the cultivation and exploitation of forests, the investigation team formulated a programme where polls would be held in all grassroots units of the seven forestry reform pilot counties and the public's opinion taken fully into account. Consequently, all votes from those grassroots units resulted in the forestry reform policy of all-round allotment, which officially represented the beginning of forestry reform in Jiangxi Province.

Three years later, director Y received a report showing that Jiangxi's forestry industry had gone through tremendous changes over the previous 2 years. Markets had been built up for forestry property rights trading and a further processing industry of forestry resources. At the same time, the forest owners' burden had been greatly reduced and their income had markedly increased. In the year 2005 alone, the reduction in forestry tax and fees aggregated to RMB 1,127,000,000, which is expected to reach RMB 1,461,000,000 this year. Over 70 per cent of the reduction was returned to forest owners, about RMB 156,000,000 fulfilled in 2005. According to a sample survey made by the Statistical Bureau, by the end of this spring, a Jiangxi farmer's per capita net income from forestry in 2005 had reached RMB 370.26, a growth of 33 per cent over the previous year, RMB 353.88 of which was cash income, an increase of 41 per cent over the previous year. About 3.29 million mu of land had been afforested throughout Jiangxi, three times more than before. When the new rural construction observation group visited Jiangxi in 2006, they were met by green forests and happy farmers. A harmonious and healthy new countryside with sustainable forestry is emerging on the horizon in Jiangxi, a Green Bank benefiting future generations.

Summary

Nothing impressed me more deeply than the tri-circle theory when I was studying at Harvard University. It was with the help of this model that this investigation was completed after numerous surveys and studies. There is no doubt that the realization of forestry property rights reform is so valuable that it means not only an inevitable alternative for Jiangxi forestry development but also an inexorable requirement for building a harmonious new socialist countryside. But the biggest difficulty in its implementation has been insufficient skill and support, as well as a small policy Nike zone. In the previous case, it may be found out that, in order to settle this problem, the government improved its skills in management and policy implementation by means of assembling capital, transfer payments and returning interests to people; on the other hand, it won maximum support from the public by giving full attention to their opinion and finally succeeding in implementing reform. This achievement not only accounts for the validity and universality of the tri-circle theory as an analysing tool in the process of establishing a harmonious society, but also shows that Harvard training plays quite a significant role in developing our cause and improving our skills.

Originated in 2005 and revised in 2006

35 The dispute over taxi managerial rights

Wu Zhenglong

In order to regularize taxi transport, the Wanzhou government of Chongqing municipality decided in December 2001 to manage the taxi trade, namely through keeping 150 of the 1,100 managerial rights quotas and granting the others to five companies. When the licences of the former individuals expired, the government would take back their managerial rights quotas. However, the plan caused a series of contradictions. One interest group was strongly opposed to the policy. Some individual taxi operators went on strike, blockaded traffic, appealed to the higher authorities for help. Some 137 people went to Beijing to appeal against the policy, and 364 people sought litigation against the government. The dispute over the taxi trade's managerial rights became not only an extensive problem affecting social stability, but also a potential issue affecting the whole province and the stability of the capital. How to solve this age-old problem was a test for Jia Mingzhi, a new leader of Wanzhou District.

At the end of 2004, Jia Mingzhi, who had worked in Chongqing municipality, was assigned to Wanzhou district, which was the largest city to undergo resettlement. As a young leader, although he knew that this was a major challenge, he was glad to accept it. He even regarded it as a privilege to participate in resettling millions of people, as well as constructing the second largest city in Chongqing municipality. Therefore, he entertained great hopes of success when he came to the city and made up his mind to complete this important task successfully. He promised that he would never fail to live up to the credence of the organization and the expectations of the Wanzhou people.

A difficult problem

As Jia Mingzhi had worked in the provincial departments of Chongqing municipality, he knew something about Wanzhou.

Wanzhou was located at the junction of the upper river and the middle reaches of Changjiang river, the centre of the Three Gorges Dam Area. It was 327 kilometres away from the upper river Chongqing City and 321 kilometres away from downstream Yichang City. Wanzhou got its name from 'having collected thousands of rivers and merchants'. At one time, it was a subordinate government of Sichuan Province as Wanxian district and Wanxian prefecture-level city. It even shared the same reputation with Chengdu and Chongqing, as the people had named them Cheng-Yu-Wan collectively at that time. It then became Wanzhou district under the direct control of Chongqing when Chongqing became a municipality. The district had a total population of 1,700,000 in 2004, 550,000 of whom were urban citizens. It was the second largest city in the municipality.

Some 250,000 people needed to be resettled with the construction of the Three Gorges Project. After the accomplishment of the Three Gorges Project, the dams controlling the flooding of the middle and lower reaches of the Changjiang river will improve the incidence of a flood every 10 years to a flood every 100 years, saving more than 80 million lives; thirty-two generators with 700,000-kilowatt machines were installed, which produce 104,200 million kilowatts an hour; the transportation ability of the upper Changjiang river has increased fivefold and reduced costs by one-third. The 'Golden Waterway' has become increasingly valuable as a result and will be of benefit to future generations. However, the key point is the resettlement of millions of people in the area, known as a world problem. As the central government leader repeatedly emphasized, resettlement depended on whether the Three Gorges Project could be processed on time. The resettlement project was testament to whether the project was successful or not. It was difficult to move people from their homes, but it was even more difficult to resettle them satisfactorily in new areas. As a result, Wanzhou attracted national and international attention.

The Three Gorges Project brought new opportunities for the development of Wanzhou: a superhighway, railway, deep-water port and airport have been built and are now fully operational. Thus, a three-dimensional transport network has been formed; the city has improved as a result, and the urban area has expanded to 39 square kilometres. Since the foundation of Wanzhou district, its GDP has increased by an average rate of 10.6 per cent every year, 3.2 percentage points higher than the national GDP and one percentage point higher than that of Chongqing municipality. What is more, its GDP continues to rise. The economic situation in Wanzhou is getting better and better.

However, because the Three Gorges Project was under discussion for many years and the nation neither invested in important infrastructure projects nor planned major industrial projects in the area, the political and economical base of Wanzhou City was very weak. Wanzhou continued to fall further and further behind other major cities in politics and economic development. In 2004, the per capita GDP of Wanzhou was $777, which was 60 per cent of the average national level and two-thirds of Chongqing's. Wanzhou had 60,000 laid-off workers, 60,000 people living on benefits and 60,000 people living in rural poverty. Some 17.8 per cent of the population in Wanzhou were unemployed. Furthermore, the contradictions of resettlement, bankruptcy and closures of enterprises during those years accumulated gradually. On 18 October 2004, a couple masquerading as civil servants beat up a Biandan (who earns a living by portering and is also called a Bangbang in Chongqing) and caused a serious public incident.

Change occurred faster than planned and, when Jia Mingzhi prepared to conduct a thorough investigation, his work was disrupted by the dispute about taxi managerial rights, which lasted for 2 years. Hundreds of taxi drivers were continuing to appeal to the higher authorities, and even stopped taxi transportation and blockaded traffic, which severely affected the social stability of Wanzhou, and even that of Chongqing and the capital. The Municipal Party Committee and municipal government attached great importance to it and demanded that the Wanzhou government deal with it as soon as possible so as to maintain stability in Wanzhou. Jia Mingzhi was in charge of transportation at the time, so he had to try to deal with the problem shortly after he began his work in Wanzhou.

The reason for the dispute

No investigation, no right to speak. So Jia Mingzhi decided to investigate the root of the dispute. First, he found out that there had been three phases of taxi industry development in Wanzhou.

- Phase 1: The free development of individual operations. At the beginning of the 1990s, self-employed taxi drivers began to operate in Wanzhou City. At that time, no matter who individuals, groups or enterprises were, as long as they could afford to buy a taxi and obtain a driving and operating licence from the transportation department and traffic police department, they could work as taxi drivers. Generally speaking, the licence was for an unlimited period. In October 1996, the number of taxis in Wanzhou increased to 771. Most of the drivers were victims of bankrupt and closed enterprises due to the resettlement, and laid-off workers.
- Phase 2: Compensating managerial rights for a limited period. During phase 1, the numbers of taxi drivers grew at an amazing rate. In addition, the taxis they drove varied in make and model, and there was no standard tariff. Competition among drivers and cheating passengers happened frequently. The market was in disarray. In order to standardize the taxi trade, the government contributed towards the funds of public establishment construction, as the government regarded the trade as a public resource. In 1996, Wanzhou City carried out the policy of compensating managerial rights for a limited period. The government stipulated that, after 17 October 1996, all newly registered taxis should pay 30,000 yuan for a 5-year licence to operate; the managerial rights of the taxi drivers did not include those who had received compensation, and would be repealed when their cars had been scrapped. From 1996 until 2000 in Wanzhou City, there were 216 new quotas of taxi managerial rights, and

200 repealed and renewed quotas. The government received all the 416 quotas' compensated rent of 30,000 yuan per year, and used the money to fund road construction in the city and countryside. In the meantime, a taxi managing department was set up, which encouraged individual taxi drivers to join a taxi company. At the end of 2000, the total number of taxis in Wanzhou city had reached 987 and there were thirteen taxi companies. There were 987 taxis in Wanzhou City alone. Of the total taxis, those operated by taxi companies numbered 125, accounting for 12.7 per cent, and those operated by individual drivers or in the name of a company totalled 862, accounting for 87.3 per cent.

- Phrase 3: Promoting taxi operation by companies. During this period, the government controlled the total number of taxis, standardized tariffs and encouraged drivers to join companies. However, as the thirteen taxi companies varied in size and ability and the individual operators were not under effective management, they continued to cheat their passengers, and the taxi service grew progressively worse. Customers complained repeatedly about the taxi service. Therefore, Wanzhou began to promote large-scale taxi management by companies by referring to the taxi managerial experiences of other cities in 2001. The government stipulated that: (1) the number of taxis in Wanzhou district would be limited to within 1,100 in 4 years; (2) the quotas and the renewed quotas of the scrapped taxis would be granted by the guidance of government and the needs of the market; (3) the taxi market would be operated by three to five major companies, and they would get quotas according to market principles; (4) the drivers' licence to operate would be for a period of 8 years, and user fees paid would be at least 50,000 yuan; (5) the government would recommend one or two non-local enterprises to participate in the taxi service in Wanzhou.

On 28 December 2001, the Wanzhou government awarded the taxi operation qualification to five companies, namely one non-local company (Xishu Company), a company trading in the district (Wanyun Company) and three companies from three resettlement developing zones (Longteng Company, Shenming Company and Bai'an Company). By retaining 150 quotas from the total 1,100 quotas of taxi managerial rights (in fact the municipality had only approved 1,040 quotas in 2002), the other 950 were assigned to the five companies, namely Xishu Company 400 quotas, Wanyun Company 100 quotas, Longteng Company 280 quotas, Shenming Company 120 quotas and Bai'an Company 50 quotas. From then to September 2003, the government recalled the 438 expired quotas of taxi managerial rights and granted them to the five companies. The five companies then rented the taxis to individual operators after obtaining the quotas. By the end of 2004, the total number of taxis operating in Wanzhou City was 774. Of the total taxis, those operated by the companies numbered 438, accounting for 57 per cent; and those operated by individual operators or in the name of a company numbered 336, accounting for 43 per cent. According to the odometer, effective passenger transport was around 50 per cent, but was about 60 per cent in practice.

Jia Mingzhi found that, before the end of 2001, during phase 1, and even in phase 2, there was no contradiction between the individual taxi operators and the government. The clash occurred gradually after phase 2.

The dispute concerning managerial rights became increasingly fierce

During the third period, the dispute concerning managerial rights became increasingly fierce.

A comrade working in the Wanzhou People's Court told Jia Mingzhi that he had been acquainted with several individual taxi operators because he had dealt with many lawsuits concerning the issue. Some taxi owners charged the Wanzhou Transport Management Department with managerial rights in October 2002 and demanded that the accused should go through the procedures and allow them to continue taxi operations. At the end of 2002, others were also charged in the Wanzhou People's Court and protested that it was illegal for Wanzhou Transport Management Department to award the taxi transport licence to a third party (Xishu Company). However, the first-instance sentence in Wanzhou People's Court and the second-instance sentence in the Chongqing Municipality Second Intermediate People's Court ignored these demands. In August 2003, 364 individual taxi operators took action to the Provincial Second Intermediate People's Court to demand that the illegal decision of Wanzhou government be rescinded and to allow the accused to work in the taxi service, which was also ignored. At last, on 27 June 2005, the Provincial Superior People's Court upheld the primary judgements.

The comrades working in the Department of Appeal and the Transport Management Department of Wanzhou were not happy about the prospect of receiving hundreds of appeals from individual taxi operators. Since the government's promotion of a standardized taxi service run by companies, the individual taxi operators had continued to appeal to the government and relevant departments, especially when the government granted 200 taxi managerial rights quotas to Xishu Company from April to August 2002. On 7 July 2003, hundreds of taxi drivers bearing banners with the slogan, 'the Three Gorges Resettlements lost their jobs' and 'return my taxi managerial rights' stormed the gates of the government buildings. On 11 August 2003, forty individual taxi operators went to Chongqing to appeal. They claimed that they would not return to Wanzhou unless they achieved their aim. They even threatened to go to Beijing and commit suicide.

The City Management Department and the Transport Management Department were also in deep trouble. In order to put pressure on the government, the individual operators gathered together to stop taxi transportation and blockade traffic, and almost achieved traffic gridlock in Wanzhou on several occasions. At 8:00 p.m. on 20 November 2003, more than 200 taxi drivers halted taxi transport and drove their cars downtown. The City Management Department and the Transport Department managed to disperse them until 3:00 a.m. the following day. On the morning of 21 November 2003, more than 100 taxis gathered in the main streets and blocked the traffic; this was dispersed until 12:00 noon. At the end of 2003, on hearing that certain national leaders would be visiting Wanzhou to comfort the victims of a recent natural disaster in neighbouring counties, some individual operators prepared to block the roads and appeal to the leaders. Luckily, their plan was discovered and stopped in time.

Wanzhou government took action to deal with these issues. (1) To strengthen the government's ability to receive and deal with the appeals, the main district government leaders went to Chongqing and Beijing to persuade the people to return home. (2) The government gave the taxi drivers wide publicity and explained the situation to them in an effort to calm them down. (3) The government consulted the five companies with a view to renting taxi managerial rights at favourable terms to the 238 laid-off workers whose licences had expired. (4) The public security bodies punished and educated the leaders of the disturbances with the legal system as well as those who had bypassed local government in order to appeal for their rights. In addition, about ten people who had contravened the law were arrested, and one leader was sentenced to 4 years' imprisonment.

These measures went some way towards easing the contradictions and maintaining social stability. However, the fundamental problem remained unresolved. In April 2005, when the Provincial Second Intermediate People's Court made the judgement, 137 individual taxi operators went to Beijing to appeal to the higher authorities and tried to cause some disturbances. Some even encouraged a cancer sufferer to commit suicide in order to put pressure on the government. In June 2005, when the Provincial Superior People's Court made the final judgement, the taxi drivers continued their actions. Another thirty people went to Beijing to appeal for taxi managerial rights.

Complex contradictions

One morning at the beginning of 2005, Jia Mingzhi went to work on foot. As soon as he entered the gates of the government buildings, he was recognized and surrounded by the crowds who were appealing to the higher authorities for help and demanded to speak to him about the situation. Some were furious, and it took some time to calm them down. On hearing that they were independent taxi operators, Jia Mingzhi invited some of them as representatives to ask their opinions and tell him what they knew.

The independent taxi operators were under the impression that their managerial rights had been obtained legally. When they had purchased their taxis years ago, the government had not yet issued terms of agreement on the expiry of managerial rights, so they believed the government had no right to cancel their rights. In addition, the drivers told Jia Mingzhi that because the individual operators were unable to obtain their managerial rights after their taxis had been scrapped, they had to rent the rights from one of the appointed five companies at a cost of between 50,000 yuan and 80,000 yuan and to pay the deposit fee in advance if they wanted to continue to operate. This meant that their income would decrease by 30,000 yuan a year compared with their status as independent taxi drivers.

Zhang Shizhong, who lived in the resettlement zone in the Pipaping area of Wanzhou, had been an individual taxi operator for many years. In 1996, he and his wife were laid off. In order to support themselves, they used the compensation due to them for their length of service and their savings to buy a Santana and started their own taxi business after going through the necessary procedures. The couple and their two children had made a comfortable living from the business for several years. In 2004, his taxi scrapped and his managerial rights withdrawn, Zhang had to spend 60,000 yuan to rent a taxi from Longteng Company in order to earn a living. As Zhang said, one year's net income of 50,000 yuan had previously funded a comfortable lifestyle. But now he had to pay rent of 5,000 yuan to the company every month, as well as fuel and maintenance. Nowadays, he could earn around 20,000 yuan a year if he worked long hours. What is more, his children were attending university, and the family's life was not as good as it once was.

For many years, Li Jinwei, Xiong Bingsheng and other independent taxi drivers, who had not understood the regulations of government, had appealed to the government and the taxi management department for help, and even participated in the disturbances at the Xishu Company when their cars were scrapped and they lost their managerial rights. They believed that they were right, because they were Wanzhou citizens who had been driving taxis for many years, and they felt that the government had no right to withdraw their managerial rights. Furthermore, the country was developing an individual economy. It was not reasonable for the local government to limit independent taxi operation.

The individual operators told Jia Mingzhi that most of them were resettlement or laid-off workers, so they lived a hard life. If the government cancelled their taxi managerial rights, there would be no way forward for them.

In order to understand the reality of their problems, Jia Mingzhi visited some individual taxi operators' families and obtained various information. Some had bought their cars and set up in business with the settlement allowance due to an enterprise's bankruptcy or resettlement in order to support their families. Their lives would be in deep trouble if they had to give up their businesses. Others had started up their businesses since 1996 and lived in better conditions with some savings. Some had bought a second-hand taxi to run as a business for just a few years or even a few months. As a result, if their taxi managerial rights were taken back, they would earn nothing or even lose all their original capital. The proportion of each circumstance is approximately one third.

Jia Mingzhi realized that the foundation of the contradiction was their loss and gain of interest, which was also the key to solving the problem. So he decided to carry out further investigations of the companies, and was surprised to learn that they too were not satisfied. They felt it unfair that they should receive no quota for entering the taxi service market. Meanwhile, in order to relieve the contradiction between the independent taxi operators as well as maintaining the stability of society, the government stopped granting the other 512 quotas out of the 950 to the five companies before the end of 2003 as the agreement stipulated, which was strongly required by the five companies, otherwise the government would be prosecuted, as the companies had incurred huge financial losses.

Furthermore, Jia Mingzhi discovered a further contradiction among the five taxi companies. When Liu Changjiang, He Guodong and the four other taxi drivers of Xishu Company were transporting passengers on 4 January 2005, they were beaten up for no apparent reason. What is more, Liu Changjiang's taxi was deliberately damaged. When the police investigated these trouble-makers, it was found that they were taxi drivers from Wanyun Company and Longteng Company. Meanwhile, members of the public called the police and told them that some taxi drivers from other companies had also attacked Xishu Company's passengers on the street and even caused mass fighting.

It seemed that all the contradictions focused on Xishu Company, but why? Jia Mingzhi started his investigations once the spring festival holiday was over. Both Longteng Company and Wanyun Company complained about Xishu Company. The leaders said that the other four companies out of the five companies who received managerial rights thought that Xishu Company received too many quotas: 263 of the granted quotas, which was almost two-thirds of the total. Furthermore, the 200 quotas granted to Xishu in 2001 cost 50,000 yuan each, while the 238 quotas granted to the companies in 2003 increased to 70,000 yuan each. As a result, they felt they were involved in illegal competition. They complained bitterly about Xishu Company and asked the government to grant them the other quotas as soon as possible.

However, Xishu Company told Jia Mingzhi that it was a non-local enterprise from Chongqing and had invested a large amount in Wanzhou's taxi market after signing certain formal agreements. Of all the companies, they had invested the most, provided the best service, managed in the most standardized ways and even paid 10 million yuan in advance to the government, but the government had failed to carry out the agreement properly.

Jia Mingzhi also found that a contradiction between the company taxi drivers and the companies was intensifying. In fact, the five companies failed to agree on a transport policy once they received the quotas. They chartered the quotas and taxis to individuals and received rent and security cash deposits in return. However, the charter parties complained that the high rents and cash deposits were the means by which the companies transferred risks to them and occupied most of their interest. On the other hand, the companies complained that the charters were difficult to manage and they even acted against their daily management intentionally. By taking taxis in person, Jia Mingzhi also heard complaints from the taxi drivers who were employed by the charters. They said they could earn only about 1,000 yuan per month by working day and night. A large proportion of their earnings was taken by the companies and charters. If the government could allow them to operate taxis independently, they could earn more and would not have to work as hard.

These contradictions made Jian Mingzhi's head spin. Unexpectedly, when he was ready to harmonize every part and plan to solve the problem, another interest group emerged. In May 2005, more than 200 people had appealed to the government to be allowed to operate taxis. What had happened? Jia Mingzhi knew that Xishu Company and Longsheng Company had sold the quotas in advance for 50,000 to 80,000 yuan deposit to more than 230 citizens without telling the government. Because the government had not granted the companies the full quotas on time, they did not get the ones the companies had promised. So they demanded that the government take back the expired individuals' quotas and carry out its promise to the companies. In order to successfully gain their quotas, they did something almost as crazy as the independent taxi operators. They appealed to the government, organized demonstrations and even went on hunger strike.

Let us hear other people's opinions. Some believed that the quotas should be sold by auction and that the taxi service should operate in an open market, which would be fair to all; some said the individual operators should be satisfied because they had earned enough; some pitied the individual operators who had lost their jobs and could not support their families. Most citizens hoped the government would deal with the situation as quickly as possible.

This information moved Jia Mingzhi deeply. He realized that the government was in an embarrassing position as every contradiction focused on it, because it was the government that had promoted the collective management of the taxi service. If the government did not keep its promise to the five companies, it would not only lose face but also be responsible for the companies' financial losses. However, if the government kept its promise, the individual operators, who were from all walks of life, would fight the government until they were allowed to operate taxis again. It would be hard to satisfy both sides.

An attempt to explore the new style of standardization management

Jia Mingzhi knew that the government's basic remit was to administer and solve the problems according to the laws and policies. So he studied certain relevant national, ministry and commission laws and regulations on taxi management.

National laws and regulations

1 *Law of the People's Republic of China on Administrative Permission,* carried out on 1 July 1 2004, says in Article 12: 'the following should be set by the administrative permissions ... (2) The use and development of the limited natural resources, the distribution of public resources and the entrance to a particular trade market which have a direct relation to the public's interest'. Article 53 says: 'The administrative organs should take the fair competition methods such as public bidding and auction to realize the administrative permission mentioned in the second item of Article 12'.

2 *Regulations of People's Republic of China on Administration of Land Transport,* carried out on 1 July 2004, says in Article 6: 'It is encouraged by the nation to manage land transport enterprises intensively and on a large scale. No organization or individual has the right to blockade or monopolize the land transport market'.

3 *Notice of a Deeper Regulation on Taxi Management by the General Office of the State Council (Guobanfa [2004] No.81)* requires: 'No city is allowed to carry out a new policy on compensated transfer of taxi managerial rights. The city which has compensated the transferred taxi managerial rights should check and regularize those managerial rights amount, money, allotted time, examining and approving procedure, usage of the selling income and the transferred mortgage as well as the parties' relationship in it after hearing suggestions from the concerned profession's workers, passengers and other people, better by holding an evidentiary hearing'. Meanwhile, it says: 'The following are prohibited: from transferring the risk of investment and management and gain of sudden huge profits to the drivers by selling quotas, collecting risk deposits, property deposits, operation income, earned income and high contract rents'.

Regulations of ministries and commissions

1 On 1 December 2004, *Regulations on 15 Administrative Permissions which Should be Taken by the State Council* issued by the Ministry of Construction stipulates the conditions of self-employed taxi drivers obtaining a taxi operation certificate: (1) The means of operation should accord with the pertinent regulations. (2) The quality of passenger traffic vehicles or devices should conform to the pertinent regulations. (3) The vehicles and the related devices and signs should tally with the pertinent regulations issued by the nation, ministries and commissions and local governments. (4) Enough money should accord with the regulations. (5) A standard parking place. (6) Ability to take civil liability on one's own. (7) Other terms according with the local laws and regulations.

2 *The Views to Strengthen the Management of City Taxi Industry (Jiancheng [2002] No. 43),* carried out by the Ministry of Construction stipulates:

'The city or section whose utilization ratio of effective mileage is lower than 70 per cent should principally not grant new transportation quotas by permission, auction or other disguised forms'. It also says: 'The taxi management organs should actively lead the taxi operating enterprises to adjust and optimize their operation methods. By reorganizing, annexing and large-scale operating, the organs should solve the problem that the taxi operating companies are too many, too scattered and too small'.

Regulations of Chongqing municipality

1   *Temporary Measures for the Administration of Taxi Managerial Authority and Certificate in Chongqing Municipality (Yufufa [2004] No. 2)* stipulates in Article 12: 'In Chongqing City a new taxi managerial authority and certificate should be granted if the practical taxi passenger transport rate is higher than 60 per cent. However, the transportation administrative departments and the transport managing department should measure and calculate the newly granted amount to make sure that the practical taxi passenger transport rate is no lower than 55 per cent'. Article 49 says: 'The other district, city and county governments (except Chongqing City) should work out measures of administration for the taxi managerial authorities in their administrative areas'.

2   *Notice of the People's Government of Chongqing Municipality to Approve and Promulgate Chongqing Municipality Transportation Committee's Work Plan on Reforming the Administrative System of Taxi Managerial Authority in Chongqing City (Yufufa [2003] No. 85)* says: 'The current taxi operators can get a 25-year taxi management licence after paying a 50,000 yuan managerial authority fee'.

3   *Guiding Comments of the People's Government of Chongqing Municipality for a Further Shake-up on Taxi Passenger Transport (Yufufa [2005] No. 27)* says: 'The new taxi management licences should be granted only when the application for granting new licences is approved by the Municipality Government. Furthermore, the application should be submitted after an evidentiary hearing for granting new taxi management licences when the average practical taxi passenger transport rate is higher than 60 per cent per year'.

From those regulations, Jia Mingzhi discovered that the management of taxis had been a gradually regulated process from an unlimited market to a regulated one. The laws and regulations, no matter whether the national ones, the ministry's and commission's or the Chongqing municipality's, were regulated principally and in draft, and only focused on the problems that had emerged thus far. There were no operating and identical stipulations in explicit terms on regulating the market.

Jia Mingzhi realized that taxi management was a problem that had emerged in all cities. He might be able to gain some enlightenment from other cities. After the investigation, he found that different cities solved the problem in different ways.

The government of Beijing, capital of China, began the controlling of taxi aggregates and promoting the company management of taxis in 1996. It permitted the established individual taxi operators to continue their work, but did not allow newcomers to set up their own businesses.

The government of Zhengzhou, in He'nan province, sold the compensated taxi services at a cost of 60,000 yuan every 8 years. Only companies could operate taxi services. However, most taxis and managerial authorities were bought by individual investment while the individuals signed contracts with the taxi companies. In fact, the operation is just under the name of the managing company.

The government of Wenzhou, in Zhejiang Province, allowed people aged 18 and over who had a registered permanent residence in Wenzhou, or an organization registered in Wenzhou, to bid for managerial authority by auction.

It seemed that it was impossible for Jia Mingzhi to find a ready-made solution to the problem in Wanzhou.

Final resolution of the dispute

In order to end the dispute concerning managerial rights in Wanzhou, Jia Mingzhi held an evidentiary hearing following full investigation. However, opinion still differed. He tried to formulate a perfect or partially perfect plan, but failed. Finally, he worked out six plans with his colleagues.

Plan 1:   Continue to promote the taxi operation by company. Based on the current regulations, no individual could receive managerial rights. The expired licences would be taken back and granted to the five companies. These companies continued to operate the taxi service in Wanzhou.

Plan 2:   Reform the taxi managerial rights system. A taxi operator could drive a taxi for 25 years after paying 50,000 yuan for a taxi management licence.

Plan 3:   Grant more quotas on taxi management. On the basis of the 1,040 quotas approved by the municipality in 2002, the government could grant more quotas to meet the needs of both individuals and companies.

Plan 4:   Sell all the quotas in public auction. All the quotas, both the expired and the newly granted ones, would be sold in auction publicly and fairly Taxi companies, individual operators and ordinary citizens would have the right to take part in the bidding.

Plan 5:   No limitation on the quotas and open up the market completely. The government would open up the taxi service market completely without any limitation on quotas, duration or parties and permit selling of the rights. The government would only take responsibility for supervision of the market.

Plan 6:   Solve the various problems in different ways and try to give consideration to all parties. The quotas should be renewed by way of *Time to Space* and *3 to 1*. Companies and individuals could obtain a 24-year managerial authority licence through three 8-year certificates. Every quota would still be sold at a cost of 70,000 yuan each. The new quotas would be granted by public auction.

The plans had some advantages and disadvantages. There would inevitably be some difficulties if any was adopted.

In considering the advantages and disadvantages, Jia Mingzhi and the Wanzhou government decided to adopt Plan 6, which seemed to satisfy every party's interests. The plan was accepted by all the interest groups and eventually implemented, although it did not satisfy each group's interests completely. At the end of September 2005, the work had been basically finished and no more problems emerged. The dispute concerning taxi managerial rights was finally over.

Epilogue

Some problems left over from the past are sure to emerge while our country is in the process of transferring from a planned economy to a market economy. In order to solve those problems, we should respect history and face reality, and administrate fairly and according to the law. In other words, the way to solve such problems is to be people oriented, which means considering the people's interest first and coping with the legal interest relationships among different groups.

Written in 2005

36 Storm at Huigao Company

Li Lecheng

The deputy mayor of the city of Jingmen who was in charge of industry had become restless of late. It was the fourth time in a month that some of the workers laid off by the Huigao Company had come to the municipal government to stage sit-in complaints. Although actions of this nature were nothing new to this old industrial base, it was the first time that such an action had been launched by the workers of a key state-owned enterprise. Accordingly, this action produced considerable social impacts on the city of Jingmen. The chief leaders of the municipal Party committee and government all paid close attention to this action, the ordinary people had diverse views, and the leadership of the Huigao Company reported orally or in writing to the municipal government several times, requesting it to handle the incident. At the same time, some laid-off workers who participated in the sit-in were also inciting a complaint visit to the provincial government. All these issues placed the deputy mayor under tremendous pressure.

Jingmen's new reform of state-owned enterprises

A new round of reforms of the small and medium-sized state-owned enterprises had been going on for several years in the city of Jingmen. The new round highlighted the reform of property rights. The municipal Party committee and government were determined to push forward these reforms. To guide the new round of corporate reform, they drew on the experience of other places and worked out the 2000–2026 document. Entitled the *Notice on the Dissemination of the Opinions of the Office of the Municipal Leading Group for Corporate Reform and Development on Further Promoting the Reform of the Property Rights of the Small and Medium-sized State-owned Enterprises*, the document was issued in the name of the general office of the Jingmen municipal people's government. In addition, the municipal government set up a leading group for corporate reform, which was headed by the deputy mayor in charge of industry and participated in by the officials of the economic and trade committee, the economic restructuring office and the finance, audit, labour and trade union departments.

The group would be specifically responsible for guiding and approving the reform plans of various enterprises in accordance with the 2000–2026 document. Thanks to the efforts in publicity, demonstration, responsibility assignment and phased solutions, the reform advanced rapidly. By the end of 2002, the reform of the city's small and medium-sized state-owned enterprises was largely completed. Despite persistent contradictions and frequent complaint sit-ins, the workers' understanding and tolerance of the reform increased as a result of the continuous improvement in the reform plans of various enterprises and the implementation of the social security measures. The reformed enterprises became more dynamic and the overall efficiency of the reforms became gradually visible. Practice indicated that this round of reforms broke through the barriers of property rights and laid a sound system foundation for the city's economic development. Jingmen's experience in reforming these enterprises won praise from the leaders of the provincial government and attracted people from other places to learn from them. However, the reform of the state-owned enterprises that highlighted the privatization of property rights also brought about a host of problems. (1) The change in their 'state-owned' status brought a psychological shock and a sense of loss to many workers. (2) The contradictions accumulated in the past by these state-owned enterprises could not be solved within a short time. For example, as the planned economy pursued a policy that emphasized high accumulation and low consumption, many workers and especially the older ones felt that they had worked selflessly in the past because they would reap the benefits later. Now, as they became sick and unable to work, nobody cared about them. This was hardly acceptable. (3) As the reform emphasized higher efficiency through lay-offs, many workers had left their work posts and found it difficult to find new jobs. These laid-off workers, who were usually in financial difficulties, were emotionally unstable. (4) Although the city's enterprises had unified standards for lay-off compensation, some enterprises paid the compensation in full while others were unable to do so. Furthermore, the allowance in addition to the compensation also differed greatly from enterprise to enterprise. When the laid-off workers from different enterprises made comparisons among themselves, those who received less compensation became angry. In particular, the compensation given by the central and provincial enterprises to their laid-off workers was several times or a dozen times higher than that given by the municipal enterprises (the compensation for the workers with the same length of service could be over 100,000 yuan higher). This angered the workers of the municipal enterprises: 'We are all the masters of the country so why is our welfare so different?' They had doubts about this reform. Other similar problems also constituted a headache for the deputy mayor but they were resolved after stirring up some minor storms. None of them lasted as long as the storm hitting Huigao or produced repercussions as wide-ranging as this one.

Huigao Company

In fact, the emotions of the workers of the Huigao Company had been unstable for some time. At first, they limited their actions within their company, blocking the plant gates and presenting demands to the principal leaders of the company. When they saw no progress after 1 month, they went to the municipal government to complain. As the reply from the municipal government did not satisfy them, they began blocking the gate of the municipal government and vowed to go to the provincial government to lodge their complaints.

Huigao was a key state-owned industrial enterprise in the city of Jingmen. It was also a key industrial enterprise placed under the regulation of the provincial government. The company grew out of a small state-owned chemical plant, which mainly produced industrial chemicals. In the early 1990s, the plant was turned into a limited liability company, and the state owned about 90 per cent of its equity capital. From the mid-1990s on, the company began to produce medical products. Its leading new product, a medical raw material, enjoyed a fairly large share of the world market. In Asia, Huigao was the largest supplier of this raw material. Huigao had many subsidiaries in China. It had its headquarters and three subsidiaries in Jingmen, which were located in Jingmen's urban areas and its county cities. In particular, the subsidiary in the urban area employed more than 1,200 workers. The company's research and development (R&D) centre and marketing office were located in the provincial capital. Over the years, while the company had been expanding, its stock rights structure also underwent changes, with the proportion of state-owned stock rights declining gradually. In 2001, the company reformed its property rights, meaning that its employees were no longer 'state-owned' and had to sign time-limited labour contracts with the enterprise. In 2002, the proportion of the state-owned stock rights held by the Jingmen State-Owned Chemical Assets Management Company in Huigao's total equity capital dropped to about 42 per cent. But the assets management company remained Huigao's largest stockholder. As the company turned increasingly towards manufacturing medical products, Huigao's demand for capital skyrocketed. As there were growing calls for the withdrawal of state-owned assets from the competitive sectors, the assets management company had no strong desire and no sufficient capacity to inject new investment into Huigao. Accordingly, Huigao's capital shortfall became increasingly acute and incapable of meeting the demand of market competition by relying on its own fund accumulation. Therefore, the company's operators and its main stockholders, especially the assets management company, decided to introduce strategic investors after winning the approval of the Jingmen municipal people's government. Thanks to long investigations and hard bargains with the investors, the assets management company signed an agreement of intent on the transfer of stock rights in December 2002 with the Rixin Investment Company, a private company in a coastal city. The agreement was to be fully operational within 6 months, after which Rixin would become Huigao's largest stockholder, and its stake in Huigao would rise to 46 per cent. The assets management company would become the second largest stockholder, having a stake of 23 per cent. In fact, as a considerable proportion of Huigao's stocks was held by its employees, Rixin actually held two-thirds of the company's corporate stocks and became Huigao's de facto absolute controller. After the agreement on the transfer of stock rights was signed, Huigao established a new board of directors, with the chairman of Rixin's board of directors working concurrently as its chairman and the former chairman of Huigao's board of directors working as the general manager. After the new chairman arrived, he conducted investigations and subsequently declared that the company's performance was poor and that it was grossly overstaffed. Therefore, management must be tightened and institutions streamlined. He requested the subsidiary in the urban area to lay off 300 people in phases and instructed the general manager to be responsible for this move. In this process, the board of directors studied the relevant documents of the governments at various levels. They noted that Article 5 of the *Regulations of the Ministry of Labour on the Economic Compensation for the Violation and Cancellation of Labour Contracts* provided that, if the parties to a labour contract reached agreement through consultation, the labour contract would be cancelled by the employing unit, and the employing unit should pay economic compensation to the workers according to their length of service at the unit. The economic compensation would be 1 month's wages for a full year and would be 12 months at most. The service for less than a full year would be deemed as service for a full year. The *Notice on the Dissemination of the Opinions of the Office of the Municipal Leading Group for Corporate Reform and Development on Further Promoting the Reform of the Property Rights of the Small and Medium-sized State-owned Enterprises* (document 2000–2026) issued by the general office of the Jingmen municipal people's government provided that one lump sum severance compensation would be paid. For each full year of service, the compensation would be 1 month of the enterprise's per capita monthly wage in the preceding 3 years (the worker's wage and the per capita monthly wage were based on those set by the labour department; if the wage was less than 400 yuan, the wage would be based on 400 yuan), and should not be more than three times higher than the city's average annual wage for enterprise workers in the preceding year. With regard to those who took early retirement, the document provided that, for the workers who retired early (before a specific date) 5 years or less before their mandatory retirement ages, the living allowance, pension, unemployment and medical insurance premiums and housing reserve fund should be calculated up until their retirement ages and should be deducted from the net assets of the former enterprise for the transformed new enterprise. The new enterprise would be responsible for paying their living allowance, pension, unemployment and medical insurance premiums and housing reserve fund. When the workers reached their mandatory retirement ages, the new enterprise would handle their retirement formalities. The workers who retired early (after a specific date) should be treated in the same way as on-the-job workers. For workers who resigned from their posts, the document provided that the former enterprise should pay their pension, unemployment and medical insurance premiums and housing reserve fund before they resigned and then cancel their labour contracts. The economic compensation due to them should be paid from the net assets of the former enterprise, based on their length of service before they resigned. The compensation would be 1 month of the enterprise's per capita monthly wage in the preceding year for each full year of service and would be 12 months at most. In addition, the 2001–15 document of the municipal government provided that, for the workers who were laid off more than 5 years and less than 10 years before their mandatory retirement ages, the enterprise might reach agreement with the workers through consultation that the enterprise might pay their social insurance premiums in full up until their mandatory retirement ages, cancel labour relations with them and pay economic compensation according to the regulations, or might pay one lump sum severance compensation before cancelling labour relations with them.

After familiarizing itself with the relevant provisions, the company decided to work out its own rules on efficiency enhancement through lay-offs. The chairman and the company's leadership all held that Huigao was a large, well-performing enterprise and the wages of its workers were relatively high in the city of Jingmen. As the workers in general were reluctant to leave the enterprise, some incentives were indispensable. Privately, the chairman and other members of the company's management also tacitly agreed that it would be enough if the company could lose 200 employees. To implement this plan, the company introduced the *Implementing Rules for Enhancing Efficiency through Lay-offs*. The rules were as follows.

The company would encourage employees to seek other jobs. Those who met the following conditions would be deemed as being those whose labour contracts were cancelled by the company when the enterprise's stockholding underwent changes. In addition to paying them 1 month's economic compensation for each full year of service according to the provisions of the *Regulations of the Ministry of Labour on the Economic Compensation for the Violation and Cancellation of Labour Contracts* (from August 2001 when the enterprise changed its property rights to June 2003), the company's major stockholders would pay 10,000-yuan compensation for early cancellation of labour contracts and a compensation of 1 month's wages if:

1   they participated in the reform of the company's property rights and held the company's stocks;
2   they were currently employees of Huigao's enterprise in Jingmen's urban areas and had labour contracts with the enterprises;
3   they would voluntarily cancel their labour contracts with the company.

At the same time, the company would make one lump sum capital stock payment to the stockholders who would leave the company and pay all the insurance premiums for them up until the month when their labour contracts were cancelled. With regard to those who left the company voluntarily within 5 years of their mandatory retirement ages, the company would also carry out the following:

- If employees voluntarily cancelled labour relations with the enterprises within 5 years of their mandatory retirement ages and met the above conditions in category 1 (namely the three conditions described above), the company would, on top of all preferential policy treatment, make one lump sum payment to them and the medical insurance, pension and housing reserve fund would be paid by the enterprise, according to the standards and ratios of premium contributions before they resigned, up until the month of their retirement.
- If those employees who had labour disputes with the enterprises and who met the condition of being within 5 years of their mandatory retirement ages were willing to cancel labour relations with the enterprise, the company would execute the rulings rendered by the Jingmen Arbitration Committee for Labour Disputes and their preferential policy treatment, as the situation of those people who had resigned would remain unchanged.

When the plan was made public, the company conducted extensive publicity. Within 2 weeks, 307 people had applied for voluntary redundancy. This figure did not include certain experienced university graduates and skilled workers, who were persuaded privately by the company not to apply for redundancy in order to avoid a brain drain. The fact that there were so many people applying for voluntary redundancy surprised the company's leadership. But the chairman was relieved, and instructed that redundancy formalities should be handled for these people as soon as possible. After 10 days, about 220 people had completed their formalities by 28 March 2003. Because this date fell at a weekend, the remaining eighty people were supposed to complete the formalities the following week. In the meantime, several dozen more planned to apply for redundancy. It was at this point that some problems started to emerge.

First, the leaders of the production workshops complained about manpower shortages. A medical chemical company such as Huigao operated in shifts and its manpower requirement was basically stable. A considerable proportion of the workers who had applied for voluntary redundancy were frontline workers. Those who had completed the formalities had already left their posts, those who had applied for voluntary redundancy were 'absentminded' in their work, and those remaining in their posts were not in a stable mood. In this situation, shift rotation became difficult, especially for the late-night shift. The workshop directors had to do that shift personally.

After some days, they became exhausted and had insufficient time for day-to-day management. Safety management was extremely important for chemical production, and any degree of negligence could cause problems. In addition, the unstable mood of the skilled workers also brought potential threats to production and quality. Therefore, nearly all workshop directors demanded that this wave of enhancing efficiency through lay-offs be brought to an end as soon as possible.

Those who had applied for redundancy also had second thoughts. Of these people, thirty were workers who were within 5 years of their mandatory retirement ages. Most were long-time employees of the company, but a few of them had been transferred to the company through connections and had worked for the company for only a few years. This triggered other people's discontent with the company's provision that all the insurances for the thirty people would be paid up until their mandatory retirement ages. They demanded equal treatment. They argued that the older workers should not receive more and, in particular, those who had joined the company through connections and made fewer contributions to the company should not receive so much compensation. Therefore, they began soliciting support and organized about 100 people on 31 March to see the general manager, claiming they did so on behalf of all those who had voluntarily resigned. They put forward three demands. (1) The company should pay compensation to all the voluntarily resigned workers on the basis of the average amount of the additional insurance premiums given to those who were within 5 years of their mandatory retirement ages. (2) The company should give monetized housing subsidies to all laid-off personnel. (3) The company should make one lump sum severance payment to all the voluntarily resigned personnel. After being approved by the chairman who was elsewhere at the time, the general manager gave them the following replies.

1   The special treatment given to the workers who were within 5 years of their mandatory retirement ages conformed to the spirit of the documents of the central, provincial and municipal governments and also to the Chinese tradition of respecting the aged. The demands of other people to be treated in the same way did not conform with the provisions of the policies and laws, and should not be accepted.

2   Monetized housing subsidies had not been introduced by Huigao or other enterprises in the city of Jingmen. In addition, the document issued in 2001 by the general office of the municipal government stated that the reform to monetized housing subsidies should be postponed in Jingmen. Therefore, the company should not carry out this reform. The company promised that, if this reform was to be carried out in the future with the permission of the provincial and municipal policies to be introduced, proper compensation would be made to the personnel who resigned this time. The company was willing to issue letters of commitment to the laid-off workers.

3   When the company reformed its property rights in 2001 and signed new labour contracts with the workers, it made a lump sum severance payment to all the workers at the rate of 826 yuan for each full year of service. While the 2000–2026 document of the general office of the municipal government provided that this lump sum severance payment should not be more than three times that of the average wage of the city's enterprises in the preceding year, Huigao's offer was more preferential and had no ceiling. For this reason, the current reform of the company that emphasized efficiency enhancement through lay-offs did not involve the issue of lump sum severance pay.

The laid-off personnel were dissatisfied with the reply from the general manager. They held that the first point avoided the question of 'equity', while the second point was an empty promise. Besides, as the enterprise was now privately controlled, nobody would be responsible, even if housing subsidies were to be monetized in the future and the promise would carry no legal effect. The central government had issued documents long ago on the reform of monetized housing subsidies, and the municipal government had no power to postpone it. The third point was also unacceptable. They held that the standard for lump sum severance pay set by the documents of the higher authorities was the minimum guarantee, and the enterprises might decide to give higher lump sum severance pay for the laid-off workers according to their operational conditions. In the city of Jingmen, the enterprises run by the central and provincial governments already set a precedent, and the enterprises run by the municipal government also differed from each other when implementing severance compensation. Huigao's operational efficiency was good and the company should implement the higher standards. The laid-off personnel further noted that, when the general manager was working as the company's legal representative, he always pursued a policy of high accumulation and low consumption. As a result, the workers' wages were low and their housing conditions were poor (some workers even alleged that the general manager may have abused his powers for selfish gain). Should the enterprise not repay the welfare debt it owed to its workers? While the laid-off employees stuck to their demands, the company's leadership refused to give in. Those who had applied for voluntary resignation became not so enthusiastic about taking voluntary redundancy, and only a few completed their formalities in the ensuing weeks. During this period, the laid-off personnel went to the general manager's office once every 2 days or simply blocked the company's office building for 1 or 2 hours. Even though there was no bodily contact, the war of words became increasingly fierce between the two sides. This was unprecedented in Huigao's history and caused quite a stir in the company. Even the company's salesmen in other provinces and cities were worried, believing that the instability would damage the company's image among its customers and affect the marketing of the company's products. They hoped that this incident would be brought to an end as soon as possible.

After learning of the problems arising from the company's efforts to enhance efficiency through lay-offs, the chairman, who was elsewhere at the time, indicated that, as a private enterprise, Rixin already offered more preferential treatment than that specified by the regional governments to those who preferred voluntary resignation when it took over Huigao and could not offer any other preferential commitments. Besides, the current cash flow of the company was insufficient to allow monetized housing compensation. If the laid-off personnel continued to be unreasonable, the company would report the issue to the Jingmen municipal people's government and request it to solve the issue and stabilize the situation in the company. Otherwise, Rixin would find it difficult to continue to invest in Huigao in such a poor climate and the aforementioned agreement on stock transfer would also have no social environment for performance. Therefore, while the company's leadership continued a dialogue with the laid-off personnel from its own position, it also reported the matter to the deputy mayor who was in charge of industry, hoping the government would support the enterprise's position and adopt compulsory measures to bring the enterprise into normal production and operation. In the meantime, the laid-off personnel also planned to lodge their complaints with the municipal Party committee and government if their demands were not met, hoping the municipal Party committee and government would help them and meet their demands.

Jingmen economic and trade committee

After reading Huigao's report, the deputy mayor immediately instructed the municipal economic and trade committee to handle the matter. In fact, the committee noticed this situation when Huigao's laid-off workers began gathering. Deputy director A of the committee, who was in charge of corporate reform, held that what happened in Huigao was entirely an internal matter and should be handled by the company itself. The government could not act as a 'granny' and handle everything. At the same time, he held that Huigao's handling of its workers' welfare in the past was not so good. After this incident, the matter would be solved if both sides could make some concessions and if the enterprises could invest a little more money. This deputy director explicitly expressed the above views when the deputy mayor left Huigao's leaders to report the issue to the economic and trade committee. The deputy director also criticized the enterprise's management for not acting according to the requirement of the municipal government when working out its own document. Therefore, the enterprise deserved the blame and must spend money to solve the problem.

These remarks greatly disappointed Huigao's leaders. When some laid-off workers went to the economic and trade committee to lodge complaints, the deputy director told them that the matter should be handled by the enterprise itself because it was the enterprise that had caused the problem and the government had no need to handle it on the enterprise's behalf. When some laid-off workers consulted the Jingmen housing reform committee, a few staff told them that the enterprises might decide whether to conduct the reform to monetize housing subsidy according to their own economic conditions. Those with economic conditions might conduct the reform first. All this made the laid-off workers feel that the fundamental reason for the failure to meet their demands rested squarely with Huigao's leadership and, accordingly, they intensified their protests at the company. They blocked the general manager in his office for a whole day on two occasions. They also prevented other employees from going to work. After the company refused to meet their demands, they went twice to the municipal government to stage sit-ins.

Within the Jingmen economic and trade committee, not all officials agreed with the views of deputy director A. Some officials held that, if Huigao's reform was a corporate action, what happened to Huigao was no longer an isolated matter because it involved a host of policy issues, and whether these issues could be solved would have impacts on other reforming enterprises in the city. They also believed that Huigao's 10,000-yuan additional compensation paid to each employee who resigned was improper, which brought trouble not only to this company but also to the stability of other enterprises in the city. For example, what if other enterprises that had reformed their property rights tried to keep up with it? In particular, the laid-off workers of those enterprises even failed to receive their lump sum severance pay in full. What if they tried to do what those at Huigao were doing? Besides, if Huigao carried out the reform to monetize housing subsidy, the workers in other enterprises and administrative public institutions would also demand the same treatment. After all, the strength of other enterprises in Jingmen and the financial resources of the municipal government at the time meant that the company was in no position to comprehensively push forward the reform to monetize housing subsidy. Therefore, the problem confronting Huigao was no longer an internal matter. The government must intervene and supervise the enterprises to act in accordance with the requirements of the documents of the municipal government. As if to prove their worries, a growing number of workers from the reformed enterprises in the city lodged complaints with the municipal government. Their visits also became more frequent. This also convinced them that the government should intervene. In addition, they also feared that, as one of the leading enterprises in the city, Huigao's downslide in production and operations would impede the fulfilment of the city's industrial and economic targets for the year. An investor such as Rixin had been attracted to this city with great difficulty. If the company gave up halfway, it would be a heavy blow to Jingmen's image in attracting investment.

Huigao's leadership felt that the inaction of some government departments had increased the enterprise's difficulty in stabilizing the situation. They felt that no more compromises should be made with the laid-off personnel. Otherwise, the prestige of the company's leadership would be eroded and its future work would become more difficult. If the level of compensation was raised, more workers would wish to leave. The company's production and operations would inevitably be affected and the consequences would be hard to estimate. The issue of monetizing housing subsidy was even more out of the question. They knew this incident must be solved as soon as possible. If the laid-off workers were allowed to carry on like this, the company's internal and external images would be adversely influenced and its future operations would be affected. Therefore, they decided that, if the laid-off workers felt they were being unfairly treated, they could return the compensation they had received and resume their original posts. The laid-off personnel were indifferent to this new decision, and none of them was willing to return to his former post. Some of them said that, after this storm was over, Huigao would inevitably need skilled workers and they would return then. Accordingly, the company's leadership more determinedly rejected the three demands of the laid-off workers. At the same time, they submitted a report directly to the deputy mayor in charge of industry to seek the help of the municipal government.

Deputy mayor

When Huigao's report was received, Huigao's laid-off workers were staging a sit-in in front of the municipal government and the deputy mayor was about to end a dialogue with the workers from another enterprise. That enterprise used the same power supply line for production and living. As the enterprise and some workers owed energy bills, the power supply for the residential area was cut off for several days. This prompted the workers to complain to the municipal government. The deputy mayor requested the power supply department to resume power supply first and to guarantee the living demands of the workers. At the same time, he reached an agreement with the workers through consultation that power supply for production and living should be separated. Intelligent meters would be installed for the power supply for living requirements, and the expenses arising from power supply rewiring would be shared between the power company and the enterprise. The workers would only pay the cost of the intelligent meters. This solution won support from all sides and the deputy mayor was pleased.

Now the deputy mayor planned to handle the complaint from Huigao's workers immediately and personally. Therefore, he asked the leaders of the economic and trade committee and Huigao to come over to discuss the issue. The officials from the committee voiced their opinions but were unable to form a unified view among themselves. On the other hand, Huigao's leaders asked the deputy mayor to intervene and requested the city's public security department to dispatch police officers to help maintain order in the company, although they were cautioned that the move would have a long-standing unfavourable impact on the company's image. This placed the deputy mayor in a dilemma. With regard to the impact of the Huigao incident, the deputy mayor had other considerations. For example, if the workers of Huigao went to the provincial government to lodge their complaints, this would have an impact on the whole city of Jingmen and would provoke the workers of the enterprises that had reformed their property rights. The demands of Huigao's laid-off workers were so strong and their attitude so stubborn that they would probably have staged demonstrations in front of the provincial government if their demands were not met. There were rumours that some people were preparing leaflets in private and were collecting some money from the laid-off workers to purchase uniform clothing and prepare banners and slogans but, if their demands were met, the possible consequences thus arising would be hard to predict. He held that, overall, the demands of the workers did not conform to the provisions of the existing policies. He felt that the Huigao issue was no longer an isolated incident. Furthermore, as the Huigao issue had dragged on for some time and as the related parties had become emotionally radical, the incident could get out of hand if not properly solved. Therefore, he allowed the government office to notify the sitting-in workers to send their representatives to the conference room for a dialogue. He thought that face-to-face contact might help find a solution.

Afterword

After a dialogue was held between the representatives of Huigao's laid-off workers and the deputy mayor, some laid-off workers remained dissatisfied with the reply of the municipal government. They went to the provincial government to lodge complaints. After hearing the explanations from the municipal government, Huigao and the complainants, the relevant department of the provincial government firmly and clearly indicated support for the opinions of the municipal government and patiently explained the relevant policies to the complainants. The complainants were persuaded, returned and staged no more collective complaints. Huigao also offered additional help to those laid-off workers who were in financial difficulties. After the storm was over, the company's production and operations steadily improved, and labour relations became relatively harmonious. Rixin increased investment in Huigao, as the company was now demonstrating an excellent development momentum.

Written in 2003

Index